Prophets
of Extremity

Prophets of Extremity

Nietzsche, Heidegger,
Foucault, Derrida

Allan Megill

UNIVERSITY OF CALIFORNIA PRESS
Berkeley · Los Angeles · London

University of California Press
Berkeley and Los Angeles, California
University of California Press, Ltd.
London, England
© 1985 by
The Regents of the University of California
Printed in the United States of America

1 2 3 4 5 6 7 8 9

Library of Congress Cataloging in Publication Data

Megill, Allan.
    Prophets of extremity.

    Bibliography: p.
    Includes index.
    1. Modernism (Aesthetics). 2. Philosophy, Modern—
19th century. 3. Philosophy, Modern—20th century.
4. Nietzsche, Friedrich Wilhelm, 1844–1900.
5. Heidegger, Martin, 1889–1976.
6. Foucault, Michel, 1926–1984.
7. Derrida, Jacques. I. Title.
BH301.M54M44 1985   190   84-8518
ISBN 0-520-05239-0

For Jason, Jessica, and Jonathan

No one knows who will live in this cage in the future, or whether at the end of this tremendous development entirely new prophets will arise, or there will be a great rebirth of old ideas and ideals, or, if neither, mechanized petrification, embellished with a sort of convulsive self-importance. For of the last stage of this cultural development, it might truly be said: "Specialists without spirit, sensualists without heart; this nullity imagines that it has attained a level of civilization never before achieved."

(Max Weber, *The Protestant Ethic and the Spirit of Capitalism,* trans. Talcott Parsons, with a foreword by R. H. Tawney [New York: Scribner's, 1958], p. 182.)

When we try to examine the mirror in itself, we discover in the end nothing but things upon it. If we want to grasp the things, we finally get hold of nothing but the mirror.—This, in the most general terms, is the history of knowledge.

(Friedrich Nietzsche, *Daybreak: Thoughts on the Prejudices of Morality,* trans. R. J. Hollingdale, with an introduction by Michael Tanner [Cambridge: Cambridge University Press, 1982], §243.)

Contents

ing the force and justice of much of what these writers said, but a tension remained between their stance and mine.

In the Conclusion, I discuss how I arrived at this stance and how I seek to justify it. I confine myself here to pointing out the effect that this stance has had on my commentary. Briefly, the reader will find a division between exegesis and critique. I frequently move from the exegetical mode to the critical mode and back again. These moves will be very obvious; indeed, they will all but leap out at the reader. Here I only want to make clear that I do not see these criticisms as arbitrary. They *do* have a rationale. If the reader is unwilling to accept my stance, he ought at least to be able to understand why I have adopted it.

Finally, I wish to point out the ironical result of what might otherwise seem to be an unequivocal attempt to demolish both aestheticism and the crisis view on which aestheticism is based. Firstly, this book—which ends in the triumph of an antihistoricist Derrida—is itself an example of historicist thought, since it turns out that the four prophets of extremity follow the developmental pattern of the "four-term" dialectic supplied by Derrida. Secondly, the book is an instantiation of aestheticism. In Derrida, it sees a triumph over modernist and postmodernist assumptions. This interpretive construction is aestheticist, and also therapeutic, for it creates a world that the reader would not have been able to anticipate before opening these pages; and it is, I hope, liberating, in that it frees from old and constraining views. Evident, too, is the fact that both elements of aestheticism are manifested in the interpretation of Derrida that it puts forward: awe and rapture before a truth unveiled by Derrida, and radical creativity evoked in response.

In writing this study, I incurred some important debts. I first of all thank Eugene Kamenka and Bob Brown for the congenial atmosphere that they provided for me during my time as Research Fellow in the History of Ideas Unit, Research School of Social Sciences, Australian National University. Without the opportunity for unhindered research that the History of Ideas Unit gave me, I could not have written this study. I found myself free, in that marvelous garden city of Canberra, to proceed as I wished; at the same time, comments and criticism were available when these were called for. I also thank Sam Goldberg, Ferenc Fehér, and Bob Berki, all connected with the History of Ideas Unit during my stay there, who read large sections of this manuscript, especially in its earlier drafts. I presented some of those drafts in seminars given in the History of

Ideas Unit. In addition, it gives me pleasure to thank Preston King for inviting me to give a paper arising out of this project in a political theory seminar in the Department of Political Science, University of New South Wales, and David Band for a similar invitation to discuss this work in another theory seminar in the Department of Political Science, Faculty of Arts, A.N.U. The Department of History in that faculty provided a pleasant teaching environment; thanks go to John Molony and Bruce Kent, among others.

At the University of Iowa, I have benefited greatly from the comments, criticism, and other help provided by members of our Colloquium on Applied Rhetoric. Those who contributed in this way include Ken Dowst, Evan Fales, Sarah Hanley, Paul Hernadi, David Klemm, Gene Krupa, John Lyne, Don McCloskey, Mike McGee, Alan Nagel, John Nelson, Bill Panning, Ira Strauber, Steven Ungar, and Geoffrey Waite. The liberal individualism and the yawning gulf between disciplines that are so much a feature of our universities tend to destroy genuine intellectual community. Fortunately, the rhetoric colloquium proved an exception to the rule. I thank Alan Nagel for inviting me to participate in a colloquium on Foucault sponsored by the University of Iowa School of Letters. John Nelson invited me to give a paper at a conference on the future of political theory, an exercise that contributed in unexpected ways to the present project. Over a period of several years, I have learned much from conversation with Thomas S. Smith, even though our perspectives on many of the issues treated in this book are radically different. At a late stage in its development, Walter Knupfer gave the manuscript a perceptive editorial and critical reading and thus helped me to sharpen both its language and the thought behind that language. I also owe a great deal to the critical reading of David Klemm and to the meticulous copyediting by Paul Weisser. Luther H. Martin and Patrick H. Hutton contributed to the final articulation of this work by inviting me to the University of Vermont in October 1982 to participate in a seminar on Michel Foucault.

I am indebted to Bob Berki for the contrast between the competing idealisms of nostalgia and imagination, a notion of which I make considerable use. Berki develops this contrast in *On Political Realism* (London: Dent, 1981), parts of which I read in draft form. Berki's work was decisive in helping me to see how Nietzsche, Heidegger, Foucault, and Derrida might be seen as modifications of a single perspective. From John Nelson I borrowed the idea of a fourth moment of the dialectic, which I then rediscovered in Derrida.

Portions of this study have appeared elsewhere in different form. I am grateful to the University of Chicago Press for permission to use material originally included in my article "Foucault, Structuralism, and the Ends of History," *Journal of Modern History*, 51 (1979), 451–503, as well as a very brief passage in a review article, "Recent Writing on Michel Foucault," forthcoming in the same journal. Denis Dutton, the editor, likewise granted permission to use material included in "Nietzsche as Aestheticist," *Philosophy and Literature*, 5 (1981), 204–225. Finally, the State University of New York Press gave permission to use several pages of another article, "Martin Heidegger and the Metapolitics of Crisis," in John S. Nelson, ed., *What Should Political Theory Be Now?* (Albany: State University of New York Press, 1983), pp. 264–304.

The University of Iowa assisted the completion of this book by giving me a summer fellowship and a semester free from teaching and administrative duties. Earlier assistance, a debt of long standing, was provided by the Canada Council. Linda Boyatzies and Pete Brokaw of the University of Iowa's Weeg Computing Center dealt patiently with a number of technical problems in the preparation of the manuscript, as did John Kolp of the University's Laboratory for Political Research. Joseph McGing and Susan Lilly helped with the proofreading and indexing.

Readers should note that I make frequent use of abbreviations in the text. The Key to Abbreviations appears immediately following this preface.

Key to Abbreviations

As a convenience to the reader, I have placed many of my references in the text, using abbreviations for this purpose. These abbreviations are given below. The reader will find, however, that most references will be clearly enough identified in the text itself, so that the annoyance of having to refer constantly to the abbreviations list ought to be avoided. When page references are separated by a slash, those preceding the slash refer to the original French or German work, while those after the slash refer to the English translation.

Friedrich Nietzsche

AC   *The Anti-Christ*. In *"Twilight of the Idols" and "The Anti-Christ,"* trans. R. J. Hollingdale. Harmondsworth, England: Penguin Books, 1968.

BGE   *Beyond Good and Evil: Prelude to a Philosophy of the Future*. Trans. Walter Kaufmann. In Nietzsche, *Basic Writings,* ed. Walter Kaufmann. New York: Modern Library, 1968.

BT   *The Birth of Tragedy*. Trans. Walter Kaufmann. In Nietzsche, *Basic Writings*.

EH   *Ecce Homo*. Trans. Walter Kaufmann. In Nietzsche, *Basic Writings*.

GM   *On the Genealogy of Morals*. Trans. Walter Kaufmann and R. J. Hollingdale. In Nietzsche, *Basic Writings*.

GS   *The Gay Science, with a Prelude in Rhymes and
              an Appendix of Songs.* Trans. Walter Kaufmann.
              New York: Random House, 1974.
HAHI;   *Human, All-Too-Human: A Book for Free Spirits,*
HAHII   Part I, trans. Helen Zimmern; and Part II, trans.
              Paul V. Cohn. In *The Complete Works of Friedrich
              Nietzsche,* ed. Oscar Levy, Vols. VI and VII. New
              York: Russell & Russell, 1964.
KGW   *Werke: Kritische Gesamtausgabe.* Berlin: de
              Gruyter, 1967—.
NBW   *Basic Writings of Nietzsche.* Ed. Walter Kauf-
              mann. New York: Modern Library, 1968.
"OTF"   "On Truth and Falsity in an Extra-Moral Sense."
              In Nietzsche, *Early Greek Philosophy and Other
              Essays,* trans. M. A. Mügge (*The Complete Works
              of Friedrich Nietzsche,* ed. Oscar Levy, Vol. II).
              New York: Russell & Russell, 1964.
TI   *Twilight of the Idols.* In *"Twilight of the Idols"
              and "The Anti-Christ,"* trans. R. J. Hollingdale.
              Harmondsworth, England: Penguin Books, 1968.
TZ   *Thus Spoke Zarathustra: A Book for Everyone
              and No One.* Trans. R. J. Hollingdale. Har-
              mondsworth, England: Penguin Books, 1961.
WP   *The Will to Power.* Trans. Walter Kaufmann and
              R. J. Hollingdale; ed. Walter Kaufmann. New
              York: Random House, 1967.

Martin Heidegger

B&T   *Being and Time.* Trans. John Macquarrie and Ed-
              ward Robinson. New York: Harper & Row, 1962.
DT   *Discourse on Thinking.* Trans. John M. Anderson
              and E. Hans Freund. New York: Harper & Row,
              1966.
EGT   *Early Greek Thinking.* Trans. David Farrell Krell
              and Frank A. Capuzzi. New York: Harper & Row,
              1975.
E&B   *Existence and Being.* Introduction and analysis by
              Werner Brock; trans. Douglas Scott, R. F. C. Hull,
              and Alan Crick. Chicago: Regnery-Gateway, 1949.
EP   *The End of Philosophy.* Trans. Joan Stambaugh.
              New York: Harper & Row, 1973.

HBW   *Basic Writings* (from *Being and Time* [1927] to "The Task of Thinking" [1964]). Ed. David Farrell Krell. New York: Harper & Row, 1976.

I&D   *Identity and Difference.* Trans. and with an introduction by Joan Stambaugh. New York: Harper & Row, 1969.

IM   *An Introduction to Metaphysics.* Trans. Ralph Manheim. New Haven: Yale University Press, 1959.

NI; NII   *Nietzsche.* 2 vols. Pfullingen: Neske, 1961. Part of the first volume is available in English, edited and translated by David Farrell Krell, as *Nietzsche, Vol. I: The Will to Power as Art* (New York: Harper & Row, 1979). So also is part of the second volume: *Nietzsche, Vol. IV: Nihilism* (San Francisco: Harper & Row, 1982).

OWL   *On the Way to Language.* Trans. Peter D. Hertz. New York: Harper & Row, 1971.

PLT   *Poetry, Language, Thought.* Trans. and with an introduction by Albert Hofstadter. New York: Harper & Row, 1971.

PT   *The Piety of Thinking.* Ed. and trans. James G. Hart and John C. Maraldo. Bloomington: Indiana University Press, 1976.

QT   *The Question Concerning Technology and Other Essays.* Trans. and with an introduction by William Lovitt. New York: Harper & Row, 1977.

QB   *The Question of Being.* Trans. and with an introduction by William Kluback and Jean T. Wilde. New Haven: Yale University Press, 1958.

T&B   *On Time and Being.* Trans. Joan Stambaugh. New York: Harper & Row, 1972.

WCT   *What Is Called Thinking?* Trans. Fred D. Wieck and J. Glenn Gray, with an introduction by J. Glenn Gray. New York: Harper & Row, 1968.

Michel Foucault

AS   *L'Archéologie du savoir.* Paris: Gallimard, 1969. English trans.: *The Archaeology of Knowledge.* Trans. Alan Sheridan. New York: Random House, Pantheon Books, 1972.

HF1   *Histoire de la folie à l'âge classique.* Paris: Plon, 1961.
        English trans.: *Madness and Civilization: A History of Insanity in the Age of Reason.* Trans. Richard Howard. New York: Random House, Pantheon Books, 1965. (This translation is a much abridged version of the original.)

HF2   *Histoire de la folie à l' âge classique, suivi de "Mon corps, ce papier, ce feu" et "La folie, l'absence d'oeuvre."* Paris: Gallimard, 1972.

LCMP   *Language, Counter-Memory, Practice: Selected Essays and Interviews.* Ed. Donald F. Bouchard; trans. Donald F. Bouchard and Sherry Simon. Ithaca, N.Y.: Cornell University Press, 1977.

MC   *Les Mots et les choses: une archéologie des sciences humaines.* Paris: Gallimard, 1966.
        English trans.: *The Order of Things: An Archaeology of the Human Sciences.* Trans. anon. New York: Random House, Pantheon Books, 1970.

NC   *Naissance de la clinique: une archéologie du regard médical.* Paris: Presses universitaires de France, 1963.
        English trans.: *The Birth of the Clinic: An Archaeology of Medical Perception.* Trans. Alan Sheridan. New York: Random House, Pantheon Books, 1973.

OD   *L'Ordre du discours: leçon inaugurale au Collège de France prononcée le 2 décembre 1970.* Paris: Gallimard, 1970.

P/K   *Power/Knowledge: Selected Interviews and Other Writings, 1972–1977.* Ed. Colin Gordon; trans. Colin Gordon, Leo Marshall, John Mepham, and Kate Soper. New York: Random House, Pantheon Books, 1980.

SP   *Surveiller et punir: naissance de la prison.* Paris: Gallimard, 1975.
        English trans.: *Discipline and Punish: Birth of the Prison.* Trans. Alan Sheridan. New York: Random House, Pantheon Books, 1977.

VS   *Histoire de la sexualité, 1: La Volonté de savoir.* Paris: Gallimard, 1976.
        English trans.: *History of Sexuality,* Vol. I: *An Introduction.* Trans. Robert Hurley. New York: Random House, Pantheon Books, 1978.

Jacques Derrida

CARTE   *La Carte postale de Socrate à Freud et au-delà.*
           Paris: Aubier-Flammarion, 1980. I cite an English
           translation of one of the essays in this book, "Le
           Facteur de la vérité," translated as: "The Purveyor
           of Truth," trans. Willis Domingo, James Hulbert,
           Moshe Ron, and Marie-Rose Logan. In *Yale
           French Studies* 52 (1975), 31–113.

DISS   *La Dissémination.* Paris: Seuil, 1972.
           English trans.: *Dissemination.* Trans. Barbara John-
           son. Chicago: University of Chicago Press, 1981.

E&D   *L'Écriture et la différence.* Paris: Seuil, 1966.
           English trans.: *Writing and Difference.* Trans. Alan
           Bass. Chicago: University of Chicago Press, 1978.

GLAS   *Glas.* Paris: Galilée, 1974.

GRAM   *De la Grammatologie.* Paris: Minuit, 1974.
           English trans.: *Of Grammatology.* Trans. Gayatri
           Spivak. Baltimore: Johns Hopkins University
           Press, 1976.

MARGES   *Marges—de la philosophie.* Paris: Minuit, 1972.
           English trans.: *Margins of Philosophy.* Trans. Alan
           Bass. Chicago: University of Chicago Press, 1982.

ORGEO   Translation and introduction to Edmund Husserl,
           L'Origine de la géométrie. Paris: Presses universi-
           taires de France, 1962.
           English trans.: *Edmund Husserl's Origin of Ge-
           ometry: An Introduction.* Trans. John P. Leavey.
           Stony Brook, New York: N. Hays, 1977.

POS   *Positions.* Paris: Minuit, 1972.
           English trans.: *Positions.* Trans. Alan Bass. Chi-
           cago: University of Chicago Press, 1981.

SPURS   *Spurs: Nietzsche's Styles* (bilingual edition). Intro-
           duction and preface by Stefano Agosti; drawings
           by François Loubrieu; trans. Barbara Harlow.
           Chicago: University of Chicago Press, 1981.

VenP   *La Vérité en peinture.* Paris: Flammarion, 1978.

V&P   *La Voix et le phénomène: introduction au pro-
           blème du signe dans la phénoménologie de Hus-
           serl.* Paris: Presses universitaires de France, 1967.
           English trans.: *Speech and Phenomena and Other
           Essays on Husserl's Theory of Signs.* Trans. David
           B. Allison. Evanston, Ill.: Northwestern Univer-
           sity Press, 1973.

Introduction

A few thinkers in the history of the West have put forward transcendent and compelling cultural visions. These visions are transcendent in that they break from previous thought, and compelling in that they force subsequent thinkers to attend to them with great seriousness. The thinkers who articulate such visions are properly characterized as agenda setters: they set the order of intellectual priorities for those who follow. They live on the boundaries, in the hope of discovering something new. Obviously, Nietzsche is one such thinker. The vision that he presented in his writings set the agenda not only for the three other thinkers whom I shall be considering in this book but for the whole of modernist and postmodernist art and thought. The impact of this style of thought is not confined to the sphere of intellectual life. Ideas do have consequences. These consequences are often of a quite material kind. The daring sortie of one generation is the universally accepted commonplace three generations later. On such commonplaces worlds are built or lost.

Though the vision with which I am here concerned is an influential one, it has never, to my knowledge, been systematically explored. The sequence from Nietzsche to Derrida has, I believe, a unity of its own—a unity that helps make sense of a large part of recent Western intellectual history. With Nietzsche something finishes and something new begins, while with Derrida the new beginning seems to me to come to an end. Moreover, this sequence connects in a number of interesting ways with other, increasingly well-accepted realities in our intellectual history. Looking to the past, it connects with what has come to be called the "failure" of the Enlightenment.[1] Looking to the present, it connects with many of the assumptions that late twentieth-century artists and intellectuals still hold. These assumptions—the assumptions of modernism and postmodernism—are put forward in their most powerful and consistent form by the thinkers with whom we are concerned here. To examine these assumptions as they appear in Nietzsche, Heidegger, Foucault, and Derrida is to examine views that are still current. In criticizing these thinkers, we are indirectly criticizing ourselves.

Aestheticism

Looking at these thinkers together, one is struck by how they are all peculiarly aesthetic, or "aestheticist," in their sensibility. This may not always be clear when one looks at them separately, but we shall have occasion enough to see that a multitude of connections exists between them, and that considering them as a group makes a great deal of sense. As it is usually employed, the word *aestheticism* denotes an enclosure within a self-contained realm of aesthetic objects and sensations, and hence also denotes a separation from the "real world" of nonaesthetic objects. Here, however, I am using the word in a sense that is almost diametrically opposed to its usual sense. I am using it to refer not to the condition of being enclosed within the limited territory of the aesthetic, but rather to an attempt to expand the aesthetic to embrace the whole of reality. To put it in another way, I am using it to refer to a tendency to see "art" or "language" or "discourse" or "text" as constituting the primary realm of human experience. This tendency has become pervasive in much recent avant-garde thought. The irony that pervaded modernism tried to uncover a Man or Culture or Nature or History underlying the flux of surface experience. In postmodernism, this has given way to a new irony, one that holds these erstwhile realities to be textual fictions. We are seen as cut off from "things" and confined to a confrontation with "words" alone.

At this preliminary point, I cannot proceed further in defining the aestheticist stance. For it is a question of different modes of aestheticism, and a further attempt at definition would embroil us prematurely in these differences. To these different aestheticisms, we might plausibly attach the names Nietzsche, Heidegger, Foucault, and Derrida. But in order to help the reader see more clearly what I have in mind, I can at least point to a few characteristically aestheticist statements in the four writers in question.

When Nietzsche says in *The Birth of Tragedy* that "it is only as an *aesthetic phenomenon* that existence and the world are eternally justified," and when in a *Nachlass* fragment he characterizes "the world" as "a work of art that gives birth to itself," he is adumbrating an aestheticist position. This is also true of the various *Nachlass* fragments in which he suggests, or seems to suggest, that "facts" and "things" are created, Orpheus-like, by the interpreter himself. Nietzsche expressed these possibilities in a somewhat tentative way, and it is not my argument that he was unequivocally an aestheticist. Rather, aestheticism is one of the possibilities that his work suggests (though for us, I think, it is the most compelling possibility).

By way of contrast, in later Heidegger the notion of the ontologically creative potential of "art" becomes absolutely decisive. In the middle 1930s, Heidegger came to lay great stress on "the work of art." Extremely important in this regard is his essay "The Origin of the Work of Art," which he gave in lecture form in 1935–36 and published in 1950 as the first essay in *Holzwege* (*Woodpaths*). Here art is seen as bringing worlds into existence. As Heidegger puts it, "towering up within itself, the work opens up a *world* and keeps it abidingly in force." After the 1930s, Heidegger characteristically attributes this world-creating force not just to the work of art but to "language" in general.

The French successors to Nietzsche and Heidegger also work within— and now, increasingly, against—aestheticism. The aestheticist foundations of Foucault's position are most clearly visible in his first major work, *History of Madness* (1961). A recurring motif in this book is Foucault's concern with the experience of the artist and with the embodiment of that experience in the work of art. But whereas in Heidegger the relationship between work and world is harmonious, in Foucault it is antithetical. Thus, Foucault tells us at the end of *History of Madness* that from now on "the world . . . becomes culpable (for the first time in the Western world) in relation to the work; it is now arraigned by the work, obliged to order itself by its language, compelled by it to a task of recognition, of reparation." As those familiar with Foucault's career will know, this incipient concern with "the work of art" soon gave way to a concern with "discourse." But Foucault's "discourse," like Heidegger's "language," stands as the successor to the work of art. Just as, in the post-Romantic aesthetics upon which these writers depend, the work of art creates its own reality, so too does language/discourse. One thinks of Nietzsche's reflections on the relationship between "fact" and "interpretation," which I shall consider in Part I, below. Art, language, discourse, and interpretation can be viewed as ultimately the same. Each makes the world that ostensibly it only represents.

Finally, there is Derrida, perhaps the most puzzling and elusive of the four. When Derrida avers that "there is nothing outside of the text," he is working within an aestheticist perspective, even as he parodistically tries to reduce that perspective to absurdity. Such, in brief, is the strand of thought that we shall here explore.

My reading of Nietzsche, Heidegger, Foucault, and Derrida is unusual. But it is not altogether new, for both the aestheticist notion itself and the particular genealogy that I attribute to it have been anticipated by other writers. I am thinking especially of Stanley Rosen's book, *Nihilism: A Philosophical Essay.* Rosen published the book in 1969, before Foucault and Derrida were at all well known outside France. Not surprisingly, he says nothing about these two more recent writers. But he discusses Nietzsche and Heidegger in some detail. From the standpoint of the present study, this discussion has two main points of interest. Firstly, Rosen repeatedly emphasizes the role that the poetic plays in the work of both writers. He sees the notion of radical creativity as central to their projects. He refers to Nietzsche's "cosmogonical poetry" and to the "onto-poetic historicism" that both writers share.[2] Secondly, he connects Nietzsche and Heidegger with the earlier project of Kant. In particular, he sees Kant's third critique, the *Critique of Judgment,* as foreshadowing the positions of the two writers.[3] In both respects, I find Rosen to be importantly right, though we shall not be able to see precisely how he is right until we have worked our way through all four thinkers.

Yet, my focus is different from Rosen's. Rosen attempts to show that nihilism has arisen because we have gotten away from the classical linkage of the good, the true, and the beautiful. He contends that in modern intellectual life the concept of reason has been illegitimately separated from that of good, and that the two need to be brought back together again. I cannot aspire to such a wide-ranging critique of the Western tradition. Instead, I see the present book as a study of the continuing impact on us of the thought of the Enlightenment. I see Nietzsche, Heidegger, Foucault, and Derrida (but especially the first two of these thinkers) as responding (at one remove) to the Enlightenment pretension to construct a science of society modeled on natural science. The intellectual problems that this Enlightenment project gave rise to are most clearly embodied in the writings of Kant. Rosen's complaint about the separation from each other of the good, the true, and the beautiful is translatable into a complaint about the Kantian separation of the practical, the theoretical, and the aesthetic. Indeed, we can see our four thinkers as responding, both positively and negatively, to Kant—or, more accurately, to the tradition to which Kant gave rise. They engage in a rebellion against Kant, even as they exploit the intellectual resources that Kant gave them.

Romanticism

To refer to Nietzsche, Heidegger, Foucault, and Derrida in this way is implicitly to connect them with another movement that rebelled against Kant and yet used Kant's own resources in that rebellion—namely, Romanticism. The Romantics were the first to argue that the Enlightenment had failed—and not for adventitious reasons but because its program was fundamentally flawed. I am acutely aware, let it be noted, that nothing is more difficult to pin down than Romanticism. The term is usually applied to certain aspects of European intellectual life in the late eighteenth and early nineteenth centuries—between, say, 1790 and 1850. But just which aspects of intellectual life in that period actually define the movement is a matter of much disagreement.

This is so partly because Romanticism took different forms in the different countries in which it appeared. In England, for example, it was almost entirely an aesthetic movement, concerned with breaking down artistic and poetic conventions that its protagonists regarded as unnatural and stultifying. In France, under Rousseau's inspiration, it was mainly a protest against *social* convention, with the aesthetic aspects of the movement (often dated from the first performance of Victor Hugo's *Hernani* in 1830) coming very late. Finally, in Germany it began as an aesthetic movement but quickly broadened out to become an explicit and comprehensive world-view. Moreover, within each country there were great differences between the individual sponsors of the movement. In consequence, it is extremely difficult to isolate any single collection of beliefs that one might willingly identify as the Romantic credo. This difficulty has led some commentators to argue that there were Romanticisms, but no "Romanticism" in the singular, and that its use as a general term ought to be abandoned.[4]

But whatever the problems with the term, in the context of the present study its use cannot be avoided. Fortunately, we do not need to define in all its complexity the whole of late eighteenth- and early nineteenth-century intellectual history. We need only look at the Romantic period with an eye to the connection with crisis thought. For our prime concern is with Nietzsche, Heidegger, Foucault, and Derrida, not with their precursors.

What is first of all worthy of note is the extent to which intellectuals circa 1800 saw themselves as living in a period of radical change. Looking back on these years from the perspective of the late twentieth century, we continue to see them as decisive in the shaping of the modern world. Politically, we still live in the shadow of the so-called Atlantic Revolution—

American and Western European—of the late eighteenth century. And beneath the clear disjunctions occurring in the politics of that time, we can also detect the workings of longer-term economic and demographic forces that were destined to bring into being the distinctly urban and industrial civilization that dominates the modern West. The social and political changes evident by the early nineteenth century had a great impact on intellectuals in that period.

But however important these changes were, the fact remains that ideas also have a history of their own. Looking at the particular history in question here, one is struck by the degree to which it can be viewed as historically independent. One can understand this history without continually referring to social and political events, though admittedly those events did impart an air of urgency to it. Leonard Krieger notes how the Enlightenment synthesis was already showing signs of dissolution as early as the 1770s, well before the social and political upheavals of the last years of the century.[5] It is tempting to regard this dissolution as a kind of organic process. But such a view is relatively unilluminating. I prefer to see the shift from the Enlightenment to its successoral movements not as a natural process of decay and rejuvenation but rather as a conscious attempt to bring to light and to respond to theoretical inadequacies in the Enlightenment position. In short, it is a matter of the "failure" of the Enlightenment, and of various attempts to confront that failure. Viewed from this perspective, the decline of the French Revolution into Terror might be seen as merely the most striking manifestation of the inadequacy of the Enlightenment's social, moral, and political theory.

Certainly, this was the way that many thinkers of the time, including those whom we consider Romantics, saw the matter. Focusing on the inability of Enlightenment thought to provide the hoped-for synthesis, they viewed their own time as an age not of established truth but of transition. The notion that European consciousness was on the way to something fundamentally new and unprecedented was decisive for the major intellectual projects of the time. A similar conviction is decisive for the four thinkers with whom we are concerned here, with one crucial difference. For whereas the Romantics and their contemporaries entertained a good deal of hope for the future, Nietzsche and his successors have not. The notion of an "age of transition" entails a *limited* crisis, a crisis contained by a unifying dialectic or by some similar promise of return. Nietzsche and his successors find no such promise. They are thus linked to the Romantics, but at the same time divided from them.

A second point of contact between the Romantics and the four thinkers at issue here is to be found in the role played by the aesthetic. As Erich Auerbach points out, Romanticism "presents rather a unity of poetic atmosphere than a systematic unity whose contours can be clearly delineated."[6] From the point of view of the present study, the aesthetic or poetic character of Romanticism is extremely important. It is not simply that the poet and artist, now liberated from the arid rules of a restrictive and overly conventionalized classicism, was seen as the epitome of Romantic freedom. This was certainly an important aspect of the Romantic view, but of greater interest to us is the elevation not only of the artist but of art itself, not only of the singer but the song. Many Romantic thinkers saw art as a manifestation, even a source, of truth—one that rivaled and ultimately surpassed the analytical reason of the Enlightenment. Wordsworth, with his intimations of immortality and his animadversions on analysis ("We murder to dissect"), is the representative of this position most familiar to the reader of English. Consider also Shelley's "Defence of Poetry," with its ringing assertion that poets are "the unacknowledged legislators of the world." The German Romantics were even more insistent on the central role that poetry played in human culture, as we shall see. Finally, one needs to note how the Romantic idea of genius, with its stress on the unconscious, unlearnable character of artistic creation, appeared to suggest that even the artist himself was unequal to his work. Thus, art was elevated above artist. As the objective embodiment of fleeting, inarticulate insight, art was seen as allowing access to a dimension of reality from which the merely analytical understanding was entirely barred. Finding its highest expression in poetry, art pushed well beyond the limiting confines of the calculative and prosaic spirit of the Enlightenment.

I am well aware that the connection that I wish to establish between the Romantics on the one hand and Nietzsche and his successors on the other will evoke challenge. The problem is not that the connection has never been made before, but rather that it has been made with an all too polemical intent. One thinks especially of Georg Lukács's *Destruction of Reason*, which presents Nietzsche and Heidegger as participants in an 'irrationalist" current of thought having its roots in Schelling.[7] *The Destruction of Reason* is surely the crudest of Lukács's writings. Nonetheless, Lukács seems to me to be on the right track in attempting to find the antecedents of their thought in Romanticism.

Of our four thinkers, Nietzsche is of most interest for this problem of antecedents. He inaugurates the strand of thought with which we are concerned in this study, and as its inaugurator he stands closest to what precedes it. In my essay on Nietzsche, I shall explain how, exactly, I view his

project. This will allow me to consider in some detail its affinities with
and differences from the earlier Romantic project. I cannot anticipate
that task here. Instead, leaving my own Nietzsche interpretation in abeyance, I shall content myself with appealing to the sound scholarship of
two other interpreters, Ernst Behler and Benjamin Bennett. Both have
explored, with great tact and learning, the relation between Nietzsche
and the Romantics.

In his very substantial essay, "Nietzsche and the Early Romantic
School," Behler examines the connection between Nietzsche's thought
and the thought of those figures who, in the years 1795–1800, gathered
around the journal *Athenaeum:* Friedrich and August Wilhelm Schlegel,
Novalis, Wackenroder, Tieck, and Schleiermacher. Behler demonstrates
that many themes that are importantly present in Nietzsche's writings
appeared earlier in the writings of the Schlegel circle. He notes a similar
cult of the mythical, manifesting itself in the search for a "new mythology," a similar divinization of art, a similar scorn of philistinism, a similar
predilection for a fragmentary or aphoristic style, a similar desire for an
"aesthetic revolution" based on a recovery of the Greek spirit, a similar
search for an "aesthetic thinking," and a similar anticipation of a "philosophy of the future" that would somehow draw on the resources of art.[8] As
is well known, throughout most of his intellectual career Nietzsche attacked "Romanticism." One of the great merits of Behler's essay is his
account of what Nietzsche seems to have had in mind in his use of this
term. Certainly, he did *not* have in mind the early German Romantics.[9]

Bennett deals with similar issues in his essay, "Nietzsche's Idea of Myth:
The Birth of Tragedy from the Spirit of Eighteenth-Century Aesthetics."
But whereas Behler focuses on the affinities between Nietzsche and Friedrich Schlegel,Bennett emphasizes those between Nietzsche and that proto-
Romantic, Friedrich Schiller. Bennett sees Nietzsche's idea of myth as an
extension of Schiller's idea of art—as "an attempt to go further toward
Schiller's avowed but not achieved goal, toward a conception of absolute
validity and necessity in art, a conception of art as the true generating center of human existence, serving no purpose higher than itself."[10]

In short, important connections can indeed be established between
Nietzsche and the late eighteenth-century proto-Romantics and Romantics. They are united, most obviously, by their common aesthetic concern.
In fact, it was the late eighteenth-century thinkers who invented aesthetics as a field of thought. Prior to that time, there were many attempts at
the philosophical criticism of art. One prominent example of this was the
abbé Dubos's *Réflexions critiques sur la poésie et sur la peinture* (first

edition, 1719). But there was little or nothing that could be called aesthetics in the sense of a philosophical consideration of art as such. Most works focused, as the *Réflexions critiques* did, on one or more particular arts, not on art in general. Only toward the end of the century did a general, philosophical aesthetics become established. The rise of such an aesthetics was a matter of immense significance for the thought of the time, especially in Germany. As Wilhelm Windelband notes in his classic *History of Philosophy,* "problems and conceptions of aesthetics" now came to play a decisive role in German philosophy: "aesthetic principles gained the mastery, and the motifs of scientific thought became interwoven with those of artistic vision to produce grand poetical creations in the sphere of abstract thought."[11] This development is significant for aestheticism, for it was on the ground of aesthetics that aestheticism came into being.

Kant

At this point, it becomes necessary to recur to Kant, who stands as the crucial linking figure between the Enlightenment, Romanticism, and the new thought initiated by Nietzsche. As one recent commentator notes, Nietzsche wrote in the wake of the "Kantian revolution."[12] In Nietzsche's eyes, Kant was a deeply subversive thinker, who had unwittingly undermined the optimistic logic of the Englightenment (see, e.g., *B.T.* chap. 18; *NBW,* p. 112). And it is interesting how important a role Kant plays in the writings of Heidegger, Foucault, and Derrida. As I have noted, all four thinkers can be viewed as attempting, in one way or another, to respond to Kant. But Nietzsche and his successors were far from being the first to respond to this thinker. On the contrary, the honor of priority goes to the Romantics, whom Kant heralded without in any way intending to do so. To understand Kant's importance for the emergence of aestheticism, we must look at his project within the wider context of Enlightenment thought. Kant is in some ways a profoundly ambivalent philosopher. His ambivalence is perhaps best seen in the light of the tension between his first and second critiques, the *Critique of Pure Reason* (1781) and the *Critique of Practical Reason* (1788). In the former work, he explores the territory of theoretical, or scientific, reason, analyzing to its very limits our understanding of the empirical world of nature. In the latter work, he explores the territory of practical, or moral, reason, seeking to constitute an independent moral realm.

We need not concern ourselves here with the details of Kant's theories of science and of morality. Rather, we are concerned with the more general problem of the relationship of the two theories to each other—a problem (admittedly, not the only problem to come out of Kant) deeply felt by the Romantics and their successors. The problem can be posed in the following way. Natural science attributes a determinism to the objects of its concern. If things were free rather than determined, they could not be the objects of science. Newton was able to explain the workings of the physical universe in terms of the theory of universal gravitation because the objects within that universe operate according to the pre-given laws of nature. Central to the whole project of Enlightenment thought was the ambition to do for the human world what Newton had done for the natural world. In other words, enlightened philosophers aspired to construct a science of society analogous to Newton's science of nature. At the same time, the philosophers of the Enlightenment also believed in the legitimacy of moral codes. But the existence of a moral code presupposes that people are free to govern their own actions, since entities incapable of governing their own actions obviously cannot be judged in moral terms. There was thus a radical contradiction between the Enlightenment project for a science of society on the one hand and its continuing belief in morality and freedom on the other.

To state the problem in another way, science can be seen as dealing with a realm of unfree objects, and morality as dealing with a realm of free subjects. Posing the disjunction in this way, we can place Kant within the broader context of post-Cartesian thought. Descartes views the world in rigidly dualistic terms: a substance that thinks but has no extension confronts a substance that has extension but does not think. Thus, in both the Cartesian and the Kantian perspectives there is a sharp dichotomy between subject and object. It is true that Kant attacked Descartes's view that mind and body are separate in substance. But looking at him in broader perspective, we can see that he was simply carrying out a further development of the Cartesian frame of reference. Moreover, by dealing explicitly with the problem of morality—as Descartes did not—he made glaringly obvious the contradictions raised by the Enlightenment project for a science of society.

Readers familiar with Heidegger will be well aware of this way of locating Kant historically. In *Being and Time* (1927), Heidegger is largely concerned with attacking what he sees as the modern West's deeply ingrained tendency to look at the world in terms of the subject/object division. Heidegger traces this tendency back to Descartes; and whatever the differences between the two thinkers, he sees Kant as continuing along the same road. Against the Cartesian and Kantian insistence on looking at the world in terms of the subject/object division, he proposes the notion of "Being-in-the-world." As will be seen in the Heidegger section of the present book, I am much more interested in the later Heidegger than in the Heidegger of *Being and Time,* for only in his later writings does he turn in an aestheticist direction. But the concern with the subject/object division, so well epitomized in the tension between the "practical" and the "theoretical" in Kant, is of tremendous importance for Heidegger throughout his career.

It is also important for Nietzsche, Foucault, and Derrida. To be sure, the preoccupation with circumventing the subject/object division is less obvious in these other writers than it is in Heidegger. But it is nonetheless present, particularly in their various discussions of the process of interpretation and in their polemics against (and residual attraction to) phenomenology. In short, there is an important connection between Kant and our four thinkers. All four can be seen as working against Kant, as trying to respond in an un-Kantian way to a problem that Kant made obvious. Nor were they the first to concern themselves with this problem of the subject/object opposition. On the contrary, the German idealist philosophers were preoccupied by precisely this issue. In their respective philosophical systems, Fichte, Schelling, and Hegel all tried to attain a unity of subject and object, of ego and non-ego. And it was not only the philosophers who became caught up in the issue. When Wordsworth notes that it was his attempt to apply "formal *proof*" to matters of morality that brought about the breakdown in which he "yielded up moral questions in despair," he, too, shows how preoccupied he was by the question of how a free, moral subject can exist within the deterministic world of science.[13]

If Kant, more than any other eighteenth-century thinker, poses this problem in a clear and systematic manner, he also seems to suggest a solution to it. Indeed, he seems to suggest several solutions, though only one of these is of any interest to us here. In the eyes of many of Kant's readers, his third critique provided a way out of the dilemma that the first and second critiques had so baldly posed. Admittedly, the *Critique of Judgment* is far less forceful and original than the two critiques that preceded it. As an intellectual performance, it is clearly inferior to them, especially to the first. Yet, it had a greater impact on Kant's contemporaries than did the first two critiques. It proved immensely suggestive for poets, artists, philosophers, and aesthetic theorists alike.

From the perspective of the present study, the *Critique of Judgment* is important because it unequivocally maintains the autonomy of aesthetic judgment. In so doing, it appears to suggest that there exists an independent realm of the aesthetic, a realm quite distinct from the other realms of morality and of nature. On the one hand, Kant opposes those previous theorists, such as Hutcheson and Shaftesbury, who by portraying both aesthetic judgments and moral judgments as matters of feeling or sentiment had in effect assimilated the former to the latter. On the other hand, he opposes any tendency to assimilate art to physiology or psychology, as would have been the case had he identified aesthetic pleasure with sensual pleasure. Thus, he diverges from such seventeenth- and eighteenth-century writers as Saint-Evrémond and La Mettrie. This divergence is reflected in his definition of aesthetic pleasure as "*disinterested* satisfaction" (*interesseloses Wohlgefallen*) and in his conception of form in art as "purposiveness *without purpose*" (*Zweckmässigkeit ohne Zweck*). To be sure, Kant denies that there exists any third realm of being, distinct from the realms of nature and freedom.[14] Nonetheless, he can be read—and *was* read—as insisting on the existence of an autonomous realm of the aesthetic, a realm whose function is to mediate between the other two. Something of this sense of art as mediator underlies Nietzsche's contention, in *The Birth of Tragedy*, that in aesthetics "the whole opposition between the subjective and objective . . . is altogether irrelevant" (*BT*, chap. 5; *NBW*, p. 52).

A second matter, in addition to mediation, is the issue of whether art in any way conveys truth. Kant's insistence on the autonomy of aesthetic judgment leads him to deny that art has "truth value." Art is a matter of pleasure (albeit a disinterested pleasure), not of knowledge. At the same time, however, some of his statements in the *Critique of Judgment* can be taken as contradicting this view. For he does hint that while art certainly cannot supply us with knowledge in any logical sense, it can put us into contact with something that cannot be fully presented in experience or grasped through concepts.

Note Kant's contention that aesthetic judgments make a claim to universal validity. In other words, when someone says, "this is beautiful," he is saying that the judgment that he has just made ought to have universal assent. Thus, a beautiful object is one that excites a delight that is not only disinterested but also necessary and universal. In establishing this point, as he attempts to do in the final stages of his transcendental deduction of the judgment of taste, Kant touches on issues of morality. Specifically, he argues that underlying the judgment of aesthetic taste is the concept of the purposiveness of nature. The "determining ground" of this concept, he says, "lies perhaps in the concept of that which may be regarded as the supersensible substrate of humanity."[15]

This is the same substrate that he uncovers, through his analysis of our moral judgments, in the *Critique of Practical Reason*. In consequence, beauty is "the symbol of the morally good."[16] Only when we view it in this light can we grasp its claim to universal acceptance. Beauty thus points toward the realm of morality, of which it gives sensual intimations. Also important is Kant's conception of the "aesthetic idea." An "aesthetic idea" is a "representation of the imagination which occasions much thought" but for which "an adequate concept can never be found," and which consequently "cannot be completely encompassed and made intelligible by language."[17] This conception points toward a view of art as expressing the inexpressible, as manifesting the ineffable. Thus it, too, suggests that art is something more than a mere purveyor of pleasure.

Schiller, Schelling

In rather different, yet at the same time in complementary ways, Schiller and Schelling develop and extend Kant's discussion of the aesthetic. Schiller is important in the present context because he was the first to take up Kant's inchoate suggestions of a higher role for art. As Richard Kroner puts it, Schiller was the first to see "that 'aesthetic unity' has shown itself to be active not only in art but also in thought itself"—the first to see "that the philosopher can only entirely fulfill his calling if he not only separates, but also once again unites what was separated."[18] In his highly influential *Letters on the Aesthetic Education of Man* (1794–95), Schiller puts forward nothing less than a history of the whole of Western culture. His heroes are the Greeks, whose lives, in his view, combined fullness of form with fullness of content, the "first youth of imagination" with "the manhood of reason." By way of contrast, modern man is divided from himself, for the unity of human nature has been destroyed by the advance of culture.[19] In short, Schiller is one of the first theorists of the idea of modern alienation, now a commonplace of cultural commentary.

Schiller argues that the cure for this alienation lies in art. He holds that there are two fundamental drives in man: the sensuous drive (*sinnliche Trieb*), which is always pressing for change; and the formal drive (*Formtrieb*), which insists on "unity and persistence."[20] Both need to have limits placed upon them, the former so that it does not encroach upon the domain of moral law, the latter so that it does not encroach upon that of feeling. Stated in slightly different terms, both need to be relaxed, but this relaxation must spring from an abundance of feeling and sensation rather than from physical or spiritual impotence. Such a harmonization can only be accomplished by the operation of a third, "play" drive (*Spieltrieb*), which exerts upon the psyche a constraint that is at the same time moral and physical. This constraint annuls all contingency. Indeed, it annuls constraint itself, setting man both morally and physically free.

According to Schiller, it is in art that the play drive emerges. Whereas the object of the sensuous drive is life and that of the formal drive form, the play drive has as its object "living form." The concept of living form designates "all the aesthetic qualities of phenomena and, in a word, what in the widest sense of the term we call *beauty*."[21] Only in the play of art are the sensuous drive and the formal drive brought together. Only in contemplating the beautiful is man harmonized, for only here does the psyche find a happy medium between the moral law on the one hand and physical exigency on the other. Beauty, for Schiller, offers us an instance of moral freedom being compatible with sense. It leads the sensuous man back to form and thought, while bringing the spiritual man back to the world of sense.

In all of this, Schiller hews to Kant's distinction between the aesthetic and the nonaesthetic. He treats art as a matter of *Schein,* of semblance or illusion. It is the "free play" of art, not any supposed revelation of truth, that draws us to it. Indeed, he explicitly declares that any blurring of the distinction between art and not-art is dangerous. In his tenth letter, he entertains the objection to his theory that "just because taste is always concerned with form, and never with content, it finally induces in the mind a dangerous tendency to neglect reality [*Realität*] altogether, and to sacrifice truth and morality to the alluring dress in which they appear. All substantial difference between things is lost, and appearance alone determines their worth."[22] In his twenty-sixth letter, he tries to meet this objection, noting that there are two kinds of semblance, the aesthetic and the logical. Logical semblance is marked by a confusion with "actuality [*Wirklichkeit*] and truth." In aesthetic semblance, on the other hand, we distinguish between semblance and truth, and love the semblance because it is semblance and not because we take it to be something better. Aesthetic semblance is play, while logical semblance is mere deception. Nor can aesthetic semblance ever be prejudicial to truth, for "one is never in danger of substituting it for truth, which is after all the only way in which truth can ever be impaired."[23] Indeed, Schiller sees the delight in pure formal beauty as protecting the autonomy of truth, for by keeping sem-

blance clear of actuality, it at the same time sets actuality free from semblance. In this way, it preserves intact "the frontiers of truth."[24]

Schiller is thus not an aestheticist. That is to say, he does not take up a
position wherein notions articulated on the basis of a distinction between
the aesthetic and the nonaesthetic are then employed as if that distinction had not been postulated. On the contrary, he explicitly asserts that
the poet must not "transgress his proper limits."[25] But Schiller's was only
one of several possible ways of moving beyond the *Critique of Judgment.*
In their development of Kant, his *Aesthetic Letters* suggested to a number
of younger thinkers that art could indeed be a source of truth, and that
philosophy ought in consequence to become aesthetic. Such a view was
expressed by Hölderlin, for example.[26] It also finds expression in a document crucial for the history of German idealism, the so-called "Earliest
Systematic Program of German Idealism." Dating from 1796–97, and
probably written by Hegel, this document anticipates the systems that
Hegel and Schelling would construct a few years later.[27] Most important
from our perspective is the fact that the author of the "Systematic Program" declares that the highest Idea is that of beauty and that the "highest act of reason" is "an aesthetic act." It follows that "the philosophy of
the spirit is an aesthetical philosophy" and that the philosopher "must
possess just as much aesthetic power as the poet."[28]

It was the Schelling of circa 1800–1803, however, who most insisted
on the need to turn philosophy in an aesthetic direction. The crucial work
for this theme is his *System of Transcendental Idealism* (1800). Schelling
starts out from the problem that Kant's philosophy had made so obvious,
that of relating subject and object—which is also the problem of relating
freedom and necessity, ego and nature, Idea and actuality, practical and
theoretical. He finds the means for overcoming these oppositions in the
Critique of Judgment. With respect to natural philosophy (which does
not concern us here), he finds this bridge in the section of the third critique
dealing with teleological judgment. With respect to transcendental philosophy, which does concern us, he finds it in the conception of art that
Kant puts forward in the critique of aesthetic judgment.

But whereas in Kant the primacy of the aesthetic is only formal or
regulative, in Schelling it is substantive. Schelling contends that nature on
the one hand and the work of art on the other are the product of one and
the same activity, an activity that is in its essence aesthetic. The only difference between the world and the work of art is that in the former the
creative activity is unconscious whereas in the latter it is conscious. As
Schelling puts it, "the objective world is only the original, still uncon-

scious poetry of the spirit."[29] In short, Schelling anticipates Nietzsche's views on the aesthetic character of reality. Whereas Nietzsche's closest predecessor, Schopenhauer, sees the world as "idea" or "representation" (*Vorstellung*), Nietzsche, like Schelling, sees it as a work of art. Though it is to Schopenhauer that Nietzsche is customarily linked, he in fact reaches back to the earlier, Schellingian moment in the history of Romanticism.

Given Schelling's conviction that reality is poetic, we are not surprised to find that he sees philosophy as culminating in art. Philosophy starts out from the principle of absolute identity, as in A = A. Absolute identity can be grasped in self-consciousness, for in self-consciousness the subject of thought and the object of thought are one and the same: ego = ego. This identity can only be grasped directly, through intellectual intuition; it cannot be grasped indirectly, through the mediation of concepts. Hence, intellectual intuition is "the organ of all transcendental thought."[30] But this raises a problem, for the intuition of absolute identity in the ego is purely subjective. Where is its external, objective manifestation to be found? In Schelling's view, it is to be found in the "aesthetic product." The aesthetic product starts out from "the feeling of a seemingly insoluble contradiction." But it ends (as all artists, and all who share their inspiration, know) in a feeling of infinite harmony that serves to indicate "the complete resolution of the contradiction."[31]

In other words, the aesthetic product gives us a vision of identity. Indeed, it gives us an objectification of identity, since it clearly exists outside the ego. As Schelling puts it, the "generally recognized and entirely undeniable objectivity of intellectual intuition is art itself. For aesthetic intuition is nothing other than intellectual intuition become objective. The work of art only reflects to me what otherwise is reflected through nothing, that absolute identity which already in the ego has divided itself."[32] In consequence,

> art is the sole organon, both true and permanent, and document of philosophy, which always and in continually new forms sets forth what philosophy cannot represent outwardly.... For this ... reason art occupies the highest place for the philosopher, since it opens up to him the holy of holies, so to speak, where in primal union, as in a single flame, there burns what is sundered in nature and history and what must eternally flee from itself in life and action as in thought.[33]

Only art can make objective what the philosopher represents in thought. Schelling therefore suggests that philosophy, having completed this task of representation, is about to return, along with all the other sciences, to "the universal ocean of poetry from which it started out."[34] The sciences began in poetry; in poetry they will conclude.

Unity and crisis

Schelling's appeal to poetry is an indication of his strong connections with German Romanticism. The German Romantics held that the intellectual and creative fragmentation of the modern world, pointed out by Schiller, could be cured through poetry. In his *Athenaeum* fragments of 1798, Friedrich Schlegel speaks of a "progressive universal poetry" that not only will reunite all the separate literary genres but will also put poetry and philosophy back into touch with each other. Thus, a breach that has existed for 2,500 years will be repaired. Indeed, Schlegel looks forward to a "completely new epoch of sciences and arts" to be dominated by a "symphilosophy" and "sympoetry" in perfect harmony with each other.[35]

This theme of a breaking down of the barriers between literature and philosophy is also pervasive in Nietzsche and his successors. Derrida in particular has become the master of a hybrid discourse that combines a "literary" exposure of the residual metaphors imbedded in philosophical texts with a "philosophical" dissection of the themes displayed in texts of literature. The same tendency is also to be found in Heidegger and in Foucault. Admittedly, it is somewhat concealed in Heidegger by the sharp division between the early and later stages in his intellectual career and by the apparent philosophical emptiness of many of the later writings. Similarly, it is concealed in Foucault by the seeming scientism (which is, in fact, a parody of science) of much of his work. Nonetheless, both writers point, like Derrida, to a *brouillage* of "literary" and "philosophical" discourse—to an apparent liberation from the restrictions of each by a conscious confusion of both. Finally, almost all recent Nietzsche criticism has stressed how in Nietzsche the traditional distinction between literature and philosophy is broken down. As one example among many, J. P. Stern notes that, in the past, some have seen Nietzsche as a "conceptual philosopher," though a confused one, while others have seen him "as a poet— either . . . as a heroic poet of the German soul . . . or as a pre-fascist poet manqué." Stern observes that this alternative, poet versus philosopher, is misleading. He suggests that Nietzsche invents a "middle mode of language, which I suppose we may call 'literary-philosophical.'"[36] This seems to me an entirely accurate way of putting it. Even if it were not accurate, it would still be significant, for almost all those contemporary intellectuals who look to Nietzsche are attracted by the strangeness of his linguistic vision.

Yet, at the same time, there is an immense gulf between the prophets of extremity and their Romantic predecessors. Readers familiar with both Nietzsche and the young Schelling will know that these are radically different thinkers. How ought we to characterize this difference? Perhaps the most obvious point is that whereas the young Schelling seeks rest in the comforting, restoring unity of intellectual intuition, any such unity is anathema to Nietzsche. Consider Nietzsche's *Birth of Tragedy*. Here the symbol of reunion is Dionysus, who constitutes one side of the Apollonian/Dionysian polarity that is central to that work. As is well known, this polarity was earlier exploited by the Romantics.[37] But Nietzsche gives to the polarity a nihilistic turn, for Dionysian immediacy turns out, in his view, to be unbearable. Schelling's system of 1800 culminates in the benign immediacy provided by intellectual intuition. For Nietzsche there can be no such culmination, and hence no system. Indeed, Nietzsche attacks the very idea of a philosophical system: "The will to a system is a lack of integrity," as he says in *Twilight of the Idols* (*TI*, "Maxims and Arrows," §26). A similar rejection of system—of closure in any form—also permeates the writings of Heidegger, Foucault, and Derrida.

The difference between Nietzsche and the Romantics can be stated in another, different way. Here it is a question of origins rather than of culmination, though these are clearly two sides of the same coin. For if the Romantics believed that a philosophical system could in some sense "culminate," they also believed that this culmination took the form of a return. Illuminating on this notion is M. H. Abrams's *Natural Supernaturalism: Tradition and Revolution in Romantic Literature*. Abrams shows how important a role the motif of a "circuitous journey" back to the beginning (or rather, to a higher stage of the beginning) played in Romantic thought. Abrams's favorite bearer of this motif is Wordsworth, whose *Prelude* he examines in some detail. We begin our lives in communion with nature, become separated from it, and finally make our way back. We move from alienation, through spiritual crisis, to a redemptive reintegration with the cosmos and with our own possibilities. As Abrams demonstrates, a similar story is told by dozens of other Romantic, proto-Romantic, or post-Romantic thinkers. We can discover a circuitous journey in the plot lines of Schiller's *Aesthetic Letters* and Hegel's *Phenomenology;* in Hölderlin's *Hyperion;* in Goethe's *Faust;* in Novalis's romances; in Blake and Coleridge and Shelley and Carlyle.[38]

"All process, Romantic thinkers believed, moves forward and also rounds back."[39] What do we find when we turn to the prophets of extremity? Here we have a circuitous journey without return, a crisis without resolution, a dialectic without reintegration. This is most clearly visible in Nietzsche. Far more than his successors, Nietzsche exploits Romantic motifs. But in doing so he radically alters their character. The equivalent in Nietzsche of the circuitous journey is the doctrine of eternal return. This doctrine, as we shall see, is ultimately unintelligible. It cannot in any way be portrayed. It is a kind of antimythic myth, a parody of the hopes that Nietzsche's predecessors entertained. Above all, eternal return does not "round back." On the contrary, it stands as a kind of perpetual crisis, in which the desire to round back is countered by the conviction that all paths are broken.

In *The Order of Things,* Foucault characterizes Nietzsche's place in nineteenth-century thought in terms that underscore both his affinity with and his radical difference from the Romantics. As Foucault puts it, in nineteenth-century thought prior to Nietzsche, "the flow of development, with all its resources of drama, oblivion, alienation, [is] held within an anthropological finitude." In other words, it is held within a finite, closed circle that promises "an end to History." But what happens in Nietzsche's thought? The notion of an end to History is transformed into "the death of God and the odyssey of the last man." Anthropological finitude gives way to "the prodigious leap of the superman." The "great continuous chain of History" is broken by "the infinity of the eternal return." And Foucault continues:

> It is in vain that the death of God, the imminence of the superman, and the promise and terror of the great year take up once more, as it were term by term, the elements that are arranged in nineteeth-century thought and form its archaeological framework. The fact remains that they sent all these stable forms up in flames, that they used their charred remains to draw strange and perhaps impossible faces; and by a light that may be either—we do not yet know which—the reviving flame of the last great fire or an indication of the dawn, we see the emergence of what may perhaps be the space of contemporary thought. (*MC,* pp. 274–275/262–263.*)

As confirmation of the complex relationship that pertains between Nietzsche and the Romantics, it is worth pointing to the polemic concerning the nature of Romanticism that has lately arisen among some literary

---

*When page references are separated by a slash, those preceding the slash refer to the original French or German work, while those after the slash refer to the English translation. The translations that I have used are indicated in the Key to Abbreviations, above.

critics. Abrams sees Romanticism as translating into a secular idiom the "great circle" of Neoplatonic Christianity, with its vision of a return from sin to primal unity.[40] Redemption, in the Romantic view, comes not through an external Redeemer but through the workings of man's own divine creativity. The important thing, though, is that redemption *does* come: there is a genuine theodicy at work. Other critics have vehemently attacked this view. It has been argued—most incisively by J. Hillis Miller —that Abrams misses the disturbing underside of Romanticism. As Miller puts it, Abrams "perhaps takes his writers a little too much at face value, summarizes them a little too flatly, fails to search them for ambiguities or contradictions in their thought, does not 'explicate' in the sense of unfold, unravel, or unweave."[41] On the one hand, Romanticism appears as a confident secularization of Christianity; on the other hand, as a worried anticipation of twentieth-century uncertainty.

Interesting is the role that Nietzsche plays in this polemic. In *Natural Supernaturalism,* Abrams presents Nietzsche as a late Romantic, who along with Marx, Eliot, and Lawrence puts forward yet another version of the circuitous journey.[42] In short, Abrams interprets Nietzsche in the light of Romanticism. Miller, for his part, interprets Romanticism in the light of Nietzsche. In the various hesitations and uncertainties of the Romantics, he sees a denial of the notion of primal unity to which, on a manifest level, they seem to be solidly committed. Instead, he sees an awakening to the idea of primal difference or differentiation that Nietzsche and his successors put forward. I am quite sure that it is Miller, much more than Abrams, who is right about Nietzsche. As to who is right about Romanticism, this is a more difficult issue, and one that we do not need to resolve here. But one thing is certain. If Abrams romanticizes Nietzsche, and if (as seems possible) Miller nietzscheanizes the Romantics, they do agree that the relation between Nietzsche and the Romantics is an important one. Thus, they both point to the relation that the prophecy of extremity bears to earlier thought.

Gadamer and aestheticism

My argument that we can find the roots of Nietzschean and post-Nietzschean thought in late eighteenth- and early nineteenth-century intellectual history is to some extent confirmed by the work of the hermeneutic theorist Hans-Georg Gadamer. Indeed, I was for a time tempted to include a major consideration of Gadamer in the present study, for the notion of aestheticism is more easily and immediately applicable to Gadamer than it is to the other writers. Partly for this reason, I finally decided against dealing extensively with Gadamer's work. The reader can make the necessary connections for himself, whereas in Nietzsche, Heidegger, Foucault, and Derrida these connections are sometimes very difficult to see. I also decided against dealing with Gadamer because, finally, he rejects the notion of radical crisis. In Gadamer's view, life as it is actually lived has its own forms of solidarity, which persist even in the face of the hubris and confusion of intellectuals.

Still, Gadamer is of interest to us for at least two reasons. He is interesting firstly because of the light he casts on Heidegger. Heidegger's aestheticist side gets obscured by the presence within his corpus of competing strands of thought. I think especially of *Being and Time,* a work that preceded his turn to aestheticism and that tends to divert attention away from the writings, often of Delphic obscurity, in which an aestheticist position is suggested. Gadamer is a more single-minded thinker than Heidegger. In consequence, we simply cannot help seeing how centrally important the aesthetic concern is for him. Yet, at the same time, his work develops in a reasonably straightforward way out of Heidegger's work. It is not, I think, inaccurate to say that he synthesizes the hermeneutical or interpretive dimension of *Being and Time* with the preoccupation with the work of art that we see Heidegger manifesting in "The Origin of the Work of Art." His investigations are marked by an analytical concern that Heidegger himself abandoned when he made his "turn" to aestheticism. In working out the details of his own position, he says things that Heidegger himself might have said had he been content, in his post–*Being and Time* incarnations, to play a less oracular role. Indeed, Heidegger himself notes of Gadamer's afterword to the 1960 Reclam edition of "The Origin of the Work of Art" that it "contains a decisive hint for the reader of my later writings" (*PLT,* p. xxiv). Gadamer perhaps gets us as close as we are going to get to an authorized interpretation of the later Heidegger. And in this interpretation, Heidegger appears unequivocally as an aestheticist.

Secondly, Gadamer is interesting because of the light he casts on the historical background to aestheticism. It is this aspect of his work that most especially interests me here. Heidegger tends to obscure the antecedents of aestheticism by his penchant for seeing himself as one of a select company of world-historical thinkers. He is so eager to draw out his relation to, for example, Parmenides and Heraclitus, that he hardly deigns to cast his eyes on nearer, lesser figures. Thus, he never suggests an affinity between his thought and that of the Romantics, though he wrote and lectured on the Romantics, particularly on Schelling. Indeed, his si-

lence concerning the matter of possible affinities between his thought and
that of the Romantics is so striking that one is tempted to accuse him of
deliberate concealment.[43] Gadamer, on the other hand, explores the immediate origins of the aestheticist view in some detail. Dealing extensively
with the Romantics and with Kant, he helps us to see how aestheticism is
connected with the emergence of aesthetics in the late eighteenth and
early nineteenth centuries.

As Gadamer makes clear both in his major work, *Truth and Method*
(1960), and in his various scattered essays on hermeneutic themes, his
main concern is to attack what he regards as the incursion of the methods
of modern natural science into the study of the social and cultural world.
Against this incursion, he appeals to the "historical and cultural sciences" as they emerged from German Romanticism in the early nineteenth century. Though he sees the historical and cultural sciences as in
part contaminated by the natural sciences, he also finds that they "maintained a humanistic heritage which distinguishes them from all other
kinds of modern research and brings them close to other, quite different,
extra-scientific experiences, and especially those proper to art."[44] Gadamer's strategy, as I see it, is to bring about a revaluation of this artistic
dimension. His central argument is that the experience of the work of art
is the model for all experience. Time and again in *Truth and Method* and
in his other, related writings, he appeals to this experience as providing a
norm for the whole process of human understanding and interpretation.

In carrying out this enterprise, Gadamer both follows the Romantics
and departs from them. It is his departure from the Romantics that is the
more evident. He is widely and quite rightly seen as a critic of Romantic
and late Romantic hermeneutics and of the German tradition of historiography that was so clearly a product of the Romantic cast of mind. If one
needs to attach names to what he attacks, he is the critic of Schleiermacher, Ranke, and Dilthey. These figures had in common the assumption
that through a process of empathetic understanding the interpreter can
arrive at an immediate grasp of the objects that he is interpreting. In textual hermeneutics, this was taken to mean that the interpreter can come
to grasp the mind of the author; in historiography, it meant a recovery of
the past "as it actually was." To be sure, immediacy in understanding may
be difficult. But through a combination of empathy on the one hand and
scientific procedure on the other, it is nonetheless attainable.

Gadamer rejects this view. Romantic hermeneutic theory conceives of
understanding as "the reproduction of an original production."[45] From
Gadamer's perspective, any such reproduction is simply impossible; for

however much we try, we cannot place ourselves back into the context within which the original production took place. The task of the interpreter, then, is not the recovery of something that cannot be recovered. Rather, his task is to make the object of his interpretation intelligible to himself and to the audience for whom he intends that interpretation. He accomplishes this task by looking at the object in the light of his own knowledge and concerns. In so doing, he quite legitimately gives new meanings to the object—meanings that may go far beyond anything that the original textual authors or historical actors could have conceived of. Thus, the Romantic notion of empathetic understanding, with its concern for mere reproduction, gives way to a notion of "active" or "productive" interpretation—of which, as it turns out, Nietzsche was the first great exponent.

Gadamer's adoption of this distinctly post-Romantic conception of interpretation should not be read, however, as a total rejection of the Romantic view. In the first place, one does not need to look very hard to find that the Romantics themselves seriously doubted the possibility of immediate, empathetic understanding. The surface commitment to transparency that runs through Romantic thought tends to be undercut by an uneasy sense of the obstacles standing in the way of this transparency.[46] Unfortunately, I cannot pursue this theme here, since it would take us too far into those difficult questions concerning the interpretation of Romanticism that I broached above, and would lead us away from our main concern, aestheticism.

More to the point is the fact that Gadamer himself finds a foreshadowing of his hermeneutics in Romantic theory. Specifically, he finds it in the Romantic "aesthetics of genius." The notion of the artist as someone who creates with a serene lack of consciousness—as someone who is unable to articulate the rules of his own creation because he works at the behest of higher or deeper forces—has important implications for the interpretation of works of art. It suggests that the interpreter of a work of art makes a serious mistake if he sees his task as the recovery of the mind of the work's author. For if the mind of the author is itself incapable of grasping the work, then the recovery of that mind is, if not irrelevant, at the very least inadequate to the work's interpretation. In short, the aesthetics of genius already suggests Gadamer's position. This is why Gadamer is able to tell us that "the aesthetics of genius has done important preparatory work in showing that the experience of the work of art always fundamentally surpasses any subjective horizon of interpretation, whether that of the artist or that of the recipient. The *mens auctoris* is not admissible as a yardstick for the meaning of a work of art."[47] Gadamerian hermeneutics takes this implication of Romantic aesthetic theory and applies it not only to works of art but to all interpretive objects.

If Gadamer's position has roots within Romanticism, it also has roots in the philosophy of Kant. Kant's *Critique of Judgment* was a major inspiration for the Romantic aesthetics of genius.[48] Thus, the aesthetics of genius, and Gadamer's use thereof, point directly to a consideration of Gadamer's relation to Kant.

Looked at superficially, Gadamer appears to stand in radical opposition to Kant, just as he appears to stand in radical opposition to the Romantics. For he follows Heidegger in attacking what he sees as Kant's sharp distinctions between the theoretical, the practical, and the aesthetic. In particular, says Gadamer, Kant was wrong to carve out a separate and independent aesthetic sphere. While on the one hand Kant thus mapped out an area in which the idea of taste could claim independent validity, on the other hand, according to Gadamer, he excluded from the aesthetic sphere all considerations of truth or knowledge. In Gadamer's words, he "limited the concept of knowledge to the theoretical and practical use of reason."[49] Against Kant, Gadamer argues strenuously for the "truth value" of art. Far from being merely a delightful residue of the playfulness of its author, the work of art embodies a knowledge quite distinct from anything its author may have intended. Gadamer speaks at one point of "the overwhelming presence of works of art."[50] Among other things, this "presence" means that the work of art transcends its historical origins. It exceeds the subjective intentions of its author. Thus, *The Merchant of Venice,* for example, has a meaning for those who live in the late twentieth century that Shakespeare did not intend and could not even have imagined. This is not to deny that authors' intentions exist. But as Gadamer puts it in one of his essays, "the work of art is the expression of a truth that cannot be reduced to what its creator actually thought in it."[51]

And yet, if this view is clearly anti-Kantian, it is nonetheless necessary to note the extent to which it still remains dependent on Kant. As we have seen, Kant's theory of genius and his closely related assertion that art can embody "aesthetic ideas" already suggest the "truth value" notion. Even more important, by granting autonomy to the aesthetic, Kant laid the groundwork for Gadamer's project—and for the aestheticist project in general. Gadamer's central move is his application of the notion of aesthetic interpretation to interpretation in general. Without the distinctions that Kant first postulates, such a move would be inconceivable. Three of our four thinkers are, like Gadamer, similarly indentured to a Kantian beginning.

They seek to free our minds from Kant—or, perhaps better, from a certain interpretation and development of Kant. They also seek to free our minds from Hegel, though we have not yet entered into that part of our story. But they still remain within a Kantian (and Hegelian) framework. Only Derrida, of these thinkers, begins to move us away from Kant and Hegel. But this is to anticipate an argument that, if it is to be convincing, will require us to work our way through the projects of all four thinkers.

PART I

Friedrich Nietzsche as Aestheticist

The world as a work of art that gives birth to itself——

—Nietzsche

CHAPTER 1

Nietzsche and
the Aesthetic

The view of Friedrich Nietzsche (1844–1900) that I advance in this essay will strike many readers as perversely out of tune with their own prior knowledge of him. At any rate, it will seem out of tune to those who have not yet confronted Foucault or Derrida, for these writers (especially the latter) project a view of Nietzsche that is in some ways close to my own. In the usual view, Nietzsche was a naturalistic philosopher, one whose aim was to recommend and cultivate an immediacy of sentiment and action, a congruence between human culture and a passionately desiring human nature. One can easily derive such a view from Nietzsche's text. For example, the casual reader of *The Genealogy of Morals* is apt to see it as presenting an argument concerning the bad effects of a repressive Christian morality on human life. Christianity, the argument goes, is in fundamental discord with human nature; men must learn to act "naturally," and a healthy culture will then emerge. The argument is clear and simple—or at any rate appears so. We see here Nietzsche the diagnostician, Nietzsche the critical analyst of contemporary culture. Here is the Nietzsche who tells us that existing morality is "anti-nature," who speaks of a "return to nature," and who recommends "affirmation of life even in its strangest and sternest problems" (*TI,* "Morality as Anti-Nature"; "Expeditions of an Untimely Man," §48; "What I Owe the Ancients," §5).

It is this Nietzsche that Walter Kaufmann emphasizes in his *Nietzsche: Philosopher, Psychologist, Antichrist* (first published in 1950). Kaufmann's book rescued Nietzsche from the view that he was a proponent of German militarism and a proto-Nazi, and thus did much to rehabilitate his reputation in the English-speaking world.[1] Many English-readers have approached Nietzsche through Kaufmann. Because Nietzsche is such a fragmentary thinker and so puzzling at first reading, one feels a real need for a coherent and easily read commentary. For a long time, Kaufmann's book seemed to fill this need. Moreover, most English-readers come to Nietzsche by way of Kaufmann's translations. In consequence, the impact of Kaufmann's interpretation of Nietzsche has been considerable. Admittedly, with increasing frequency people have been approaching Nietzsche independently of Kaufmann. They have become skeptical of Kaufmann's tendency to deny everything in Nietzsche that struck him as too extreme and questionable. But even many of these people have still been inclined to view Nietzsche as essentially a critic and analyst, concerned with exposing the antinatural character of the dominant moral code, and, by implication, concerned also with replacing that antinatural morality with a natural one.

But such a reading vastly underrates the complexity and subtlety of Nietzsche's position. Since many of Nietzsche's statements lend themselves to a naturalistic interpretation, one is inclined to postulate a certain hesitancy on Nietzsche's part, an unwillingness to depart from a position having recognizable philosophical antecedents. Or perhaps what looks like a residual naturalism is really only a matter of rhetorical strategy, by which Nietzsche attempts to appropriate for his own position the more familiar language of earlier revolutionaries—just as Foucault, Nietzsche's closest successor, has at times appropriated the language of Marxism. We may concede Nietzsche's appeals to "nature," his panegyrics of "life," his calls for an immediate and uncomplicated mode of behavior. But what does "nature," or "life," mean? And what would be the content of a "natural" or "life-affirming" morality? In fact, Nietzsche gives us no content, and he declines to do so because it is precisely the notion of a "natural" morality that he rejects. In Nietzsche's view, the notion of a morality that would somehow be given by nature is untenable. It is untenable because in any culture that has become sufficiently self-conscious about its behavior to articulate moral theories, the very notion of naturalness will have become so distant as to be all but useless, except as propaganda.

Nietzsche's experience is also that of many who live within late twentieth-century Western culture. After Freud, with his attempt to reach down into formerly unknown strata of human thought and action, what can we say about the "naturalness" of human nature? Where does the natural end and the cultural, the artificial, begin? And, supposing one could have it, would one *want* a "natural" morality? Surely all morality, by the very fact of its being a morality, is in some basic sense unnatural. If this is so, what grounds do we have for choosing between one unnatural moral code and another? Freud's preferences were clear, but in subsequent thinkers preferences have blurred. To take an obvious example—one much stressed by Foucault—why have certain modes of sexual behavior been defined as "natural" (good, acceptable) while other modes have been defined as "unnatural" (bad, unacceptable)? In the nature of things, it now comes to be argued, one has no ground for choosing one mode of behavior over another, for morality is not a question of "the nature of things." Or, as Nietzsche puts it in *Beyond Good and Evil,* "there are no moral phenomena at all, but only a moral interpretation of phenomena ——" (*BGE,* §108).

How, then, does one choose between competing modes of behavior? Nietzsche's answer is that the choice ultimately has to be made on aesthetic grounds. The idea of the free creativity of the artist is decisive in this choice. More than anything else, Nietzsche abhors an inartistic subjection to the given. Notwithstanding his naturalistic rhetoric in attacking moral codes of which he disapproves, it is this, rather than lack of conformity to a supposedly given "nature," that bothers him. The great initiators of moral codes (most obviously, Jesus) escape his reproaches, for it is only the later rigidification that he objects to. Indeed, he sees the whole of culture as an essentially aesthetic product. Thus, he tells us in *The Genealogy of Morals* that the state was created by conquerors having the egoism of artists, who imposed on a formless "reality" their own image of how the world ought to be ordered. As Nietzsche characterizes them, such natures "come like fate, without reason, consideration, or pretext; they appear as lightning appears, too terrible, too sudden, too convincing, too 'different' even to be hated. Their work is an instinctive creation and imposition of forms; they are the most involuntary, unconscious artists there are." Such figures do not feel compelled to justify their work on grounds of its naturalness or utility or rationality, for their "terrible artists' egoism . . . knows itself justified to all eternity in its 'work' [*Werke*], like a mother in her child" (*GM,* 2nd Essay, §17).

Nietzsche is here attributing to art an ontogenetic, that is, a world-making significance. What comes into being does so as a result of artistic will; the "given," "natural" materials of this creation have no more significance than the blank emptiness of the artist's canvas as he starts to paint. As Nietzsche puts it in a fragment included by his editors in *The Will to Power,* "One is an artist at the cost of regarding what all non-artists call 'form' as *content,* as 'the thing itself' [*die Sache selbst*]. To be sure, then one belongs in a topsy-turvy world: for henceforth content becomes something merely formal—our life included" (*WP*, §818 [translation altered]; *KGW*, 8. Abt., 2. Bd., pp. 251–252). Here we have much more than a hint how we ought to interpret Nietzsche's conception of nature. For as these passages indicate—and as further passages confirm—he conceives of "nature" and of "the natural" as human creations. In his view, the world in which we live is a work of art that is continually being created and recreated; what is more, there is nothing either "behind" or "beyond" this web of illusion. This is the thought that underlies his dictum, to be found twice in the main body of *The Birth of Tragedy* and repeated in the 1886 preface, to the effect that "it is only as an *aesthetic phenomenon* that existence and the world are eternally *justified*" (*BT*, "Attempt at a Self-Criticism," §5, chaps. 5, 24; *NBW*, pp. 22, 52, 141). And it is a thought that persists throughout his career.

Such, at any rate, is one way of looking at Nietzsche. I am not convinced that this "aestheticist" view of Nietzsche totally sums up his thought, for I am not convinced that he had a single, conclusive doctrine. On the contrary, I detect in his writing, besides an aestheticism, a lingering commitment to the critical and analytical tradition of the Enlightenment. Nor am I even certain that this is the "best" Nietzsche interpretation among the various imperfect alternatives. If there are some texts that support it, there are others, especially those in which Nietzsche declares his commitment to the search for truth as the end and goal of philosophy, that need to be subjected to some interpretive violence if they are to be made consistent with aestheticism. Perhaps for some readers the naturalistic view of Nietzsche will continue to seem more convincing. At the same time, however, I am persuaded that a large measure of historical and critical legitimacy is granted to my attempt to view Nietzsche "as aestheticist" by the fact that this side of Nietzsche marks out the perspective in terms of which some influential later thinkers, most notably Heidegger, Foucault, and Derrida, work.

Moreover, it is the aestheticist and not the naturalist who is the crucially original Nietzsche, the thinker marking an epoch in the thought of the modern period. Others before Nietzsche called for an immediate relation between thought and "life." Others before Nietzsche spoke of the primacy of irrational forces in nature or in man. Others before Nietzsche attacked established codes of morality and rejected bourgeois convention. But no one else made the aestheticist move, though Schelling, at least, came close to it. Like Schelling, Nietzsche sees the world as a work of art. But in Schelling there was an author standing behind the work: as Schelling puts it, the world is "the original, still unconscious poetry *of the spirit.*" In Nietzsche, all authorship is excluded. The world is "a work of art"—but one that, as a consequence of the crisis of God's death, "gives birth to itself" (*WP*, §796; *KGW*, 8. Abt., 1. Bd., p. 117). The notion of the world as aesthetically self-creating constitutes an absolutely stunning innovation in thought, laying the basis for much of what follows Nietzsche—not least Heidegger, though Heidegger himself refused to acknowledge any such affinity. To put it in the simplest terms: Nietzsche stands as the founder of what became the aesthetic metacritique of "truth," wherein "the work of art," or "the text," or "language" is seen as establishing the grounds for truth's possibility.

Crisis

The notion of crisis is crucial for our understanding of Nietzsche's project, for it is this notion that opens the way to his aestheticism. The paradigm of crisis is the "death of God." Nietzsche's announcement of the death of God should not be mistaken for an empirical observation concerning the decline of Christian belief in the nineteenth century. On the contrary, it is a statement of faith, albeit a negative faith. In announcing the death of God, Nietzsche is declaring his conviction that the present is in a state of absolute dereliction, that it lacks any redeeming features, anything that might allow us to reconcile ourselves to things as they are. Many of Nietzsche's commentators, less favorably inclined to him than Kaufmann was, have seen him not only as a naturalist but also as an irrationalist, and they have pointed to his attack on values, his rejection of rational order, and his glorification of the will to power as evidence of this irrationalism. But as I have indicated, these various Nietzschean doctrines do not take us to the center of his thought. It is not so much the content of that thought as its style that suggests characterizing him as an "irrational" or (better) a "nonrational" thinker. And the style of Nietzsche's thought finds its justification in the conviction of crisis.

This conviction embraces a condemnation of the present world as null. The recognition of this nullity is what we know as nihilism. But as Nietzsche points out, there are two kinds of nihilism. On the one hand, there is a nihilism that fails to respond to what Nietzsche sees as the opportunity offered by the world's nullity. This nihilism views the devaluation of all present values as oppressive and burdensome. We look upon the void, we shudder, we draw back. We try to dull the reality of crisis, pretending that nothing has happened, that the world is still turning on its axis. In short, we adopt a passive and anaesthetic attitude. On the other hand, there is an active, aesthetic nihilism. Nietzsche prescribes this nihilism as the appropriate attitude for modern, and postmodern, existence. Instead of drawing back from the void, we dance upon it. Instead of lamenting the absence of a world suited to our being, we invent one. We become the artists of our own existence, untrammeled by natural constraints and limitations. It is this that Nietzsche has in mind when, in a *Nachlass* fragment, he declares that "the most extreme form of nihilism" is the view that there is "no *true world*," and hence that everything is "a *perspectival appearance* whose origin lies in us" (*WP*, §15; *KGW*, 8. Abt., 2. Bd., p. 18). Accepting this view, we see the necessity of lies; and accepting the necessity of lies, we embark upon a divine—that is, a creative—way of thinking.

In viewing Nietzsche "as aestheticist," I am not concerned with "Nietzsche's views on art," but rather with the role that notions generally seen as proper to the aesthetic play in his thought as a whole. These notions are utterly pervasive, going far beyond what one usually thinks of as the bounds of art. Foucault, Derrida, and their followers have already done much to suggest the importance of this aspect of Nietzsche's project. But they do so from inside the aestheticist perspective, and hence from a standpoint that is certainly not concerned with "correctness" in interpretation. I propose here to cast a scholarly eye on the Nietzschean beginnings of aestheticism. I propose to look at the wide-ranging aesthetic dimension of his work, and likewise at the mythological or broadly prophetic framework within which this aesthetic dimension is set.

This exploration of Nietzsche requires that we distinguish between the different phases of his career. We must avoid on one hand the view that his writings constitute a pure "anarchy of atoms," and on the other the view that they ought to be seen in terms of a single, coherent philosophy. Both views are defective; both obscure our perception of what is constant and what changes in Nietzsche's standpoint. The most important distinction is between the "early" Nietzsche of circa 1872–1876 and the "mature" Nietzsche of 1883 and after. The former period includes *The Birth of Tragedy* and the four *Untimely Meditations;* the latter, all the works from *Thus Spoke Zarathustra* through to his last, *Nietzsche contra Wagner* (finished 1888; published 1895). Between these two periods lies what is sometimes called Nietzsche's "positivistic" or "scientific" phase, which has its high point in *Human, All-Too-Human* (1878), and which runs through to *The Gay Science* (1882)—though this last work already foreshadows the Nietzsche of *Zarathustra.* The view that Nietzsche's career ought to be divided into "early," "middle," and "late" periods is by no means new, and I see no need to justify it here. In any case, my reasons for adopting this division will become clear as we proceed.

I do, however, differ from previous critics and commentators in my view of the relationship between the three periods, or at least in my view of the relationship between the "early" and the "mature" Nietzsche. Most readers of Nietzsche tend to look upon his early writings as interesting but as not indicative for his "mature" position. It is perfectly true that in these works Nietzsche has not yet come into his own. He is not yet entirely sure of the intellectual territory he inhabits. But at the same time, important aspects of his "mature" position are already in place in the early writings. And the historical roots of that position are much more clearly visible in the early than in the later writings. The aesthetic and mythological preoccupations of early Nietzsche are obvious, whereas the similar preoccupations of the mature Nietzsche are all too often overlooked.

What are the main parallels between these two phases in Nietzsche's career? Firstly, he is concerned in both his early and his late writings with attempting a "return to myth." Admittedly, the myth is in each case different, and in the late writings the very idea of myth tends to be undermined. But the fundamental concern with returning to myth, or to some simulacrum thereof, persists. In consequence, there is a structural identity between early and mature Nietzsche, a homologism in which much is transformed but in which the underlying principle remains the same. Secondly, in his early writings Nietzsche is clearly concerned with art as subject matter, but he is also concerned with art as style and method. While the former concern largely drops out of the "mature" writings, the latter becomes all the more important. As for Nietzsche's "middle" period, which stands outside this homologism, we shall be able to consider its significance only when we have examined in some detail the role of the aesthetic in his thought.

The centrality of the aesthetic

The most important element in Nietzsche's attraction to the aesthetic is the notion of creativity. Time and again, he glorifies the artist. Overflowing with strength and well-being, the artist transmutes reality. He transforms the brute material of existence into something made after his own image. He sees "nothing as it is, but fuller, simpler, stronger" (*WP*, §800; *KGW*, 8. Abt., 3. Bd., p. 87). This facet of Nietzsche's conception of art is important because he extends it to his own activity, conceiving of himself in his "mature" phase not simply as an observer of art but as an "*artist*-philosopher" (*WP*, §795; *KGW*, 8. Abt., 1. Bd., p. 87).

We here see the Romantic theme of the reunification of poetry and philosophy, which turns out to mean a reunification of poetry and philosophy under the domination of poetry, a return of philosophy to "the wide ocean of poetry," and not the reverse.[2] The theme of reunification is explicitly stated by Nietzsche himself in *The Gay Science*. In this work, he envisages a joining together of "the artistic energies and the practical wisdom of life" with "scientific thinking," the whole to form an organic unity that will far surpass present-day scholarship, medicine, legislation, and art (*GS*, §113). In *The Gay Science,* this is viewed only as a remote possibility, and not one to which Nietzsche himself would directly contribute. But *Thus Spoke Zarathustra,* whose first and second parts were written the following year, marks an important reorientation in Nietzsche's position, for here philosophy turns into art, with Nietzsche playing the artist-philosopher's role. It is all but impossible to read *Zarathustra* except as a very peculiar sort of artwork, so little is it a matter of philosophical or historical argument, so much a matter of "poetic" image and metaphor. Little wonder that in *Zarathustra* itself Nietzsche refers to the Zarathustrian project as poetry and to Zarathustra as a poet, and that in *Ecce Homo,* where he reviews all his previous writings, he attributes *Zarathustra* to a specifically poetic inspiration. And lest the poetic inspiration manifested in *Zarathustra* seem something peripheral, it is worth pointing out that Nietzsche regarded that work as the "highest" and "deepest" of his writings—indeed, as the "greatest gift" ever given to mankind.[3] Thus, Nietzsche himself saw his thought as, in some fundamental sense, aesthetic in character, and viewed that aesthetic element as central to his own significance as a thinker.

Underlying this insistence on the centrality of the aesthetic is a variant of the Romantics' commitment to immediacy, of which the Dionysian was one symbol. An important notion among the Romantics was the idea of art as promising an immediate knowledge—a knowledge that did not proceed along the killing path of mediation, the path of analysis and concepts. Nietzsche accepts this longing for immediacy, this suspicion of the analytical mind. But at the same time, there is a radical difference between Nietzsche and his Romantic predecessors. Whereas the Romantics were inclined to believe that art actually *could* penetrate to the truth of things, bringing subject and object together in a supreme moment of aesthetic insight, Nietzsche denies any such possibility. In Nietzsche's view, art is a vehicle not of truth but of illusion. Indeed, in one of his *Nachlass* fragments, he links the "will to art" to the will "to lie, to flight from 'truth,' to *negation* of 'truth'" (*WP,* § 853, pp. 451–452; *KGW,* 8. Abt., 2. Bd., p. 435). This is a view to which such figures as Schelling or Friedrich Schlegel never adhered, for they took art too seriously to regard it in its illusionistic aspect. Nietzsche is committed to immediacy, but only in the sense of feeling an unrequitable longing for it. He values art because it is nonconceptual, but recognizes that it gives us only the semblance of reality and not reality itself—whatever "reality itself" might mean.

To my mind, the French novelist and literary critic Maurice Blanchot gets things right when he notes that Nietzsche "thinks or, more precisely, writes . . . under a double suspicion that inclines him to a double refusal: refusal of the immediate, refusal of mediation."[4] Blanchot here conveys the peculiar duplicity of Nietzsche's position. Nietzsche sees immediacy as unattainable, but still desires it; he views concepts as undesirable, but also as necessary. This puts him in an odd position, opposing the reduction of concepts to immediate vision and intuition, but at the same time refusing to forget vision and intuition when dealing with the world of concepts. In response to these tensions, he extends the notion of art as illusion to the whole of the conceptual world, with "metaphysics, religion, moralities, science" viewed as products of an underlying aesthetic will to falsification (*WP,* §853; *KGW,* 8. Abt., 2. Bd., p. 435).[5] Here we see the basis for his radical attack on conventional scholarship; the source, too, of the inventive capacity that is so striking a feature of his own writing. Caught in a no-man's-land between an impossible immediacy and a rejected mediation, Nietzsche opts for the one thing that seems to remain: the style, the inner workings, of the text itself. In Blanchot's terminology, Nietzsche comes to the practice of a "*parole de fragment,*" an "*écriture fragmentaire*" that says nothing outside itself, that delights in the play of language for its own sake, that subverts the "spirit of gravity" and undermines the other side of the Nietzschean text, the "philosophical discourse" in which Nietzsche presumes to convey a coherent philosophical message. (It is no accident, incidentally, that Blanchot's work has a close affinity with later Heidegger, and that his impact is in turn visible in both Foucault and Derrida; for often those who are within the aestheticist circle see, in Nietzsche, elements that other commentators are inclined to miss.)[6]

But I am moving forward too quickly, anticipating elements of my argument that I have not had time to develop. Let us begin our consideration of the aesthetic dimension in Nietzsche by exploring his peculiar commitment to and refusal of immediacy. From this we can move on to his analogous treatment of mediation. Nietzsche's complex attitude toward imme-

diacy is best approached through his use of the opposition between
Apollo and Dionysus. *The Birth of Tragedy* is constructed around this
"extraordinary contrast" (*BT*, chap. 16; *NBW*, p. 100). Hence, the contrast is essential to any understanding of "early" Nietzsche. Moreover,
Nietzsche's attachment to it is suggestive in its foreshadowing of the later
dualisms of existentialism and of modernism in general. And while the
Apollonian (though not the Dionysian) all but drops out of the "mature"
Nietzsche, an analogous contrast remains, as we shall see, in his sometimes contradictory attempts to come to terms with the reality and practice of interpretation.

Apollo and Dionysus

Nietzsche believes that the Apollonian/Dionysian opposition allows
him to gain such an unusual insight into the Hellenic character that the
pretensions of present-day science—a science based, in his view, on
"classical-Hellenic" foundations—are called into question (*BT*, chap. 16;
NBW, pp. 100–101). But what exactly does this opposition amount to?
As soon as one begins to analyze it, one sees how slippery and elusive it is.
The Apollonian and the Dionysian are symbols rather than concepts,
multivalent centers of meaning rather than denotatively exact tokens designating a determinate "X" and a determinate "Y." Indeed, the Apollo-
nian/Dionysian contrast contains within itself at least three subsidiary
oppositions, each of which moves off in a direction quite different from
the other two.

The opposition that most consistently attracts the attention of Nietzsche's readers (one that is already to be found, though under a different
name, in Schiller) is between Apollonian formalism and Dionysian formlessness. Apollo is the form-giving force, who seeks to "grant repose to
individual beings . . . by drawing boundaries around them," and Dionysus
is the force that from time to time destroys these "little circles," lest the
Apollonian tendency "congeal the form to Egyptian rigidity and coldness" (*BT*, chap. 9; *NBW*, p. 72). Notwithstanding its highly suggestive
and inexact character, there are circumstances under which this opposition has a certain analytical usefulness. For example, we shall see how the
form/formlessness contrast serves as a way of ordering the historical
oeuvre of Michel Foucault and of illuminating certain of its contradictions and underlying tendencies.

Another aspect of the Apollonian/Dionysian contrast, less frequently
exploited but in some ways equally suggestive, is the conflict between the

visual bias of Apollo—"the 'shining one,' the deity of light"—and the nonvisual or "nonimagistic" (*unbildlich*) bias of Dionysus, who rules over the realm of music (*BT*, chap. 1; *NBW*, pp. 33, 35). I shall make use of this opposition, too, in discussing Foucault, for it connects with the metaphoric of light, as I shall call it, that appears in and later disappears from Foucault's work. Nor is it only in Foucault that such can be found, for Derrida (and, more recently and restrainedly, Richard Rorty) has attempted to identify the entire tradition of Western thought with just such a metaphoric. Apollo, conceived of as the god of light and wisdom, serves as a convenient symbol for this reading of the Western philosophical tradition. Let me emphasize again that these two oppositions—between form and formlessness and between the visual and the nonvisual—are by no means rational or conceptual; but because neither Foucault nor Derrida adheres to a conceptual logic, these oppositions do, in some sense, "fit" their thought, where logical categories do not.

Here, however, I wish to focus not on these oppositions but on another that is equally a part of the contrast between the two gods, and that in the present context is of decisive importance. For if in Nietzsche's eyes Apollo is "the 'shining one'" (*der "Scheinende"*), he is also the god of illusion (exploiting, here, the ambiguity of the German *Schein*, which means not only "light" but also "semblance" or "illusion"). He is the god who wraps man in "the veil of *māyā*" and thus protects him from the harsh realities of his altogether frightening and pitiful existence (*BT*, chap. 1; *NBW*, pp. 35–36). And if Apollo creates the illusions without which we cannot go on living, then Dionysus "annihilates" the veil of *māyā* and thus opens the way for a direct and unmediated participation in reality (*BT*, chap. 3; *NBW*, p. 40). This polarity, too, is part of the aesthetic heritage of Romanticism. It is the polarity between reality and dream, between the desire to participate in the "really real" and the apparently contrary desire to revel in the irrealistic realm of fantasy.

As I have already noted, Nietzsche gives to the Apollonian/Dionysian, illusion/reality distinction a nihilistic turn, for he finds Dionysian immediacy to be unbearable. In *The Birth of Tragedy*, he rejects the then-conventional belief, articulated by Winckelmann, Goethe, Matthew Arnold, and others, that the essence of Greek culture is to be found in its "noble simplicity" and "calm grandeur"—that is, in its specifically Apollonian characteristics. Aware of this, and aware also of the role that the Dionysian plays in the writings of the later Nietzsche, the casual reader might well be inclined to view the work as a paean to the Dionysian element in culture.

But Nietzsche is in fact far more interested in the cultural role played by

the Apollonian. In Nietzsche's view, all primitive peoples are amply endowed with Dionysian energies. In all quarters of the ancient world, one
can find Dionysian festivals of one sort or another, most of them centering
on sexual licentiousness and on the unleashing of savage natural instincts.
What distinguished the Greeks from their barbarian counterparts was their
attachment to Apollo, whose imposing figure "held out the Gorgon's head
to this grotesquely uncouth Dionysian power" (*BT*, chap. 2; *NBW*, p. 39).

Apollo did not destroy Dionysus but only tempered him. The Dionysian orgies of the non-Greeks consistently turned into crudely natural dis-
charges. In contrast, those of the Greeks became "festivals of world redemption and days of transfiguration," in which Dionysian revelry, with
its destruction of the *principium individuationis* that normally separates
man from man, took on the character of an artistic phenomenon (*BT*,
chap. 2; *NBW*, p. 40). To put it briefly, it was the "figure of Apollo" that
made the difference between barbarism and culture. The barbarians remained barbarians because their Dionysian impulses were left unrestrained. The Greeks became Greeks because, under the influence of
Apollo, these impulses were redirected and transformed, becoming an
ingredient of culture rather than a mere expression of nature.

To say that Apollo protected the Greeks from barbarism is also to say
that Greek culture was founded on illusion. More than this, it is to say
that culture in general is so founded, for in Nietzsche's view the Greeks
provide the model for culture. I won't bore the reader by quoting all those
passages in which Nietzsche identifies the Apollonian with dream, fantasy, semblance, illusion, madness, and deception. Suffice it to say that
the identification is pervasive. According to Nietzsche, the Apollonian
veil of *māyā* seeks to shield us from the harsh realities of existence. It
restores us with "the healing balm of blissful illusion [*Täuschung*]." It
gives us a "splendid illusion [*Illusion*] that would cover dissonance with a
veil of beauty" (*BT*, chaps. 21, 25; *NBW*, pp. 127, 143). But with equal
zeal, Dionysus seeks to tear aside the Apollonian veil, opening the way to
"the Mothers of Being," to "the mysterious primordial unity" (*BT*, chaps.
1, 16; *NBW*, pp. 37, 99). Nietzsche characterizes the Dionysian as the
"intoxicated reality" (*rauschvolle Wirklichkeit*) that calls a halt to Apollonian dreaming (*BT*, chap. 2; *NBW*, p. 38). As it turns out, however, the
Dionysian is much more "intoxicated" than "realistic": Nietzsche
stresses the element of frenzy, excess, and jubilation much more than he
does the Dionysian contact with reality. Consequently, the latter tends to
be overborne by the former, so that, as Nietzsche puts it, a "chasm of
oblivion" comes to separate "the worlds of everyday reality and of Dio-

nysian reality" (*die Welt der alltäglichen und der dionysischen Wirklich-keit*) (*BT*, chap. 7; *NBW*, p. 59).

In any case, the Dionysian tearing aside of the veil, if it is persistent, is also intermittent—for a continuous unmediated glance into the depths of reality would be so horrifying as to precipitate a reversion from culture to barbarism. Within the confines of culture, then, the tendency is toward a continual return of the Apollonian, a continual recurrence of illusion. In Nietzsche's view, there are three types of culture, each of which requires the presence of illusion if the more nobly formed and sensitive natures are not to fall victim to their own loathing and displeasure at existence. "It is an eternal phenomenon," Nietzsche says: "the insatiable will always finds a way to detain its creatures in life and compel them to live on, by means of an illusion [*Illusion*] spread over things." In "Socratic" culture, men are chained by the delusion (*Wahn*) that through the love of knowledge they will be able to "heal the eternal wound of existence." In "artistic" culture, they are ensnared by a "seductive veil of beauty" fluttering before their eyes. In "tragic" culture, they are given "metaphysical comfort" by the belief that "beneath the whirl of phenomena eternal life flows on inde-structibly." Nor are these the only illusions that "the will" has at hand (*BT*, chap. 18; *NBW*, p. 110). Nietzsche's tendency in *The Birth of Tragedy* is to move on the Apollonian plane of illusion—to see the magic moun-tain of Olympian fantasy as an absolute necessity of culture. In Nietz-sche's view, men cannot bear the full burden of reality. Consequently, only in illusion does culture flourish or even survive.

Yet (to move into the critical mode), a manifest illogicality runs through this attempt to portray Apollonian illusionism as a genuinely protective element in culture—indeed, as the element making culture possible. Let me approach the problem by asking *how* Apollonian illu-sion protects us from the reality of existence, an issue that Nietzsche does not manage to deal with very clearly. Suppose that the protective illusion is one that we know to be an illusion—a plausible view, if Dionysian real-ity is continually impinging upon consciousness. On this supposition, Nietzsche's account appears to break down immediately; for if we know the illusion to be illusion, then presumably its entire protective force will be lost. Suppose, on the contrary, that the illusion is one that we do not know to be an illusion. Here, again, Nietzsche's case breaks down, for the concept of illusion seems to presuppose a contrary concept, that of "real-ity." It seems to presuppose, too, that at some point there will be contact between the two, whether it be with "Dionysian" reality or with "every-day" reality. But this contact is bound to be shattering, precisely because the illusion *is* illusion, and hence by definition in discord with "reality." In fact, the only contact that would not be shattering is the contact between reality and a correct belief regarding that reality—"Dionysian" reality being bearable only when one understands that it *is* Dionysian reality, and the same with "everyday" reality.

To make the same point in slightly different terms: one can call everything "illusion" if one wishes, just as one can call everything "discourse" or "text." But this does not abolish the distinction between, say, an interpretation of the experience of being run over by a truck and the experience itself—a distinction which every language, if it is to function on something more than a purely fantastic level, must somehow accommodate. Focusing on interpretation and attempting to abstract itself away from reality entirely, aestheticism fails to give to this distinction the weight that it "normally" has. Foucault, for example, finds himself in exactly the same position as Nietzsche when he maintains that his historical works are fictions written with the aim of bringing about political effects in the present. If Foucault's readers know that his allegedly historical writing is fictional, then that writing cannot by any rational standards have the desired effect on their politics. On the other hand, if his readers do not know that his writing is fictional, they will be brought up short at their first contact with an intransigent reality—even if we choose to call that reality, too, a fiction.

There is one context, however, in which the position embraced by Nietzsche and Foucault makes sense: the aesthetic context. In the realm of the aesthetic, we engage in the willing suspension of disbelief. We view the play or read the novel as if the events it depicts are real events. We know and at the same time do not know that the illusion is an illusion. We enter the world of the artwork, and for a time the nonaesthetic world becomes irrelevant, or at least peripheral, to consciousness. Admittedly, this may not be the dominant experience of all art at all times (take, for example, the initial impact of "Guernica," and of all "committed" art). But I nonetheless see it as a crucial aspect of the aesthetic experience, for we do tend to distinguish art from a propaganda so caught up in its own message that it is of no interest aside from that message. Nietzsche, and Foucault after him, generalize this aesthetic context to cover the whole of the social and political world, the whole range of personal and human experience. There is much that one can learn from such a move. At the same time, it can be seen as provisionally dangerous and, because it ultimately comes up against its contradiction, finally self-defeating.

The aesthetic dimension in the later writings

So far, I have looked at the early, not the "mature" Nietzsche. It might be thought that in his later writings Nietzsche abandoned the aestheticism that we see in *The Birth of Tragedy*. True, there is an important shift from his early to his later writings. Confining ourselves to the theme of art (leaving myth to one side for the moment), the shift can be viewed as a manifestation of Nietzsche's liberation from Schopenhauer. Nietzsche observes in a note of 1887 that "around 1876" he first came to realize that his instinct "went into the opposite direction from Schopenhauer's: toward a *justification of life,* even at its most terrible, ambiguous, and mendacious" (*WP,* §1005; *KGW,* 8. Abt., 2. Bd., pp. 18–19).

Admittedly, in the 1886 preface to *The Birth of Tragedy* and in the section discussing that work in *Ecce Homo* (written in 1888), Nietzsche claims that his attachment to Schopenhauer had been only terminological (*BT,* "Attempt at a Self-Criticism," §6; *NBW,* p. 24; *EH,* "BT," §1; *NBW,* pp. 726–727). But this is contradicted by any careful reading of the work itself, which (whatever Nietzsche's intentions in writing it may have been) is deeply marked by Schopenhauer's philosophy. To raise the most obvious point first, in his employment of the opposition between Apollo and Dionysus, Nietzsche allows the former to take on the characteristics of Schopenhauer's "world as representation," and the latter those of his "world as will." Insofar as the Apollonian power to create form is also associated, in *The Birth of Tragedy,* with the creation of illusions—and the association is pervasive—it is equivalent to the illusory world of phenomena. Insofar as the Dionysian power to destroy form is associated with the primal ground of being, it is equivalent to the world as will.

Indeed, one can go even further than this, for there is another opposition running through *The Birth of Tragedy,* the opposition between a combined Apollonian/Dionysian art on the one hand and a chaotic and threatening reality on the other. This, too, is a repetition of Schopenhauer. In manifest opposition to his predecessor, Nietzsche tells us that art (more specifically, the art of tragedy) ought to lead not to the denial but to the affirmation of reality. Yet, he in fact follows Schopenhauer by seeing art as will-less and disinterested, and then attributing to it the role of protecting man from the terrors of an "interested" reality (*BT,* chaps. *t, 6; NBW,* pp. 48, 55). Knowledge of that reality, Nietzsche suggests (and here we see his refusal of immediacy), kills action. "Action requires the veils of illusion" (*zum Handeln gehört das Umschleiertsein durch die Illusion*). Fortunately, art comes to the rescue; for art, "a saving sorceress, expert at healing," alone knows "how to turn these nauseous thoughts about the horror or absurdity of existence into notions with which one can live" (*BT*, chap. 7; *NBW*, pp. 59–60).

The "mature" Nietzsche, having abandoned Schopenhauer, tempers this sharp opposition between art on the one hand and reality or life or truth on the other. To be sure, the opposition does occasionally reappear. For example, in a characterization of *The Birth of Tragedy* dating from the fall of 1888, he observes that he was the "first to become serious about the relation of art to truth," and he notes, further, that "even now I stand with a holy horror before this conflict" (*KGW*, 8. Abt., 3. Bd., p. 296). Similarly, there is the well-known fragment of 1888, in which he tells us that "*Wir haben die Kunst,* damit wir nicht an der Wahrheit zu Grunde gehn"—*We have art* lest we perish of the truth (*WP*, §822; *KGW*, 8. Abt., 3. Bd., p. 296).[7] But his more general tendency, abandoning the simple illusion/reality dichotomy of his early career, is in fact to view everything under the aspect of aesthetic illusion. In short, there is a movement from art in the sense of the "work of art" to art in the broader sense of a primordial illusion-creating tendency. (Admittedly, there was already warrant for such a view in his early writings.) Thus, any distinction between "metaphysics, religion, moralities, science" on the one hand and "art" on the other is blurred; *all* are manifestations of "the will to art, to lie, to flight from 'truth,' to *negation* of 'truth'" (*WP*, §853, pp. 451–452; *KGW*, 8. Abt., 2. Bd., p. 435). This amounts, as we shall later come to see, to a movement from the strongly modernist tendency of *The Birth of Tragedy* to a position that is distinctly postmodernist in character.[8]

Nietzsche continues to view art, in both the narrow and the wide sense, as a mode of protection from the harsh realities of life. But he now comes to distinguish between two ways of taking advantage of this function. As he says in *The Gay Science* (in a passage added to that work in 1887), "every art and every philosophy is a remedy for sufferers." But there are two kinds of sufferers. On the one hand, there are those who suffer from "*the impoverishment of life.*" These seek "rest, stillness, calm seas, redemption from themselves through art and knowledge, or intoxication, convulsions, anaesthesia, and madness." Nietzsche identifies this view with "romanticism" in general and with the "romantic pessimism" of Schopenhauer and Wagner in particular. On the other hand, there are those who suffer from "*the over-fullness of life,*" and who want "a Dionysian art and likewise a tragic view of life" (*GS*, §370, p. 328). Here the conception of art as a protection from life somewhat contradictorily tries to join itself to the opposing conception of art as an affirmation of life, as "an excitation of the animal functions through the images and desires of intensified life," as "an enhancement of the feeling of life, a stimulant to it" (*WP*, §802; *KGW*, 8. Abt., 2. Bd., p. 58).

Significantly, Nietzsche's reference here to the Dionysian is not accompanied by any reference to the Apollonian. Indeed, the alteration in his view of art as one moves from his "early" to his "mature" writings (which is by no means as sharp as the concurrent alteration in his view of myth) is most clearly indicated by the all but total disappearance of the Apollonian: the word occurs only twice in all the works that Nietzsche published, or prepared for publication, in the 1880s. In *Twilight of the Idols* (1888), he compares the Apollonian artistic state, which "alerts above all the eye," to the Dionysian state, in which "the entire emotional system is alerted and intensified" (*TI*, "Expeditions of an Untimely Man," §10). In *Ecce Homo,* he characterizes "the antithesis of the Dionysian and the Apollonian" as reeking too much of Hegel and Schopenhauer (*EH*, "BT," §1).[9] The "extraordinary contrast" that in *The Birth of Tragedy* had served as the basis for an entire theory of culture now appears as, at most, merely one aspect of the "psychology" or "physiology" of art that Nietzsche hoped to write in this period.[10] It is significant, for example, that in the 1886 preface to *The Birth of Tragedy* Nietzsche does not even mention the Apollonian/Dionysian contrast but instead characterizes the work as concerned with the question "what is Dionysian?" (*BT*, "Attempt," §§3, 4; *NBW*, p. 20). Similarly, in the discussions of *The Birth of Tragedy* in *Ecce Homo* and in *Twilight of the Idols,* its elucidation of the role of the Dionysian within Greek culture is seen as its greatest merit (*EH*, "BT," §§1–4; *NBW*, pp. 726–731; *TI*, "What I Owe to the Ancients," §5). Indeed, the Dionysian comes to play something of the same symbolic role for the later Nietzsche as the Apollonian and Dionysian together had played for the earlier.[11]

It is presumably because of this that Kaufmann interpreted the later Dionysus as a synthesis of the earlier Apollonian and Dionysian. This alleged synthesis radically transformed Dionysus, changing him from "the deity of formless frenzy" into the representative of "passion controlled"—a composite deity now standing in opposition to the extirpation of the passions recommended by "the Crucified," by Christianity.[12] But there is no textual support for such an interpretation.[13] It is far better, I think, to see the later Dionysus not as the consequence of any union with Apollo but rather as the product of a shift of emphasis within the Diony-

sian itself, one that reflects Neitzsche's movement away from the Schopenhauerian variant of Romantic aesthetics. As I have already noted, in *The
Birth of Tragedy* Nietzsche envisions the Dionysian as an "intoxicated
reality," with the emphasis being placed very much on the intoxication,
on the destruction of the individual and his redemption through "a mystic
feeling of oneness" (*BT*, chap. 2; *NBW*, p. 38). When Euripides, for example, attacks the Dionysian element in tragedy, he is attacking not the realism of Dionysus (for it is precisely this that he denies) but rather the ec-
stasy, the intoxication, that separates the Dionysian from the everyday
world (*BT*, chap. 12; *NBW*, p. 81).

In Nietzsche's later writings, Dionysus certainly remains an ecstatic
being, but at the same time Nietzsche comes to place a much greater
emphasis on his "realistic" aspect. For the most prominent characteristic
of the later Dionysus is his "affirmative" attitude toward "reality," toward
"life." The notion of "saying Yes" to reality—a notion that is absolutely
central in the later writings—first appears in *The Gay Science*, where
Nietzsche presents us with a New Year's resolution: "*Amore fati*: let that
be my love henceforth! I do not wish to wage war against what is ugly. I do
not want to accuse; I do not even want to accuse those who accuse. *Looking away* shall be my only negation. And all in all and on the whole: some
day I wish only to be a Yes-sayer" (*GS*, §276). In *Zarathustra*, the notion is
further developed; indeed, it underlies the "central conception" of that
work, the doctrine of eternal return, which for Nietzsche is the "highest
formula of affirmation that is at all attainable" (*EH*, "TZ," §1).

What is especially important here is that as early as 1886, when Nietzsche refers to Zarathustra as "that Dionysian monster," Dionysus becomes the symbol of this "affirmative" attitude (*BT*, "Attempt," §7;
NBW, p. 26). As Nietzsche tells us in *Twilight of the Idols*, looking back
upon *The Birth of Tragedy* (and in the process distorting its message,
reading the later position into the earlier), "affirmation of life even in its
strangest and sternest problems, the will to life rejoicing in its own inex-
haustibility through the sacrifice of its highest types—*that* is what I called
Dionysian, *that* is what I recognized as the bridge to the psychology of the
tragic poet" (*TI*, "What I Owe," §5). Similarly, in the section on *The
Birth of Tragedy* in *Ecce Homo*, Nietzsche finds that "in the Dionysian
symbol the ultimate limit of affirmation is attained" (*EH*, "BT," §1). Or,
to return to the fragment in which Nietzsche speaks of the alteration in
his thought that occurred "around 1876": "I grasped that my instinct
went into the opposite direction from Schopenhauer's: toward a *justifica-*

tion of life, even at its most terrible, ambiguous, and mendacious; for this I had the formula '*Dionysian*'" (*WP*, 31005; *KGW*, 8. Abt., 2. Bd., pp. 18–19).

Nietzsche's shift away from Apollonian illusionism toward Dionysian realism is not a shift toward any kind of conceptual analysis of "reality." For despite their apparent radical opposition, the Apollonian and the Dionysian, as essentially aesthetic categories, have in common a rejection of the mediated understanding provided by concepts. The Dionysian symbolizes an impulse toward a direct, not a mediated, participation in the reality of experience; the Apollonian symbolizes an impulse toward the attainment of a similar immediacy through submergence in the irrealistic world of dream and fantasy, a world that is seen as embodying a truer and deeper reality than that of "normal" experience. In short, the Apollonian and Dionysian opposites join each other in a rejection of the "stepping back" that is implicit in all theorizing, a rejection of the mediation that comes with concepts. Both sides of the opposition (not simply the Dionysian) pertain to reality—the Dionysian to the reality of action and suffering, the Apollonian to the reality of dream and illusion—but neither reality fits well with conventional rationality, attached as it is to a specifically theoretical understanding. Not only in his early, Apollonian phase but also in his later Dionysianism, Nietzsche turns insistently away from the articulation of any *structure* of understanding, opting instead for a radical antistructuralism that constitutes his true affinity with the "poststructuralism" of Foucault and Derrida, as also with the anticonceptual bent of the later Heidegger.

"On Truth and Lie"

I have considered Nietzsche's longing for and refusal of immediacy, as manifested in his employment of the opposed yet allied symbols of the Apollonian and the Dionysian. I propose now to turn to his concurrent refusal of the mediation that comes with concepts. There are important links between Nietzsche's reflections on this issue and the wider field of nineteenth-century epistemology. As Maurice Mandelbaum points out, many nineteenth-century critics of the intellectual powers of man shared a common feature that one does not find in such previous epistemologists as Locke, Hume, or Kant—namely, "a distrust of the conceptual aspect of thought, a doubt that the concepts we employ in the sciences and in the practical affairs of everyday life are really adequate to the tasks which we ordinarily assume they perform." This distrust had its origin in the feeling of these critics that "our empirical concepts do not adequately delineate the characteristic features of what it is that we take them as representing."[14]

Mandelbaum links this distrust to Romanticism: "In the Romantic movement in the late eighteenth and nineteenth centuries, and subsequently in other movements as well, it was assumed that genuine knowledge necessarily involves some form of immediate apprehension, in which what we know must be both directly present and grasped in concrete detail." On this assumption, "any knowledge which merely *represents* an object, without *re*-presenting it, is never adequate: it merely stands for, or symbolizes, that which we seek to know."[15] Mandelbaum goes on to note that the full force of this commitment to immediacy, and of the disdain for conceptual knowledge that accompanies it, is to be felt only where the existentialist movement has gained a dominant intellectual position. Yet, at the same time, as he also notes, a distrust of conceptual knowledge—a feeling that it is a *defect* in concepts that they do not give us contact with the immediacy of things themselves, and a related tendency to view concepts as subjective projections upon nature—has manifested itself in many writers having no connection with existentialism; for example, Helmholtz and Spencer. Nietzsche's epistemological views ought to be seen within this wider context of opinion.

These views are radically different, however, from the views of neopositivists, pragmatists, and existentialists, for Nietzsche is separated from these other critics of conceptual thought by his aesthetic bent. From Kant's third critique onward, it has been common to emphasize the ultimate ineffability of the aesthetic experience, its tendency to resist enclosure in words and concepts. Nietzsche shares this view: the realm of the aesthetic offers, in his opinion, an alternative to the mediating and complexifying influence of concepts. This is brought out most clearly in his essay of 1873, "On Truth and Lie in an Extramoral Sense," a work which, after having been long ignored, has recently and quite rightly come to attract the attention of his commentators. Nietzsche never had occasion to publish the essay, but it is a finished, even a polished piece of work, and one that he still had in mind in the 1880s.[16]

Nietzsche reflects in this essay on what he considers to be the "wretched, transitory, purposeless, and fanciful" character of cognition. The human intellect, he maintains, is essentially a dissimulating power, one that claims to give us a true knowledge of the world when in fact it does not. Every concept, he holds, is a falsification of what it purports to represent. In Nietzsche's words, "every concept originates through equating the unequal": *Jeder Begriff entsteht durch Gleichsetzen des Nicht-Gleichen* ("OTF," p.179).[17] The world, in Nietzsche's view, is made up of absolutely individualized fragments: no thing, no occurrence, is exactly the same as any other thing or occurrence.

Take, for example, a leaf. Every leaf differs, however slightly, from every other leaf. It follows that the concept *leaf* can only be formed through an omission of these differences—an omission that Nietzsche holds to be entirely arbitrary. Thus, the concept *leaf* is a falsification of the reality of leaves. First, according to Nietzsche, it imputes to reality an entity of which reality knows nothing—in this case, the concept and form of the leaf, *the leaf* in general. We think, Nietzsche avers, that in addition to the multiplicity of actual leaves there exists in nature *the leaf*. Second, it involves taking away from reality elements that are actually there—in this case, the arbitrarily omitted qualities that differentiate all individual leaves from one another.

In short, concepts do not give us a true, genuine knowledge of reality. On the contrary, they are bare schemata that rob reality of its multiplicity and human experience of its original richness and vitality. But one must not stop with individual concepts, for, as Nietzsche points out, these are used by men to build a "great structure of concepts" (*der grosse Bau der Begriffe*), a "pyramidal order of castes and grades," a "new world of laws, privileges, sub-orders, delimitations" that shows "the rigid regularity of a Roman columbarium and in logic breathes forth that rigor and coldness which we find in mathematics" ("OTF," pp. 181–182). This structure, too, is an illusion, a repetition on a higher and more complex level of the falsification to be found in each individual concept. We think that the laws of nature are in nature, when in fact they are imposed by men upon nature. Moreover, we think that these impositions comprehend nature in its totality, when in fact nature, in its infinite individuality and creativity, far transcends them. The whole structure of human knowledge, then, is in doubt, except as the indicator of a purely human reality, as the reflection of purely human preoccupations.

Underlying this account of concepts is the belief that genuine knowledge must have the same characteristics as that which it represents, that it must somehow be what it represents, that it must (to follow Mandelbaum's formulation) *re*-present the thing in its very essence. But it would be a serious error, and would lead one to miss what is truly original about Nietzsche's project, were one to identify his position with the Romantic glorification of immediacy. For if Nietzsche hungers after immediacy, he also holds immediacy to be unattainable, even momentarily; and unattainable, too, is genuine knowledge—that is, a knowledge of things as they actually are. In the Nietzschean universe, men are irremediably shut out from "reality." About themselves they are almost completely ignorant: nature "threw away the key" to the mechanism of the human body, while human consciousness remains a mystery. As for the external world, the situation is equally hopeless. In Nietzsche's words, men "are deeply immersed in illusion [*Illusion*] and dream images; their eyes glance only over the surface of things and see 'forms'; their sensation nowhere leads to truth, but contents itself with receiving stimuli and, as it were, with playing a game of touch [*ein tastendes Spiel*] on the back of things" ("OTF," p. 175).

What status, then, can we accord to human knowledge, to the "structure of concepts"? Nietzsche's answer is that it has an essentially aesthetic status—that it arose through an aesthetically creative human impulse. This differs fundamentally from Schelling's view as put forward in the *System of Transcendental Idealism*. To be sure, both thinkers give primacy to the aesthetic, but they do so in an entirely different spirit. Schelling sees art as the culmination of philosophy because art alone, in his view, can give us an immediate insight into reality. Nietzsche, on the other hand, accords primacy to the aesthetic precisely because it does not give us insight into "reality." Indeed, it does not even claim to do so. On the contrary, it is explicitly a realm of illusion, and as such it stands in opposition to the unacknowledged illusion of logic and dialectic. Man, in Nietzsche's view, has no access to reality whatsoever. He is only arguably a rational being. His much-vaunted abstractions turn out to be metaphors in disguise, and his language, far from embodying logical truth, embodies rather his innate talent for aesthetic creation.

There is, indeed, a division in Nietzsche between language and "reality" analogous to the division that he also wants to see between art and "reality"—and a corresponding tendency toward the legitimation of what becomes, in parts of Foucault's corpus and in the later Heidegger, the notion of the "essence" or "being" of language. In Nietzsche's view, language is emphatically not the "adequate expression of all realities" ("OTF," p. 177). Rather, it is completely out of contact with reality and only conveys the illusion of such a contact by inventing a self-contained world of its own. Thus, we imagine, says Nietzsche, that the word *Schlange,* or "serpent" (from the Latin *serpere*), is somehow an adequate expression of the thing that it represents. But it is, in fact, an entirely arbitrary designation that chooses to emphasize one, and only one, of the serpent's characteristics: its sinuosity. According to Nietzsche, "when we talk about trees, colours, snow, and flowers, we believe we know something about things themselves [*den Dingen selbst*], and yet we possess nothing other than metaphors of things, and these metaphors do not in the least correspond to the original essentials"—just as Chladni figures do not in the least correspond to musical tones ("OTF," p. 178). In short, the construction of language "did not . . . proceed on logical lines, and the whole material in which and with which the man of truth, the investigator, the philosopher works and builds, originates, if not from cloud cuckoo land, at any rate not from the essence of things" ("OTF," p. 179). (One notes the absence here of any attempt to canvass possibilities intermediate between X and Y, between "cloud cuckoo land" and "the essence of things.") We may imagine man to be a rational being if we wish, but his supposedly rational status depends on his capacity for "causing concrete [*anschaulich*] metaphors to evaporate into a schema, and thus resolving an image into a concept." Out of these schemata, he builds that "world of laws, privileges, sub-orders, delimitations," which he imagines express the reality of things but which are in fact a purely human creation. This conceptual world "confronts the concrete world of first impressions as the more fixed, general, known, human of the two and therefore the regulating and imperative one" ("OTF," p. 181). But however stern and solid it may seem, the conceptual world is only the hardened product of "a mass of images that originally poured forth, in a fiery fluidity, from the primal faculty of human fantasy" ("OTF," p. 184).

Whereas in Schelling subject and object are brought together by the unifying force of aesthetic intuition, in Nietzsche there is no "adequate expression of an object in a subject," for "between two absolutely distinct spheres, as between subject and object, there is no causality, no accuracy, no expression, but at most an *aesthetical* relation, I mean a suggestive transposition, a stammering translation into a quite distinct foreign language" ("OTF," p. 184). Once more: "truth" tells us nothing about reality but only about man's aesthetic apprehension of reality. As Nietzsche puts it in what has become one of his most celebrated statements, truth is "a mobile army of metaphors, metonymies, anthropomorphisms: in short a sum of human relations which have been poetically and rhetorically intensified, transposed, adorned, and after long usage seem to a nation fixed, canonical, and binding; truths are illusions of which one has forgotten that this is what they are; metaphors which have become worn out and have lost their sensual power; coins which have lost their pictures and now are no longer of account as coins but merely as metal" ("OTF," p. 184).

Nietzsche has a peculiarly double attitude toward this devolution of metaphors into concepts and toward the whole logical order that is in consequence thrown up. On the one hand, he acknowledges that the conceptualizing ability has been absolutely necessary to man's survival. Indeed, he maintains that the exigencies of survival led to the emergence of this power in the first place. Only by generalizing his impressions into concepts is man able "to attach to them the ship of his life and actions" (or subject them to his will to power, as he would have said in his later period); only by "evaporating" metaphors into schemata is he able to stand out from the animal world. By turning vivid metaphors into pale, cold concepts, man attains the "invincible faith that *this* sun, *this* window, *this* table is a truth in itself"; and through this faith, he is able to live "with some repose, certainty, and consequence" ("OTF," p. 184). "The man of action," Nietzsche goes on to say, "binds his life to reason and its concepts, in order to avoid being swept away and losing himself," while the seeker after truth "builds his hut close to the building site of the tower of science, in order to be able to help with its construction and to find protection under its bulwarks" ("OTF," p. 187). Thus, the structure of concepts—the "truth"—that man has created plays an absolutely indispensable role in human life. Indeed, as Nietzsche also argues at the beginning of his "On the Uses and Disadvantages of History for Life" (1874), it is only by escaping from the flux of immediate, present experience that man becomes man.[18]

Conceptual thought can thus be regarded as good, as performing an entirely necessary and essential function. But it also has a negative side, for people forget that the structure of concepts is entirely man-made and that its relation to everything outside man is purely aesthetic. Instead, they take it to be a portrayal of reality itself. This turns it into a rigidifying influence, one that impairs the richness and immediacy of "experience," of "life." (Once again, we can recur to "The Uses and Disadvantages of History." Here history is seen as providing useful illusions about the past. But it is also seen as absolutely essential that no particular illusion should gain the upper hand, since this would rigidify our experience, and use, of the past.)

Nietzsche's attitude, under these circumstances, is an ironic one. On the one hand, he seeks to demonstrate the wholly illusory character of concepts. He seeks to show that the "infinitely complex cathedral of concepts" is built "on a movable foundation and as it were on running water" ("OTF," p. 182). But on the other hand, far from wishing to eliminate the conceptual world, he envisages a "freed intellect"—one that, precisely because it recognizes the illusory status of concepts, will be able to use them in a truly creative and artistic way. Thus, "that enormous framework and hoarding of concepts, by clinging to which the needy man saves himself throughout life, is to the freed intellect only a scaffolding and a toy for his most daring feats; and when he smashes it to pieces, throws it into confusion, and then puts it together again ironically, pairing the most alien, separating the closest items, then he reveals that . . . he is no longer led by concepts but by intuitions." A free play of intellect begins: one that does not lead into "the land of spectral schemata, of abstractions," but delights rather in play for its own sake, in bringing forward "forbidden metaphors" and "unheard-of combinations of concepts" ("OTF," p. 190). In short, Nietzsche envisages not the destruction of the conceptual world but rather (to borrow Derrida's terminology) its deconstruction— that is, its transformation into a realm of aesthetic illusion and play.

It is important to distinguish between the view that Nietzsche puts forward in "On Truth and Lie" and the view that Kant advances in the *Critique of Pure Reason,* for Nietzsche's account of knowledge may remind some readers of Kant. Kant argues that men have knowledge only of appearances and are inescapably ignorant of things-in-themselves, and he further argues that the categories in terms of which men understand appearance are in fact imposed by them upon it. Nietzsche's view differs from Kant's in two crucial respects. First (though this is a point that I do not propose to develop here), there is a generality in Kant that we do not find in Nietzsche. The Kantian categories are derived from a human mind that is conceived as being the same in all men, whereas in Nietzsche the process of "constructing" reality is portrayed as an arbitrary and individual matter. In other words, Kant's epistemology is attached to a conception of human nature; it embodies, to use the terminology of Heidegger and Foucault, an unacceptable "humanism" or "anthropologism." Second, Kant views the imposition of the categories upon the noumenal realm as an ordering of reality, whereas Nietzsche views it as a *Verstellung*—that is, as a dissimulation, or (to attempt a more literal translation) as a displacing or disarranging.

How does Nietzsche arrive at this notion of dissimulation? There is a peculiarly antidialectical dialectic at work in his epistemological reflections. He begins with the assumption that only immediate knowledge is genuine. He then perceives that, except on the most primitive level, immediacy is unattainable. But instead of abandoning immediacy as the criterion of genuine (or "adequate") knowledge, he makes his move to the aesthetic, portraying knowledge as the expression of an aesthetically creative power in man. Knowledge is not for Nietzsche a theoretical comprehension of reality, as in Kant, but rather an entirely self-contained set of anthropocentric illusions. Thus, Nietzsche tells us that "truth" is essentially the creation of the language we employ: "that which henceforth is to be 'truth' is now fixed; that is, a uniformly valid and binding designation of things is invented and the legislation of language gives also the first laws of truth; . . . here, for the first time, originates the contrast between truth and lie." It is within a linguistic context, and within such a context alone, that truth can be said to exist. The liar is one who uses "the valid designations, the words, in order to make the unreal appear as real," one who "abuses the fixed conventions by convenient [*beliebige*] substitution or even inversion of terms." The linguistic realm in question is an aesthetic realm, language itself being the product of man's penchant for creating metaphors. And since we are within the realm of the aesthetic, men do not hate deception itself; they hate only "the evil, hostile consequences of certain species of deception." In Nietzsche's view, they covet "the agreeable life-preserving consequences of truth"—that is, truth as useful illusion; but toward "pure, ineffective knowledge"—that is, truth in a scientific, theoretical sense—they are indifferent or even hostile ("OTF," pp. 176–177).

Against theory

Nietzsche's aesthetic standpoint, as manifested in "On Truth and Lie," is crucial to understanding his enterprise as a whole, for his commitment to immediacy,[19] and the countervailing movement to aesthetic illusion, underlie the persistently antiphilosophical, antiscientific strand in his thought. The first and clearest expression of this antiscientific animus is to be found in *The Birth of Tragedy*. In one of its aspects, this work is an attack on Socrates, and on the whole logical-philosophical enterprise for which Socrates, in Nietzsche's eyes, stands. In Nietzsche's account, Socrates was the inventor of logic and dialectic, the practitioner of a "rationalistic method" who believed firmly in clear concepts, in intelligibility, in a purely conscious knowledge. So impressive was he as a logician and dialectician that he managed to impart to Greek culture a "penetrating critical process," an "audacious reasonableness" (*verwegene Verständigkeit*) that destroyed Greek art (*BT*, chap. 12; *NBW*, p. 84).

Here a new symbolic meaning of the Apollonian comes into view: the Apollonian not as illusion nor even as form, but rather as the light of theoretical learning, seeking to open up to clear visibility all aspects of human experience, seeking to create order through *nous*, through understanding. Apollonianism in this sense—which Nietzsche identifies with Socratism—is irremediably hostile to art. The philosophical expression of this hostility is to be found in Plato. Plato "almost always speaks only ironically of the creative faculty of the poet, insofar as it is not conscious insight." Indeed, he denies that the poet, as poet, is even capable of conscious insight. Rather, poetry demands that the poet become "unconscious and bereft of understanding" (*BT,* chap. 12; *NBW,* pp. 85–86). The aesthetic expression of this hostility—perhaps more interesting precisely because it *is* aesthetic—is to be found in Euripides. It was he, Nietzsche maintains, who brought rationalism onto the Greek stage. Placing himself in opposition to the unconscious creativity of Aeschylean-Sophoclean tragedy, he supplemented Socrates' dictum that "to be good, everything must be conscious [*bewusst*]" with the further dictum that "to be beautiful, everything must be conscious." He then attempted to show the world "the reverse of the 'unintelligent' [*unverständigen*] poet" (*BT,* chap. 12; *NBW,* p. 86). With his "*critical* talent," with "all the brightness and dexterity of his critical thinking," he viewed the masterpieces of his great predecessors and saw in them "something incommensurable, . . . a certain deceptive distinctness and at the same time an enigmatic depth, indeed an infinitude, in the background. Even the clearest figure always had a comet's tail attached to it which seemed to suggest the uncertain, that which could never be illuminated" (*BT,* chap. 11; *NBW,* p. 80). It was precisely the incommensurable that Euripides sought to eliminate from his own dramatic productions, for it sinned against Socratic reasonableness. Unfortunately, in his un-Dionysian penchant for clarity in art, he "went astray and became naturalistic and inartistic" (*BT,* chap. 12; *NBW,* p. 83).

But it is not simply that the conscious, theoretical mind—the mind that works in concepts, that cultivates a distance from its immediate perceptions and instincts—is hostile to art. The gravamen of Nietzsche's charge is that it is hostile to culture in general. For the critical mind, in his view, is essentially uncreative. In all normally constituted men, creativity comes from the instincts, the passions, the unconscious—from the dark, hidden recesses of the human spirit. Socrates himself had some inkling of this, for, says Nietzsche:

> The most acute word . . . about this new and unprecedented value set on knowledge and insight was spoken by Socrates when he found that he was the only one who acknowledged to himself that he knew *nothing*, whereas in his critical peregrinations through Athens he had called upon the greatest statesmen, orators, poets, and artists, and had everywhere discovered the conceit of knowledge. To his astonishment he perceived that all these celebrities were without a proper and sure insight, even with regard to their own professions, and that they practiced them only by instinct. (*BT,* chap. 13; *NBW,* p. 87.)

In Nietzsche's opinion, Socrates here glimpsed what for Nietzsche is the most fundamental of all facts: that the basis of human culture is instinctual. Unfortunately, Socrates failed to face up to this fact. Instead, he chose to view the instinctual character of culture as a defect: "'Only by instinct': with this phrase we touch upon the heart and core of the Socratic tendency. With it Socratism condemns existing art as well as existing ethics. Wherever Socratism turns its searching eyes it sees lack of insight and the power of illusion; and from this lack it infers the essential perversity and reprehensibility of what exists" (*BT*, chap. 13; *NBW*, p. 87). Socratism therefore sought, according to Nietzsche, to "correct existence" (*das Dasein corrigieren*). It sought to do this by building, on top of the real world and as, in effect, a denial of it, a whole structure of theories and concepts. In doing so, it dared to negate the Greek genius—a genius that, in Homer, Pindar, and Aeschylus, in Phidias, in Pericles, in Pythia and Dionysus, in the "deepest abyss" and the "highest height," commands "our astonished veneration" (*BT*, chap. 13; *NBW*, pp. 87–88). For it is precisely in the instinctual—in the immediacy of *unconscious* creativity—that the Greek genius arose. Without the unquestioning sureness of touch that came from his lack of consciousness, it could not have survived.

To be sure, in Socrates himself consciousness does become creative. But Socrates was a monstrosity, in whom the "superfetation" or hypertrophy of the logical was so great that consciousness became the creative force, with instinct playing the critical and dissuasive role that consciousness normally performs. Thus, Socrates represented a total inversion of Greek culture. This inversion imparted such a flood of power to the "logical urge," rivaling the power of the greatest instinctive forces, that it "was absolutely prevented from turning against itself" (*BT*, chap. 13; *NBW*, p. 88). Indeed, Socrates was the founder of an entirely new system of culture, the culture of "theoretical man." Theoretical man finds his deepest pleasure in the search after truth. He is sustained by the "profound *illusion*" (tiefsinnige *Wahnvorstellung*) that "thought, using the thread of causality, can penetrate the deepest abysses of being." He believes that he can "correct the world by knowledge, guide life by science, and actually confine the individual within a limited sphere of solvable problems, from which he can cheerfully say to life: 'I desire you; you are worth knowing'" (*BT*, chaps. 15, 17; *NBW*, pp. 95, 109).

Yet—to look at Socratic culture in a negative sense again—there is too much that it misses, that it deliberately excludes from its purview. After all, the sphere of solvable problems is a narrow one. The Socratic turn thus represented a restriction, even a perversion, of the Apollonian tendency, its withdrawal into "the cocoon of logical schematism" (*BT,* chap. 14; *NBW,* p. 91). And this meant that the Dionysian, too, was impaired, for the clear-seeing but narrow-visioned "Cyclops eye" of Socrates, in which "the fair frenzy of artistic enthusiasm had never glowed," was incapable of gazing into "the Dionysian abysses" (*BT,* chap. 14; *NBW,* p. 89). Socratic culture sets out to destroy art and (as we shall see more clearly in Chapter 2), to dissolve myth, for given the individual's confinement within the sphere of solvable problems—a confinement that carries the Apollonian *principium individuationis* to its extreme—he has no need for either.

But again we can shift our point of focus and look at Socratic culture in a positive light, for by the very extreme to which it carries the pursuit of science it generates a new and more insistent need, and capacity, for art. In Nietzsche's words, "the influence of Socrates... again and again prompts a regeneration of *art*—of art in the metaphysical, broadest and profoundest sense;... its own infinity also guarantees the infinity of art" (*BT,* chap. 15; *NBW,* p. 93). This is so because the "sublime metaphysical illusion" (*Wahn*) that accompanies science—namely, the illusion that it can penetrate and correct being—leads it "again and again to the limits at which it must turn into *art*—*which is really the aim of this mechanism*" (*BT,* chap. 15; *NBW,* pp. 95–96). In short, science itself turns into art, taking art in the broadest sense of that word.

At this point, we ought perhaps to reflect on the general bearing of Nietzsche's account of Socratic culture and of the science to which it pays obeisance. (Admittedly, my summary of this account hardly does justice to the suggestiveness of *The Birth of Tragedy* or to its peculiar reversals and juxtapositions, but justice will only be done when the reader goes back to it himself.) Underlying Nietzsche's account is a view of the relation between art and science, between art and philosophy, between (in the most general terms) art and critical thought, that is virtually the opposite of that put forward by Hegel. Perhaps it seems odd that I should introduce Hegel here, since Hegel's explicit presence in Nietzsche's texts is very modest indeed. As we shall see, however, Hegel is a tremendously important point of reference for Heidegger, Foucault, and Derrida. Hegel makes possible the "crisis" view that is central to their work—and to Nietzsche's as well. My interest here, however, is more with Hegel's view of art than with his view of history. In reaction against Schelling, Hegel places philosophy, conceived of as a conceptual and analytical enterprise, above art, religion, love, and whatever other forms of the immediate and intuitional may present themselves.[20] In contrast, Nietzsche places art above philosophy. In this regard, *The Birth of Tragedy* can be seen as a mirror image of Hegel's *Aesthetics*. Whereas the *Aesthetics* views art from the perspective of *Wissenschaft* (science), *The Birth of Tragedy* (as Nietzsche tells us) views *Wissenschaft* from the perspective of art (*BT,* "Attempt," §2).[21] Indeed, in the original preface to the work (addressed to Richard Wagner), Nietzsche declares art to be "the highest task and the truly metaphysical activity of this life" (*BT,* Preface; *NBW,* pp. 31–32).

Ultimately, *The Birth of Tragedy* has very little to do with the historical reality of Greek culture but a great deal to do with what Nietzsche regards as the reality of his own time—for, as with his historical emulator, Foucault, his reflection on the past is really only a pretext for a reflection on the presumed present. The present, Nietzsche believes, bears witness to the triumph of scientific culture. The impulse to destroy art and (even more) the primal myth in which art has its roots is now pervasive. The dialogues of Plato, which gave us, Nietzsche says, the model of that unpoetic modern art form, the novel, accord to poetry "the same rank in relation to dialectical philosophy as this philosophy held for many centuries in relation to theology; namely the rank of *ancilla.*" In Plato, and in post-Platonic thought in general, *"philosophic thought"* thus "overgrows art and compels it to cling close to the trunk of dialectic" (*BT,* chap. 14; *NBW,* p. 91).

Nietzsche clearly envisages a reversal of this situation, a revaluation that would once more grant to art the governing position. Since scientific culture has now reached its extreme—its outer boundaries—such a revaluation is now in sight. In Nietzsche's words, "modern man is beginning to divine the limits of this Socratic love of knowledge and yearns for a coast in the wide waste of the ocean of knowledge" (*BT,* chap. 18; *NBW,* p. 11). This coast, this haven, will be provided by myth, for like his Romantic predecessors, Nietzsche views myth as giving that ground of certainty and of implicitly accepted images that the artist, and the man of culture, needs if he is to be freely and confidently creative.

Unmasking logic

Such, then, is the view of knowledge that animates the early Nietzsche. But this view, essentially aesthetic in character and reflecting his commitment to the criterion of immediacy, is by no means confined to his early, "aesthetic" period. On the contrary, it persists throughout his intellectual career, continuing as an important element in his "mature" thought. Indeed, in its critical, destructive aspect, the whole of his later enterprise can be characterized as a sustained effort to "unmask" concepts, and logic in general, carrying them back to their presumed origin in the immediacy of the will to power.

Many of Nietzsche's most striking comments in this direction occur in the *Nachlass,* and are thus in that portion of his corpus that for the most part cannot be regarded as "definitive"—as representing his considered final position. Nonetheless, these comments are eminently worth noting. In many cases, they cast light on, and are confirmed by, passages that Nietzsche actually did publish, or at least intended for publication. What is interesting at this point, however, is the extent to which they recall the views on knowledge and culture put forward in the early writings. For example, in fragment 440 of *The Will to Power,* Nietzsche once again opts for the immediacy of instinct over the mediation implicit in concepts, averring that

> genius resides in instinct; goodness likewise. One acts perfectly only when one acts instinctively.... Scientific integrity is always ruptured when the thinker begins to reason.... It could be proved that all conscious thinking would ... show a far lower standard of morality than the thinking of the same man when it is directed by his *instincts.* (*KGW,*8. Abt., 3. Bd., p. 215.)

Raising the question of adequacy, Nietzsche asks in fragment 516 whether "the axioms of logic" are "adequate to reality," or whether they are "a means and measure for us to *create* reality, the concept 'reality' ['*Wirklichkeit*'], for ourselves" (*KGW,* 8. Abt., 2. Bd., p. 53). His answer is that since we do not have "a previous knowledge of being," the latter possibility is the only one that we can accept; in consequence, "logic is the attempt to comprehend the actual world by means of a schema of being posited by ourselves; more correctly, to make it formulatable and calculable for us———" (*WP,* §516 [translation altered]). Conceptual thought, then, is a falsification of the world, a convenient fiction. What is more, it is an artistic fiction, the result of an aesthetic gift in man. Man is an artist, and his metaphysics, religion, morality, and science are

> all of them only products of his will to art, to lie, to flight from "truth," to *negation* of "truth." This ability itself, thanks to which he *violates reality* by means of *lies,* this *artistic ability par excellence*—he has it in common with everything that is. He himself is after all a piece of reality, truth, nature; how should he not also be a piece of *genius in lying!* (*WP,* §853, pp. 451–452 [translation altered]; *KGW,* 8. Abt., 2. Bd., p. 435.)

In these various fragments, we find reproduced, in its essential points, the intellectual configuration that we have already found in the early writings: first, the commitment to immediacy as the true criterion of knowledge; second, an admission that conceptual knowledge cannot live up to this criterion; and third, an enthusiastic acceptance of the view that such knowledge is a purely fictional creation, having nothing to do with any supposed "real" world existing outside the interpreter.

In the published works of Nietzsche's later period, we find similar views expressed, especially in *Beyond Good and Evil* and *Twilight of the Idols*. In the former, Nietzsche speaks of the "fictions of logic" and of the "purely invented world of the unconditional and self-identical" that logic creates for us. But though our judgments may be false, this is "not necessarily an objection" to them, for what counts is the extent to which a judgment is "life-promoting, life-preserving, species-preserving, perhaps even species-cultivating" (*BGE*, §5). Every great philosophy, Nietzsche maintains, has been nothing more than "the personal confession of its author and a kind of involuntary and unconscious memoir," the result not of a "drive for knowledge" but rather of eminently self-interested considerations (*BGE*, §6). Again, a gulf is postulated between our rational understanding and primal experience: on the one hand, "pale, cold, gray concept nets"; on the other, "the motley whirl of the senses" (*BGE*, §14). Again, the accusation is made that mankind has wrongly taken concepts for the world as it really is—that we have created a "symbol world" of cause, sequence, relativity, number, and the like, which "we project and mix . . . into things as if it existed 'in itself'" (*BGE*, §21).

In *Twilight of the Idols*, Nietzsche devotes a chapter to what he calls "'Reason' in Philosophy," where he raises again the question of the adequacy of concepts to reality. Philosophers, he tells us, refuse to accept the evidence of the senses, which show us that reality is in constant flux; instead, they insist on mummifying experience in concepts: "All that philosophers have handled for millennia has been conceptual mummies; nothing actual has escaped from their hands alive" (*TI*, "'Reason' in Philosophy," §1). Moreover, in his chapter on "The Problem of Socrates," Nietzsche returns to the specifically *historical* thesis of *The Birth of Tragedy*, reflecting again on the "superfetation of the logical" that Socrates brought with him. Once more, he views Socrates and Plato as "symptoms of decay," as *"declining types"* who heralded the dissolution of Greek culture. Once more, he views them as, at the same time, cultural creators, men who perceived that Greek culture was suffering from an anarchy of instincts and was going to collapse in any case, and who sought to thwart this collapse by fostering an absurd rationality, a rationality that viewed every yielding to the instincts as a defeat and that opted for "the daylight of reason," in which one strove to be "prudent, clear, bright at any cost" (*TI*, "The Problem of Socrates," §§2, 4, 10).

Thus Spoke Zarathustra

This anticonceptual, antiscientific perspective underlies the work that Nietzsche himself saw as his most important, *Thus Spoke Zarathustra*. Any interpretation of Nietzsche, if it is to claim validity, must come to terms with this text. Those who, following Kaufmann, view Nietzsche as essentially a critic and analyst are unable to do this, for *Zarathustra* simply will not fit a critical or analytical framework. The most striking thing about the work is the extent to which it is set within a frankly assertorial mode. It is far more peremptory than, say, *Beyond Good and Evil* or *The Genealogy of Morals*, which are the works that contemporary readers of Nietzsche seem, generally speaking, to find most interesting and suggestive. In the words of Zarathustra himself, "I am not one of those who may be questioned about their Why" (*TZ*, Pt. I, "Of Poets," p. 149). Instead of reasons, Nietzsche gives us images; instead of arguments, allegories. As Tracy B. Strong puts it, "at the end of *Zarathustra*, the reader has a distinct feeling of dissatisfaction; something has happened to Zarathustra, but Nietzsche does not say what it is."[22]

The central image of *Zarathustra* is eternal return. Around this image are located a number of other images, of which the most important are the Superman, the will to power, and the Higher Man. But Nietzsche fails to make these images part of any coherent argument. Each image constitutes a kind of vision, something that, without our knowing why, simply comes to be. Thus, Zarathustra introduces the Superman in a bare, declarative proclamation ("I teach you the Superman"), as he does the death of God that allegedly makes the Superman necessary (*TZ*, Pt. I, "Zarathustra's Prologue," §§2, 3). The will to power is brought in as if it were of no great importance, and its actual nature (the relation, for example, between "will," "power," and "will to power") is never properly explained (*TZ*, Pt. II, "Of Self-Overcoming," pp. 136–138). What Zarathustra calls his "abysmal thought" (*abgründlicher Gedanke*), the eternal return, rises up from the bottomless depths of his unconscious, only to nauseate his conscious self (*TZ*, Pt. III, esp. pp. 178, 183, 232–240 ["The Convalescent"]; also Pt. II, "Of Redemption," p. 162). The Higher Man, for its part, is forced upon him by an ambiguous and threatening exterior (*TZ*, Pt. IV, esp. "The Cry of Distress," pp. 254–256).

Nor are the connections between these separate, unexplained visions ever made clear. To be sure, the Superman is one who overcomes himself, and the will to power is nothing other than this self-overcoming; but the linkage between these two conceptions depends all too much on the verbal similarity between the words *Übermensch* (Superman or, literally, Overman) and *überwinden* (to overcome). Superman and will to power on the one hand and eternal return on the other stand as entirely separate revelations, unconnected by any perceptible chain of argument; and while the Higher Man is said to be a bridge to the Superman (*TZ*, Pt. IV, "The Greeting," p. 293), we are never told how this is so. Zarathustra did not argue; he merely spoke. Nietzsche aptly characterizes the book as a work of inspiration: "One hears, one does not seek; one accepts, one does not ask who gives; like lightning a thought flashes up, with necessity, without hesitation regarding its form" (*EH*, "*TZ*," §3).

To be sure, every intellectual project begins in intuition. But the important thing about Nietzsche's project is that it never proceeds beyond this initial intuitional stage. As a Heideggerian commentator points out, seeing this as one of the book's chief merits, *Zarathustra* "contains no facts or empirical arguments and no metaphysical axioms from which Nietzsche purports to deduce eternal verities"; it "develops not through the presentation of arguments but through the development of events in the life of Zarathustra."[23] Another way of putting this is to say that *Zarathustra* is a work of literature, an imaginative aesthetic creation in which Nietzsche's vision of crisis and "return" finds its highest expression. This is not to say that *Zarathustra* can somehow be taken as a paradigm of what literature is, but only that the category of literature seems to be the only one within which *Zarathustra* fits at all—and Nietzsche does refer to himself as "the poet of *Zarathustra*" (*EH*, "*BT*," §4). The important question here, however, is whether *Zarathustra* can also be regarded as a work of philosophy. Nietzsche clearly intended it to be so regarded, and Nietzsche's Heideggerian, Foucauldian, and Derridean commentators agree that it conveys a philosophical message, or at least some sort of philosophical standpoint.

But this leads to a problem. For in its refusal to articulate arguments, in its disdain for "facts" (and this word has a larger ambit than might at first glance seem the case), the Zarathustrian mind cuts itself off from argument with other minds, stopping at the level of the assertorial "this is so." It *demands* that we accept its view of the universe; it does not attempt to argue for such an acceptance. That the world actually is as Zarathustra portrays it—a world in which the death of God is a reality dwarfing all others—is presumed to be obvious to all sensitive souls. Those who accept Zarathustra's vision put themselves within the Nietzschean realm of discourse; those who do not are beyond the pale. The Zarathustrian mind is a mind so convinced of the correctness of its vision that it seeks only to work out the implications of that vision, not to establish its grounds. Relating to actuality only aesthetically, it stands as an absolute to itself, naively self-confident, delighting in its own free play, which it seeks, without further justification, to impose upon the world.[24] In *The Genealogy of Morals,* Nietzsche declares that whoever is completely an artist is "to all eternity separated from the 'real,' the actual [*von dem 'Realen,' dem Wirklichen*]." But this condition, he continues, is a difficult one, and the artist sometimes grows weary of the "eternal 'unreality' and falsity of his innermost existence." When this occurs, he "may well attempt what is most forbidden to him, to lay hold of actuality, for once actually to *be*" (*GM,* 3rd Essay, §4).

Such, according to Nietzsche, had been Wagner's course, and (as was inevitable) he had failed miserably in his undertaking. But Nietzsche's analysis of Wagner's failure is really only an analysis of his own, for the Zarathustrian poet, too, transgresses the domain of the aesthetic. Like the artist, he strives to bring off "inventions and feats"; unlike the artist, he imputes these inventions to the world of actuality. To be sure, in *The Gay Science* Nietzsche mounts a defense of this undertaking, declaring that "it is enough to create new names and estimations and probabilities in order to create in the long run new 'things'" (*GS,* §58). But *is* this a sufficient means for creating new things? To be sure, our "discourse" does have creative force. It can enlighten us; at the same time, it can mislead, preventing us from seeing "things" that we ought to see. But if "discourse" (or "language" or "art" or "interpretation") is to have any real meaning, there must be something that is not-discourse, not-language, not-art, not-interpretation. The truck that is coming down the road is fundamentally different from the interpretation "Here comes a truck." To believe otherwise—and the aestheticist does believe otherwise, or, for heuristic or revolutionary purposes, claims that this is his belief—is to risk becoming trapped in an implausible and highly artificial form of historical idealism.

The imputation of a purely aesthetic reality to the world itself can be regarded as the first of the two moments making up Nietzsche's aestheticism. The second moment—which perhaps better explains the psychological appeal of the Nietzschean position—marks a contrary movement away from the world. For the aestheticist perspective claims to liberate its adherents from mundane reality, from all those forces that seek to constrain the individual. Nietzsche's remedy for all oppression is a simple one: become an artist. In the Nietzschean world of ideas, nothing is ever humanly desirable in itself; all such qualities are imputed to things by man, who, functioning as an artist, accommodates the supposed "in itself" to the human eye. With artists in the narrow sense (who do not greatly interest Nietzsche), this power "comes to an end where art ends and life begins" (*GS*, §299); what Nietzsche wants is the abolition of any such distinction between art and life.

So far, we are still within the moment of imputation; but the point of this imputing is precisely that it "frees" us, that it leads to the moment of supposed liberation. Art, for Nietzsche, is the "cult of the untrue" that makes bearable for us the general untruth and mendaciousness of the world. It is the "*good* will to appearance" that protects us from an imperfect reality. Against what is "grave and serious" in human beings—what Nietzsche refers to in *Zarathustra* as the "spirit of gravity"—it is "exuberant, floating, dancing, mocking, childish, and blissful." It gives us, in Nietzsche's view, a "*freedom above things*," an ability to detach ourselves from "reality," to view "reality" as somehow irrelevant to our own aesthetic laughter and play (*GS*, §107). As Nietzsche asks in another passage, "what is 'reality' ['*Wirklichkeit*'] for an artist in love? . . . That mountain there! That cloud there! What is 'real' ['*wirklich*'] in that? Subtract the phantasm and every human *contribution* from it, my sober friends. If you can! . . . There is no 'reality' for us—nor for you either, my sober friends" (*GS*, §57).

Here Nietzsche's idealism is glaringly obvious, whatever his naturalistic rhetoric. (So far as I know, Danto is the only commentator to have drawn explicit attention to this idealism. At the end of *Nietzsche as Philosopher*, he links the names of Nietzsche and Berkeley—a linkage far less outrageous than it seems.)[25] But—to raise a "normal" objection to Nietzsche—if "art" cannot create reality, neither can it declare our freedom from reality. Ultimately, there is no "freedom above things," except in the limited domain of the aesthetic itself, the domain of an aesthetic utopian vision. (It is this that Marx, the most realistic of all utopians, so clearly understood.) In his Dionysian mode, Nietzsche imposes his own vision upon the world; while in his Apollonian mode, he abstracts himself away from the world. But both modes, confined as they are within the aesthetic, are distinctly limited in their signification. Nietzsche himself recognized this, and reached down from his laughing, dancing heights— but not toward things, or arguments, or "facts." He reached rather to the chthonic realm of myth. It is in myth that he seeks the rootedness of art. Myth promises to divest the perspective of the artist of its arbitrary character and connect the separate aesthetic illusions together in a powerful common vision. We must turn, then, to the role of myth in Nietzsche's thought. This is not a departure from aestheticism, for (as we shall see) Nietzsche views myth as itself a form of art.

CHAPTER 2

Nietzsche and Myth

Nietzsche regards myth as the ground of art, the foundation on which all aesthetic creation must be built. Just as art is always seeking to reemerge, even within the confines of a culture that regards itself as wholly scientific in bearing, so also is myth. In the "early" Nietzsche, art and myth are both linked to the "fundamental impulse of man"—his impulse toward the formation of metaphors, toward the continually creative substitution of one element for another within his language. This primitive impulse has now been overlaid by a rigid structure of concepts, but it has not thereby been defeated or even subdued, for it "seeks for itself a new realm of action and another river-bed, and finds it in *Mythos* and more generally in art" ("OTF," p. 188).[1]

In the "later" Nietzsche, there is a much greater stress on creating myth consciously, and much less of a tendency to rely on a supposedly automatic process of remythification. The Romantic circle is explicitly crossed out. It is placed *"sous rature,"* as Derrida would put it. Moreover, one also finds what can best be termed a "denaturalization" of myth, an attempt to create myth *ex nihilo* rather than out of already extant mythic resources. But whatever the differences, myth remains, for the later Nietzsche as for the earlier, an absolutely central element of culture—indeed, the only escape from the malaise from which he believed "modern man" was suffering.

The "positivistic" Nietzsche

Nonetheless, with regard to myth, the shift from "early" to "mature" Nietzsche is much more marked than it is when we approach him via the theme of art. This means that we must now go back and examine the phase in his thought that divides these two phases, his "middle" or "positivistic" period. Here, especially in the first part of *Human, All-Too-Human* (1878), we find a reaction against the aestheticizing and mythifying tendency of *The Birth of Tragedy*. Nietzsche now tends to define himself much more as a critic and analyst of contemporary culture and much less as a purveyor of a new art and myth. As he says in the preface to the second part of the second edition of *Human, All-Too-Human* (1886), that work represented a "spiritual cure." It represented an "anti-Romantic home treatment that my instinct, which had always remained healthy, had itself discovered and prescribed against a temporary illness occasioned by the most dangerous form of Romanticism"—namely, that of Wagner (*HAHII*, Preface, §2 [translations altered, here and following]).

The first edition of *Human, All-Too-Human* is dedicated, significantly enough, to Voltaire. In the book itself, Nietzsche praises "the spirit of science," "scientific knowledge," "scientific methods," the "clear thinking of reason," "rigorous thought, cautious judgment, and logical conclusions," and "the spirit of enlightenment" as opposed to "Romanticism" (*HAHI*, §§36, 37, 635, 130, 265, 110). This aspect of Nietzsche's thought was to continue to have its impact on the later writings. Clearly, a process of de-Romanticization had taken place, leaving in its wake a harder and sterner Nietzsche, one who was decidedly post-Romantic rather than Romantic. Yet, at the same time, Nietzsche's supposed embrace of science by no means signaled the abandonment of his earlier hostility to "Socratic" theoreticism, with its coldly visual apprehension of the world.[2]

To be sure, at first glance *Human, All-Too-Human* seems to represent a radical rejection of all that Nietzsche had earlier stood for. A peculiar reshuffling occurs, a revaluing of the great opposing entities with which he had concerned himself in *The Birth of Tragedy*—namely, art and science. He had previously viewed art as the higher activity, the activity to which the scientist attains when he has become truly free and creative. He now views it as a potentially dangerous distraction from more pressing and important cultural activities. Art "makes heavy the heart of the thinker," inducing in him a longing for religion and metaphysics (*HAHI*, §153). Since the development of a perfect work of art is in essence inexplicable, it encourages a cult of genius. It thus leads to an undervaluing of the systematic and methodical work of the scientist and to a misguided attachment to the apparent miracle of "intuition" (*Intuition*) (*HAHI*, §162). Nietzsche had previously looked forward to a rebirth of tragedy and to the emergence of a better and more serious art. He now envisages—with equanimity and even with approval—the decline of tragedy, and suggests that a "new, higher grade of humanity" will not necessarily produce "the highest form of art" (*HAHI*, §§108, 239). He had previously viewed the artist as promising to save our culture from dissolution into mythlessness by embodying, in his art, a new and more believable myth. He now sees the artist as a suspect figure, weak and backward and at the same time dangerous.

Artists, he suggests, are intellectual lightweights. The artist "does not stand in the front rank of the enlightenment and civilization of humanity," for he remains a child or youth throughout his life, his development having been arrested "at the point where he was overcome by his artistic impulse" (*HAHI*, §147). Artists are "always of necessity *epigoni.*" They lighten the burdens of life, but their healing is only temporary, and in the meantime it has the unfortunate effect of discouraging men "from working toward a genuine improvement in their conditions" (*HAHI*, §148). Their backward, childish condition leads to a belief in gods and daemons, to a spiritualization of nature, to a hatred of science (*HAHI*, §159). Above all, since he is an habitual practitioner of deception, the artist's "sense of truth" is defective:

> With regard to recognition of truths, the artist has a weaker morality than the thinker; he will on no account let himself be deprived of sparkling and profound interpretations [*Deutungen*] of life, and defends himself against simple methods and results. He is apparently fighting for the higher worthiness and meaning of mankind; in truth he will not renounce the *most effective* suppositions for his art, the fantastical, mythical, uncertain, extreme, the sense of the symbolical, the overvaluation of personality, the belief that genius is something miraculous: he therefore holds the continuance of his kind of creation as more important than scientific devotion to truth in all its forms, however simple this may appear. (*HAHI*, §146.)

Indeed, throughout *Human, All-Too-Human,* Nietzsche portrays art and science as existing within an historicist framework that seems uncannily Hegelian. Mankind has undergone an historical progression leading from religion and metaphysics (and presumably also myth) to art, and finally to science; and at the "apex of the entire pyramid of science" stands philosophy, which in its true form seeks to give "the greatest possible depth and meaning to life and action" (*HAHI*, §6). These stages are reproduced, according to Nietzsche, in the cultural development of individuals today. As children we begin with religious temperaments. We are then overcome by a "metaphysical philosophy," which we eventually abandon in favor of an attachment to art. Finally, we are driven to "the most rigorous methods of knowledge" by an ever more imperious scientific sense (*HAHI*, §272). The earlier stages in human history had a legitimate, indeed a necessary role to play. For in Nietzsche's view it was error that made men culturally inventive: "pure knowledge," had they possessed it, would simply have generated in them "the most disagreeable disillusionment" (*HAHI*, §29). As individuals, we therefore ought not to feel ashamed of having once loved religion and art, for these experiences will help us to follow the history of humanity with a clearer understanding. They will give us access to that "ground of clouded thought" upon which "many of the most glorious fruits of older civilizations" have grown (*HAHI*, §292).

In the present context, I am mainly interested in Nietzsche's account of the historical roles of art and science. The former he sees as beneficently providing a bridge from religion to science; without it, the transition to "a really liberating philosophical science" would have been far more difficult (*HAHI*, §27). According to Nietzsche, art "raises its head where religions decline. It takes over a crowd of feelings and moods engendered by religion, lays them to its heart, and itself becomes deeper, more full of soul" (*HAHI*, §150). Art has taught us, says Nietzsche, to "take pleasure in existence and to regard human life as a piece of nature"—just as, earlier, religion brought about an "exalting and intensifying of temperament" (*HAHI*, §22).

But we are now making the transition to science; and from the methodologically more demanding standpoint that is coming into being, art plays a retrograde role. Nietzsche contrasts the "rigorous method" of our own age with the "joy-diffusing and dazzling errors" that arise from "metaphysical and artistic times and peoples." More specifically, he contrasts this new rigor with an earlier pleasure in "symbols and forms": "Formerly the spirit was not occupied with rigorous thought, its seriousness then lay in the spinning out of symbols and forms. This is changed; that seriousness in the symbolical has become the mark of a lower culture" (*HAHI*, §3). The hegemony of art is over. Indeed, Nietzsche goes so far as to suggest (again, as Hegel had before him) that art is a thing of the past. Admittedly, the "intensity and multiplicity of the joys of life" that art has implanted in us will still demand satisfaction. But the satisfaction will be found in science, which will now come to play the culturally creative role that was formerly reserved for art (*HAHI*, §222). We are witnessing, Nietzsche declares, the "evening glow of art": soon, in its relation to us, art will be like "a touching memory of the joys of youth. Perhaps never before was art so deeply and soulfully grasped as now when the magic of death seems to play around it. . . . The artist will soon come to be regarded as a splendid relic. . . . [T]he sun has already set" (*HAHI*, §223).

The "positivistic" Nietzsche does depart, then, from the explicit elevation of art to be found in the earlier and later writings. But this alteration
in perspective is much less profound than appears at first glance, for
Nietzsche's anticonceptualism, which, as we have seen, is closely connected with his attraction to art, persists throughout the whole of his intellectual career. His view of science embraces the anticonceptualist
theme. In *Human, All-Too-Human,* as in the earlier and later writings, he
remains committed to the view that logic is a fiction, that concepts falsify
the world. For example, he points out (as he had done, in much the same
language, in "On Truth and Lie") that logic and mathematics are
"founded on suppositions to which nothing in the actual world corresponds." Most importantly, they are founded on "the supposition of the
equality of things, and the identity of the same thing at different points of
time" (*HAHI*, §11).

Nietzsche's point is a valid one; the difficulty is rather with the direction in which he takes it. Here again is raised the problem of the logicality,
in the conventional sense, of his position. In his "positivistic" writings, as
elsewhere, he experiences the mediacy of concepts as a loss, even though a
necessary one. His ideal remains that of an immediate contact with "reality." But since he recognizes the effective unattainability of such contact,
he is forced to think in terms of a rigidly dichotomous relation between
"knowledge" and "reality," in which man creates a reality of his own
precisely because he cannot know reality as it actually is. Nietzsche characterizes language as a "would-be [*vermeintliche*] science," for in it man
"has placed a world of his own beside the other, a position [*Ort*] which he
deemed so fixed that from it he might lift the world that remains over off
its hinges and make himself master of it" (*HAHI*, §11). In another passage of similar bearing, Nietzsche suggests that what we now call the
world is in fact the result of "a crowd of errors and fantasies which arose
gradually in the general development of organic being . . . and are now
inherited by us as the accumulated treasure of all the past" (*HAHI*, §16).
These errors are not only inescapable but are also, as the last phrase suggests, a benefit to mankind. Indeed, our humanity depends upon them,
for it is only such errors (above all, the suppositions of equality and of
identity) that have allowed the development of human reason.

In all of this, there is a strange mixture of approval and disapproval, a
recognition of the necessity of the process but at the same time a regret,
even a nostalgia, for the reality that has been lost. As Nietzsche says in
Daybreak, in an aphorism entitled "honouring reality [*Wirklichkeit*]":

"If we are not to lose ourselves, if we are not to lose our *reason,* we have to flee from experiences. Thus did Plato flee from reality and desire to see things only in pallid mental pictures."[3] It is perfectly true that the "positivistic" Nietzsche praises science again and again, but the science that he praises is really only a mode of the aesthetic, a mode characterized by more rigorous rules of play and by more widely useful illusions than are to be found elsewhere.

In short, even in his "positivistic" period, Nietzsche views science from the perspective of art—as he had done before in *The Birth of Tragedy* and would do again in the later writings. Why, then, does he insist on distinguishing between the two, elevating the former over the latter? The paradox can be explained in purely biographical, though not entirely trivial terms, as the product of his estrangement from Wagner. Disillusioned by the vulgarity of the first great festival at Bayreuth, Nietzsche now came to see Wagner as "human, all-too-human," where formerly he had been Nietzsche's hero. When Nietzsche attacks "the artist" for being retrograde and for having "a weaker morality than the thinker," as he does in the fourth part of *Human, All-Too-Human,* "Concerning the Soul of Artists and Authors" (§§145–223), it is clear that he has one particular artist in mind.

Ultimately, however, the paradox transcends biography. It does so because in Nietzsche's early writings "Wagner" represents much more than the person of Wagner: he represents, in fact, the prospect of the rebirth of myth, just as Schopenhauer represents an appreciation of the aesthetic. When Nietzsche "lost" Wagner, he also lost the prospect of that rebirth, a prospect that was absolutely crucial to his early position. In essence, the "positivistic" Nietzsche was in search of a myth to replace the one that Wagner had seemed to offer. For a time, he thought (in common with many other nineteenth-century thinkers) that the required myth, or at least a plausible substitute for it, was to be found in science. He did not believe that art itself could serve as myth, for in common with his Romantic predecessors he still held that art must accept its guiding images from myth, within whose liberating confines the artist, if he is to be truly creative, is obliged to work. This explains, I think, Nietzsche's attempt to distinguish science from (and raise it over) art, even while viewing it in terms that made it essentially a mode of art.

The tactic was a daring one, but it was carried out *faute de mieux,* and after *Human, All-Too-Human* its impact very quickly spent itself. For Nietzsche was never really convinced of the mythic potential of science, even in that most proscientific of all his writings. Thus, he notes that a drawback accompanying the cessation of what he calls "metaphysical views" (by which he means myth) is that "the individual looks upon his short span of life too exclusively and receives no stronger incentive to build durable institutions intended to last for centuries; he himself wishes to pluck the fruit from the tree which he plants, and on account of this he no longer plants those trees which require regular care for centuries and which are destined to afford shade to a long series of generations." In contrast, "metaphysical views" furnish an unquestioned basis of cultural assumptions; they furnish the belief that "the last conclusive foundation has been given, upon which henceforth all the future of mankind is compelled to settle down and establish itself; the individual furthers his salvation when, for instance, he founds a church or convent; he thinks it will be reckoned to him and recompensed to him in the eternal life of the soul."

But can science arouse a similar faith in its results? Nietzsche is cautious in his answer. Science, he observes, "needs doubt and distrust as its most faithful auxiliaries," rather than faith. At the same time, he suggests that eventually science may come to furnish a "sum of inviolable truths" sufficiently great that "one may determine to found thereupon 'eternal' works" (*HAHI*, §22). He exhibits a similar caution when, in contemplating "the future of science," he declares that the men of a higher, scientific culture will need two entirely separate brain chambers, one to "feel" (*empfinden*) science and the other to "feel" nonscience. Science alone will not be enough to give a sustained impulse to the culture that it is bound to bring into being. To be sure, it gives much pleasure to its devotees, but this pleasure will diminish and then cease as all its important truths become "commonplace and everyday matters." Thus, men will need a nonscientific brain chamber. Heated by illusions, by one-sided judgments, and by passions, this part of the brain will preserve the consolations of metaphysics, religion, and art against science's analytical, dissolving effects, while still being held in check by the scientific part of the brain. If this bifurcation and mutual balancing off do not occur, science will be ruined, says Nietzsche; illusion, error, and imagination will reconquer their former territory, and culture will relapse into barbarism (*HAHI*, §251). In short, Nietzsche remains very uncertain about the mythic potential of science. Only under the most delicate circumstances will science be able to serve as the mythic basis of culture.

Myth and culture

In discussing Nietzsche's "positivism" and its limitations, I have been forced to anticipate, to some extent, a proper account of the early Nietzsche's commitment to myth. It is time, by looking again at *The Birth of*

Tragedy, to make good this omission, for in one of its aspects that work chronicles the fate of myth in Greek society and by extension in our own. Nietzsche's account of the efflorescence and decline of Greek tragedy is set within the larger context of what he regards as the all but inevitable tendency of culture to move from an initial mythic apprehension of the universe to an apprehension that is critical, skeptical, and ironical. A culture begins by believing in myth. More precisely, myth begins by creating culture, for culture could not have come into existence without the "concentrated image of the world" that myth gives to men, without myth's true and sacred tradition, without its comprehensive guidance to the ordering of life (*BT*, chap. 23; *NBW*, p. 135). But gradually the sacredness of myth—the haunting awareness of myth as an intimation of transcendent forces—is worn away. In the initial phase of this process, myth is not so much denied as trivialized, through the reduction of its eternal truth to specific historical fact. In Nietzsche's words, "it is the fate of every myth to creep by degrees into the narrow limits of some alleged historical reality, and to be treated by some later generation as a unique fact with historical claims" (*BT*, chap. 10; *NBW*, p. 75). This is the way, Nietzsche declares, that religions customarily die out: under the influence of an orthodox dogmatism, the mythical premises of the religion "are systematized as a sum total of historical events; one begins apprehensively to defend the credibility of the myths, while at the same time one opposes any continuation of their natural vitality and growth; the feeling for myth perishes, and its place is taken by the claim of religion to historical foundations" (*BT*, chap. 10; *NBW*, p. 75).

At this stage, there is at least a continuation of the formal structure of myth, even though the "feeling for myth" is gone. But the process continues. Eventually, all hint of transcendent meaning is lost, mythic fabulation is reduced to mere fiction, and myth as a living reality totally disappears from the horizon of the culture. According to Nietzsche, the decline of Greek mythic consciousness provided the occasion for the rise of tragedy. At the time of tragedy's birth, the great Homeric myths—the "juvenile dream" of the Greek people—were losing their hold on the Greeks, and their devolution from manifestations of inherited cultural wisdom into trivial historical realities, into an "historico-pragmatical *juvenile history*," was only a matter of time (*BT*, chap. 10; *NBW*, p. 75). Tragedy, Nietzsche holds, brought an infusion of new life into this waning tradition. Noting the parlous state of mythic consciousness and seeing his opportunity, the Dionysian artist seized upon the dying myths of his people and forced them into the service of the new deity, with Dionysian truth taking over "the entire domain of myth as the symbolism of *its* knowledge" (*BT*, chap. 10; *NBW*, p.

74). The force that served to revitalize the old myths and to transform them into a vehicle of Dionysian wisdom was music—not the older Apollonian music, that "Doric architectonics in tones," but rather the new, awesome, terrifying music of Dionysus (*BT*, chaps. 2, 10; *NBW*, pp. 40, 75). For tragedy is a combination of two elements, music and myth, each of which reinforces the other. Tragedy absorbs "the highest ecstasies of music," while through the tragic myth—and more specifically, through the tragic hero—it "knows how to redeem us from the greedy thirst for this existence," reminding us of "another existence and a higher pleasure for which the struggling hero prepares himself by means of his destruction" (*BT*, chap. 21; *NBW*, p. 125). The secular decline of myth was halted. Indeed, myth attained "its most profound content, its most expressive form," in tragedy (*BT*, chap. 10; *NBW*, p. 75).

But the resurgence of myth—and the great flowering of Greek culture that resulted therefrom—was only temporary. Hardly had tragedy been born than it died, and myth died with it. Immediately responsible for this turn of events was Euripides. Failing to see that it was precisely the mythic character of tragedy that gave it its impact, he turned it in a naturalistic direction by getting rid of the tragic hero and bringing the spectator—the "everyday man"—onto the stage (*BT*, chap. 23; *NBW*, p. 137). Euripides, however, was only a stalking horse for something much greater: the logical impulse within culture represented by Socrates.

We have already seen how the Socratic orientation, with its demand for clarity and rationality, was in Nietzsche's eyes inimical to art. He considers it to be even more inimical to myth. Even more than art, myth revels in instinct and in the incommensurable and depends on an unquestioning acceptance of its own veracity. In short, myth is too irrational in its bearing to live up to the logical canons of Socratism. It is simply not "reasonable." When Socratism triumphed and reason took the place of a disintegrated instinct, the art that remained (now deprived of its paradigmatic expression, tragedy, and of the mythic substratum that had made such an achievement as tragedy possible) was forced to seek an alliance with dialectic.

As consequences of this move, the Apollonian tendency withdrew into the "cocoon of logical schematism," while at the same time the Dionysian departed entirely from the horizon of culture and was replaced by an "un-Dionysian myth-opposing spirit" (*BT*, chaps. 14, 18; *NBW*, pp. 91, 108). Thus, the new, "Alexandrian" culture—the culture of "theoretical man"—came into being. Substituting "earthly consonance" for "metaphysical comfort," Alexandrian culture "combats Dionysian wisdom and art" and "seeks to dissolve myth" (*BT*, chap. 17; *NBW*, p. 109).

In his later writings, Nietzsche continues to view culture as moving from myth to logic, with the latter still seen as inimical to the former. Admittedly, for reasons that will soon become evident, he no longer attributes to tragedy the important role that he did in *The Birth of Tragedy*, but in the present context this is a peripheral issue. What is important is that the *mythos/logos* distinction, and the antilogical impulse that underlies it, are retained. Even in *Human, All-Too-Human*, Nietzsche expresses his regret at the decline of myth, declaring that "it is only where the ray of myth falls that the life of the Greeks shines. . . . The Greek philosophers are now robbing themselves of this myth." He here goes on, however, to say that the philosophers were not opposed to myth *per se*, but were seeking another, brighter myth, that of knowledge and truth (*HAHI*, §261). In the later works, the belief in a myth of knowledge or science disappears, and the negative valuation of the movement to logic returns in full force: Nietzsche regrets the devolution, even while admitting its necessity. In *Human, All-Too-Human*, he praises those "free spirits" and "free thinkers" who, instead of simply following tradition, "demand reasons" for their actions (*HAHI*, §225, also 230; the subtitle of *HAH* is "A Book for Free Spirits"). In the later works, he repudiates this position and returns to the view adhered to in *The Birth of Tragedy*, where the authentic act is the instinctual one, the one that is in accord with the "native myth" of a people, with "the unconscious metaphysics of its previous existence" (*BT*, chap. 23; *NBW*, pp. 135, 137).

In a fragment included in *The Will to Power*, Nietzsche views the Socratic taste for reasons as a veritable decline: "Before Socrates, the dialectical manner was repudiated in good society; one believed it compromised one; youth was warned against it. Why this display of reasons? Why should one demonstrate? Among others one possessed authority. One commanded: that sufficed. Among one's own, *inter pares*, one possessed tradition, *also* an authority; and finally one 'understood one another'!" (*WP*, §431). The section on "The Problem of Socrates" in *Twilight of the Idols*, for which this *Nachlass* fragment was clearly a preliminary, runs in the same direction. Most important, there is *Thus Spoke Zarathustra* itself, which is nothing if not a repudiation of "logic," of the whole drive to give reasons for our actions (in Nietzsche's terms: to *rationalize* them). When Zarathustra tells us that he is "not one of those who may be questioned about their Why," he separates himself from the antimythical dialecticians. And he does so because he—or, more properly, his author—aspires to the creation of a new myth, on whose basis alone a new culture can be created.

We thus arrive at what is clearly Nietzsche's real concern: not Greek antiquity but the supposed present. Nietzsche claims, as we have already in part seen, that present-day culture remains essentially Socratic and Alexandrian. He holds, in fact, that practically nothing of cultural importance has happened since the beginning of the Hellenistic period. Among other things, this means that we live in a culture within which the binding force of myth has been loosed. According to Nietzsche, present-day culture is critical, rational, skeptical, and ironical—in sum, antimythical. The clearest expression of this antimythical drive is to be found in the way we approach our past. Our inclination, according to Nietzsche, is to examine the past in a critical and scientific spirit. In so doing, we have made mythic consciousness all but impossible. In Nietzsche's words, "it is probable . . . that almost everyone, upon close examination, finds that the critical-historical spirit of our culture has so affected him that he can only make the former existence of myth credible to himself by means of scholarship, through intermediary abstractions" (*BT*, chap. 23; *NBW*, p. 135). Instead of living by a common native myth, which would give to our culture a firm foundation and protect it from the dissolving effects of the historical process, we try to live by a naive optimism and by faith in knowledge.

This, in Nietzsche's view, is a disaster. For Nietzsche believes myth to be absolutely essential to the health of a culture:

> Without myth every culture loses the healthy power of its creativity: only a horizon defined by myths completes and unifies a whole cultural movement. Myth alone saves all the powers of the imagination and of Apollonian dream from their aimless wanderings. The images of the myth have to be the unnoticed omnipresent demonic guardians, under whose care the young soul grows to maturity and whose signs help the man to interpret his life and struggles. Even the state knows no more powerful unwritten laws than the mythical foundation that guarantees its connection with religion and its growth from mythical notions. (*BT*, chap. 23; *NBW*, p. 135.)

Indeed, Nietzsche sees the historical curiosity of his own century as a symptom of cultural disease. He holds that we are the products of a Socratism that, by destroying myth, has robbed our culture of any "fixed and sacred primordial site." Lacking a limiting and ordering myth, man "digs and grubs for roots": "The tremendous historical need of our unsatisfied modern culture, the assembling around one of countless other cultures, the consuming desire for knowledge—what does all this point to, if not to the loss of myth, the loss of the mythical home, the mythical maternal womb? Let us ask ourselves whether the feverish and uncanny excitement of this culture is anything but the greedy seizing and snatching at food of a hungry man" (*BT*, chap. 23; *NBW*, pp. 135–136).

The recovery of myth

The problem, then, is to recover myth, and thus to restore the lost vitality of culture. This problem is central for both the "early" and the "mature" Nietzsche—the focus of his entire enterprise. Admittedly, as he enters into his final phase he attacks the problem in a manner radically different from his earlier approach. As a result, the underlying continuity of purpose—his retention of the belief in the cultural indispensability of myth—is apt to be entirely missed.

It is just this oversight that lies at the back of the two most fateful misinterpretations of Nietzsche's thought. The first of these is the view, which we have already encountered in one of its aspects, that Nietzsche is an essentially critical and analytical thinker. In this view, if Nietzsche's main concern is not (in anticipation of certain strands in twentieth-century Anglo-American philosophy) to analyze and thereby relieve us of philosophical problems, it is to lay bare, with a purely critical intelligence, the crass and philistine culture of his contemporaries. The second is the view that since his thought (at least in its later phase) lacks an explicitly political dimension, he is an entirely unpolitical thinker, one whose work has no relevance at all to the political world. Our examination of the aesthetic element in Nietzsche has given us some insight into the limitations of the first view. Its limitations will become even clearer as we perceive how myth remains important for him throughout his career. The second view similarly crumbles in the face of Nietzsche's persistent attachment to myth. The difficulty, however, is that in the later Nietzsche myth appears in such a deromanticized form that it can hardly be recognized as myth. In fact, I am tempted to speak in terms of functional equivalency rather than in terms of myth as such. And since the writings of the later period are quite rightly seen as providing the benchmark for any serious Nietzsche interpretation, with the earlier writings playing a largely preliminary role, it is easy to see why the mythic pretensions of Nietzsche's thought have so often been overlooked or discounted.

Yet, myth stands as the culmination of Nietzsche's project as an artist-creator. It goes almost without saying that Nietzsche idealized—and idolized—the classical Greeks, whom he saw as having created a culture unequaled either before or after their own time. In his view, myth—specifically, the tragic myth—gave them a unity of purpose that made their cultural achievements possible. It gave their culture its unity of purpose—its "public" bearing, in contrast to the allegedly purely private bearing of present-day culture.[4] This was a view to which Nietzsche always adhered, though the practical conclusions that he drew therefrom changed over the course of his intellectual career. In his early period, he envisaged, as a cure for the fragmentary and undirected state of modern culture, a revival of the tragic myth. It is on this account that Nietzsche refers not to the birth but to the rebirth of the tragic myth in contemporary life, and assures us that the process by which myth was lost is now to be followed by "*the reverse process, the gradual awakening of the Dionysian spirit* in our modern world!" (*BT*, chap. 19; *NBW*, p. 119). There is a strong element of nostalgia here, of which Greek culture is the object: from the Greeks we started out, and to them we shall return. Admittedly, it is not customary to view Nietzsche as a nostalgic thinker, and this element does largely disappear from his mature writings, except in the more general sense in which I shall define Dionysus and the eternal return as nostalgic. Nonetheless, it is an aspect of his thought that ought not to be ignored, not so much because of its function within the Nietzschean text as because of its illuminating connections outside that text.

Nostalgia is central, for example, to the thought of Heidegger and of such followers of Heidegger as Hannah Arendt. Nor should its importance for some of the cruder political movements of the twentieth century be underestimated, as we shall see in Part II. Going back in time, it was a prominent feature in the thought of the Romantics, who, especially in their forays into the political sphere, also tended to idealize one or another past historical period (fifth-century Greece, the Middle Ages, the Renaissance) and use it as a standard against which to measure the present. But Nietzsche's affinity with the Romantics can be more precisely characterized than this. It is a question not simply of nostalgia in general. It is a question of Nietzsche's reworking of the pervasive Romantic motif of the "circuitous journey" from *mythos* to *logos* and back. If the early Nietzsche, at least in his mythological dimension, is to be understood at all, he has to be viewed in the light of the Romantic concern with a return to myth.

To be sure, in his early writings Nietzsche rarely referred to the Romantics; and when he did refer to them, it was in pejorative terms.[5] There is thus no question of his having consciously worked within the Romantic tradition. Yet, *The Birth of Tragedy* appears a strangely, even an inexplicably self-contradictory work unless one views it as a restatement of this Romantic theme. Kaufmann, who vehemently denies any Romantic connection, is forced to distinguish between Nietzsche's account of the character of classical Greek culture, which he regards as illuminating and important, and his account of the rebirth of tragedy in the modern world, which he regards as an embarrassing mistake. According to Kaufmann, it was a mistake that Nietzsche could easily have avoided, simply by leaving out chapters 16 to 25 of *The Birth of Tragedy* and ending it "with [chapter] 15, as an early draft did and as the book clearly ought to" (*NBW*, p. 13).

It is entirely true that Nietzsche later regretted the introduction of "the most modern problems" into his account of "the grandiose *Greek problem*" (*BT*, "Attempt," §6; *NBW*, p. 24). But to read *The Birth of Tragedy* with the "modern problems" left out is to misconstrue the book entirely. Notwithstanding the interest that subsequent generations of classical scholars have taken in it, it is not primarily a scholarly treatise on the Greeks. Rather, it is a protest against a contemporary culture that Nietzsche thought to be "analytical and inartistic."[6] Its account of the birth of tragedy, far from being its "main thesis,"[7] sets the stage for something that in Nietzsche's view is far more important: the prospect of tragedy's rebirth. It is clear why Kaufmann should want to repudiate the latter aspect of the work, for the whole notion of an artistic-mythical rebirth ill accords with the view of Nietzsche that Kaufmann wants to convey, a Nietzsche who would find cultural salvation in the revitalization not of myth but of critical thought. Moreover, Nietzsche's account of the rebirth of tragedy, quite apart from its general failure to accord with any such view, is intellectually and personally embarrassing in its attribution of the long-awaited rebirth to the beneficent workings of Richard Wagner. Nietzsche sees Wagner as a modern Aeschylus, performing the same wonders with German myth that his classical predecessors had performed with the Greek. There can be absolutely no doubt that Nietzsche was wrong—and disastrously so—about Wagner. The easiest way of "saving" Nietzsche from his faux pas is to view this aspect of *The Birth of Tragedy* as, in Kaufmann's words, "a reflection of Wagner's neo-Romantic aspirations," and as "not in harmony with Nietzsche's own basic intentions."[8]

But it is exceedingly difficult to sustain such a view. There are really two points at issue here. The first is the question of whether early Nietzsche was in any sense a Romantic. Although Kaufmann, for one, denies this connection, *The Birth of Tragedy* is importantly marked by Romantic motifs. In fact, the role that Wagner plays in the work is all but inexplicable unless one views it in terms of the Romantic hope (which I explored in my Introduction) that the poet will bring consciousness back to its prelapsarian, unified condition. One is reminded of the Schelling of *The Ages of the World* (1811), who looked forward to a "golden age" when "truth becomes fable and fable truth," envisaging the appearance of one who would "sing the greatest heroic poem, comprehending in spirit what was,

what is, what will be, the kind of poem attributed to the seers of yore."
This might almost be an announcement for *The Birth of Tragedy*, while
mutatis mutandis it fits *Thus Spoke Zarathustra* and indeed the whole
aestheticist project of an "integration" of literature and philosophy.[9] To
be sure, as Paul de Man has argued, Nietzsche simultaneously undermines such a reading of *The Birth of Tragedy*, particularly in his *Nachlass*
fragments of the same period.[10] But this is no denial of Nietzsche's explicit attachment to the Romantic motif.

Moreover, looking back on *The Birth of Tragedy* in his 1886 preface,
Nietzsche himself had no reservations about characterizing it as a work
infected by Romanticism. His appeal to Wagner, he now held, had been
nothing short of folly. The "German music" in which he had placed his
hopes for the rebirth of the tragic myth he now saw to be "romanticism
through and through," and hence the "most un-Greek of all possible art
forms" (*BT*, "Attempt," §6; *NBW*, p. 25). Nor does the underlying motif of
a "return to myth" escape Nietzsche's censure: "How now? Isn't this the
typical creed of the Romantic of 1830, masked by the pessimism of 1850?
Even the usual romantic finale is sounded—break, breakdown, return and
collapse before an old faith, before *the* old God. How now? Is your pessi-
mists' book not itself a piece of anti-Hellenism and romanticism?" (*BT*,
"Attempt," §7; *NBW*, p. 26).

One can still escape characterizing the early Nietzsche as a neo-
Romantic by maintaining, as Kaufmann does, that the neo-Romantic elements in his thought were not part of his "basic" intention. This is the
second point at issue, for while there is no doubt that the mature Nietzsche
found his earlier Romantic enthusiasms embarrassing, there is simply no
textual warrant for distinguishing between the early Nietzsche's "basic"
intentions and those that were not so basic, and attributing the "Romantic"
features of *The Birth of Tragedy* to the latter category. Indeed, it is difficult
to see what would be left of the work if its "Romantic" features were
removed.

Nor do we need to confine ourselves to *The Birth of Tragedy*, for two of
Nietzsche's *Untimely Meditations* are directly concerned with the fate of
myth and the prospect of its return. To begin with, there is the second
Untimely Meditation, "On the Uses and Disadvantages of History for
Life" (1874). Here he deals at much greater length than he had in *The
Birth of Tragedy* with the critical, antimythical spirit that he sees as dominating "modern" life. He believes this spirit to be most clearly manifested
in the way we approach our past. The illusions that are destroyed by the
"unrestrained historical sense" are in the first instance the mythic illu-

sions that establish the ground of a culture, for the historical mind is simply incapable of leaving the sacred foundations of a culture untouched.
Moreover, as in *The Birth of Tragedy,* Nietzsche envisages a return from
logos to *mythos,* from a debilitating skepticism and ironism to a renewed
ground of certainty. As he says at the beginning of the final chapter of the
essay: "Mindful of this situation in which *youth* finds itself I cry Land!
Land! Enough and more than enough of the wild and erring voyage over
strange dark seas! At last a coast appears in sight: we must land on it
whatever it may be like, and the worst of harbours is better than to go
reeling back into a hopeless infinity of scepticism."[11] Admittedly, "The
Uses and Disadvantages of History" deals far more with the alleged dangers of the critical spirit than it does with the mythic spirit that is destined
to take its place, so that we never actually learn why Nietzsche believes
that "the coast is at last in sight." Indeed, a fact that was much to the
master's annoyance, the name of Wagner is not even mentioned.

But these omissions are more than made up for in the fourth and last
Untimely Meditation, "Richard Wagner in Bayreuth" (1876). Like "The
Uses and Disadvantages of History," this also is a coda to *The Birth of
Tragedy,* though one that develops the positive rather than the negative
possibilities that the earlier work claimed to uncover. Once again, Wagner is portrayed as the great artistic and poetic genius who will lead us
back into the realm of myth. His task is "to restore to myth its manliness,
and to take the spell from music and bring it to speech."[12] His "*poetic*
element," says Nietzsche, "is disclosed by the fact that he thinks in visible
and palpable events, not in concepts; that is to say, he thinks mythically, as
the folk has always done." It is commonly believed that some particular
thought lies at the bottom of a myth, but according to Nietzsche this is an
error. A myth "is itself a mode of thinking; it communicates an idea [*Vorstellung*] of the world, but as a succession of events, actions, and suffer-
ings." The *Ring of the Nibelungen,* for example, constitutes "a tremendous system of thought without the conceptual form of thought"—a
system whose appeal is not to the "theoretical man" but to "the folk."
Wagner had "forced language back into a primordial state in which it
hardly yet thinks in concepts and in which it is itself still poetry, image,
and feeling." In so doing, he had transported us into a realm that Nietzsche views as far more vivid and immediate, and in consequence far more
authentic, than the "non-mythical sphere"—the sphere of concepts and
of theory—that we customarily inhabit.[13] Or, as Nietzsche says in another passage, Wagner was a "counter-Alexander," one who, through his
revitalization of myth, was bringing about a cultural unity that had not

been seen since the time of the Greeks. On this account, he had to be reckoned among the "truly great cultural masters," dominating the arts, religion, and the histories of the various nations.[14]

The image of the circuitous journey back to myth is the major point of affinity between Nietzsche and his Romantic predecessors. To this we can add the prophetic, quasilegislative role that he attributes to the poet; the contrast, widely accepted by the Romantics, between the emotive and poetic languages of primitives and the abstract and restrained language of advanced civilization; and, of course, the Apollonian/Dionysian polarity. These latter affinities disappear from the later writings. The motif of a "return to myth," however, persists, with Nietzsche-Zarathustra playing the remythifying role that in the early writings is played by Wagner. Admittedly, as I have already suggested, the motif of return is "crossed out." It is crossed out by the thought of crisis, which breaks the circle and makes any actual return supremely problematic. To put this in another way, it is not origin but difference that now rules. Myth itself is almost completely ironized away, reduced to an ideal insubstantiality that we sense can never become real. But these observations are no denial of the project's Romantic roots.

The parallel that I am here suggesting is also suggested by Nietzsche himself, in a passage in *Ecce Homo* that is rarely remarked upon, and then usually in support of a point quite different from mine. Here Nietzsche tells us that in "Richard Wagner in Bayreuth" Nietzsche alone is being discussed in "all psychologically decisive places; . . . one need not hesitate to put down my name or the word 'Zarathustra' where the text has the word 'Wagner.' The entire picture of the dithyrambic artist is a picture of the pre-existent poet of *Zarathustra*, sketched with abysmal profundity and without touching even for a moment the Wagnerian reality [*Realität*]. Wagner himself had some notion of that; he did not recognize himself in this essay" (*EH*, "BT," §4). It is possible to read this passage with apologetic intent, as showing that Nietzsche's high praise of Wagner had not been meant for Wagner at all. In this way, one can explain away the early Nietzsche's enthusiasm for a man whose social and political views were little short of despicable.

But the passage does not "explain away" Wagner at all. Quite apart from the fact that it gives a highly implausible account of what Nietzsche actually meant when, in 1876, he attached certain qualities to the name *Wagner*, it confirms, from the perspective of 1888, the homologism that I have been insisting exists between the early and the mature Nietzsche. Nietzsche may have *thought* that in countenancing a substitution of the names

Wagner and *Nietzsche* he was distancing himself from his erstwhile hero. But it is equally plausible to interpret this substitution as indicating not that the early Nietzsche was not a "Wagnerian" but rather that the mature Nietzsche was—with the most prominent indication of the later Nietzsche's Wagnerianism to be found in the persistence of his concern with re-mythification. Nietzsche's further comments on the parallel between "Richard Wagner in Bayreuth" and *Thus Spoke Zarathustra* support such a view, for he goes on to tell us that the former work anticipates both the "style" and the "event" [*Ereigniss*] of Zarathustra, that the "idea of Bayreuth" was transformed in the later work into the Zarathustrian noontide "at which the most elect consecrate themselves for the greatest of all tasks," and that consequently "Richard Wagner in Bayreuth" is "a vision of my future" (*EH,* "BT," §4; also *EH,* "The Untimely Ones"). To be sure, it is necessary almost on principle to regard Nietzsche's self-interpretations with considerable suspicion. But it seems to me that in this instance Nietzsche is entirely right—that his concern with myth persists fundamentally unchanged as one moves from the early to the later writings.

The mythos of the future

It is in *Zarathustra* that Nietzsche introduces the "mythos of the future,"[15] the myth destined to save us from the nihilism that he believes has cast its shadow over Western culture. This myth, the doctrine of eternal return (or recurrence), is calculated to impart to human life something that in his opinion it no longer has: a meaning, a pattern.[16] It will thus allow us to confront nihilism, this "uncanniest of all guests" who "stands at the door" (*WP,* §1; *KGW,* 8. Abt., 1. Bd., p. 123). Some indication of how this desirable turn of events will be accomplished is to be found in *The Gay Science,* where, as I noted earlier, numerous hints of the Zarathustrian perspective are already to be found. Among other things, Nietzsche here attacks what he calls the "ridiculous overestimation and misunderstanding of consciousness" in modern culture, and suggests that the most important task for the future is that of "incorporating knowledge and making it instinctive" (*GS,* §11). It is here that myth will play its role, for myth's value is that it provides, in Nietzsche's view, a system of unconscious, nonconceptual knowledge, a pattern of immediate response uniting all participants in a given culture. Such was what Nietzsche saw in the amphitheater of Greek tragedy; such is what he wants to see within the larger sphere of the present.

One can accept as valid a good deal of what Nietzsche wants to say about myth and its relation to culture, for without a basis of unquestioningly accepted patterns of civility, coherent social life would undoubtedly become impossible. One can also accept a more strictly existential interpretation of Nietzsche's point, for it is equally clear that if the individual had to think out from its beginnings every act that he wished to perform, his life would become impossible. An ability to take things on faith—to act without continually trying to make explicit the grounds and assumptions of one's actions—is an absolute necessity in both social and individual life. In the absence of this ability, we enter the realm of pathology. To put the point in slightly different terms, we often find ourselves operating on the plane of Apollonian illusion, accepting "image" or "discourse" as adequately conveying reality without pursuing them down to their real ground. The problem with Nietzsche's position is that this tends to become a permanent condition, unchecked by a critical effort of thought or by any attempt to measure image against reality (hence, for example, the failure of latter-day Nietzscheans to explain to us exactly *how* the Nietzschean "death of God," on which they lay such great emphasis, manifests itself in social and political life).[17] A total self-containedness sets in. It is significant that Nietzsche can see man's fundamental impulse as directed not toward making his way in the world but rather toward the substitution of one linguistic element for another, an operation that in the later Nietzsche becomes the prime expression of the will to power. We never step outside language and its apparently infinite creativity. The truck never comes down the road, though we may find ourselves talking endlessly about the grounds for the possibility of our knowledge that it is coming.

The consequences of this for Nietzsche's project will perhaps be best seen if we look at the doctrine of eternal return itself. Nowhere in Nietzsche's text is there any clear indication of what eternal return in fact means, or of why Nietzsche thought himself justified in valuing the doctrine so highly, or of how it embodies the social dimension that, as myth, it presumably ought to have. Aside from the accounts of eternal return in *Zarathustra* and in the work that was effectively Nietzsche's finale, *Ecce Homo*, we find no discussion of the doctrine in any of his books.[18] The interpreter of Nietzsche is thus tempted to underplay "this most dubious doctrine,"[19] and to emphasize instead the apparently more intelligible conception of the will to power. But Nietzsche himself held it to be the "fundamental conception" of what he saw as his most important work (*EH*, "TZ," §1). In view of this evaluation of the doctrine, we have to take seriously what Nietzsche says about it, however extravagant and unreasonable those assertions may appear.

It is obvious, of course, that Nietzsche intended eternal return as a denial of both the Christian myth of redemption and the nineteenth-century bourgeois myth of progress. Thus, we do have a kind of negative characterization of the doctrine. But when one tries to move from a conception of what eternal return is not to a conception of what it is, one runs into trouble. For example, in *Zarathustra* Nietzsche goes out of his way to reject the view that eternal return involves a cyclical conception of time. He does this not, one suspects, because he thinks such an interpretation wrong, but because he thinks it too clear (or, to take a more Nietzschean approach, too glib and easy). Admittedly, we do learn in *Ecce Homo* that eternal return is the "highest formula of affirmation that is at all attainable" (*EH*, "TZ," §1). But again one wonders what such a formula could possibly mean. Normally, we speak of an affirmation "of" something— of *X* or *Y* or *Z*; to speak of affirmation *tout court* is odd, though hardly inconsistent with Nietzsche's perspective as I have been trying to unveil it. (It is worth noting, parenthetically, that one has the same problem with Foucault, Derrida, and the later Heidegger. The "fundamental conceptions" of all these writers turn out to be so elusive that every attempt to define them, along the lines of "*X* is . . . ," will necessarily be wrong. At most, one can say that "*X* is . . . ," with the *is* "crossed out," to follow Derrida's tactic. Alternatively, one can say, as Foucault is wont to do, that "*X* is neither *Y* nor *Z*," with no more positive option presented.)

The problem of interpretation

To get to the roots of this perspective, we must look more closely than we have done so far at Nietzsche's account of interpretation. The problem of interpretation is central to the whole aestheticist strand of thought. It is a recurring preoccupation in all four of our writers. But it is a preoccupation especially important for anyone attempting to come to grips with Nietzsche in particular. In confronting it, we get some indication of the complexity of his enterprise, of the sheer difficulty of pinning it down in any determinate way.

Nietzsche has often been characterized, and in fact characterized himself, as adhering to a perspectivist view of interpretation. It is not clear, however, how radically one ought to interpret his various perspectivist statements. Sometimes he seems to be holding that there is no single correct interpretation of any given thing, but rather a variety of correct interpretations, each of which can be considered valid within its own frame of reference. But this tends continually to verge over into something quite

different, into the view that there is no such thing as correct interpretation. Or to formulate the difficulty in different, and perhaps tendentious-
sounding terms, sometimes he seems to be a "demystifying" interpreter,
one whose aim is to clear away symbols and masks and illusions in an
attempt to get down to the true and solid reality of "things." At other
times, he appears as a *re*-mystifier, as one who wants to say that there is no
such thing as a thing—that every "thing" is only a mask for some other
"thing," which in its turn will be seen to be only a mask as well.

In this latter instance, the center of interest is not the presumed reality
that interpretation seeks to uncover, but the process of interpretation itself—a process infinite in its unfolding, for the ground is never reached,
the "original" or "transcendental" signified never uncovered. (I am using
a terminology common to Foucault and Derrida, a shared language suggesting that despite their vast differences of style, they inhabit similar
territories.) Indeed, interpretation itself becomes part of a growing system of concealments, an obfuscation, yet another mask. It is this aspect of
the Nietzschean project that Foucault celebrates in his lecture of 1964 on
"Nietzsche, Marx, Freud."[20] It is presumably this, too, that Derrida has
in mind when he declares that Nietzsche "contributed a great deal to the
liberation of the signifier from its dependence or derivation with respect
to the logos and the related concept of truth" (*GRAM*, pp. 31–32/19).

I cannot deal in detail with all the exegetical and conceptual difficulties
involved in the attempt to interpret the Nietzschean interpretation of interpretation. Nonetheless, I can say enough about Nietzsche's account of
interpretation to establish that notwithstanding his obvious failure to
think through in a systematic way all the issues involved, and notwithstanding, too, certain hesitancies and retreats, Nietzsche really did in an
important sense adhere to the second view that I have outlined.

I have been much helped, in coming to grips with Nietzsche's interpretation of interpretation, by John T. Wilcox's *Truth and Value in Nietzsche: A Study of His Metaethics and Epistemology.* Wilcox's study is not
the only one to deal extensively with the problem of interpretation in
Nietzsche, but for two reasons it is the one most useful for my purposes.
In the first place, Wilcox takes a position on Nietzsche that is radically
opposed to the view being put forward here, since he argues for the "rationalist" as opposed to the "irrationalist" character of Nietzsche's
thought (or, to use Wilcox's more frequent terminology, for his "cognitivism" as opposed to his "noncognitivism").[21] As Wilcox puts it, "there is
so much rationalism in Nietzsche's thought and rhetoric, in his avowals
and in his polemics, that it cannot be overlooked or explained away."[22] At

the same time, however, Wilcox tends to undercut his own argument. He recognizes the "antinomies, direct and indirect, in Nietzsche's thought," his "many-sidedness," even his "outright inconsistency."[23] Hence, if in Wilcox's view Nietzsche's "cognitivism" is dominant, he also finds much that simply will not fit a cognitivist reading. He is in consequence forced to conclude that Nietzsche wanted some sort of still-undefined union of the cognitive and the noncognitive—a "*trans*-cognitive approach, we might say."[24] This is already to retreat very seriously from the notion that Nietzsche ought to be viewed as a cognitivist. In the second place, Wilcox is useful in the present context because, if his highly literalistic and pedestrian approach to Nietzsche prevents him, in my opinion, from seeing what Nietzsche is really pointing toward, it also makes him extremely careful about his documentation. He fully documents every point he makes. What is more unusual, he also adduces all the negative evidence that he can find in relation to any given point. In short, he lets us know exactly how he comes to his conclusions, and gives us a good deal of the evidence needed to challenge those conclusions.

Let us look at some of the passages in Nietzsche that deal explicitly with the problem of interpretation. The most striking of these are to be found in *The Will to Power*. Admittedly, since Nietzsche himself never published these writings, they must be treated with some caution. But their unpublished status does not rob them of a certain indicative force. In any case, they are paralleled and reinforced, as we shall see, by other passages that Nietzsche did publish.

In fragment 560 of *The Will to Power*, Nietzsche suggests that it is an "idle hypothesis" to imagine "that things possess a constitution in themselves quite apart from interpretation [*Interpretation*] and subjectivity" (*KGW*, 8. Abt., 2. Bd., p. 17). On the contrary, as he says in fragment 556, "the essence of a thing is only an *opinion* about the 'thing,'" and the question "what is that?" an "imposition of meaning from some other viewpoint" (*KGW*, 8. Abt., 1. Bd., p. 138). Indeed, he declares in fragment 567, it is a mistake to believe that if all the perspectives on the world were deducted, a world "would still remain over" (*KGW*, 8. Abt., 3. Bd., p. 163). The subject alone is "demonstrable," he suggests in fragment 569, where he hypothesizes that the "object" is "only a kind of effect produced by a subject upon a subject—a *modus* of *the subject*" (*KGW*, 8. Abt., 2. Bd., p. 60). Expressing the same idea in slightly different terms, he suggests in fragment 560 that "the objective is only a false concept of a genus and an antithesis *within* the subjective" (*KGW*, 8. Abt., 2. Bd., p. 17). We are thus not surprised when he opines, in fragment 604, that "there are no facts [*es giebt keinen Thatbestand*], everything is in flux, incomprehensible, elusive; what is relatively most enduring is—our opinions" (*KGW*, 8. Abt., 1. Bd., p. 98). Nor are we surprised when, in opposition to the "positivistic" view that "there are only *facts* [*Thatsachen*]," he declares in fragment 481 that "no, facts are precisely what there is not, only interpretations [*Interpretationen*]. We cannot establish any fact [*Factum*] 'in itself': perhaps it is folly to want to do such a thing" (*KGW*, 8. Abt., 1. Bd., p. 323).

Wilcox argues that most of these passages, along with some similar, though for our purposes less interesting ones in the published writings, can be explained as rejections of the Kantian thing-in-itself and of the whole Kantian distinction between the noumenal and the phenomenal worlds. Insofar as it is *this* that Nietzsche is concerned with, he is "not rejecting the possibility of *empirical* knowledge; he is merely rejecting the possibility of any *transcendent* knowledge, in Kant's sense."[25] I do not wish to deny that this may be part of what Nietzsche intended in these passages. Nor do I wish to deny that there is a great deal of cognitivist rhetoric running through Nietzsche's writings: one of the merits of Wilcox's book is that he makes it clear just how pervasive this rhetoric is.

Yet, specifically with regard to the passages quoted above, it is necessary to make two points. In the first place, though it is clear that Nietzsche had Kant in mind when he composed some of these passages, he does not say that it is only the Kantian thing-in-itself, and only the possibility of transcendent knowledge, that he is attacking. And while in composing these passages he may have meant something less than the second version of perspectivism, what he says frequently does add up to such a view—to the view that the "thing" is entirely the invention of the interpretive act or series of acts, or (to put the matter in a slightly harder form) to the view that there is "nothing" outside interpretation.

Second, and connected with this first point, some of the above passages are marked by Nietzsche's tendency to think in terms of opposed extremes. Time and again in Nietzsche, one encounters an inclination to postulate opposites and assume that these exhaust the possibilities: "If not *X*, then *Y*; if not *Y*, then *X*." Other possibilities, whether medians between, or totally unrelated to, *X* and *Y*, are consistently ignored. This tendency is most evident in the two passages above where Nietzsche postulates his distinction between "fact" and "interpretation" (or "opinion") and then opts entirely for interpretation—that is, for interpretation conceived as a total imposition of meaning and "reality" upon the world. But the other passages also bear the marks of this extremist tendency. Note, for example, Nietzsche's statement that the "essence of a thing" is *only* an opinion about the thing, and the object *only* "a kind of effect produced by a subject upon a subject." This gets us back to my previous point, for it is precisely this tendency that opens up the gap between what Nietzsche meant (or rather, may possibly have meant, since of his actual intentions we cannot always be certain) and what he says. Admittedly, it is possible that had he sought to work out systematically the implications of some of these statements, he would have modified them. He might have concluded, for example, that there are both subjects and objects, both things and opinions, both facts and interpretations. But he never did. To imagine him doing so, we would have to imagine a thinker radically different from the thinker whose corpus now lies before us.

Art and interpretation

I now move on to a more general issue, for the main deficiency in Wilcox's consideration of the problems of truth and interpretation in Nietzsche is his failure to take account of the aesthetic dimension of Nietzsche's project. At the end of his book, Wilcox lists all the passages that he cites from Nietzsche. It is telling that he has three times more citations from Nietzsche's most "positivistic" work, *Human, All-Too-Human,* than from the central, but dense and gnomic *Zarathustra.*[26] It is all very well to look at Nietzsche from the perspective of Kant. But one must not forget that, as thinkers, Kant and Nietzsche are entirely different in spirit. Kant saw himself as a critic. Nietzsche saw himself as an artist and mythmaker (which is not to deny that he was also, in some respects, a critic; but the critical, demythologizing part of his enterprise was entirely subordinate to his remythologizing).

I have already noted that whereas Kant views the imposition of categories on the world as an ordering, Nietzsche views it as a dissimulation—a *Verstellung.* Nietzsche's evident delight in *Verstellung* (tinged, admittedly, with regret at the impossibility of grasping the world as it really is) is the product of what most clearly distinguishes him from Kant, his aesthetic conception of his own project. It is this perspective that enables him to *rest* in dissimulation, for within art *Verstellung* (sometimes referred to as "poetic license") is accepted as legitimate. One might almost say that it is the *Verstellung* that makes art into art, that introduces the impedances, the darkness, the gulf between saying and meaning, without which the work of art would be a mere statement of fact. The artist is an interpreter, but not one who is compelled to a "correct" interpretation of what he observes—for in art it is the interpretation itself that interests us. Take, for example, the case of modern painting, which runs the gamut from abstractionism to realism. The irrelevance of "correctness" to abstract painting is obvious. But even in so-called realistic styles of art, the interest is to be found in the divergences between "art" and "reality" that the artist introduces or discovers—even when, as in the recent style of photo-realism, he is apparently concerned with an exact reproduction of things. To be sure, the works of art that are thus produced may enable us to "see" reality more clearly and more fully than we did before. But this is not to say that what makes them works of art is their fidelity to reality. Indeed, one could construct an entire theory of the aesthetic as utopia—a utopia liberating us, through its disorder, from the oppressiveness of what is extant, actual, established, and determined. To some extent, by such thinkers as Herbert Marcuse, this has already been done.

More important here, however, is the distinction that one can make between aesthetic interpretation and nonaesthetic interpretation. It is now necessary to shift from the perspective of the creator of the work of art to the perspective of its observer. There is an important difference between the way we interpretively approach a work of art and the way we approach a "mere thing." Put briefly, we see ourselves as having a far greater freedom in interpreting the former than the latter. This is because, in contrast to the utilitarian contexts that dominate most of our lives and that tend to pare away meanings from objects, we see in art a richness of meaning. We are free to choose, from among a multiplicity of possible meanings, those that the work of art will have for us. As post-Romantics and post-Kantians, we tend to feel that the "meaning" of the work is the meaning that it has for us as individual interpreters, whereas we do not feel this, or do so only to a much lesser degree, with "mere things." (Of course, we can also treat a work of art as an object of scholarly investigation, but this is a different matter, and one that is not relevant to the present case. Scholarship, at least in its conventional, that is, non-Nietzschean forms, is not aesthetic in character—even when the objects that it investigates happen to be works of art.) The fact that the "Mona Lisa" is a work of art rather than a passport photograph makes irrelevant to our consideration of it as a work of art such questions as who exactly the woman is, whether Leonardo accurately portrayed her, and why she is smiling. (And the "Mona Lisa" is a work of art mainly because we take it to be a work of art; we could also envisage passport photographs, or urinals, or Brillo boxes being viewed, under certain circumstances, as works of art.) Indeed, the fact that we do not know who the woman is or why she is smiling, and are thus free to invent our own interpretations, adds to the work's aesthetic charm.

What is distinctive about Nietzsche is that he takes this conception of interpretation and extends it far beyond what we normally take to be the boundaries of the aesthetic realm. For Nietzsche, *all* interpretation is of the aesthetic sort, detached from "things," from any indenture to the referent. It is no accident that his central work is a piece of prose poetry, the whole of which, he says, "may be reckoned as music" (*EH*, "TZ," §1). Nor is it accidental that he characterizes the major work of his early period, *The Birth of Tragedy*, as music, and declares that it should be sung and not spoken (*BT*, "Attempt," §3). Nietzsche's conception of interpretation is determined by his underlying aesthetic perspective—by his tendency to look at the world in aesthetic terms, indeed his tendency to view art as a kind of self-justifying recreation of the world. It is this concern that establishes his vocation as an "*artist*-philosopher." It is significant, moreover, that the art in terms of which he most often defines this vocation is the art of music—the most self-contained and abstract of all the arts, in which the quantum of invention far outweighs the quantum of "pure" representation (if any such were possible). I turn again to a passage from *The Gay Science* that I quoted in part at the end of Chapter 1, where Nietzsche addresses himself "to the realists"—those "sober people" who think that reality is an object passively waiting for man to unveil it. Against such objectivism, Nietzsche declares that the world has been created by man himself: "That mountain there! That cloud there! What is real in that? Subtract the phantasm and every human *contribution* from it, my sober friends! If you *can!* If you can forget your descent, your past, your training—all of your humanity and animality. There is no 'reality' for us—nor for you either, my sober friends" (*GS*, §57).

Furthermore, it is as an *artist* that man creates. Nietzsche's artist has little in common with Marx's worker, who humanizes nature (and in the process naturalizes himself) through patient, collective labor. "We artists!" Nietzsche declares. "We ignore what is natural. We are moonstruck and God-struck. We wander, still as death, unwearied, on heights that we do not see as heights but as plains, as our safety" (*GS*, §59). In the same work, he attacks what he calls "the fancy of the contemplatives"—that is, the delusion, from which "the higher human being" suffers, that he is a mere "*spectator* and *listener* who has been placed before the great visual and acoustic spectacle that is life." Yet, "he himself is really the poet who keeps creating this life." As poets, we "continually fashion something that had not been there before: the whole eternally growing world of valuations, colors, accents, perspectives, scales, affirmations, and negations." Whatever has value in our world has value only because it has been given value by man. Indeed, "only we have created the world *that concerns man!* [*die den Menschen etwas angeht*]." Unfortunately, continues Nietzsche, we are always forgetting that *we* are the creators of the world. As a result, "we are *neither as proud nor as happy* as we might be" (*GS*, §301).

Nietzsche pursues a similar line in *Beyond Good and Evil*, the other published work in which we find him dealing explicitly with the problem of interpretation. One notes, firstly, the dichotomy that he sets up between explanation (*Erklärung*) and interpretation (*Auslegung*). Explanation would depict the world as it objectively is. Interpretation, on the other hand, is purely subjective ("to suit us, if I may say so") (*BGE*, §14). It is true that on occasion (though very rarely) Nietzsche seems to suggest that an observer with sufficient scientific rigor could indeed produce an account of a thing that was entirely objective, entirely without interpretation.[27] But for all practical purposes he finds only the subjective side of the dichotomy interesting or even in the least degree relevant. In section 14 of *Beyond Good and Evil*, he maintains that contemporary thinkers are only just beginning to grasp that physics is interpretation rather than explanation, and he goes on to suggest that there is a positive enjoyment and nobility in the attempt to throw a net of interpretation over the world. Similarly, in section 22, he condemns what he regards as the "bad modes of interpretation" (*schlechte Interpretations-Künste*) practiced by physicists, who imagine, according to Nietzsche, that the laws of nature actually exist *in* nature. He declares these supposed laws to be "interpretation, not text," and adds that "somebody might come along who, with opposite intentions and modes of interpretation, could read out of the same 'nature,' and with regard to the same phenomena, rather the tyrannically inconsiderate and relentless enforcement of claims of power." To be sure, an objector could protest that this view, too, is "only interpretation"—to which Nietzsche responds, "well, so much the better" (*BGE*, §22).

What clearly matters for Nietzsche is not the objective "correctness" of the interpretation but rather the courage and daring of the interpreter and his ability to pursue his insights at length and in "a *single* direction" (*BGE*, §188). Indeed, Nietzsche holds the notion of correctness to be basically nonsensical. There is no "essential opposition" between the true and the false, but only "degrees of apparentness [*Scheinbarkeit*]," while the preference for "truth" over "mere appearance" (*Schein*) is nothing more than a "moral prejudice" (*BGE*, §34). Once more, Nietzsche suggests that "the world *that concerns us*" is a fiction (*BGE*, §34). Once more, he adopts what he calls an "anti-realist" stance. Once more, he rejects as vain the attempt to acquire a certain and objective knowledge and opts instead for the "beautiful possibilities" that interpretation brings with it (*BGE*, §10).

Nietzsche is convinced that philosophers will more and more come to acknowledge the total subjectivity and individuality of the interpretive process. Already the "stronger and livelier" thinkers are coming to speak of "perspective" with a new arrogance (*BGE*, §10). The "philosophers of the future," for their part, will justify all their conclusions with the words, "My judgment is *my* judgment" (*BGE*, §43). In *Beyond Good and Evil*, Nietzsche has less to say about art than he does in *The Gay Science*, but it is nonetheless clear that the aesthetic connection remains decisive for him. He speaks, for example, of the "artistic power" that will enable men to rise above, and not return to, actuality (*BGE*, §10). He refers to the need to form men "as artists" (*BGE*, §62). He remarks approvingly on the artist's familiarity with lying and invention (*BGE*, §192). All of this suggests that *Beyond Good and Evil*—and in some of its aspects, *The Gay Science*— ought to be seen as a kind of prosaic, "theoretical" exposition of the artistic-philosophical practice that we find exemplified in *Zarathustra*.

It is worth noting that an illusionistic side still persists in Nietzsche's later writings, even though the initial embodiment of illusion, the Apollonian, all but disappears. Admittedly (in a move that we have already encountered), Nietzsche evaluates cultural products—interpretations included—in terms of their "value for life" (*BGE*, §2). Here we see the naturalistic Nietzsche, the Nietzsche who seeks to "translate man back into nature" (*BGE*, §230) and who judges things "healthy" or "unhealthy" insofar as they may help or hinder this aim. In wishing to translate man back into nature, he presumably countenances something outside interpretation into which man is capable of being translated. This naturalistic orientation, had it been consistently maintained, would presumably have made Nietzsche into a pragmatist. As is well known, many commentators have seen pragmatic elements in his thought. But it is impossible to derive a straightforward pragmatism from Nietzsche's admittedly fragmentary statements on epistemological issues. The difficulty is that he does not identify utility with truth; as he says in fragment 483 of *The Will to Power*, "a belief can be a necessary condition of life and still be false" (*KGW*, 7. Abt., 3. Bd., p. 326).[28] Such statements as this should not, however, be seen as committing Nietzsche to some aspect of a correspondence theory of truth, as if he were a pragmatist who lacked the courage of his convictions. Rather, they are evidence of the continuing role in his thought of an aesthetic commitment. This commitment inevitably takes him beyond the bounds of "normal" philosophical discourse. Time and again, he characterizes intellection as a matter of veils and masks and caves and concealments, of "foreground estimates," of "provisional perspectives" (BGE, §2). If he sometimes justifies these concealments on grounds of their "value for life," he is equally likely to apply to them the aesthetic criteria of creativity, elegance, richness, and subtlety.

There are many passages in which Nietzsche speaks of the supposed necessity of illusion. For example, he tells us in Beyond Good and Evil that no philosopher has as yet been proved right; flee, therefore, into concealment—"and have your masks and subtlety [Feinheit], that you may be mistaken for what you are not, or feared a little" (BGE, §25). Indeed, he doubts whether a philosopher could possibly have "ultimate and real" opinions, suggesting rather that "behind every one of his caves" there must be "another deeper cave—a more comprehensive, stranger, richer world beyond the surface, an abysmally deep ground behind every ground, under every attempt to furnish 'grounds'" (BGE, §289). He speaks, too, of the readiness of the spirit to let itself be deceived and to deceive in its turn. Being deceived, one may very well have a "capricious intimation of the fact that such and such is not the case," but one nonetheless "accepts . . . a delight in all uncertainty and ambiguity, a jubilant self-enjoyment in the arbitrary narrowness and secrecy of some nook, in the all too near, in the foreground, in what is enlarged, diminished, displaced, beautified." Deceiving, one manifests the "continual urge and surge of a creative, form-giving, changeable force: in this the spirit enjoys the multiplicity and craftiness of its masks, it also enjoys the feeling of its security behind them" (BGE, §230). Similarly, in Daybreak, he characterizes "all our so-called consciousness" as "a more or less fantastic commentary on an unknown, perhaps unknowable, but felt text." What he values, it seems, is not the correctness of the commentary—since this is indeterminable—but rather its freedom, which he compares to the freedom of dreams.[29] Similarly, in the "poetic prelude" to The Gay Science, he has a quatrain in which he makes fun of "the thorough who get to the bottom of things," those "heavy" thinkers who keep falling until they reach "the ground" (GS, "Jokes, Cunning, and Revenge," §44).[30]

Nietzsche's ideal is quite otherwise. The true thinker is one who escapes an academic gravity and seriousness, who is able to remain airborne, spinning out interpretations of a reality that lies irremediably beyond human ken. Nor, in Nietzsche's view, should this be regarded as a mere frivolity.

"Anyone who has looked deeply into the world may guess how much wisdom lies in the superficiality of men," he declares in section 59 of *Beyond Good and Evil*; for those who stand most in need of "the cult of surfaces" must "at some time have reached *beneath* them with disastrous results." A similar opposition appears in section 230. Here he contrasts the "will to mere appearance [*zum Schein*], to simplification, to masks, to cloaks, in short, to the surface" with "that sublime inclination of the seeker after knowledge who insists on profundity, multiplicity, and thoroughness." This is nothing other than the old opposition between the Apollonian and the Dionysian, with the same emphasis on absolute immediacy and the same retreat to forms, illusions, and surfaces. So that here, again, the aesthetic emerges as a determining element in Nietzsche's project.

Language

I find myself being led back to the issue of language, on which I touched in the course of discussing "On Truth and Lie." For language provides the nexus between interpretation and myth in Nietzsche, opening the way to an understanding of the role that the latter plays in his thought. Like his perspectivism, Nietzsche's preoccupation with matters of language is widely known. But once again we must be careful in interpreting this concern. On the one hand, his account of language can be viewed as running in an analytical direction, continuing the tradition established by such earlier writers as Locke and Condillac and anticipating twentieth-century ideal language philosophy. In short, Nietzsche can be viewed as arguing that language is unfortunately a less than perfectly transparent medium for thought, but that transparency is the ideal, and that if we are to get at the truth we must compensate for the distortions that it introduces.

Nietzsche does insist that language distorts. The most fateful instance of such distortion is to be found, he holds, in the effect that the sharp distinction in Indo-European languages between subject and object has had on the development of Western philosophy. He expresses this idea succinctly in fragment 484 of *The Will to Power*, where he attacks the *cogito ergo sum* of Descartes: "'There is thinking: therefore there is something that thinks': this is the upshot of all Descartes' argumentation. But that means positing as 'true *a priori*' our belief in the concept of substance—that when there is thought there has to be something 'that thinks' is simply a formulation of our grammatical custom that adds a doer to every deed" (*KGW*, 8. Abt., 2. Bd., p. 215). Similarly, in *The Gene-*

alogy of Morals, he tells us that "our entire science still lies under the misleading influence of language and has not disposed of that little changeling, the 'subject'" (*GM,* 1st essay, §13). Similarly, in *Beyond Good and Evil,* he declares that it is a "falsification of the facts of the case to say that the subject 'I' is the condition of the predicate 'think.' . . . One infers here according to the grammatical habit: 'Thinking is an activity; every activity requires an agent; consequently——'" (*BGE,* §17).

Nietzsche sometimes seems to envisage an escape from this entrapment in grammar. When he is operating as a critic, he seems to want to suggest that it is an "*unconscious* domination and guidance by . . . grammatical functions" (*BGE,* §20) that leads us into these predetermined patterns of thought. By becoming conscious of this domination, we nullify its effects, escaping from the net that language seeks to weave around us. "I shall repeat a hundred times: we really ought to free ourselves from the seduction of words!" (*BGE,* §16). But this is only part of the story, for the *prophetic* Nietzsche consistently takes up a position that would make such a move not so much impossible as totally inconceivable. He seems to want to say not that language distorts reality but that it *is* reality—with nothing outside language to be distorted. We can see this view already in place in "On Truth and Lie," where language is regarded not as the "adequate expression of all realities" but rather as an independent world that, through its metaphors, metonymies, and anthropomorphisms, creates truth.[31] In this vein, the truth of language is *in* language, not outside it. Language is a prison from which escape is utterly impossible. If we employ *one* language, we will have beliefs congruent with that language, while with another language we will have other beliefs—and to both sets of belief the question of correctness will be irrelevant. When he is operating in this mode, Nietzsche's linguistic point is not that the message and the medium ought to be carefully distinguished, but rather that the two are one and the same thing. In short, we see a repetition of the peculiar self-containedness that we have already observed in his account of interpretation—and a repetition, too, of his fascination with illusion. For a language is nothing other than a system of interpretation or (what amounts to the same thing) a set of illusions; and just as Nietzsche sees interpretation and illusion as aesthetically self-justified, so also does he see language itself.

These matters of language bring us to the center of Nietzsche's enterprise. It is Foucault who most clearly puts his finger on this. In *The Order of Things,* he links Nietzsche to Mallarmé. In both writers, he perceives a "radical reflection upon language." Through this reflection, language itself, as distinguished from the "things" that language represents or signifies, comes to the fore. Nietzsche asks the question, "who is speaking?" Mallarmé replies that what speaks "is, in its solitude, in its fragile vibration, in its nothingness, the word itself—not the meaning of the word, but its enigmatic and precarious being." Thus, thought is "brought back, and violently so, towards language itself, towards its unique and difficult being." Thus does it come about that "the whole curiosity of our thought now resides in the question: What is language, how can we find a way around it in order to make it appear in itself, in all its plenitude?" What matters is language, and language alone—its "vast play . . . contained once more within a single space." The discovery of this play means, according to Foucault, a "decisive leap towards a wholly new form of thought" (MC, pp. 316–318/305–307).

Here we see language conceived not as signification or as representation, but aesthetically, as itself a work of art. Here we see the gaze resting not on what language means but on how it speaks. Similarly, with any work of art not reducible to pure propaganda, we focus our attention not on what it says but on how it says it—for the interest of the work of art, like the interest of language taken in its Foucauldian (and Heideggerian) sense, lies in the enigma that it manages to sustain. I have a great deal to quarrel with in Foucault. I believe him to be pursuing a course that is in some ways mistaken. But he seems to me to be right in this characterization of Nietzsche's significance, perceiving what is truly original and important in his thought.

We now return, finally, to the "dubious doctrine" of eternal return. Nietzsche's conception of language as active, independent being, speaking what is allegedly its own truth, provides the framework within which we are able to grasp the role that this "doctrine" plays in his thought. Nietzsche sees himself, clearly, as a critic of the regnant values of bourgeois Christian civilization. But the genuine philosopher must be a creator of values as well as a critic. In Nietzsche's words, "*genuine philosophers . . . are commanders and legislators: they say, 'thus it shall be!' . . .* With a creative hand they reach for the future, and all that has been becomes a means for them, an instrument, a hammer. Their 'knowing' is *creating,* their creating is a legislation, their will to truth is—*will to power*" (BGE, §211). But how is such creation, such legislation, to come about? It is clearly not to come about through rational argument, though once established it will obviously be supported by appropriate rationalizations. It will come about, rather, through the creation of a new language—that is, through the creation of a comprehensive system of inter-pretation that will somehow impose itself upon men.

Nietzsche tells us in *The Gay Science* that the adherents of "the old religion and religiosity" have "determined linguistic usage hitherto" and have thus given opposing systems of belief a "bad reputation even among the freest spirits" (*GS*, §23). The Nietzschean legislator seeks to establish a new linguistic usage within which his own system of belief will be em-bodied and from which opposing systems will be excluded. This is the point of that well-known statement in *Twilight of the Idols*, where Nietz-sche tells us that "I fear we are not getting rid of God because we still believe in grammar" (*TI*, "'Reason' in Philosophy," §5). There is a great deal implied in this striking but at the same time puzzling assertion. In order to understand its implications, the reader needs firstly to realize that the connection between "God" and "grammar" is provided by the notion of the subject. Nietzsche believes that the notion of the subject arose from the distinction in grammar between subject and object. But since "God" is nothing other than the supreme subject, the idea of God, too, is grammatical in origin. And since the idea of God is grammatical in origin, to get rid of it we must destroy our present grammar and replace it with a new one. There seems to be no question here of a distinction be-tween "conscious" and "unconscious" determination by language. That is to say, Nietzsche is not suggesting that by becoming aware of the biases that the language we speak introduces into our view of reality, we shall be able to cancel out their effects. In other words, it is not a matter of "cor-rectness" or "incorrectness." It is instead a matter of interpretive will to power, one that arbitrarily declares that some *new* language will simply *be*. And this new language will constitute a new system of interpretation that by virtue of its very existence will bring into being the new reality corresponding to it. If in that early idealist, Berkeley, the world is seen as a "divine visible language," in Nietzsche it is seen as language *tout court.*

This new language has, in fact, the status of myth, in the peculiar sense in which Nietzsche understands the term. Prior to Nietzsche, aesthetic thinkers viewed myth as the unconscious ground of image and metaphor upon which art is able consciously to raise itself. Nietzsche reverses this order, viewing myth not as the unconscious product of human nature but rather as the conscious product of art itself—as a justificatory art, one that sets the limits and determines the direction of a given culture.[32]

We have seen how in the Preface to *Ecce Homo* Nietzsche characterizes *Thus Spoke Zarathustra* as the "greatest gift" ever made to mankind

(*EH*, Preface, §4). This is not a mere momentary conceit, for in the chapter of *Ecce Homo* that is devoted specifically to *Zarathustra* he goes on to elaborate. Here he tells us that in Zarathustra the "concept of the 'Dionysian' . . . became a *supreme deed;* measured against that, all the rest of human activity seems poor and relative." Goethe and Shakespeare "would be unable to breathe even for a moment in this tremendous passion and height." Compared with Zarathustra, Dante is "merely a believer and not one who first *creates* truth, a *world-governing* spirit, a destiny." The poets of the Veda are "not even worthy of tying the shoelaces of a Zarathustra." Indeed, if all the "great souls" in the world were added together, they "would not be capable of producing one of Zarathustra's discourses. The ladder on which he ascends and descends is tremendous; he has seen further, willed further, been *capable* further than any other human being" (*EH*, "TZ," §6).

Nietzsche attributes an equally high significance to himself as creator of *Zarathustra*. "I know my fate," he says in the chapter of *Ecce Homo* entitled "Why I am a Destiny": "One day my name will be associated with the memory of something tremendous—a crisis without equal on earth, the most profound collision of conscience, a decision that was conjured up *against* everything that had been believed, demanded, hallowed so far. I am no man, I am dynamite" (*EH*, "Why I am a Destiny," §1). Kaufmann suggests that such assertions are "embarrassing" and leaves matters at that (*NBW*, p. 661). But the embarrassments are obviously *there*, an indubitable part of the Nietzschean text. They were certainly intended by Nietzsche. Moreover, along with the last ten chapters of *The Birth of Tragedy*, they can be shown to be consistent with "Nietzsche's own basic intentions," or at any rate with what we are able, through the Nietzschean text, to understand of those intentions. For Nietzsche saw Zarathustra as promulgating, in the doctrine of eternal return, the new myth—or (what is the same) the new world-governing and world-creating language.

In Nietzsche's words, *Zarathustra* is "the first language for a new series of experiences." In consequence, it is destined not to be understood by Nietzsche's contemporaries. From the one side, Nietzsche explains this incomprehensibility as resulting from the fact that no one has yet shared the Zarathustrian experience: "Ultimately, nobody can get more out of things, including books, than he already knows. For what one lacks access to from experience one will have no ear." But from the other side, he seems to want to suggest that the language itself, if it were truly accepted, would provide the experience that would make *Zarathustra* comprehensible: "having understood six sentences from it— that is, to have really experienced them— would raise one to a higher level of existence than 'modern' men could attain" (*EH*, "Why I Write Such Good Books," §1). Somehow, the language will be its own disclosure. Nietzsche wants us to *try* his language, to live in it—and once living in it, we will be transformed into beings entirely different from what we are now. But the process whereby we would come to grasp Nietzsche's language remains unclear. As Danto points out, there can be "no lexical bridge between our language and any that Nietzsche might frame."[33] At the same time, ostensive definition would obviously also be ruled out, since the work of art/language/interpretation creates the reality to which it apparently only refers.

Myth

Under these circumstances—since Nietzsche's position seems to me ultimately unintelligible—perhaps the best that I can do is point out the parallel between the Zarathustrian myth and the Christian myth that it is destined to replace. At first glance, such a parallel might seem farfetched. But Nietzsche does view *Zarathustra* as comparable to the Bible: it is this thought, in fact, that underlies his suggestion that someday university chairs will be set aside solely for the purpose of interpreting it (*EH*, "Why I Write Such Good Books," §1). Nietzsche's true predecessor as a mythmaker is Jesus. Admittedly, as Nietzsche points out in *The Birth of Tragedy*, Socratic science also turned into myth; but since the rationalism of Socrates was in its foundations hostile to the mythic element in human culture, this result was entirely inadvertent. In contrast, like Nietzsche himself *(Ecce homo!)*, Jesus deliberately set out to create a myth. And how, in Nietzsche's view, does this mythmaker speak? As Nietzsche makes clear in *The Anti-Christ,* he speaks as an "antirealist." In Nietzsche's words, "It is precisely on condition that nothing he says is taken literally that this antirealist can speak at all." He is opposed "to any kind of word, formula, law, faith, dogma." He speaks only of "the inmost thing; . . . everything else, the whole of reality, the whole of nature, language itself, possesses for him merely the value of a sign, a metaphor." Indeed, this "symbolist *par excellence*" finds himself "outside of all religion, all conceptions of divine worship, all history, all natural science, all experience of the world, all acquirements, all politics, all psychology, all books, all art—his 'knowledge' is precisely the *pure folly* of the fact *that* anything of this kind exists." He puts forward no arguments in favor of this "knowledge": "Dialectics are . . . lacking, the idea is lacking that a

faith, a 'truth' can be proved by reasons." Nor is he *able* to put forward
arguments, for such a doctrine "simply does not know how to imagine an
opinion contrary to its own" (*AC*, §32).

In all of this, Jesus' mythmaking project—and by extension the mythmaking project of Zarathustra—reveals its grounding in the realm of art.
The antirealism and antiliteralism on the one hand, the symbolism and
metaphorization on the other—not to mention the opposition to reason
and to dialectics—are all evidence of Nietzsche's aesthetic concern. So,
too, is the peculiar exclusivity of the vision, for art likewise makes exclusiv-
ist claims upon us: only if we allow ourselves to be brought inside the world
of the artwork can we begin to appreciate it as art, rather than as, say, a
document in cultural or intellectual history. In short, for Nietzsche the creation of myth is an essentially aesthetic task, in his own peculiarly antiaesthetic sense of the aesthetic.[34] It is in this task that the "*artist*-philosopher"
of Zarathustra finds his highest endeavor.

In *The Birth of Tragedy* and in "Richard Wagner in Bayreuth," Nietzsche's conception of myth is still to some degree anthropological. That is to
say, he still tends to view myth as something that appears in a particular
culture at a particular time or times in its historical development and is
closely connected with the wider life of that culture. Thus, he can speak of
myth as the "unconscious metaphysics" of the previous existence of a people; he can refer—not once but twice—to a "mythical home"; and he can
look forward to a "*rebirth of German myth*," which he appears to view as
a reawakening of primitive Teutonic mythology (*BT*, chaps. 23, 24; *NBW*,
pp. 136, 137, 142). Yet, what is distinctive about the early Nietzsche's speculations on myth is the extent to which he already views myth in aesthetic
rather than in anthropological terms. Benjamin Bennett makes this point
very well when he asserts that for Nietzsche "myth—at least in its more
fully developed Apollonian and tragic stages—is essentially artistic illusion, an illusion to which we submit while still knowing it to be mere illusion"; it is an "artistic phenomenon, revealing its true nature only gradually, in the development of art."[35]

In Nietzsche's later writings, this aesthetic conception of myth takes
over completely, and the notion that myth is also characterized by anthropological elements simply disappears from sight. This explains how Nietzsche can attribute such a tremendous significance to *Zarathustra*. As
Bennett points out, in *The Birth of Tragedy* Nietzsche "appears relatively
modest about his own position in intellectual history; he does not claim to
exercise as a thinker the 'myth-creating power' of music."[36] This modesty
was made necessary by, among other things, the presence of anthropolog-

ical elements within his early view of myth. Given these elements, he could not expect to recreate myth on his own, but had rather to appeal to a hoped-for revival of myth within the culture as a whole. But when the anthropological elements disappear, and myth comes to be viewed entirely in aesthetic terms, there is no longer any compulsion to modesty. On the contrary, myth can now be created in precisely the same way that the artist creates the work of art. Such was what Jesus had done. Such is what Nietzsche-Zarathustra aspires to do.

But there is a serious problem in this final Nietzschean aestheticization of myth. As we have seen, in *The Birth of Tragedy* Nietzsche views myth as providing a solid foundation for the process of aesthetic creativity by which all culture lives. In Nietzsche's words, "myth alone saves all the powers of the imagination and of Apollonian dream from their aimless wanderings" (*BT,* chap. 23; *NBW,* p. 135). We now find, however, that what was viewed as the ground of art is itself a form of art. All ground is lost, and we are left with a free-floating aesthetic universe. Foucault, perhaps unwittingly, identifies the problem when he tells us that Nietzsche killed man and God "in the interior of his language," for here we see— once more, and in the most telling of all possible contexts—the aesthetic self-containedness that dominates Nietzsche's project (*MC,* pp. 317/306 [translation altered]).

Perhaps we *could* enter the particular interior space that Nietzsche has constructed for us, just as we can enter the interior space that is offered to us by almost any work of art. But why *should* we? After all, the claims that Nietzsche makes far exceed the claims of any artist. He promises not, as the artists does, to enliven our world or to make us see it better, but rather to change it into something that it is not. And the claim is one that Nietzsche has no ground for making. In making this claim, Nietzsche is articulating an idealism far more radical than anything in Hegel. On the one hand, the eternal return—allegedly Nietzsche's "heaviest thought" (*GS,* §341), and destined to provide a counterweight to his aesthetic laughter and play— embodies a radical idealism of nostalgia. On the other hand, the superman—and the superanthropology that presumably accompanies it—embodies a radical idealism of imagination.[37] Neither idealism is in the least degree definable. Neither connects with the world as we know it. And in important senses, we *do* know the world, and are able to function therein, even though we may not be able—as so many are eager to remind us—to establish the grounds for the possibility of our knowing it. Thus, we see why Nietzsche is unable to tell us what eternal return means; we see, too, why he must drop a definable anthropology for an indefinable superanthropology. His myth, in fact, is a form of mysticism, a purely individualistic, even solipsistic creation. Moreover, it is a creation that is bound, in its absolute utopianism, to obscure the world as it is.

There is only one condition under which we would be compelled to adopt Nietzsche's position, or any position resembling it, for our own. If it could be shown that there is an ontological parallel between the world and the work of art, between the world and the "being" of language, then we could inhabit the latter knowing that they correspond to the former. If it could be shown that the world really is an aesthetic phenomenon, then we would have to concede that in his essentials Nietzsche was right. In short, the problem is ultimately an ontological one—as Heidegger, much more than Nietzsche, was able to see. But the proof cannot be given: these things seem incapable of proof. They also seem incapable of disproof. So perhaps it is our free decision whether or not to accept Nietzsche's perspective. If we accept that perspective, the objection can then be raised that though we may visit the aesthetic world, we cannot live in it, for it utterly lacks the structures necessary for human social life. It ignores, that is, the natural and social needs of humankind for the unconstrained freedom of the artist. Yet, on the other hand, it can also be said that by its very disconnection from the world that we know and live in, the work (whether it claims to reconcile or divide) opens up a dimension that would not otherwise exist, leading us rightly to question the fullness, the oughtness, of the given. If this is so, then we may take Nietzsche as our double, just as we take the artist. No one questions the legitimacy of art. What, then, of the legitimacy of Nietzsche's art? For the world as it exists may in some ways need to be obscured—and transfigured.

PART II

Martin Heidegger and the Idealism of Nostalgia

Why is the setting up of a work an erecting that consecrates and praises? Because the work, in its work-being, demands it. How is it that the work comes to demand such a setting up? Because it itself, in its own work-being, is something that sets up. What does the work, as work, set up? Towering up within itself, the work opens up a *world* and keeps it abidingly in force.

—*Heidegger*

CHAPTER 3

Heidegger and Crisis

The writings of Martin Heidegger (1889–1976) constitute an imposing corpus. The corpus will have become even more imposing when the publication of his *Complete Works,* in a projected fifty-seven volumes, is finally concluded. The magnitude and difficulty of his writings are enough to make prospective readers shy away from him altogether. Yet, whether one agrees or disagrees with the reading of the world that he puts forward, there is no denying the richness and suggestiveness of much that he has written. He may be compared to an imaginary novelist, clumsy in his use of language and prolific in his output, whose very clumsiness seems to suggest a groping after higher and deeper meanings than could ever be intentionally communicated, and whose productivity seems to confirm that some great though only dimly perceptible mythic vein has been tapped. Such, it seems to me, is the spirit in which Heidegger—especially the later Heidegger—is best read.

As one might expect, the immensity of his corpus and the breadth of his evocations make him an extremely difficult thinker to write about, since these suggest a multiplicity of themes and starting points. Should one focus on the "early" or the "late" Heidegger? On Heidegger as existentialist, or on Heidegger as critic of technology? On the hermeneutical concern, or on the ontology? On the "thought" or on the "poetry"? Obviously, my perspective on Heidegger—which, I must point out, does not claim to exhaust his significance—is to a certain extent given in advance, and determines what I shall emphasize in his work. In the context of the present study, Heidegger is important because he tried, in his own words, "to take Nietzsche seriously as a thinker."[1] Let it be noted that he did not always see Nietzsche as such a centrally important figure. There are only three references to Nietzsche in *Being and Time* (1927), and only one of them is of any real significance (see *B&T*, pp. 264, 272*n*, 396). But from the early 1930s onward, his work begins to take on the aspect of a completion of Nietzsche, and it is the aestheticist element in Nietzsche that we find being completed.

At first glance, there seems to be little affinity, if any, between these two writers. The texts neither of the "early" nor the "late" Heidegger read in the least like Nietzsche's. The jargon-ridden ponderousness of so much of Heidegger's work contrasts sharply with the sense of lightness, ease, and spontaneity that we so often find in Nietzsche. "As Heidegger wittily remarks, in the fifth chapter of *Being and Time* . . ." is a sentence that will never appear in print. Moreover, Heidegger himself saw Nietzsche as one who stood on the nether side of a rift. In Heidegger's eyes, Nietzsche's commitment to the will to power marked what was probably the final stage in man's forgetfulness of Being. Heidegger conceived of his own project as the beginning of an attempt at Being's return. Not surprisingly, then, he always denied the existence of any "positive" relationship between his work and that of his predecessor.[2]

Nonetheless, Heidegger's envisaging of the return of Being is in many respects merely a radicalization of Nietzsche. In the earlier thinker, the anti-analytical spirit is tempered by the existence of a preliminary project of demythologization that works, or seems to work, within the tradition of the Enlightenment. In his successor, the anti-analytical spirit is ultimately given free play. At the end of "The Word of Nietzsche: 'God is Dead,'" Heidegger tells us that "thinking begins only when we have come to know that reason, glorified for centuries, is the most stiff-necked adversary of thought" (*QT*, p. 112). This is a statement that Nietzsche could never have made. Yet, it is present in Nietzsche as something "unsaid," as one implication of the Nietzschean project. Even in his most "positivistic" work, *Human, All-Too-Human*, Nietzsche had suggested that philosophers were all "tyrannized over" by logic (*HAHI*, §6, p. 19). The "later" Heidegger jumps out of the logical circle, taking up residence in the radically antilogical territory that Nietzsche limns but only tentatively enters. Though he claims to be struggling against idealism, he works out a new version of the aesthetic idealism pioneered by Nietzsche.

Admittedly, Heidegger found his way to an aesthetic turn only with some difficulty and hesitation. In consequence, he pushes hard against the interpretive framework in terms of which I propose to view his work. Yet, he is clearly a prophet of extremity—darker, more oracular, and more enigmatic than Nietzsche, but unequivocally committed to a similar notion of crisis. And though the concept of aestheticism is not helpful at all for interpreting *Being and Time,* it does illuminate the texts that follow *Being and Time* and toward which that work already in some ways points.

Some readers may want to question why I choose to deal with Heidegger at all, especially since I plan to focus largely on the later writings. If the later Heidegger is regarded as a philosopher, then from what I have just said about his antilogicality it might be concluded that a critical analysis of his arguments would be an all but pointless exercise.[3] On the other hand, if he is regarded as a very peculiar kind of poet or novelist, then however suggestive his writings may be, it is nonetheless clear that, in contrast to at least some of Nietzsche's writings, they are extremely difficult of access.

I am convinced, however, that the issues the later Heidegger raises are important enough and his actual or potential influence great enough to justify a genuine effort at comprehension. If such an effort requires learning his language, it also requires recognizing that any attempt to isolate and criticize his arguments never really reaches the ground of his enterprise, which moves on a different level. One is quite able to regard the later Heidegger as mostly mistaken, while still holding that he opens up important perspectives—perspectives that, before he appeared on the scene, either did not exist or existed only in an inchoate and undeveloped way.

Like Nietzsche before him, the later Heidegger stands as an antitype to mainstream, "conventional" scholarship. Heidegger's opposition to such scholarship is all the more pressing and immediate than Nietzsche's, for he began to write only after the tremendous explosion in humanistic and social scientific scholarship of the late nineteenth and early twentieth centuries. Briefly, he opposes all manifestations of the scientization of the study of man. In asking the "big" questions (beginning with the biggest of all, what does it mean to be?), he sets himself against those who in his view are unable to deal with anything important because they allow themselves to become caught up in methodology to the extent of letting the methodology itself determine the questions they ask. He sets himself against those who lack the imagination to break out from the boundaries that methodology is always tending to impose upon them. He sets himself against the drive of contemporary scholarship toward ever-increasing specialization, routinization, and trivialization.

Even when these banes are avoided, one still has to contend with formidable barriers to communication. These barriers are more easily accepted than challenged, so that all too often philosophers end up speaking only to other philosophers, historians to other historians, literary critics to other literary critics. Specialty barricades itself against specialty; the research report prevails over the seminar, with its connotation of seeding and cultivation; dialogue fades and then dies out. This is perhaps an overdrawn picture, but I do not think it essentially inaccurate. What is at question is the vitality of scholarship. One may hold that in opting, as I think he finally does, entirely for myth (in something very close to Nietzsche's sense) and entirely against the methodological claims of science, Heidegger is moving in a dangerous direction. But those who occupy the other territory, who fail to confront the subjective elements that enter into their own pursuit of the social sciences, are equally mistaken. If nothing else, Heidegger is important because he points out, admittedly in a manner that sometimes mystifies as much as it illuminates, the dangers that accompany the growing scientization of humanistic study.

Heidegger's attack on science, implicit in *Being and Time* and entirely explicit in the later writings, accounts for much of the influence that he has had in the past and is likely to have in the future. To be sure, in the English-speaking world this influence has been distinctly limited, for it has mainly been confined to the relatively unimportant Anglo-American offshoots of "continental" philosophy. In the European context, the whole tradition of German idealism after Kant provided a precedent for Heidegger. Indeed, it is part of my argument that Heidegger continues that tradition in important and largely unacknowledged ways. In Anglo-American philosophy, the dominant orientation has been empirical and analytical. Anyone who is part of this tradition will need to make a special effort if he is to discover worthwhile insights in Heidegger's work.

In a letter written to Alexander Bain in 1867, John Stuart Mill opined that "conversancy with [Hegel] tends to deprave one's intellect. The attempt to unwind an apparently infinite series of self contradictions not disguised but openly faced & coined into [illegible word] science by being stamped with a set of big abstract terms, really if persisted in impairs that acquired delicacy of perception of false reasoning & false thinking which has been gained by years of careful mental discipline with terms of real meaning."[4] The view of Heidegger that still largely prevails in the English-speaking world follows in the spirit of Mill's view of Hegel. The German, later American, logical positivist Rudolf Carnap pioneered this line in his well-known essay of 1931, "The Overcoming of Metaphysics through Logical Analysis of Language." Here Carnap attacks "metaphysics" in general and Heidegger's "What Is Metaphysics?" (1929) in particular as consisting of meaningless "pseudostatements." He argues that the only legitimate task for philosophy is the purely critical one of engaging in the logical analysis of propositions.[5] Such well-known and influential English-speaking philosophers as Ayer and Quine have dealt with Heidegger in a similar spirit. In other words, they see his work as irrelevant to the legitimate practice of philosophy.[6]

By the early 1960s, Heidegger's influence in Germany had greatly diminished, as his students retired from their professorial chairs and as younger philosophers, highly suspicious of what they saw as their compromised elders, turned in other directions. But this was offset by the growing interest that French intellectuals took in his work. I shall argue in subsequent chapters that the writings of Foucault and Derrida are continuations of, and confrontations with, a Nietzschean and Heideggerian perspective. I shall further argue that the new lease on life that Foucault, Derrida, and others have given to Heidegger's work closely connects with the evident instability of the modernist position in contemporary art and thought. Modernism is giving way, by and large, to other perspectives. In part, it has given way to "postmodernism." But postmodernism is even more unstable than modernism, and Derrida can be seen as articulating a critique of it. Nietzsche and Heidegger provide us with something that is rarely given—namely, an intellectual articulation of the assumptions underlying modernism and postmodernism.

Moreover, even within intellectual contexts where "continental" philosophy is ignored and where there is no explicit concern with the problems raised by modernism and postmodernism, one can sometimes still make connections with Heidegger. Consider some recent efforts in the philosophy of science. In *The Structure of Scientific Revolutions*, T.S. Kuhn is "tempted to exclaim that when paradigms change, the world itself changes with them."[7] In *Against Method: Outline of an Anarchistic Theory of Knowledge*, Paul Feyerabend attacks the notion of scientific method and declares that science is "much closer to myth than a scientific philosophy is prepared to admit."[8] These views are close to the later Heidegger (and to Foucault). Though some of Kuhn and more of Feyerabend have been subjected to intense criticism, this is not the point. The point is that Kuhn, and to a lesser extent Feyerabend, have been taken seriously by many people having no explicit interest in Heidegger or Nietzsche, or in the fate of modernism and postmodernism in art, literature, and thought. Thus, a perspective that is in some important ways Heideggerian turns out to have an impact going well beyond the intellectual territory usually designated as Heideggerian.

Similar connections can be made with other figures and movements in

addition to Kuhn or Feyerabend. From our point of view, these connections are highly important. For they help us to see that the strand of
thought that we are here examining is relevant to far more than a mere
fringe coterie of cultural extremists. They help us to see that it raises issues of the widest intellectual significance. The issues and arguments of
Heidegger (and of his fellow prophets of extremity) are central to twentieth-century thought in both the humanities and the sciences—though in
the latter they are only rarely allowed to breach dominant notions of
method. Feyerabend and Kuhn are evidence that these issues and arguments have had to be confronted even in the citadel of citadels, the philosophy of science.

The idea of crisis

Of the four thinkers with whom I am concerned in this study, Heidegger is certainly the most formidable. This is partly due to the sheer bulk of
his corpus. It is also due to the fact that in a technical sense he is the most
sophisticated philosopher of the four (though philosophers from other
traditions would be inclined to argue that his sophistication is really obfuscation). Whatever the case, his style of philosophy often makes it difficult to understand what he is trying to say. Finally, the trouble that we
have in confronting Heidegger stems from something pointed out by Hannah Arendt in an important essay, "Martin Heidegger at Eighty." As
Arendt indicates, Heidegger's thinking "acts in a peculiarly destructive or
critical way toward its own results." For Heidegger is concerned not with
knowledge or cognition but with the act of thinking itself; his is a "pas-
sionate thinking" that begins anew each time it recommences its work.[9]
To change the metaphor, his thinking is always "under way," yet never
arriving at its destination. This is because he sees the thinking itself, and
not the conclusion of the thought, as important. This view of the nature
of thinking (a view having close analogues in Romantic and post-Romantic theories of art) is well illustrated by the titles he gave to three of his
more important essay collections: *Holzwege* (*Woodpaths*); *Wegmarken*
(*Trail Markers*); and *Unterwegs zur Sprache* (*On the Way to Language*).

Clearly, such a notion of the task of thinking renders hopeless any
attempt to pin down "The Doctrine of Heidegger" or "Heidegger's Philosophy." As Heidegger himself says in his "Dialogue on Language between a Japanese and an Inquirer" (written in 1953–54, published in
1959), "I have left an earlier standpoint, not in order to exchange it for
another one, but because even the former standpoint was merely a way-

station along a way. The lasting element in thinking is the way" (*OWL*, p. 12). Moreover, if already in the notion of the self-sufficiency of thinking we see a hint of the aestheticist element in Heidegger, he did not begin as an aestheticist, and the concept of aestheticism thus cannot serve to embrace the whole of his thought. This suggests that we ought to begin by examining the not always acknowledged ground—the implicit justification—of his aestheticism. Having done this, we can then proceed to explore its shape and implications.

Such an approach to Heidegger seems to me especially promising, for the ground of his aestheticism is something that he shares with a large number of other twentieth-century intellectuals. In consequence, this approach will allow us to see how he is related to a wide and influential segment of twentieth-century thought. This in turn will help us to account for the wide resonances that his thought has evoked. But what is this ground? Karl Löwith has observed that the impact of Heidegger's analyses and interpretations is partly due to the fact that they carry "the signature of our age."[10] They carry this signature because they express, with a power unmatched in any other twentieth-century thinker, the notion of cultural crisis. This notion is to be found in everything that Heidegger wrote from *Being and Time* onward, though only after that work did the idea of crisis broaden out to become a conception of nihilism—that is to say, a conception of the absolutely alienated character of contemporary life and thought. In one or another of its versions, crisis is the most widely held assumption of twentieth-century thought. Its very pervasiveness leads to its mindless repetition. More often than not, it is evoked rather than explained and defended. Unchallenged, it is exempted from any sort of critical examination.

We have already encountered the crisis notion as it appears in Nietzsche, where its paradigm is the "death of God" and where it is deployed against the assumptions of progress and continuity that dominated nineteenth-century thought. Writing between 1870 and 1888, Nietzsche was a forerunner, one whose meditations were "untimely" mainly because they were *ahead* of their time. The most striking thing about the period from about 1890 to the 1920s is the extent to which the crisis notion was taken up, in one form or another, by many of the most important and creative European artists and intellectuals.

This was especially the case in Germany. The impact of German defeat in World War I was decisive in this regard. Yet, already before the war, the crisis view was being widely articulated in avant-garde intellectual circles. Already before the war, the younger and more "sensitive" souls saw themselves as alienated, in both a material and an intellectual/cultural sense. They saw themselves as alienated, that is, from mass society and from the technology accompanying mass society; they also saw themselves as alienated from the prevailing, establishment styles of art and literature. This sense of growing alienation partly accounts for the remarkable vogue that Nietzsche began to enjoy very soon after his lapse into insanity, as well as for the discovery (or rediscovery) of such writers as Kierkegaard, Dostoevsky, and Hölderlin. In a well-known passage in *The Man without Qualities,* Robert Musil evokes (admittedly with the benefit, and distortions, of hindsight) something of the changed mood and confusion of styles among the intellectual and artistic avant-garde of the time:

> Out of the oil-smooth spirit of the last decades of the nineteenth century, suddenly, throughout Europe, there arose a kindling fever. Nobody knew exactly what was on the way; nobody was able to say whether it was to be a new art, a New Man, a new morality or perhaps a reshuffling of society. . . . The Superman was adored, and the Subman was adored; health and sun were worshipped; people were enthusiastic hero-worshippers and enthusiastic adherents of the social creed of the Man in the Street; one had faith and was skeptical, one was naturalistic and precious, robust and morbid.[11]

The belief that all continuity had been lost and that in consequence new and unexpected possibilities had, for good or ill, been opened up was shared by many in the prewar period. But it would be a mistake to regard this feeling of crisis or discontinuity as merely a "period" concept. On the contrary, it underlies the whole of modernist and postmodernist art and literature—as Alan Wilde's illuminating study, *Horizons of Assent,* helps us to see.[12] Moreover, going beyond art and literature, the interpretive categories of modernism and postmodernism are applicable to the realm of thought as well. Modernist and postmodernist notions of crisis and of how to respond to crisis turn out to be central to such intellectual trends or movements as psychoanalysis, existentialism, structuralism, and poststructuralism.

To deal in any detail with the manifestations of the crisis notion from the 1890s to the 1920s would take me away from my main task here, which is to come to an understanding of Heidegger in particular and of aestheticism in general. This task must take precedence over any attempt at the detailed reconstruction of historical contexts, however interesting those contexts may be. Nonetheless, as a background to Heidegger's own crisis preoccupation and as an indication that the notion of cultural crisis did not come from the empyrean heights but had, on the contrary, a definite historical matrix, the main loci of the crisis idea can be quickly indicated.

Note, firstly, the transformations in artistic style that occurred in the 1890–1920s period. The very terms *fin de siècle* and *décadence* suggest a crisis of consciousness, which may or may not be resolved by the appearance of something genuinely new and creative. And beyond the aestheticism of the 1890s (I am here using the word in its conventional sense), one can observe, over a longer time span, a transition from naturalism to expressionism. The former found its inspiration in the materialistic science of the second half of the nineteenth century; the latter represented itself as an entirely new birth, one in which apocalyptic notions played an important role.[13] Secondly, there occurred in this period a crisis in the natural sciences and in mathematics. (Admittedly, this crisis had an impact on the wider reaches of intellectual culture only in the 1920s, as people became aware of the Einsteinian revolution and of those post-Einsteinian figures whose theories were, if anything, more unsettling than Einstein's.)[14] Thirdly, crisis acquired a sociological dimension as various critics and commentators began to reflect on what they saw as the effects of industrialization, urbanization, and bureaucratization on modern life. Important in this respect are Weber, Tönnies, Nordau, and, above all, Simmel. This last relentlessly explored the notion that "modern man" endures a peculiarly alienating existence, characterized by a contradiction between, on the one hand, the need for personal development and spontaneity, and on the other, the existence of an "objective" culture that confronts the individual not as a work of man but as something autonomous, impersonal, and, in its vastness, deeply oppressive.[15] Fourthly, the alienation theme (for this is what the notion of crisis here becomes) also made its appearance in the literature of the time. Think of Rilke's *Notebook of Malte Laurids Brigge* (1910), which depicts the poet's all but hopeless attempt to maintain his own "authentic" existence in the face of the anonymous reality of the city, and of Thomas Mann's various explorations of the gulf between art and life. Nor should we forget Freud, who in such works as *Studies on Hysteria* (co-authored with Joseph Breuer) and the "Dora" analysis reveals, without quite acknowledging what he is doing, the soul-destroying rigidities of late nineteenth-century upper bourgeois existence. Finally, and most directly connected with our theme, there was the "crisis of historicism," to which the growing awareness of the flux and multiplicity of history, and a growing consciousness of the subjectivity of its apprehension, gave rise. Nineteenth-century figures like Buckle and Spencer, and before them Hegel, could view history as a coherent process moving toward a rational end. But such a view was no longer possible, or at any rate no longer easy, for a Dilthey or a Weber or a Troeltsch.[16]

The experience of World War I gave to the crisis notion a much greater currency and breadth. The outbreak of the war was greeted with enthusiasm by many European intellectuals, who felt that it would provide an exciting break from the dull routine of respectable bourgeois life. But the respite turned, in fact, into a nightmare. Nietzsche's "great war" was entirely spiritual in nature (*EH*, "BGE," §1); the war that Heidegger and his contemporaries witnessed was disturbingly concrete. For the participants in the war and for its immediate observers, as well as for those who grew to intellectual maturity in the 1920s (often in the midst of great social and economic dislocation), the war served only to intensify the sense of cultural crisis. Think of Ezra Pound's characterization of Western civilization as "botched," as "an old bitch gone in the teeth." Think of Paul Valéry's diagnosis of a contemporary "crisis of spirit," following on the recognition that the present civilization and all its works are just as susceptible to destruction and oblivion as its predecessors. Think, finally, of the immense popularity of Oswald Spengler's *Decline of the West* (published in 1919–23), with its notion of inevitable cultural collapse.[17]

Integrally connected with this sense of crisis was the notion of apocalyptic change and regeneration, which had also made itself felt before the war. This notion had been especially evident in the ideology of "youth." The young were seen as having the sacred mission of destroying the corrupt, unnatural, stultifying, tension-ridden old society and creating in its place a new and regenerate one.[18] In the war's wake, ideas of apocalyptic change came to play a much greater role in the work and thought of European artists and intellectuals. For purposes of historically locating the attitude toward modern culture adopted by Heidegger, we may note that this desire for cultural regeneration could lead in two opposing directions. On the one hand, it could lead to an enthusiastic embrace of the new; on the other, to an attempt to revitalize the old. In other words, to follow the schema proposed by Robert N. Berki, the response to crisis could lead in an "imaginative," or alternatively in a "nostalgic," direction.[19] Futurism and the Bauhaus are obviously imaginative in orientation, as is (to a considerable degree) expressionism; the George circle clearly belongs in the "nostalgia" column; Georg Lukács, with his idealization of the future utopia represented by communism, is imaginative; T. S. Eliot, with his idealization of the past utopia represented by royalism and Catholicism, is nostalgic; while Dada, with its desire for a "flight out of time," can perhaps be seen as an absurdist refusal to choose either possibility.

Obviously, the intellectual movements of the prewar, war, and postwar years are far more complex than this, and it is not my intention to suggest that they ought all to be reinterpreted in terms of the nostalgia/imagination contrast. Nonetheless, especially when it is a question of dealing with the most extreme thinkers, this contrast does seem to me to have a high degree of validity. The most extreme thinkers fit the typology out of a logical necessity. They do so because, seeing around themselves the complete dereliction of the present, they can appeal only to the future or the past. (Let me note here that these are *ideal* pasts and futures, since any attempt to specify what these futures or pasts contain would entail making them real, hence present. And this would return us to our state of dereliction.) Nietzsche, as I have tried to show, embraces both sides of the opposition, never coming to a choice between them or establishing how they are related to each other. This ambiguity finds expression in his failure to make a definitive choice between the imaginative notion of the will to power and the nostalgic notion of eternal return. Foucault embraces the imaginative side of the Nietzschean heritage, announcing the possibility of a "future thought" whose shape cannot be discerned because it has not yet made its appearance (*MC*, pp. 398/386). Heidegger, on the other hand, embraces the nostalgic side of the Nietzschean heritage, constantly looking back to a mode of thinking that allegedly lies hidden in that dim period preceding the emergence of Greek philosophy.[20] Finally, Derrida occupies the impossible midpoint between the two. His is a double refusal, for, like Heidegger and Foucault, he first refuses the extant world, but then proceeds to a refusal of their nostalgic and imaginative turns. Thus, he deconstructs the Nietzschean mode of thought—as Nietzsche deconstructs the Kantian mode of thought that made his own thought possible.

In suggesting that Heidegger's assertion of crisis, and his manner of responding to that supposed crisis, ought to be viewed in the light of similar notions being put forward at the same time or slightly earlier by other thinkers, I will no doubt evoke opposition from Heidegger's more uncritical followers. Heidegger often presented his thought as arising from an encounter with "the great philosophers." In this reading, the Heideggerian notion of crisis becomes part of an awe-inspiring plot line, one that leads from Anaximander, Heraclitus, and Parmenides, through Plato and Aristotle, to Descartes, Kant, Hegel, and Nietzsche—with Heidegger writing *finis* to all this and going back to the beginning. Prophecy characteristically seeks to obfuscate its own origins. In Nietzsche this obfuscation takes the form of a denial of origins, with the animating insight seen as lying "6,000 feet beyond man and time" (*EH,* "TZ," §1; *NBW,* p. 751). In Heidegger it takes the form of an enhancement of origins, with the actual origins not so much denied as displaced.

The young Heidegger, with his resolutely rural and provincial up-bringing, came out of a very different background than did the sophisti-cated cosmopolitans of Berlin, Vienna, Munich, Prague, and Budapest. Perhaps the very modesty of this background partly accounts for his at-tempts to seek a higher genealogy for his thought. Yet, Heidegger's rela-tion to the thought of his own time, and through that thought to the social and political realities that it reflected—rapid industrialization and urban-ization, new and more efficient modes of transportation and communica-tion, new and more destructive kinds of warfare, and finally the threat of revolution—is absolutely crucial if one is to understand what drove him forward to an aestheticist position. For example, his discussion of the oppressive "they" in *Being and Time,* and his account of "technology" in his later writings, are virtually incomprehensible unless one sees how they come out of a particular time and out of an intellectual sensibility peculiar to that time.[21]

Thus, I reject the approach of those who take Heidegger's account of the place of his work within the history of philosophy more or less at face value, while neglecting to consider the problem of its place within his own time.[22] And yet, within Heidegger's work itself we can find strong argu-ments for a consideration of exactly this problem. Note, for example, how in *Being and Time* he remarks on the "fateful destiny" that one shares with one's own generation (*B&T,* p. 385, also p. 20). In accordance with this side of his highly complex intellectual persona, Heidegger some-times does discuss the intellectual milieu within which he grew to matu-rity. Significantly, the writings in which he does this are all of an informal character. It is as if he felt free, in these writings, to depart momentarily from the pose of the great philosopher engaging in a conversation with the ages. And what features of this milieu does he evoke? He notes the impact that the philosophers Brentano, Husserl, Rickert, and the tragically short-lived Emil Lask had on him. He mentions his discovery, in 1908, of a little volume of Hölderlin's poems. For the years 1910–14, he finds a num-ber of things worthy of note: the publication of the second, enlarged edi-tion of Nietzsche's *Will to Power* (first published in 1906 and reprinted in 1911); the translations of Kierkegaard and Dostoevsky that were appear-ing in that period; the reawakening of interest in Hegel and Schelling; the poetry of Rilke and Trakl; the publication of Dilthey's *Gesammelte Schriften.* In addition, he specifically notes his interest in art and his awareness of the expressionist movement.[23]

Crisis and nostalgia in Heidegger

In various of his *Nachlass* fragments, Nietzsche managed to construct at least the outlines of a theory and history of nihilism—an entity which, in a striking image, he characterized as "this uncanniest of all guests" standing at the door of Western culture (*WP*, §1). To what extent, and in what manner, does a similar notion appear in Heidegger's writings? To what extent does Heidegger, too, see Western culture as torn apart by crisis?

I propose to pursue this question chronologically, beginning with *Being and Time* and moving forward through Heidegger's political involvement of 1933–34 to his later preoccupation with "technology." I shall leave out of consideration the writings that preceded *Being and Time:* in the last of these, his *Habilitationsschrift* on *The Doctrine of Categories and Meaning of Duns Scotus* (1916), Heidegger was still working along lines charted out by the early Husserl. It is at first glance astonishing that between 1916 and the appearance of *Being and Time* in 1927 (ages 27–38) he published nothing. Yet, this did not mean that he was intellectually inactive, for from 1919 onward he was carving out, in his lectures and seminars at Freiburg and later at Marburg, his own philosophical "way." As Arendt and Pöggeler both point out, Heidegger's first postwar courses mark the true beginning of his intellectual career.[24] *Being and Time* (which he began to write in the winter of 1923–24) was the product of his reflections in this period. With its publication he became, almost overnight, a figure to be reckoned with on the European philosophical scene.

Admittedly, the impact of *Being and Time* was partly due to the fact that it introduced into philosophy preoccupations that Heidegger's contemporaries had already encountered in their reading of Kierkegaard and Dostoevsky. But to attribute its impact solely to what, on a very elevated level, was its "voguish" character is to underrate its genuine merit. It is quite clear that the work failed to do many of the things that it set out to do, as Heidegger himself was later, at least in part, to concede. But this is not to deny the intrinsic interest and importance of many of its analyses. Indeed, since in his later writings analysis tends increasingly to give way to a kind of quasi-mysticism that is very difficult to deal with analytically, there is a danger of our devoting more attention to *Being and Time* than in the present context it deserves. From the perspective of the present essay, *Being and Time* is less important than the later writings because in it Heidegger does not adhere to a posthistoricist notion of crisis. To be sure, the notion of alienation or "inauthenticity" plays a crucial role in the work, and alienation can certainly be viewed as one of the aspects of an historical crisis situation. But this is not the view that Heidegger takes in

Being and Time. Rather, he portrays inauthenticity as a permanent danger in human life. It is a falling away from one's own authentic possibilities brought on by fear of death.[25] The presence of this notion in *Being and Time* does not by itself indicate an attachment to the notion of an historical crisis.

Only after *Being and Time* does crisis in the posthistoricist sense become central to Heidegger's work. (Significantly, only after *Being and Time* does Heidegger begin to take Nietzsche seriously.) The notion of alienation and the concern with authenticity do persist in Heidegger's thought, both "early" and "late." So does his nostalgic bias, which is already obsessively present in *Being and Time,* as we shall see shortly. But the key idea underlying the project of the later Heidegger is his conviction that the whole of Western civilization is undergoing an absolute and unprecedented crisis, for which the statement "God is dead" can stand as the shorthand expression. To put it in other, equally Nietzschean terms, after *Being and Time* Heidegger becomes obsessed by the problem of "nihilism." Nihilism is something more than simple alienation. It *is* alienation, but more importantly it is the condition of living within a state of crisis, within a present that is absolutely derelict. In Chapter 4, I shall consider Heidegger's turn from the "conceptual language" and apparently "representational" approach of *Being and Time* to the complex of notions that I have designated as aestheticism ("Letter on Humanism"; *HBW,* pp. 235, 207). It is in the context of Heidegger's new preoccupation with nihilism that this turn must be seen.

In *Being and Time,* Heidegger portrays an ontological situation in which *Dasein*[26] is constantly being threatened by an alienation from its own authentic possibilities, what he calls its "ownmost potentiality-for-Being." This alienation follows from his characterization of Dasein as "falling," a term that evokes man's initial alienation from God (and, incidentally, also underscores Heidegger's major debt to Christian theology). To be sure, Heidegger avers that the "everyday publicness of the 'they' . . . brings tranquilized self-assurance—'Being-at-home,' with all its obviousness—into the average everydayness of Dasein" (*B&T,* pp. 188–189). To translate this into simpler language, he is saying that the banal and superficial life that we lead when, in the broadest sense, we are out "meeting the public" conceals from us the knowledge that we are alienated beings and makes us feel "at home" within the world.

But this feeling is entirely deceptive, and Dasein's true condition comes more clearly to light when it finds itself in a state of anxiety. In anxiety, Dasein feels *"unheimlich"*—a word that in its usual sense means "un-

comfortable" or "uncanny," but whose literal meaning is "unhomelike."
Heidegger places a strong emphasis on the literal meaning of the word; as
he puts it, "'*Unheimlichkeit*' also means 'not-being-at-home' [*das Nicht-
zuhause-sein*]." If in the context of "the 'they'" Dasein has the entirely
tranquilized sensation that it is "at home," when anxiety arises this feeling disappears and the "Being-in" of Dasein "enters into the existential
'mode' of the '*not-at-home*'" (*B&T*, pp. 188–189). Moreover, between
Unheimlichkeit on the one hand and, on the other, the tranquilized condition that characterizes Dasein in its everydayness, the "not at home"
must, from "an existential-ontological point of view," be regarded as "the
more primordial phenomenon" (*B&T*, p. 189). Or, as he puts it in a later
passage, "*Unheimlichkeit* is the basic kind of Being-in-the-world, even
though in an everyday way it has been covered up" (*B&T*, p. 277).

Heidegger does not hold that the "existential-ontological" situation
that he here portrays is something to which "modern" man, as distinguished from the previous varieties, is peculiarly subject. His notion that
Dasein is characterized by a falling away from its "authentic potentiality
for Being itself" and into "the 'world'" should not be interpreted in historical terms (*B&T*, p. 175). Every Dasein, at all times, manifests such a
fallenness. There is no notion, here, of an "age of anxiety."

Nonetheless, perhaps without being entirely conscious of what he is
doing, Heidegger does manage to introduce a temporal, or quasi-tempo-
ral, bias into *Being and Time*. For *Being and Time*, and indeed all of his
writings since that work (though for the moment we shall leave these out
of the picture), are pervaded by a metaphoric of "going back," of "return
to origins." Heidegger perpetually wants to go back, to return, to go
home again, to some earlier, more primal, more immediate, less articulate, but definitely more authentic state or condition. In short, we find in
Heidegger a persistently nostalgic orientation. If we take the word *nostalgia* in its original Greek sense of homesickness (*nostos,* return home; *al-
gos,* pain) rather than in its more attenuated contemporary sense, we can
see how the notion of *Unheimlichkeit* is one expression of this.

Heidegger's nostalgia is already firmly in place long before his post–
Being and Time preoccupation with the crisis betokened by nihilism. By
and large, though, his critics and commentators have ignored this aspect
of the work. Perhaps this is partly because many of them are in such deep
agreement with his nostalgic bias that it becomes almost invisible to
them, or at any rate seems not to require any explicit commentary.[27] And
yet, Heidegger's predilection for a metaphoric of return is, it seems to me,
more important for understanding what is going on in *Being and Time*

than is the structure of its arguments. Time and again, these arguments simply do not seem to follow, even when one grants Heidegger all of his explicit presuppositions. To analyze the arguments of *Being and Time* while ignoring the nostalgic matrix within which these arguments are imbedded is to miss the one totally sustained and self-consistent feature of the work. Indeed, one of the reasons why philosophers in the analytical tradition find it very difficult to come to grips with *Being and Time* is that they focus on the logic of the work, failing to see that what is compelling about it is its metaphorical bias, the peculiar direction of its rhetoric.

Nostalgia in Being and Time

Heidegger's predilection for "going back" is present in both the onto-logical aspect of *Being and Time,* where he is concerned with uncovering the "meaning of Being" (or at least with recovering the long-lost ques-tion), and in its existential aspect, where he is concerned with analyzing Dasein's Being-in-the-world. (Of course, I am well aware of how question-able the distinction between the "ontological" and "existential" aspects of *Being and Time* is; I entertain it here only for purposes of presenta-tion.) Let us look first at the ontological aspect of *Being and Time,* which Heidegger himself regards as the end toward which the existential ana-lytic points. As he says at the beginning of Division Two, Book V, "all our efforts in the existential analytic serve the one aim of finding a possibility of answering the question of the *meaning of Being*" (or of "what it means to be") (*B&T,* p. 372). Admittedly, Heidegger's search for the meaning of Being has struck many readers as peculiarly empty and abstract com-pared to the existential analytic itself. And since *Being and Time* remains only a fragment of the work that Heidegger intended to write, we do not come close to finding out what the meaning of Being is. Indeed (imitating here the later Heidegger), we do not even come close to the place from which it would someday be possible for us to ask the question. But this is no denial of the crucial importance that the search for the meaning of Being has for understanding Heidegger's work—not only *Being and Time* but also the later writings.

It is remarkable the degree to which Heidegger's discussion of Being in *Being and Time* is dominated by a metaphoric of return. This metaphoric is especially obvious in the Introduction, where he gives us his "Exposi-tion of the Question of the Meaning of Being" (*B&T,* p. 2).[28] The first section notes the need for "an explicit repetition [*eine ausdrückliche Wiederholung*] of the question of Being." This question, Heidegger informs us, "has today been forgotten." And yet, he continues, the question "is hardly an arbitrary one. It sustained the avid research of Plato and Aristotle, but from then on ceased to be heard *as a thematic question of actual investigation.* What these two thinkers gained has been preserved in various distorted and 'painted over' forms down to Hegel's *Logic.* And what formerly was wrested from phenomena by the highest exertion of thinking, albeit in fragments and first beginnings, has long since been trivialized" (*B&T,* p. 2).

In short, Heidegger wants us to find our way *back* to the question of Being. As he puts it a few pages further on, "whether the answer [to that question] is 'novel' is of no importance and remains extrinsic. What is positive about the answer must lie in the fact that it is *old* enough to enable us to learn to comprehend possibilities prepared by the 'ancients' " (*B&T,* p. 19). Here is the basis for what Heidegger sees as one of his major tasks: carrying out a *"Destruktion"* of the history of ontology. By *Destruktion* he does not mean "destruction" in the usual sense of the word (for which the German equivalent is *Zerstörung*), but rather something close to a "destructuring" or "dismantling." For in Heidegger's view, the "tradi- tion" (*Tradition*) of ontological thought has served to conceal the original sources from which it arose. As he puts it, "if the question of Being is to achieve clarity regarding its own history, a loosening of the sclerotic tradi- tion and a dissolving of the concealments produced by it is necessary. We understand this task as the *destruction* of the traditional content of an- cient ontology. . . . This destruction is based upon the original experiences in which the first and subsequently guiding determinations of Being were gained" (*B&T,* p. 22).

There is a good deal that is right in Heidegger's proceeding here, if I may stop for a moment to comment on what he is trying to do. Writing from the perspective of his own time—which in this respect is our time as well—he finds that it is so seductively easy to know *about* things that one risks not *knowing* anything at all. His dismayed realization that insight is always in danger of degenerating into something commonplace and sec- ondhand becomes an even stronger theme in his later writings (see, for example, *Discourse on Thinking,* pp. 51–52), and helps to explain the appeal that the distinctly anti-academic later Heidegger has had for some contemporary academics. For if one perceives (which is actually the case) that much of contemporary academic production is essentially trivial, contributing little that is original to our understanding of the world, then the notion that the true task of thinking is to get us back behind the tradi- tion will appear immensely attractive. It can be argued, for example, that the proper function of the study of literature is to reveal to its students the reality of, say, Shakespeare, a reality that is always in danger of being buried under mountains of commentary or, on a more elementary level, under the protest, "I know that already." (Of course, the question of what this reality *is* is always under debate.) Nor is the problem restricted to literature. On the contrary, it appears in every field of intellectual concern, once the field in question has advanced to the point where it possesses a "tradition." When Heidegger tells us in *Being and Time* that "the ultimate business of philosophy is to preserve the *force of the most elemental words* in which Dasein expresses itself, and to keep the common understanding from leveling them off to that unintelligibility which functions in turn as a source of pseudoproblems," it is the concealing power of "tradition" that he is seeking to attack (*B&T,* p. 220).

And yet, if one can concede that he has grasped an important point here, there is at the same time something disturbing about the direction in which he takes the point. The difficulty is that he engages in a mythologization of the origin. For Heidegger's "origin" turns out to be something that we have to take on faith: its assumed superior value compared to the present is entirely dependent on Heidegger's word. Heidegger tells us, for example, that "both realism and idealism have—with equal thoroughness—missed the meaning of the Greek conception of truth" (*B&T,* p. 34). But how do we know this? And how do we know that Heidegger has succeeded where the realists and idealists failed? In fact, Heidegger's Greeks are ideal rather than historical—too lost in the dark mists of time to have any historical reality whatsoever. Or again, when Heidegger says that the destruction is "based upon the original experiences in which the first subsequently guiding determinations of Being were gained," he is making the destruction dependent on "original experiences" that are accessible only by means of the destruction itself. If one accepts Heidegger's word, one can follow him in his nostalgia. But there seems little reason, beyond a prejudice that remains unexamined, for accepting it.

Nostalgia is also pervasive in the existential aspect of *Being and Time.* Take, for example, Heidegger's discussion of "the call of conscience." Conscience, according to Heidegger, calls us. But where does it call us? It calls us *back:* "In the tendency to disclosure which belongs to the call lies the momentum of a push—of an abrupt arousal. The call is from afar unto afar. *It reaches him who wants to be brought back*" (*B&T,* p. 271 [my italics]). Or again, a few pages further on: "In calling the one to whom the appeal is made, [the call] does not call him into the public idle talk of the 'they,' but *calls him back* from this *into the reticence of his existent* potentiality-for-Being" (*B&T*, p. 277). Or again: "We have not fully determined the character of the call as disclosure until we understand it as one which calls us back in calling us forth [*als vorrufender Rückruf*]" (*B&T*, p. 280). Heidegger's discussion of "resoluteness" similarly follows the motif of a "back to." Thus, he tells us that in its authentically resolute mode Dasein "comes toward itself futurally in such a way that it comes *back*. . . . Anticipation of one's uttermost and ownmost possibility is coming back understandingly to one's ownmost 'been' " (*B&T*, p. 326). In a later passage, he speaks of "the resoluteness in which Dasein comes back to itself" (*B&T*, p. 383).[29] The same motif is evident in his discussion of "care": "In our formulation of the structure of care, the temporal meaning of existentiality and facticity is indicated by the expressions 'before' and 'already' " (*B&T*, p. 328). Similarly, he tells us that in the state of anxiety "Dasein is taken all the way back to its naked uncanniness [*Unheimlichkeit*] and becomes fascinated by it" (*B&T*, p. 344). On a more general plane, his characterization of Dasein, in its "thrownness" into the world, as "Being-ahead-of-itself" has the implication that it is perpetually trying to find its way back to its ownmost potentiality-for-Being (*B&T*, pp. 191–192).

The pervasive character of the nostalgia in *Being and Time* is also indicated by the frequency with which a single, usually unnoticed word recurs in the work: the word *ursprünglich*, "original" (rendered as "primordial" in the Macquarrie and Robinson translation). The word appears dozens of times, though the reader is perhaps not likely to attach much significance to its repeated occurrence. And yet, it *is* significant, for it is a further sign of Heidegger's almost unconscious mythologization of the very idea of the origin—his "archaic" predilection. Again, our best proceeding here is simply to quote the text, in order to indicate the variety of contexts in which the word appears: "The question remains whether these interpretations of Dasein have been carried through with an original existentiality comparable to whatever existentiell originality they may have possessed" (*B&T*, p. 16). "In such an inquiry one is constantly compelled to face the possibility of disclosing an even more original and more universal horizon from which we may draw the answer to the question, 'What is "*Being*"?' " (*B&T*, p. 26). "In the averageness with which it prescribes what can and may be ventured, [the 'they'] keeps watch over everything exceptional that thrusts itself to the fore. . . . Overnight, everything that is original gets glossed over as something that has long been well known" (*B&T*, p. 127). "There emerges the necessity of reestablishing the science of language on foundations which are ontologically more original" (*B&T*, p.

165). "When Dasein maintains itself in idle talk, it is—as Being-in-the-world—cut off from its primary and originally genuine relationships-of-Being toward the world, toward Dasein-with, and toward its very Being-in" (*B&T*, p. 170). *"The original phenomenon of truth has been covered up by Dasein's very understanding of Being"* (*B&T*, p. 225). "Are we entitled to the claim that in characterizing Dasein ontologically *qua* care we have given an *original* interpretation of this entity?" (*B&T*, p. 231). "The originality of a state of Being does not coincide with the simplicity and uniqueness of an ultimate structural element. The ontological source of Dasein's Being is not 'inferior' to what springs from it, but towers above it in power from the outset; in the field of ontology, any 'springing-from' is degeneration" (*B&T*, p. 334).

But the most telling sense in which Heidegger's position in *Being and Time* is nostalgic has yet to be touched upon. It is Derrida—Heidegger's most serious reader and most telling critic—who points the way to this further sense of the nostalgic in Heidegger. As Derrida notes in his essay "The Ends of Man," Heidegger's discourse is dominated by "an entire metaphorics of proximity, of simple and immediate presence, a metaphorics associating the proximity of Being with the values of neighboring, shelter, house, service, guard, voice, and listening" (*MARGES*, pp. 156/130). In discussing Derrida, I shall explore in some detail Derrida's difference with Heidegger, a difference that finds its beginnings in Derrida's attack on Heidegger's valorization of precisely these values of proximity and presence. In the present context, I shall limit myself to pointing out the ubiquity of Heidegger's characterization of Being as presence. It is central to *Being and Time,* and, with the exception of one telling deviation, marking a persistent undercurrent in Heidegger's thought of which Derrida has made great play, it remains central to the later Heidegger as well.[30]

This raises a problem: how can Heidegger's nostalgic drive to "go back" coexist with his elevation of presence? We must distinguish here between the two senses of the word *presence.* There is the temporal sense, in which the present is distinguished from the past and the future, and the spatial sense, in which something is "present at" or "in proximity to" something else. In German, these two senses are marked off, as they are not in English, by the distinction between *Anwesenheit,* which means the presence of someone at some place or occasion, and *Gegenwart,* which may mean "presence at," but which more often means presence in the temporal sense. Heidegger himself somewhat conceals his nostalgic orientation, for notwithstanding the fact that the two senses of presence are represented in German by two separate words, he tends rather to assimilate them. As Derrida notes in another of his explorations of Heidegger,

"*Ousia* and *Grammē*: Note on a Note from *Being and Time*": "In *Being and Time* and in *Kant and the Problem of Metaphysics,* it is difficult—we are tempted to say impossible—to distinguish rigorously between presence as *Anwesenheit* and presence as *Gegenwärtigkeit*" (*MARGES,* pp. 75/64). (Macquarrie and Robinson also point out Heidegger's tendency to "fuse" the two meanings of presence; see their English version of *Being and Time,* p. 47, note 2.)

Clearly, Heidegger's notion of return to an original (if ideal) past is a departure from presence in the temporal sense. But it is not a departure from presence in the sense of proximity. Recall Heidegger's tendency to mythologize, or elevate, the origin. In his essay "Différance," Derrida refers to this as Heidegger's "myth of a purely maternal or paternal language, a lost native country of thought" (*MARGES,* pp. 29/27). Here the nostalgic cast of Heidegger's commitment to proximity, to "simple and immediate presence," becomes clear. This commitment turns out to be a longing for what is past—for what cannot be possessed in the temporal present. Thus, Heidegger joins the Dionysian side of the Apollonian/Dionysian contrast, taking the Apollonian in its active, illusion-creating sense and the Dionysian in the sense of a primitive passivity, of a complete union with the primal flux of things. In short, Heidegger's nostalgia can be read as a longing for the immediate Dionysian presence of the origin, from which all division, all separation, all difference is excluded.

Crisis in Being and Time

The emphasis that Heidegger places on nostalgic motifs already points toward something else. It points toward a crisis or (to take *crisis* in its literal sense) toward a turning that would permit a return to the primal home for which Heidegger, both in his specifically ontological attempt to reawaken the question of the meaning of Being and, more restrictedly, in the existential analytic, is always looking. As I have already indicated, Heidegger denies that his analysis of Dasein ought to be interpreted in historical terms, as portraying a Dasein extant at some specific time and place. Thus, he is not suggesting that the fundamental feature of Dasein, namely, its "falling" character, is a "bad and deplorable ontical property of which, perhaps, more advanced stages of human culture might be able to rid themselves" (*B&T,* p. 176). Nor is he saying that there was once a time when Dasein was free from "falling." Nonetheless, certain aspects of *Being and Time* do suggest precisely the sort of view that Heidegger disavows.

Let us look first at the existential analytic. Here Heidegger's discussion of "the public," which he sees as a threatening force always seeking to thwart Dasein's attempt to realize its own authentic possibilities, has a contemporary ring to it, for he seems to be evoking conditions of life that are peculiar to the modern world. The following passage is the most striking indication of this:

> In utilizing public means of transport and in making use of information services such as the newspaper, every Other is like the next. This Being-with-one-another dissolves one's own Dasein completely into the kind of Being of "the Others," in such a way, indeed, that the Others, as distinguishable and explicit, vanish more and more. In this inconspicuousness and unascertainability, the real dictatorship of the "they" is unfolded. We take pleasure and enjoy ourselves as *they* take pleasure; we read, see, and judge about literature and art as *they* see and judge; likewise we shrink back from the "great mass" as *they* shrink back; we find "shocking" what *they* find shocking. (*B&T*, pp. 126–127.)

Since there exists a vast literature stigmatizing the alleged inauthenticity of modern life—of which Kierkegaard's "The Present Age," whence Heidegger derived his conception of "publicness," is one example[31]—it is not surprising that some commentators have seen the analyses of *Being and Time* as concerned with "the anonymous and depersonalized subject of the modern industrial city."[32] But it is quite clear that in *Being and Time*, at any rate, Heidegger sees "the public" as something that can as well appear in a close-knit village as in an anonymous city. It is something that exists wherever Being-with-one-another comes into play. In other words, it exists at every moment of Dasein's existence. In his later writings, Heidegger's view changes, for he does come to link the notion of the public with "the modern age," and by extension with the notion of a specifically modern cultural crisis. This connection makes its appearance most obviously in the "Letter on Humanism" of 1947 (see *HBW*, p. 197). Heidegger thus deviates from his position in *Being and Time*. Yet, we can see how *Being and Time* prepares the ground for this new, "historical" view.

Secondly, an historical reading of *Being and Time* is also suggested by its ontological preoccupation. After all, Heidegger holds that the question of the meaning of Being "has *today* been forgotten" (*B&T*, p. 2 [my italics]). Greek ontology, which in its original form did have an insight into the question, has in the course of its history "deteriorated [*verfällt*] to a tradition in which it gets reduced to something self-evident—merely material for reworking, as it was for Hegel" (*B&T*, p. 43). Here is an outline for a history of Western philosophy—indeed, for a history of the West in general. And given Heidegger's nostalgic tendency to elevate the origin and to view subsequent developments as a deterioration, there is more than a hint here that we are somehow in, or are at least heading toward, a situation of crisis. But in *Being and Time* nihilism is not in any conscious way an issue for Heidegger; it only becomes so in the later writings.

This means, obviously, that an important change in Heidegger's views occurred sometime after 1927. Though it is impossible to pinpoint the change by referring to works published by Heidegger at the time, there is some reason to think that it occurred about 1930. Otto Pöggeler writes, in his *Philosophie und Politik bei Heidegger,* that "ever since 1929–30, when Nietzsche became a matter of 'decision' for him, his new starting point for thinking the truth of Being was dominated by the all-determining presupposition that God is 'dead.'"[33] In the Foreword to his *Nietzsche* (published in 1961, based on lectures of 1936–40), Heidegger himself expresses the hope that these volumes will grant readers "a view of the path of thought I followed from 1930 to the 'Letter on Humanism'" (*NI,* pp. 10/xvi). And in his 1964 lecture on "The End of Philosophy and the Task of Thinking," he refers to his "attempt undertaken again and again ever since 1930 to shape the question of Being and Time in a more primordial [presumably Nietzschean] way" (*HBW,* p. 373).

Especially significant in this regard is Heidegger's essay on "Plato's Doctrine of Truth," which originated as a lecture in 1930, though it first appeared in print only in 1942. Here he characterizes Nietzsche as the thinker in whom "the history of metaphysics has begun its unconditional completion," and epitomizes Nietzsche's time (and ours) as "the epoch in which the completion of the modern age begins."[34] He develops this theme at great length in his *Nietzsche,* where he portrays ours as the age in which metaphysics is completed or (what is the same thing) the age in which nihilism comes to the fore. For in our age, "Being" has been forgotten in the face of "beings," in the face of "that-which-is" (see especially the long essay "Der europäische Nihilismus" [1940], in *NII,* pp. 31–256). Of course, this echoes *Being and Time* a bit, for nihilism turns out to involve the "forgetfulness of Being" so central to the earlier work. Heidegger is right when in the "Letter on Humanism" he maintains that the "turn" (*Kehre*) in his thought since *Being and Time* is "not a change of standpoint from *Being and Time.*" Rather, he characterizes it as an arrival "at the location of that dimension out of which *Being and Time* is experienced, that is to say, experienced from the fundamental experience of the forgetfulness of Being" (*HBW,* p. 208 [translation altered]). But this forgetfulness is now presented much more pointedly as an historical event: one which produces the present crisis.

The political texts

It is in the political texts of 1933–34, and most importantly in *The Self-Assertion of the German University,* given as his *Rektoratsrede* before the students and faculty of Freiburg University on May 27, 1933, that Heidegger's new sense of crisis first comes clearly into view.[35] In consequence, within the context of the present study, these writings are more important than they might otherwise be. This is especially so in light of the fact that during the 1930s Heidegger published very little. To be specific, between 1929, when three of Heidegger's writings were published (*Kant and the Problem of Metaphysics; On the Essence of Reasons;* and "What Is Metaphysics?"), and 1941, when he published the essay "Hölderlin's Hymn, 'When, as on a Festal Day...,'" only one work—aside from the political texts—appeared in print. This one exception was his discussion of "Hölderlin and the Essence of Poetry," published in 1936 (which I shall consider in Chapter 4). The political texts number less than twenty speeches, articles, and letters, none more than a few pages long and many of them less than a page. Yet, they are virtually the only reliable evidence we have for the evolution of Heidegger's thought in this period. More than this, they also reveal, with unaccustomed clarity, some of the hidden sources and connections of his philosophy as a whole.

I cannot do justice in the present essay to the problem of Heidegger's involvement with the Nazis. Here is a man whom many consider one of the greatest philosophers of the twentieth century—perhaps the greatest. Even if one rejects as thoroughly nonsensical such assessments of his work, one cannot deny that he is the twentieth century's most influential philosopher. Indeed, next to Freud he is probably the century's most influential thinker. And yet, he lent his support to Hitler's revolution. Admittedly, his involvement lasted barely ten months, and he had no influence within the party itself, which clearly viewed him as yet another famous name to be exploited. But this is no denial of the enthusiasm with which he welcomed, in public pronouncements, a movement so primitive and chauvinistic. In defense of Heidegger, it is necessary to say that he never embraced the anti-Semitism of the Nazis; indeed, his first act as rector was to forbid the posting on university property of a Nazi placard against the Jews. But he did refer in his rectoral address to the "earth and blood strengths" of the *Volk.*[36] How could he have expected his listeners not to link this to Nazi racial ideology? Similarly, he stated in a speech of January 1934 that there is "only a single German 'station in life,' " that which is rooted "in the supporting ground of the Volk [*in den tragenden Grund des Volkes*] and in the *place of work* that is freely ordained by the historical will of the state, whose character is being shaped in the movement of the National Socialist German Workers Party."[37] It is difficult to see how Jews would find a place in such a community. Moreover, in at least one private conversation, Heidegger seems to have allowed himself to go beyond his usual discretion, for Karl Jaspers reports that when Heidegger visited him for the last time, in June 1933, the latter spoke to him of the international Jewish conspiracy and of Hitler's "wonderful hands."[38]

To be sure, one can try to construct defenses of many, at least, of Heidegger's pronouncements in this period. Heidegger himself does this in the interview he granted the German newsmagazine *Der Spiegel* in 1966 (published only in 1976, after his death).[39] But such attempts merely underscore one of the most remarkable features of his political rhetoric, its sheer equivocacy. If Heidegger never publicly called a spade a spade, he was nonetheless willing in his words of 1933–34 to play up to his audience. He was willing to speak with a studied ambiguity, knowing full well in what direction his listeners would dot his *i*'s and cross his *t*'s. In this sense, his language was, according to the argument of *Being and Time* itself, inauthentic (see *B&T*, pp. 173–175). Perhaps most disturbing, he did not hesitate to make a specifically philosophical terminology serve an immediate political, or more precisely metapolitical, function; categories that he had hitherto employed only within the context of abstract thought acquire a social, or quasi-social, content. Finally, there is the fact that in all the years that remained to him after 1945, he never "came clean" about his words and actions in 1933–34. Admittedly, he seems to have soon recognized that he was wrong about Hitler, but there is no evidence of his ever having confronted the implications—both linguistic and moral—of his own terrible equivocation.

Instead, in his later self-justifications he tended to focus on the years 1934–45, portraying himself as the increasingly harassed victim of the regime, who nonetheless managed to turn his classroom into a hotbed of anti-Nazi *Denken*. I cannot hope, and perhaps no one can, to make a definitive judgment on the precise degree of guilt or innocence attaching to his actions in 1933–34: so much depends on motives, bearings, and intentions that are at best only dimly visible to the historian. I turn aside from the issue here not because I believe it unimportant but because my consideration of Heidegger the man must in the present context remain subordinate to my consideration—and assessment—of the body of writing that the man has produced. In short, I am interested in Heidegger's involvement with the Nazis only insofar as that involvement can cast light on the main tendencies of his thought.[40]

In reading through the texts of 1933–34, one is struck by the extent to which they are permeated by a rhetoric of crisis. They are also permeated by the notion that in order to resolve this crisis we must "go back" to a largely undefined but allegedly very desirable prior condition. The motifs of crisis and return are to a certain extent continuations of the same themes in *Being and Time*. At the same time, however, one notes how much more apocalyptic Heidegger's formulations now are. One notes, too, how they are given a much more obviously historical reference. One is also struck by the equivocacy to which I have just referred. Heidegger continually moves between the abstract realm of thought on the one hand and the immediate social and political condition of Germany on the other. It is entirely fair to say that he confuses the two. Löwith conveyed something of the flavor of this confusion when he observed, shortly after the war, that Heidegger's listeners were never quite sure whether they should take up the study of the pre-Socratics or join the Storm Troopers.[41] To use the language of recent criticism, Heidegger is exploiting the trope of metabasis, but his *metabasis eis allo genos* has, as some recent critics are inclined to forget, a moral and not simply a rhetorical significance. It is of practical and not merely of rhetorical moment that in 1933 Heidegger dealt with philosophical issues of the most profound complexity, and with the immediate political situation of Germany, on the same plane and without even a pause for breath—indeed, using the same words ambiguously to refer to both. A similar blurriness runs through the whole of his later thought. In this and several other ways, the pronouncements of 1933–34, far from being left behind, mark the beginning of what for simplicity's sake I refer to as the "later" Heidegger.

Löwith and a number of other commentators have pointed out the importance of the crisis notion in the texts of 1933–34.[42] But it is worth drawing attention to its presence again. Heidegger obviously believed that Germany in 1933 stood in a state of extreme crisis. He also believed that the National Socialist "movement" was the only political force in Germany that had faced up to this fact. Most subsequent observers, looking back on the situation that prevailed in Germany at the time, would agree with Heidegger's reading of it: Germany *was* in a state of great social and political crisis in 1933. But it would be a mistake to believe that Heidegger intended his evocations of crisis to be viewed as an objective diagnosis of the condition of Germany. On the contrary, his pronouncements seem intended to accentuate and glorify the state of crisis, thereby accentuating and glorifying the role of the movement that was to master the situation, that was to "take charge." Extreme situations demand extreme responses. The old order is about to give way to the new, but the time is nonetheless one of great danger, and courageous action and hard sacrifices will be needed if the German nation is to fulfill its destiny. Such is Heidegger's language in 1933.

Take, for example, his message to "German students," published in the *Freiburger Studentenzeitung* of November 3, 1933, where he declares that:

> The National Socialist Revolution [*Revolution*] brings a complete transformation [*Umwälzung*] in our German existence. Under these circumstances, it is up to you always to remain eager and at the ready, perseverant and continuing to develop yourselves. . . . Doctrines and "ideas" shall no longer be the rule of your Being. The Führer, he and he alone, is the present and future German reality and its law. Learn this ever more deeply: From now on, each and every thing demands decision and each and every act responsibility. Heil Hitler![43]

Consider, too, his speech to representatives of the German professoriate in Dresden on November 11, 1933, the eve of the plebiscite in which Hitler asked the German people to ratify Germany's withdrawal from the League of Nations:

> German teachers and comrades! German compatriots! The German people is called by the Führer to a choice. . . . Tomorrow the people will choose nothing less than its own future. This choice cannot be compared to any previous choice. The unique quality of this choice is the simple grandeur of the decision to be taken in it. The inexorability of the simple and of the last allows no delay. This final decision reaches out to the uttermost boundaries of the existence of our *Volk*.[44]

Consider, finally, his speech of January 22, 1934, to six hundred formerly unemployed workers marched to the largest lecture hall in the university for the occasion. Here he notes that:

> There is a new, common will to throw up a living bridge between the worker of the hand and the worker of the brain. This will to bridge-building is no longer a hopeless dream—and why not? Because through the National Socialist state our entire German reality has been altered, and this has as its consequence that all previous ideas and thinking must also change into something else.[45]

Heidegger's rhetoric of crisis was not confined, however, to his observations on the political situation in the Germany of 1933, for he was convinced that the political crisis was merely one manifestation of a wider and much more significant crisis in philosophy or thought. This is brought out most clearly in *The Self-Assertion of the German University*, a work that manages to combine the attributes of philosophical manifesto and *völkisch* tract. Already in *Being and Time*, Heidegger had referred to alleged crises in mathematics, physics, biology, the *Geisteswissenschaften*, and theology. Indeed, he had asserted (without argument) that "a science's level of development is determined by the extent to which it is *capable* of a crisis in its basic concepts" (*B&T*, pp. 9–10). He took up the theme again in "What Is Metaphysics?," pointing to the fragmentation of disciplines as evidence for crisis in science as a whole.[46] In *The Self-Assertion of the German University*, he then extends this notion of crisis to all of Western culture.

According to Heidegger, the crisis had been caused by our departure from the essence of science—that is, from its Greek beginnings. In his words, "we do not at all experience the essence of science in its innermost necessity so long as we merely contest . . . the independence and presuppositionlessness of an all-too-contemporary science." We need instead to cast our eyes back, for we can grasp the essence of science only if "we place ourselves again under the power of the beginning of our spiritual-historical existence." This beginning, he continues, "is the awakening [*Aufbruch*] of Greek philosophy. Therein Western man, out of a *Volk* heritage that he possesses by virtue of his language, for the first time stands up against that-which-is as a whole and questions and grasps it as the being that it is. All science is philosophy, whether it knows and wishes it or not. All science remains bound up with that beginning of philosophy. Out of it, it creates the power of its essence, assuming that it remains at all equal to this beginning."[47]

Heidegger declares that we are now separated by 2,500 years from the Greek beginnings of science. Between us and those beginnings stand both the "Christian-theological world interpretation" and the "mathematical-technological thinking of the modern age."[48] Most important, for the first time in any of his published writings, he evokes the crisis statement of "the passionately God-seeking last German philosopher, Friedrich Nietzsche," linking Nietzsche's "death of God" with his own developing notion of "the abandonment of present-day man in the midst of beings."[49] But if God is dead and Being forgotten, Heidegger nonetheless sees the possibility of a transformation: one taking the form of a return to the origin. "The beginning is yet to be. It does not lie behind us as something long past, but on the contrary stands before us. . . . The beginning has fallen into our future, it stands there as the distant decree over us, to bring again its greatness."[50]

As I have noted, it is very striking how easily Heidegger moves back and forth in the *Self-Assertion* speech between philosophy and politics. An elevated and highly abstract consideration of the essence of science blurs into a more down-to-earth but somehow equally abstract consideration of the destiny of the German *Volk*. "German students are on the march."[51] But we never quite learn whether they are on the march toward a true understanding of the essence of science or toward the complete overthrow of the Treaty of Versailles. At the end of the speech, he tells his audience that "we only fully understand the glory and the greatness of this awakening [*Aufbruch*] when we carry within us that deep and wide reflection, out of which ancient Greek wisdom spoke the word: '*ta . . . megala panta episphale*'... All that is great stands in the storm."[52] (Heidegger here quotes the *Republic*, 497d, 9; the passage is more conventionally rendered as "All great undertakings are risky."[53]) But to which *Aufbruch* is Heidegger referring—the *Aufbruch* of Greek philosophy, or the *Aufbruch* heralded by Hitler's accession to power? Does *Sturm* refer to the difficulties with which a return to Greek philosophy is fraught or to the task of creating an entirely "coordinated" German nation?

Heidegger does not resolve the ambiguity. In effect, he has it both ways. He could later claim, without fear of textual disconfirmation, that he had intended only the more elevated meaning. In his letter of self-justification of November 4, 1945, written to the incumbent rector of Freiburg University, he notes of 1933 that "I was at that time . . . convinced that through the independent, collaborative work of men of learning [*Geistigen*] many essential beginnings of the 'Nazi Movement' could be deepened and transformed, in order to place the Movement in such a position as to be able in its own way to help to overcome the confused situation of Europe and the crisis of the Western spirit."[54] But it seems clear that most of Heidegger's listeners could only have taken his words in their "lower" sense. These words thus lent an aura of high intellectual and moral purpose to the "Nazi Movement"—that is, to the movement that actually existed, as distinguished from the hypothetical movement existing only in the mind of Martin Heidegger.

Heidegger must certainly have known that this is how his words would be taken. Why, then, did he speak in the way he did? Perhaps he enjoyed the sense of power and excitement that came from this pandering to popular prejudice. In Schneeberger's *Nachlese zu Heidegger*, one finds a somewhat disturbing photograph of Heidegger. Wearing on his lapel an eagle-and-swastika badge, he sits resolutely at his desk in what one takes to be his impression of the approved National Socialist style, his eyes focused somewhere in the middle distance to the right of and beyond the camera.[55] But there is more to Heidegger than this; he was not simply a panderer and demagogue. For he seems to have thought that words actually would bring about the higher order he envisaged—that reality would ultimately yield to *Dichten* and *Denken*. To be sure, this perspective—the perspective of aestheticism—would only be articulated later, and it would be articulated in a passive rather than in an active mode. But its roots are already visible in his pronouncements of 1933. Indeed, it is in the *Self-Assertion* speech that Heidegger first refers to *Dichten* and *Denken*. Tellingly, he includes a third element, *Glauben* or belief.[56] *Glauben* is not to be found in his later language. But it remains implicit in the whole of his later project, for that project, involving as it does the development of a Heideggerian mythology to replace the worn-out Christian mythology,[57] necessarily entails belief.

Finally, one notes the appearance in the writings of 1933–34 of something absent from Heidegger's earlier writings—a specifically social nostalgia, the longing for an earlier and simpler social order. This comes out most clearly in his radio address of early March 1934, entitled "Why Do We Stay in the Provinces?" Here he explains why he had turned down calls to the more prestigious universities of Munich and Berlin, preferring instead to remain at Freiburg: near his birthplace, near the Black Forest, near the Alps. He tells his listeners that he carries out his work in a small ski hut in a wide valley of the southern Black Forest. And why here? As he explains it:

> Philosophical work does not take its course as the aloof business of a man apart. It belongs in the midst of the work of peasants. When the young peasant drags his heavy sledge up the slope, and then guides it, piled high with beech logs, down the dangerous descent to his house, when the herdsman, lost in thought and slow of step, drives his cattle up the slope, when the peasant in his shed gets the countless shingles ready for his roof—then is my work of the same kind. It is intimately rooted in and related to the life of the peasants.

Heidegger lauds the thoughtfulness and sense of remembrance that prevail in peasant life. Moreover, he regrets that "the world of the city runs the risk of falling into a destructive error," for a "very loud and very pushy and very fashionable obtrusiveness" is abroad, passing itself off as "concern for the world and existence of the peasant." But precisely this threatens to destroy the peasant's world. The peasant, Heidegger declares, must be left alone; he does not want or need this "citified officiousness," but rather a "quiet reserve with regard to his own way of being and its independence." Finally, Heidegger notes how, after receiving his second call to Berlin, he withdrew from the city and returned to his hut: "I listened to what the mountains and the forests and the farms said. I came to my old friend, a 75-year-old-peasant. He had read about the call to Berlin in the newspaper. What would he say? Slowly he fixed the sure gaze of his clear eyes on mine, and keeping his mouth tightly shut, he placed his true and considerate hand on my shoulder—ever so slightly, he shook his head. That meant—absolutely no!"[58]

Heidegger's idealization of the fixed world of the peasant is by no means original. On the contrary, such sentiments were a commonplace in European, and especially German thought in the period. One notes, as perhaps the most famous example of this, Spengler's characterization of the peasant as historyless, eternal, having a mystical soul and a dry, shrewd, practical understanding, the source of the culture and history that grows up within the cities, but always separate from that culture and history.[59] I have argued that those disturbed by the "crisis of the European spirit" could move in either a nostalgic or an imaginative direction. That is to say, they could respond to the presumed dereliction of the present by looking toward either a mythic past or a mythic future. In the wake of World War I, many Germans opted for the former. There was much in German thought and society to incline people this way. One set of comparative statistics is perhaps worth citing: in 1871, 5 percent of the German population lived in cities of 100,000 or more; by 1925, the proportion had grown to 27 percent.[60] Inevitably, many Germans looked back to the serene and joyful, but (alas) largely imaginary period before the city had taken over. Indeed, the whole idea of the *Volk,* which in its more extreme versions idealized the primeval world of the ancient Germans, was nostalgic in bearing.[61]

In view of the political and social factors also at work, it is not surprising that in the 1920s Germany saw a flowering of neo-conservative thought, of a "conservative revolutionism" that proclaimed the bankruptcy of middle-class humanism and strove to create, by vaguely defined revolutionary means, one or another variety of nostalgic utopia.[62] Heidegger's affinities with this strand of thought are too striking to ignore. Like Spengler, like Moeller van den Bruck, like Ernst Jünger, Heidegger believed that the West stood in a state of crisis. If in his interpretation of that crisis he differed (sometimes quite radically) from these thinkers, he still shared much in common with them. Nazism, too, shared many of these same prejudices: idealization of the German past, fondness for the peasant, suspicion of rootless cosmopolitans, and (above all) commitment to the notion of crisis. The Nazis were not always consistent, but they were coherent enough in espousing and exploiting these themes for Heidegger to take them, for a time, as a vessel for his ontological hopes.

From willing to waiting: technology

Heidegger's attachment to the Nazi party did not, however, last very long. He says in the *Der Spiegel* interview that by Christmas 1933 it had become clear to him that his ambitious hopes for reforming the university (bringing it closer to the original Greek essence of science) had no possibility of attainment.[63] In any case, when in February 1934 an appropriate occasion arose, he resigned the rectorship. There is no denying his distance from the regime in the years that followed. And yet, if he now saw that he had been mistaken in his belief that Nazism could be "deepened and transformed," the preoccupations that underlay his turn to Nazism remained. Until his dying day, he still believed that the West stood in a state of absolute cultural and spiritual crisis, and he still saw the proper response to this crisis as a turning back.

Yet, there is a crucial difference between the Heidegger of 1933 and the Heidegger of, say, 1966. In 1933, Heidegger was very much an "activist." He believed strongly that human will could have an impact on the course of history. Thus, in the peroration to *The Self-Assertion of the German University*, he tells his listeners that the spiritual fate of the West hangs on "whether we as a spiritual-historical *Volk* still and again *will* ourselves—or whether we no longer will ourselves. Every single individual concurrently makes his decision on this, even when—especially when—he avoids this decision."[64] By way of contrast, in 1966 (and not only in 1966) a deep sense of regretfulness and loss, elegiac in its intensity, prevails. Thus, in the *Der Spiegel* interview, Heidegger declares that:

> Philosophy will not be able to effect an immediate transformation of the present condition of the world. This is not only true of philosophy, but of all merely human thought and endeavor. Only a god can save us. The sole possibility that is left for us is to prepare a readiness, through thinking [*Denken*] and poetic creation [*Dichten*], for the appearance of the god or for the absence of the god in the time of foundering [*Untergang*], for in the face of the god who is absent, we founder.[65]

Or as he puts it in "Conversation on a Country Path about Thinking" (based on notes of 1944–45, and published in 1959), "we are to do nothing but wait": *Wir sollen nichts tun sondern warten* (*DT*, p. 62).

Some of Heidegger's more sympathetic commentators prefer to see, in this shift from willing to waiting, a fundamental change from the Heidegger who supported the Nazis.[66] But the change is not really so fundamental, for both the crisis assumption and the nostalgia remain intact and unexamined. We find no indication in Heidegger of a questioning of the nostalgic turn. Nor do we have any questioning of the thought of crisis itself. These omissions cast doubt on Heidegger's claim that his text is something other than the expression of a *Weltanschauung*—that it is, in fact, a kind of entryway to Being. The "later" Heidegger shares with Nietzsche a peculiar readiness to view the world under the guise of catastrophe while failing to ground that catastrophe in any recognizable social order. Undoubtedly, there are biographical reasons for this shared failure, though it is not our task to examine them here. But we can certainly examine the specifically intellectual modes that facilitated the omission. And this leads us once more to aestheticism, which in the present context serves to obfuscate the relationship between text and world.

I have noted how Nietzsche's notion of language as something that creates its own reality sustains his Zarathustrian propheticism. In the later Heidegger, this notion is given full flower. But even before his linguistic move, he obfuscates. To be sure, he claims, as we shall see, to be listening to the voice of Being and to be creating nothing new himself, but this is merely a measure of the extent to which he comes to identify himself with the "Being" of language. We have seen how equivocally Heidegger speaks in 1933, and his peculiar abstractness and ease of moving from one level to another persist throughout his later work. Distinctions essential to critical thought are obliterated. Everything is portrayed through a nostalgic haze, so that, for example, in his Memorial Address in honor of the minor nineteenth-century composer Conradin Kreutzer (delivered in 1955, published in 1959) (*DT,* pp. 43–57), as in his 1933 address in honor of the Freikorps adventurer and nationalist martyr Albert Leo Schlageter,[67] the actual historical reality of these individuals is entirely lost from sight. In many of his later writings, he seems not to be saying anything at all in its minute particulars; instead, he seems to be inviting us to a kind of reverie on the text. Under these circumstances, the question of the precise intended meaning of the text becomes, as with all post-Nietzschean thinkers, extremely difficult to pursue, for the author himself endows his words with an inviting openness.

Especially since it is decisive for Nietzsche, the analogy with music is an appealing one. Though, as George Steiner points out, this is not an analogy that Heidegger himself emphasizes,[68] it is nonetheless true that the relation between Heidegger and his text seems almost like the relation between a composer and his music. Unless we happen to be amateur or professional musicologists, we do not, as listeners, ask ourselves what the composer intended; rather, we let the music carry us where it will. Certainly, in such writings as his prose poem of 1947, "Aus der Erfahrung des Denkens," or the ending of "Conversation on a Country Path about Thinking," Heidegger appears to want a musical response on the part of his readers, a response of pure, atheoretical contemplation ("The Thinker as Poet," *PLT,* pp. 1–14; *DT,* pp. 58–90).

Yet, these writings are much more than a blank slate on which we may inscribe what we will, for they do put forward certain assertions regarding the character of our culture. The most evocative of these assertions concern the role of science and technology in modern life. Once again, there is a peculiar abstractness in what Heidegger has to say. But at the same time, he seems to be speaking of and to an actually extant reality, the reality of technologism, conceived by Heidegger as an anonymous force that is gaining an ever more certain and ramified control over human life. According to Heidegger, this force has its origins in modern science. The essence of modern science is in turn grounded in the thinking of the Greeks. More specifically, it is grounded in the thinking of Plato and Aristotle, who (abandoning the initial poetizing impulse of Greek thought) initiated the process whereby the all-important distinction between "Being" and "beings" was forgotten.

But the crucial development in the emergence of modern science occurred only with Descartes, whom Heidegger sees as the great initiator of the modern age. Heidegger argues in "The Age of the World Picture" (first given as a lecture in 1938, and published in 1952) that Descartes radically altered the meaning of the notion of subject, that is, of *subiectum* or (to take the original Greek word) *hypo-keimenon.* Prior to Descartes, the *subiectum* or *hypokeimenon* was conceived as a kind of basis or foundation of beings, one that had "no special relationship to man and none at all to the I." With Descartes, however, a radical change took place (albeit a change that was in harmony with the Platonic and Aristotelian beginnings of philosophy), for Descartes turned man into "the primary and only real *subiectum.*" Thus, man became "the relational center of that which is as such" (*QT,* p. 128). Concurrently, "that which is" was now turned into an object, something viewed exclusively from the perspective of the human center.

As a result of this, beings can no longer simply "be." No longer can they "come to presence" in the way that (to anticipate our further argument with and against Heidegger) a work of art does. On the contrary, the world is reduced to a complete passivity. Far from showing *itself,* it is now violently seized upon by the Cartesian *fundamentum absolutum inconcussum,* the *ego cogito.* The theoretical consciousness (already present in Greek philosophy, but only now attaining its full power) grasps the world as a picture or model (*Bild*) standing apart from and against the human subject. It "re-presents" or sets before itself this picture, attempting to make it fixed and secure by reducing it to terms of calculability. This representation is not, Heidegger declares, a self-unconcealment of that which is; it is rather a "laying hold" or "grasping"—an "assault" of man upon beings (*QT,* pp. 149–150, also pp. 141–142). Man projects a conceptual grid onto the world, and attends only to what can fit the grid. In a later essay, "Science and Reflection" (1954), Heidegger cites a well-known statement of the physicist Max Planck: "That is real which can be measured." In Heidegger's view, this statement articulates a view that belongs to the essence of modern science (*QT,* pp. 169–170).

The consequences of the Cartesian elevation of man to the status of subject are more than merely theoretical, for by placing man at the center Descartes opened the way for the attempt at an absolute mastery of nature that constitutes the essential character of modern technology. In "The Question Concerning Technology" (preliminary lecture version, 1949; expanded version, 1953; published in 1954), Heidegger holds that in the original *technē* of the Greeks, beings were still able to presence themselves. *Technē*—as evidenced in the work of the hand craftsman, for instance—was then a form of *poiesis,* of "bringing-forth" (*QT,* pp. 12–13). In other words, Greek *technē* still allowed beings to "be." But with technology in its specifically modern form, the situation changes completely. Modern technology, says Heidegger, assaults the world in the same way that modern science does, and in so doing it brings modern science to its completion. Heidegger compares the windmill with the hydroelectric power plant, and the work of the peasant with "the mechanized food industry." The windmill and the peasant are accommodated to nature. Thus, the peasant merely places seed in nature's keeping and watches over its increase. But what of the power plant and the food industry? These challenge nature; they *set* upon it. Whereas the windmill turns only when the wind decides to blow and produces energy only on those occasions, in the power plant energy is unlocked from nature and stored up. Similarly, in the food industry all sorts of artificial procedures come into play, such as the use of fertilizers and tractors. No longer is nature something that we take care of and maintain. On the contrary, just as in modern science nature is turned into a mere object, in modern technology it is turned into a mere resource. It is turned into what Heidegger calls a "standing-reserve" (*Bestand*), whose sole justification for existing is that it can be used to satisfy man's needs (*QT*, pp. 14–17).

Moreover, not only nature but man himself is transformed into a standing-reserve, according to Heidegger. Heidegger envisages a world that has been totally reduced to technological terms, a world in which (as he puts it in the *Der Spiegel* interview) the only relationships are technological ones—relationships, that is, of pure manipulation.[69] The will to power of a purely calculative, technological thinking threatens to obliterate Being, for Being is something that can in no way be encompassed in the standing-reserve. Technological man concerns himself solely with beings, forgetting even the possibility of Being. In *An Introduction to Metaphysics* (given as a lecture course in 1935, published in 1953), the first text in which he evokes the "encounter between global technology and modern man," Heidegger unequivocally views the "technological frenzy" of the modern world as a manifestation of the "spiritual decline of the earth." This decline, he goes on to maintain,

> is so far advanced that the nations are in danger of losing the last bit of spiritual energy that makes it possible to see the decline (taken in relation to the history of "Being"), and to appraise it as such. This simple observation has nothing to do with *Kulturpessimismus*, and of course it has nothing to do with any sort of optimism either; for the darkening of the world, the flight of the gods, the destruction of the earth, the transformation of men into a mass, the hatred and suspicion of everything free and creative, have assumed such proportions throughout the earth that such childish categories as pessimism and optimism have long since become absurd. (*IM*, pp. 37–38; on "global technology," p. 199.)

In short, the nihilistic impulse lying at the foundation of Western culture finds its culmination in technology. Here is the ultimate locus of the crisis that confronts Western man.

For those who have difficulty seeing why anyone would take Heidegger—especially, the later Heidegger—seriously, much of the answer is to be found in the fact that his nostalgic, idealistic, technological catastrophism does seem in many of its aspects to accord with twentieth-century experience. The Holocaust, nuclear weapons, the growing technologization and bureaucratization of modern life—all these realities seem to confirm Heidegger's text, or at the very least can be convincingly interpreted in Heideggerian terms. There are numerous examples of writers who draw on Heideggerian notions in their attempts to come to grips with the contemporary world. Some of these are persons whom one might expect, by virtue of their sympathies and personal histories, to be radically opposed to Heidegger. For example, when Hannah Arendt viewed Eichmann as instancing the "banality of evil," she was in fact putting forward a Heideggerian interpretation of the Holocaust, for the banality of which Arendt speaks is virtually indistinguishable from Heidegger's notion of a self-directing technological routine that brings with it the "forgetfulness of Being."[70] When Herbert Marcuse portrayed advanced capitalist society as a domain of one-dimensionality, he, too, was interpreting the contemporary world in terms of Heidegger's conception of technology; indeed, that aspect of Marcuse's work owes far more to Heidegger than it does to Marx.[71] Finally, the difficulties of resource supply and the growing ecological concern of the last ten years or so can be approached in a very Heideggerian way.[72]

In short, the impact of the aspect of Heidegger's project that we are considering here is to be explained by the fact that in his work Heidegger attempts to confront what have become pervasive realities in twentieth-century life. In large measure, I think, this confrontation remains on the level of cliché. It rests on the undiscriminating invocation of a few formulae that Heidegger draws from his own intellectual and cultural past. Lest this sound too negative, let me note that a cliché can at the same time be true. Thus, on the positive side, it is possible to say that Heidegger, like our imaginary novelist, can sensitize our minds to realities that we might not otherwise perceive. A similar function is performed by the classic social theorists, such writers as Marx and Weber. Yet—if I may once more shift to the negative—Heidegger differs from the social theorists in that the latter make an attempt actually to analyze society, and their analyses can in principle be confirmed or disconfirmed. Heidegger, at least the later Heidegger, makes no analyses. But unlike the novelist, he claims that his work is much more than a fiction. He claims, indeed, that it conveys an insight into the extant world that exceeds in truth and profundity anything that conventional, "representational" thought can provide.

Underlying this claim is the notion of an elevated and sublimated art speaking a truth that is uniquely its own. I touched on this notion in considering Gadamer's version of aestheticism in my Introduction. Since Nietzsche emphasizes not the "truth value" of art but rather its role as a creative lying, this theme is one that up to now I have had to leave in abeyance. It is so critical, however, that we must now turn to it.

CHAPTER 4

Heidegger's Aestheticism

We have seen how the idea of the uniquely revelatory character of art was a prominent feature in Romantic thought. We have also seen how Nietzsche is both an heir to and a rebel against Romanticism. The connection is close between Nietzsche's hope for a new mythology and the similar hopes entertained by such early nineteenth-century writers as Hölderlin, the young Hegel, Friedrich Schlegel, Novalis, and Schelling. This connection is especially evident in *The Birth of Tragedy*. Even in the later writings, however, important aspects of the Romantic project remain intact, though myth now appears in an entirely denaturalized and dehumanized—that is, de-Romanticized—form.

Yet, there is a crucial difference between Nietzsche and the Romantics. For in adopting the crisis notion, Nietzsche turned radically against Romanticism—or at any rate against its manifestly confident veneer. From the point of view of his conception of the aesthetic, the crisis notion had important implications. Most importantly, the Romantic idea of genius implied that art is noteworthy because it is the highest expression of the genius's elevated feelings and perceptions, a view that in its subjectivity is clearly antithetical to aestheticism. Such a subjectivism does survive in Nietzsche. Indeed, it is fundamental to his whole uncompleted project for a psychology or physiology of art. Time and again, Nietzsche stresses the close relationship between "art" and "life": art is, or at least ought to be, "the great stimulant of life, an intoxication with life, a will to life" (*WP*, §851; *KGW*, 8. Abt., 3. Bd., p. 203).[1] This is not an aestheticist view but a naturalistic one. Only when Nietzsche is most thoroughly convinced of the reality of the crisis; only when he views the present in its most deeply null guise; only when he rejects the naturalism of man for the undefinable antinaturalism of the overman does aestheticism become possible, indeed necessary, for him. In short, only when man dies does art live.

It is here that Heidegger enters our range of view. By the early 1930s, Heidegger had become a herald of absolute crisis, a prophet of extremity. Crisis opens the way for his aestheticism, as it does for Nietzsche's as well—except that Heidegger is much more explicit about the relationship pertaining between art and crisis, and much more inclined to explore in detail the intellectual possibilities that aestheticism offers. In Heidegger's universe, there is a rift, a fissure, an abyss. Out of this rift comes art, conceived as a *Stiftung,* as an entirely new founding or establishing. Negative and positive go together. The complete degradation of the extant world—its *Nichtigkeit*—prepares the ground for an aesthetic creation *ex nihilo;* the notion of crisis opens up the space within which aestheticism can flourish.

After about 1935, one notes a certain cessation of movement in Heidegger's thought. One finds instead a tendency to circle round a few constant themes, with terminological innovations from time to time and an occasional acknowledgment of changing external circumstances (for example, the advent of nuclear energy and the threat posed by the atom bomb). Indeed, within the broader ambit of the crisis notion, the themes of his later writings are reducible to only two: technology and art. In the winter semester of 1939–40, Heidegger gave a lecture course on "Art and Technology," and while the manuscript of the lectures is not yet in print, the title is suggestive of the "way" of his later thought. For within certain limits (limits established by the radically absolute character of his utopianism), Heidegger sees art as the counterforce to technology. If technology is the destroying power, one that turns man into an object even as he seeks to make himself master of objects, then art stands, in Heidegger's eyes, as "the saving power." In a totally degraded, totally alienated world, a world of pure manipulation, a light gleams out: hope is not entirely lost.

Characteristically, Heidegger finds warrant for this faith in the land of the Greeks. Technology in its modern form is entirely manipulative in character. But in the original Greek form of *technē,* it was something quite different. It was a *poetic* or *revealing* art—an art that eschewed the manipulation of things and aimed instead to bring truth forth into "the splendor of radiant appearing." As Heidegger puts it in "The Question Concerning Technology": "In Greece, at the outset of the destining of the West, the arts soared to the supreme height of the revealing granted them. They brought the presence [*Gegenwart*] of the gods, brought the dialogue of divine and human destinings, to radiance. And art was simply called *technē*. It was pious, *promos,* that is, yielding to the holding-sway and the safekeeping of truth" (*QT,* p. 34). The Greeks kept themselves open to the experience of art. Heidegger envisages a return to this openness.

In the modern age, Heidegger holds, we have shut ourselves off from the revelation that art can bring us. Art, like everything else, has been subjectivized, has been subordinated to human will. Our relation to art has been turned into "aesthetics," that is, into yet another post-Cartesian science. Having adopted the standpoint of the subject, aesthetics views art as mere object, and in consequence no longer allows it to appear in its full coming-to-presence (*QT,* p. 35). And the same holds true throughout our culture. Ours is thus the time of the "flown gods," as Heidegger says at the end of "Hölderlin and the Essence of Poetry." (It is entirely characteristic of Heidegger that he should here link the essence of poetry to the presence or absence of gods, for he sees the experience of art as in a fundamental sense religious.) But our time is also that of the "approaching god"; in the depths of our alienation, we still have hope of redemption, though we have nothing else (*E&B,* p. 289 [translation altered]).

How will this redemption come to us? It will come (*if* it comes) through a remanifesting of the original, poetic essence of technology. In short, it will come through a reintegration of technology and art. I have already noted how, in the extremist perspective of the crisis notion and of aestheticism, to make a possibility present is already to corrupt it. It is thus not surprising that Heidegger says nothing about the concrete reality of this repoeticized technology: to do so would be to remove it from the pure and uncorrupted realm of possibility. Whereas Marx, for example, can perceive in the present economic and social order foreshadowings of a later liberation, such a stance is not open to Heidegger, for with his notion of radical crisis he can see no lines of connection between the degraded situation of the present and the possibility of future liberation.

Yet, for all his reluctance to be explicit, part of the interest of Heidegger's thoughts on art and technology lies in the fact that we can attribute a real and plausible content to his words. As one small example of this, instead of having a secretary type the present manuscript, I am entering it into a computer. This allows me to carry out, by myself and with a minimum of fuss, whatever revisions I should care to make in it. The equipment that I am using is cumbersome and slightly obsolete. It is last year's model, not this year's. But it does open up, for authors, a tremendous promise. It points the way toward a situation in which an author will be able to craft his own book, handling all stages in its production from the initial conception to the final typesetting. One can view this as a return to *technē* in the Greek sense, where every product of human fabrication is lovingly crafted by its maker, and where this crafting makes possible the revealing or discovery of Being. I introduce this vision of a revival of craft work only as a possibility; perhaps, for one reason or another, the possibility will not be realized. But it *is* a possibility, and it is one that can be read out of (or into?) Heidegger's writings.

Idealism and history

Still, Heidegger's perspective (like all perspectives) has its limitations, and it is important to point out just what these limitations are. This exercise should not be regarded as a condemnation of Heidegger. Nor should it be taken as implying that Heidegger ought to have gone beyond his own chosen boundaries, for these boundaries are all but inevitable, given the nature of the project in general. Rather, I point out these limitations because it seems to me that Heidegger's readers ought to be aware of crucial aspects of his work that might otherwise escape their attention, or at most would be perceived only in a vague and somewhat dissatisfying way.

Two points in particular are exceedingly important. Firstly, there is the fact that the notion of crisis, as it develops in the thought of Nietzsche and Heidegger, presupposes a certain reading of history. Specifically, it presupposes an historicist reading of history. I shall develop this point later, in discussing Derrida. But I can comment briefly on it here. In "Hölderlin and the Essence of Poetry," Heidegger suggests a past flight, and future return, of the gods. Elsewhere he makes it clear that this is a turning that occurs within the process of history itself. Note, for example, his statement in "The Anaximander Fragment" (written in 1946, published in 1959) that if we are "latecomers in a history now racing toward its end," we are also, at the same time, able to grasp the truth that the pre-Socratic Greeks speak to us (*EGT*, p. 16). As this passage suggests, behind Heidegger's notion of crisis lies the notion of history as constituting a continuous process or movement that is somehow now in the midst of being broken. This notion, as we shall see, has definite historical antecedents, whose presence is decisive for the whole enterprise of crisis theory.

The second point is one that I do want to develop here. This is the fact of Heidegger's radical idealism. To some extent, the grounds for this idealism are clear to us already. The later Heidegger is a radically ideal utopian (as are Nietzsche and, in important phases of his work, Foucault) because he feels an absolute revulsion against the present. He believes implicitly that to make our hope real is to destroy it. Unfortunately, this idealism has an obvious and not entirely desirable effect. Briefly, it tends to block out the important issues of concrete, actual power and control. How will the new technology be organized? In whose interests will it operate? These are issues that Heidegger does not deal with. Indeed, his perspective actively discourages a consideration of such issues. It all but hides actual technology behind a veil of mysticism.

In the *Der Spiegel* interview, for example, he declares that the "mystery of the superior global power of the unthought essence of technology" brings with it "the tentativeness and inconspicuousness of thought, which attempts to meditate this still unthought essence."[2] It is difficult to know what such a statement could mean. Significantly, in 1966 Heidegger could still say that National Socialism tried to move toward the achievement of just such an "adequate relationship to the essence of technology," though unfortunately the Nazis were "far too limited in their thinking" to succeed in this enterprise.[3] From a Nietzschean or Heideggerian perspective, it is perhaps legitimate to say that the problem with the Nazis was that they were not extreme enough, but it is hard to imagine any other perspective within which such a view could be maintained. Whatever Heidegger's apologists may say in defense of his later position of "unwilling," his political judgment seems to me as questionable in 1966 as it was in 1933. And the questionableness of his judgment is closely related to his tendency to think in ideal, almost mystic terms, rather than in terms of concrete actuality. The crisis of the "modern age," in Heidegger, suggests a turning. But the turning itself seems always to lie beyond our grasp. In consequence, like the characters in Beckett's *Waiting for Godot* (a work that Heidegger is said to have greatly admired),[4] we shall always be in attendance on something that will never quite appear.

If Heidegger's idealism is the product of his revulsion against the present, it also has another connection—namely, to German idealist philosophy. To be sure, these two idealisms are very different in spirit, since German idealist philosophers sought a reintegration of, in, and with the extant world, whereas the utopian idealism associated with the thought of crisis denies the possibility of any such reintegration. Nonetheless, in Heidegger the two idealisms are brought together, for Heidegger uses the German idealist tradition as a support for his type of utopian idealism. Notwithstanding his incessant talk of "technology," which might seem to suggest a role for material factors in history, Heidegger time and again characterizes spiritual phenomena as the determining ones. And he does so in a way that reminds us of the work of an earlier German philosophy professor, namely, Hegel. Indeed, it can justly be said that Heidegger "takes Hegel seriously" as much as, and perhaps more than, he does Nietzsche.[5] Ironically, Heidegger's thought turns out to be dependent on two thinkers who are virtually the antipodes of each other.

Heidegger's Hegelian-sounding statements are numerous. For example, in *An Introduction to Metaphysics*, he speaks of "the whole spiritual history of the West, that is to say, its history pure and simple" (*IM*, p. 137). Similarly, in "The Word of Nietzsche," he observes that "we have for decades now accustomed ourselves to cite the dominance of technology or the revolt of the masses as the cause of the historical condition of the age, and we tirelessly dissect the intellectual situation of the time in keeping with such views." But, says Heidegger, these views are mistaken; the more fundamental phenomenon is the rise of nihilism, and the "realm for the essence and coming-to-pass [*Ereignis*] of nihilism is metaphysics itself" (*QT*, p. 65). And in "The Age of the World Picture," he tells us that "metaphysics grounds an age, in that through a specific interpretation of what is and through a specific comprehension of truth it gives to that age the basis upon which it is essentially formed. This basis holds complete dominion over all the phenomena that distinguish the age" (*QT*, p. 115).

But just how Hegelian are these assertions? Whatever his "idealism," Hegel himself was also a "realist," concerned with coming to grips with the manifold complexity of the social, political, intellectual, and cultural world, as R. N. Berki convincingly argues.[6] This is clear from such works as his *Philosophy of Right*, his *Philosophy of History*, and his *Lectures on Aesthetics*. Taken together, these works well indicate the breadth of his vision of human history. Heidegger chooses to ignore the full range of Hegel's project. Instead, he treats Hegel as if his *History of Philosophy* were the whole of his view of history. Like the Left Hegelians before him, Heidegger finds attractive the side of Hegel that suggests, or seems to suggest, that the ideas of philosophers play the governing role in world history. Heidegger holds philosophers—especially those in or authorized by the German philosophical tradition—to be the bearers of our "spiritual history." Thus, in *An Introduction to Metaphysics*, he refers in the following terms to the turning away from idealist philosophy that occurred in the late 1840s: "It was then that occurred what is popularly and succinctly called the 'collapse of German idealism.' . . . It was not German idealism that collapsed; rather, the age was no longer strong enough to stand up to the greatness, breadth, and originality of that spiritual world, i.e., truly to realize it" (*IM*, p. 45). And in "Overcoming Metaphysics" (written in 1936–46, published in 1954), he declares that "in spite of the superficial talk about the breakdown of Hegelian philosophy, one thing remains true: Only this philosophy determined reality in the nineteenth century, although not in the external form of a doctrine followed, but rather as metaphysics, as the dominance of beingness in the sense of certainty. The countermovements to this metaphysics belong *to* it. Ever since Hegel's death (1831), everything is merely a countermovement, not only in Germany, but also in Europe" (*EP*, p. 89).

Nowhere does Heidegger seek to justify his commitment to "Hegel" (the "scare quotes" seem especially necessary here), to German idealism, or to idealism in general. This is an aspect of his thought that one has to take on faith, part of the Heideggerian version of what John Gunnell has called the "myth of the tradition."[7] One presumes that because of his socialization into the German philosophical profession and his immersion in the idealist texts, Heidegger did not see this commitment as a problem. But a problem it is, for unless one accepts Heidegger's conviction that "Hegel's" philosophy is the determining element in our history, one will have great difficulty taking him seriously.

Perhaps, at the most profound level, Heidegger does not *want* to be taken seriously. It is just conceivable that he is, by intention, a deeply concealed ironist, secretly laughing at those who insist on reading his words literally: certainly, there are elements in his thought that point in this direction. But if this is so, one wonders at the reason for the concealment, and at the evident lack on Heidegger's part of any attempt to confront its moral and political ambiguities. In short, though ironism may be able to save Heidegger from the charge that he is committed in a foolishly literal sense to idealism (and even this is debatable), it opens him up to difficulties that are just as serious. To my mind, moreover, the ironistic hints in Heidegger are so attenuated that one has little choice but to regard him in an idealist perspective.

Heidegger also takes over from Hegel—or more accurately, from the tradition to which Hegel gave birth—the notion of the end or fulfillment (*Vollendung*) of history. This notion very much contributes to the crisis idea. The canonical text, here, is the passage in the *History of Philosophy* where Hegel suggests that the history of the world in general and of philosophy in particular "seems to have reached its goal." Hegel makes this suggestion because he believes that, in the form of Hegelian philosophy, the world spirit has "at last succeeded in stripping off from itself all alien objective existence" and has realized itself "as spirit."[8] It is not entirely clear how much Hegel wants to make of this claim; he does appear to qualify it in his following paragraph. Nonetheless, as Karl Löwith has pointed out, the claim was taken up by a whole range of thinkers, including Kierkegaard, Marx, Bruno Bauer, Stirner, and Feuerbach. All of these viewed Hegel's history as, in fact, a prehistory, the completion of which would yield either an "extensive revolution" or an "intensive reformation."[9]

Heidegger needs to be added to this list, for he, too, sees Hegel as marking an end and as suggesting the possibility of a new beginning. For example, in his essay "Hegel and the Greeks" (given as a lecture in 1958, first published in 1960), Heidegger observes that "with the name 'the Greeks' we think of the beginning of philosophy, with the name 'Hegel' of its completion"; and yet, the "ruin [*Zerfall*] of philosophy is not yet the end of thinking," for "the matter of thinking is still at stake (*steht auf dem Spiel*)."[10] And in "Overcoming Metaphysics," in a move that at first thought seems surprising, he sees Hegel and Nietzsche as convergent figures, with Hegel heralding the beginning of the completion of metaphysics and Nietzsche its end (*EP*, pp. 89, 95).

As one might expect, Heidegger views the supposed "end" of philosophy in a rather different light than Hegel did. The two are agreed, to be sure, in seeing the end of philosophy as also opening up a new beginning; as Hegel puts it, "a new epoch has arisen in the world."[11] But Heidegger's beginning is radically different from Hegel's, for Heidegger gives to this notion a consistently nostalgic weight, whereas Hegel's nostalgia is intermittent and partial. Heidegger sums up the difference between the two positions when he notes in his essay "The Onto-Theo-Logical Constitution of Metaphysics" (presented in seminar and lecture form in 1956–57, published in 1957) that "For us, the character of the conversation with the history of thinking is no longer *Aufhebung*, but the step back": *Für uns ist der Charakter des Gespräches mit der Geschichte des Denkens nicht mehr die Aufhebung, sondern der Schritt zurück* (*I&D*, pp. 49, 115).

In other words, the Hegelian notion of *Aufhebung*—of a simultaneous negation/preservation/elevation of previous thought—gives way, in Heidegger, to the notion of going back before the tradition, to a time preceding philosophy's entrance into the world. Hegel insists that the beginning, of philosophy or of anything else, is "implicit, immediate, abstract, general"; it is "poorer in determinations," with the "more concrete and richer" coming later.[12] Heidegger, on the other hand, mythologizes the beginning, finding it more genuine and illuminating than subsequent appearances. As he puts it in "The Question Concerning Technology": "All coming to presence [*Wesende*] keeps itself everywhere concealed to the last. Nevertheless, it remains, with respect to its holding sway, that which precedes all: the earliest" (*QT*, p. 22).

And yet, Heidegger's nostalgia is by no means entirely foreign to Hegel or to the tradition of German idealism in general. In a *Nachlass* fragment, Nietzsche shrewdly notes that "German philosophy as a whole ... is the most fundamental kind of *romanticism* and nostalgia [*Heimweh*] there has ever been: the longing for the best that ever existed. One is no longer at home anywhere; at last one longs back for that place in which alone one can be at home, because it is the only place in which one would want to be at home: the Greek world" (*WP,* §419 [translation altered]; *KGW,* 7. Abt., 3. Bd., p. 412). In his own writings, Heidegger picks up on the Hellenophilia of Schiller, Hölderlin, and Hegel, which he moves in a Nietzschean direction by his insistence on focusing on the obscure territory of pre-Socratic philosophy.[13]

Moreover, there is yet another way in which we can connect Heidegger's nostalgia with Hegel, and this is through Hegel's notion of the pastness of art. When Heidegger says in "The Question Concerning Technology" that "in Greece, at the outset of the destining of the West, the arts soared to the supreme height of the revealing granted to them" (*QT,* p. 34), he is following Hegel. For Hegel holds that if the histories of philosophy and of religion are fulfilled with Hegelian philosophy and with the advent of Christianity respectively, then the history of art reached its fulfillment with the Greeks. Art, in consequence, is "a thing of the past" (*ein Vergangenes*).[14] The nostalgic charge that Hegel and many of his contemporaries thus gave to art helps explain why it is to art that Heidegger appeals in his own attempt to find the "saving power" that he believes the present age requires.

What is Denken?

Almost immediately after the end of his political involvement, Heidegger began to reflect on the role of poetry, of *Dichtung,* in the revealing of Being. This reflection broadened out to become a new view of language, a view of language as creative rather than merely representational, a view of language as a "work of art" and as an ontogenesis. The best point of entry into the aestheticism that this implies—a point of entry that further emphasizes Heidegger's connection with the German idealist tradition— is the "Letter on Humanism" (1947). Writing to a young French philosopher, Heidegger takes extreme pains to repudiate the humanist, that is, subjectivist, reading of *Being and Time* propagated by Jean-Paul Sartre, who by 1945–46 had become immensely famous as the spokesman of "existentialism." Heidegger declares that he was not and had never been an existentialist. In his *Existentialism is a Humanism* (1946) and else-where, Sartre had argued that man alone creates, through his engaged action, the world in which he lives. Heidegger repudiates this view. He holds instead that what principally exists is Being, and that man "ek-sists," or "stands out," only in the truth of this Being. He thus reiterates a point that ought to have been obvious to the original readers of *Being and Time* but frequently was not—namely, that the existential analytic in that work is subordinate to what Heidegger views as the larger and more important question of the "meaning of Being."[15]

But Heidegger does more than this, for he also informs his correspon-dent that there had been a "turning" or "reversal" (*Kehre*) in his thought since *Being and Time*. We have already touched on one aspect of the turn in showing that he comes more and more to interpret the forgetfulness of Being as peculiarly bound up with "the modern age." As he says in the "Letter on Humanism" (and we ought to remember, here, the tremen-dous disruption and movement of population that was occurring in Ger-many, and in central and eastern Europe in general, in the wake of the war): "Homelessness is coming to be the destiny of the world. Hence it is necessary to think that destiny in terms of the history of Being. What Marx recognized in an essential and significant sense, though derived from Hegel, as the estrangement [*Entfremdung*] of man has its roots in the homelessness of modern man" (*HBW*, p. 219). This is an evocative, and for some an appealing position. In its linking of estrangement (or alienation) with an ineffable *Seinsgeschichte*, it appears to align itself with the Marxist position on alienation, while depriving the Marxian analysis of whatever specificity and concreteness it may have. This can be linked to Marx's and Heidegger's radically different conceptions of freedom. For Marx, freedom is something to be actualized within a social order, so that the analysis of this social order becomes immensely important. But for Heidegger (as for Nietzsche), freedom is radically personal. Freedom in the Nietzschean and Heideggerian sense is the freedom of the creative artist, who has somehow managed to escape from external trammels and limitations.

Connecting with this notion of freedom, it is important to note that Heidegger's concern with the alienation of "modern man"—involving, as it does, an explicitly historical (or posthistoricist) notion of crisis—is more a precondition for the turning than the turning itself. In his own reflections on the "turn," Heidegger clearly views as crucial his altered perspective regarding the role and capacity of conceptual thought. In "Phenomenology and Theology" (given in lecture form in 1927–28, and first published in 1969), a work that we can assume articulates his view-point in the period of *Being and Time,* Heidegger tells us that "something can very well be inconceivable and never primarily disclosed through reason without thereby excluding a conceptual grasp of itself. On the contrary; if the inconceivable as such is to be disclosed properly, it can only be by way of the appropriate conceptual interpretation" (*PT,* p. 17). In the "Letter on Humanism," Heidegger for the first time explicitly announces his departure from such a position. Here he declares that the "conceptual language" (*Begriffssprache*) in terms of which *Being and Time* was conceived and written fell short of what was needed. Indeed, the whole project of a "fundamental ontology" was flawed, since ontology "does not think the truth of Being and so fails to recognize that there is a thinking more rigorous than the conceptual" (*HBW,* p. 235).

But what is the character of this "more rigorous" thinking? In the "Letter on Humanism," Heidegger refers to it as "neither theoretical nor practical"; it comes to pass, he says, before the theoretical/practical distinction. And he continues:

> Such thinking is, in so far as it is, a recollection of Being [*das Andenken an das Sein*] and nothing else.... Such thinking has no result. It has no effect. It satisfies its essence in that it is. But it is by saying its matter. Historically, only one saying [*Sage*] belongs to the matter of thinking, the one that is in each case appropriate to its matter. Its material relevance is essentially higher than the validity of the sciences, because it is freer. For it lets Being—be. (*HBW,* p. 236.)

Though Heidegger rejects such a designation, what we have here is thinking conceived under the sign of the aesthetic. As Derrida remarks in *Truth in Painting,* Heidegger is part of "the heritage of the great philosophies of art" (*VenP,* p. 14). Kant is the decisive reference here: the notion of a thinking that is neither theoretical nor practical, of a thinking that has no result, that *does* nothing, fits clearly within the scope of the discussion of art in the *Critique of Judgment.* It is Kant who opens up the intellectual space within which Heidegger's claims become possible. But Heidegger goes far beyond Kant. Whereas Kant sees art as a bridge between pure reason and practical reason, between theory and practice, Heidegger follows in the footsteps of Schelling by seeing art as constitutive of these separate territories. Moreover, like Nietzsche before him, he also goes beyond Schelling. As we saw in the Introduction, Schelling viewed "the objective world" as "the original, still unconscious poetry *of the spirit*" (my italics). As crisis thinkers, both Nietzsche and Heidegger reject this notion of an author writing the poetry. For Nietzsche, the world is a work of art "that gives birth to itself." For Heidegger, too, the world is a poem of its own making.

In "Hölderlin and the Essence of Poetry," Heidegger declares that "poetry is the act of establishing [*Stiftung*] by the word and in the word. ... Poetry is the establishing of Being by means of the word. ... Poetry is the supporting ground of history [*Dichtung ist der tragende Grund der Geschichte*], and therefore it is not a mere appearance [*Erscheinung*] of culture, and absolutely not the mere 'expression' of a 'culture-soul'" (*E&B*, pp. 280–283 [translation altered]). Heidegger here speaks of poetry, but it is clear from this and other writings that he intends poetry to stand as the highest manifestation of art. Hence, in the view that he is suggesting in this passage, the theoretical and the practical are to be seen not as preexistent territories that art manages to join together, but rather as spaces that a self-creating art itself brings into being. In Heidegger's view, one finds the unity of the theoretical and the practical by going back to that "essential ground" or "essential thinking" that is art, for everything that exists is the product of an original artistic-poetic creation. This is a significant departure from his position of 1933 (a position that has important foreshadowings in *Being and Time* itself), where it is the *Volk* that is the "*tragende Grund*" of history. We are not, I think, wrong to see here something of an evasion—a hasty retreat from the world of social and political action, which had so greatly disappointed his hopes in 1933, to another realm where hope could never be defeated.

Any attempt to engage in a logical analysis of the position that Heidegger now comes to articulate would be fundamentally uninteresting, for the logic of that position is so deeply questionable that one can hardly regard it as a logic at all. Even the exercise of trying to reconstruct an implicit argument by making unstated assumptions explicit—an exercise that to a great extent "works" with *Being and Time*—seems useless when it is a matter of dealing with the later writings. It is widely held that these writings do not constitute "philosophy" at all. If philosophy is defined as logical argument, we are forced to conclude that this opinion is correct. The "later" Heidegger seems much more a mystic than a philosopher in any normal sense. But this is not to say that these writings are nonsensical: they contain, or manifest, a meaning of sorts. They connect, as the writings of a sensitive novelist would, with a wider historical and personal experience. Heidegger is indeed obscure, but his thinking introduces and plumbs (sometimes ambiguously and sometimes explicitly and consistently) profound and disturbing problems central to twentieth-century experience, which many "logical" philosophers ignore.

We have seen how the assumption of crisis, and the preference for a nostalgic resolution of crisis, play an extremely important role in Heidegger's work. These notions are difficult (if not impossible) to establish as "correct," but neither they nor the works that express them are so incomprehensible or so absurd as Heidegger's more dismissive critics have imagined. One needs to understand, too, that Heidegger at least begins in a recognizable philosophical tradition. Admittedly, he moves away from this tradition in his later writings, where the attempt to construct arguments recognizably akin to those of other philosophers is largely abandoned. *Being and Time,* however, still retains close connections with what certain other philosophers of the period were attempting to do. In consequence, it helps to make clear for us the philosophical background to Heidegger's version of aestheticism.

In the "Letter on Humanism," Heidegger laments that the language of *Being and Time* "does not yet succeed in retaining the essential help of phenomenological seeing and in dispensing with the inappropriate concern with 'science' and 'research' " (*HBW,* p. 235). The notion of "phenomenological seeing," as displayed in *Being and Time,* is a crucial element pointing toward the "turning," toward Heidegger's later adoption of an aestheticist position; moreover, there is an important link with certain of Nietzsche's concerns earlier. "Phenomenological seeing" refers to the preoccupation of Husserl and his followers with obtaining an immediate experience of things, a preoccupation epitomized in the phenomenologists' slogan "*Zu den Sachen selbst!*": "To the things themselves!" Heidegger emphatically places *Being and Time* within the context of this enterprise, repeatedly emphasizing his concern for the disclosure of "the things themselves." In Heidegger's words, "phenomenology means *apophainesthai ta phainomena*—to let what shows itself be seen from itself. This is the formal meaning of the type of research that calls itself 'phenomenology.' But this expresses nothing other than the maxim formulated above: 'To the things themselves!' " (*B&T,* p. 34). In short, the phenomenologist eschews imposing a philosophical grid, an interpretation, upon the world. Instead, he seeks to maneuver himself into a position such that the world will reveal itself to him as it essentially is.

This essentialist preoccupation can be placed within the broader intellectual context provided by the widespread dissatisfaction with positivist and neo-Kantian orthodoxy that emerged, early in the century, in academic and extra-academic philosophical circles in Germany and elsewhere. Not only the phenomenologists but also Bergson and his students in France yearned for a philosophy that would be receptive to objects, one that would avoid the sharp dichotomy between subject and object postulated by positivists and neo-Kantians alike. Heidegger is unquestionably part of this broader movement. In *Being and Time,* a large part of his concern is with attacking what he sees as the Cartesian tendency to interpret the whole of reality as if it consisted of isolated, independent objects. It is as a counter to this dichotomization that he introduces his own, opposing concept of "Being-in-the-world."

In Heidegger's view, the problem with the Cartesian approach to the world (an approach that Kant took over "quite dogmatically") is that it leads us to ask the wrong questions. Within the framework of the subject/object division, one is faced with the problem of explaining how the knowing subject "comes out of its inner 'sphere' into one which is 'other and external.' " In fact, one is faced with the problem of "how knowing can have any object at all" (*B&T,* p. 60; see also p. 366). But this question of how the subject can make its way out of itself and achieve "transcendence" is not, for Heidegger, the really important one. He does not regard the subject/object distinction as wrong; rather, insofar as Dasein is concerned, he sees it as being insufficiently "original." When it is taken as the starting point for investigating the human world, it is allowed to function as an *a priori,* without its grounds being properly examined. After all, asks Heidegger, "what is more obvious than that a 'subject' is related to an 'object' and *vice versa?*" Unfortunately, when this "obvious" point of departure is adopted, without any attempt to go behind it, its "ontological necessity and especially its ontological meaning are . . . left in the dark" (*B&T,* p. 59).

The question that one ought to ask instead is what makes it possible for entities to be encountered in the world in the first place. And this means that one needs to examine the Being of the subject rather than, as Kant did, simply taking the subject as a given. Examining the supposed subject more closely, one sees that it is really Being-in-the-world, and that its in-the-worldness is not some sort of external accident but is, on the contrary, essential to its existence. Thus, the pseudoproblem of how the subject grasps the object disappears, since, in Heidegger's words, "Being-in is something quite different from a mere confrontation, whether by way of observation or by way of action; that is, it is not the Being-present-at-hand-together of a subject and an object" (*B&T,* p. 176). Moreover, the notion of truth is now radically altered, for truth can no longer be conceived in terms of an agreement or correspondence between a knowing subject and a known object but must rather be seen as an "uncoveredness" or "unhiddenness" of things themselves.[16] We thus return to

Heidegger's "phenomenological" preoccupation with letting things show themselves just as they actually are.

It is noteworthy how little Heidegger says in *Being and Time* about the aesthetic. Indeed, virtually his only reference to aesthetic matters is a single sentence in section 34 of the work, the well-known section on language, where he suggests that "in 'poetical' discourse, the communication of the existential possibilities of one's state-of-mind can become an aim in itself and this amounts to a disclosing of existence" (*B&T*, p. 162). Heidegger seems here to be voicing a conventionally expressivist view of art, not an aestheticist view. Yet, his concern with circumventing the subject/object dichotomy through a "phenomenological seeing," and his resulting definition of truth as "unhiddenness," in some ways already suggest an aestheticist resolution, for it is a commonplace of Romantic and post-Romantic aesthetics that art is a peculiarly immediate form of seeing, that its truth is one not of correspondence but of revelation, and that it escapes from the opposition of subject and object.

One notes, for example, Lukács's important essay "The Subject-Object Relation in Aesthetics," which appeared in the journal *Logos* in 1917–18. Working out of Kant's distinction between the logical, the ethical, and the aesthetic spheres, Lukács maintains that only in the sphere of the aesthetic is there any real connection between subject and object. (Lukács tends to overschematize Kant, but our concern here is as much with what was made of Kant's philosophy—from Schiller onward—as it is with Kant's philosophy itself.) In the realm of pure logic, Lukács holds, there is no subject at all, for the essence of logic lies in its theoretical objectivity. Logic constructs a world from which all subjectivity is excluded, except in the totally abstract sense of consciousness itself. In the realm of pure ethics, on the other hand, there is a denial of the object. Here, the ethically-acting subject is raised up out of the world of objects. That world, deprived of all inherent structure and independence, now becomes no more than an infinite field of activity for the subject. Even the supposed objectivity of the ethical norm (the "categorical imperative") turns out to be nothing other than an unconditioned interconnection of all subjects, whose "maxim" is thus a maxim of pure subjectivity. Only in the realm of the aesthetic, Lukács maintains, is there a "peaceful equilibrium" between the two. To the infinite object of the logical sphere, there corresponds an abstract subject entirely separate from any real subject, while the infinite subject of the ethical sphere is a utopian postulate that cannot be realized in the objective world of human drives and inclinations. In contrast, within the aesthetic sphere, infinity is excluded from both sides of the opposition, and an equilibrium between the two is achieved. The subject appears as a stylized, living unity embracing the fullness of experience, and this subject reaches its highest possible subjectivity in its connection to an object that corresponds absolutely to it.[17]

Implicit in Lukács's essay is the "tragic" insight that it is in art alone, and not in the world of human action, that the unity of subject and object is to be attained. This was a major theme of his 1911 essay collection, *Soul and Form,* in which he stressed the Schopenhauerian (and in part Nietzschean) notion of the conflict between art and life, arguing that only in art is perfect form attainable.[18] The aestheticist move is to transgress the boundary that is thus established between what is art and what is not-art. An attempt is made to carry over what has been won within the aesthetic into the world of human action—forgetting, in this movement, that such winnings are dependent on the existence of the boundary in the first place. It is a matter of what Derrida, in his ironic deconstruction of aestheticism, has identified as the problem of the *cadre,* or frame (*VenP,* pp. 69–94). Readers of Lukács's *History and Class Consciousness,* recalling his insistence on portraying the proletariat as the unified subject-object of history, will perceive that he himself was not entirely immune to the aestheticist temptation, notwithstanding his warning against it.[19] Our concern here, however, is with Heidegger. While the details of Heidegger's development as he moved away from his perspective in *Being and Time* are far from clear, one thing that does seem clear is that an important impetus for this shift was his concern, already central in that work, with circumventing the subject-object division and arriving at a complete receptivity to things in their "unhiddenness." When *Being and Time*'s "inappropriate concern with 'science' and 'research'" is dropped, what remains is the revelatory power of art, a power that at its extreme seeks to turn into the enclosing and defining space of myth.

The truth value of art

In many ways, the most lucid and accessible expression of Heidegger's aestheticism is his essay "The Origin of the Work of Art" (first given as a lecture series in 1935–36; first published in 1950; and republished with an addendum and minor revisions in 1960). Here Heidegger argues for the distinctive "truth value" of art. This notion of the truth of art comes as close as anything to being the central theme of his later thought, and is a major focus for many of those who have found him an important and stimulating figure. Commenting on a painting by van Gogh of a pair of peasant shoes, Heidegger argues that through the painting the Being of the shoes comes to light. How so? It is Heidegger's view that in our "normal," propositional-conceptual-representational thinking we project a grid onto the world. In seeking to understand "the thing," for example, we apply rigid definitions to it. According to Heidegger, the history of Western metaphysics has seen three attempts to answer the question, what is a thing? One answer holds that the thing is the subject, or *hypokeimenon*, around which certain properties have assembled. A second holds that the thing is the *aestheton*, that which is perceptible by the senses, so that here the thing is conceived as a collection of sense perceptions. A third holds that the thing is a unity of matter with form (*PLT*, pp. 22–26).

Unfortunately, all three definitions miss the thingness of the thing. Attempting to conceptualize the thing, they in fact assault it, but "the unpretentious thing evades thought most stubbornly" (*PLT*, p. 31). In short, as with the Nietzsche of "On Truth and Lie," conceptual thought falls short. It falsifies reality; it does not let reality be. But what happens when we turn to art? Here we have a radically different approach to the world and to the things and tools and works that populate that world. Van Gogh's painting of the peasant shoes lets the shoes be; likewise, we ourselves let van Gogh's painting be, approaching it in the same way that it approaches the world. In consequence, there is a speaking and a hearing that would not otherwise occur. In the vicinity of the artwork, we are "suddenly somewhere else than we usually tend to be"; the artwork lets us know "what shoes are in truth" (*PLT*, p. 35). Moreover, says Heidegger, it would be "the worst self-deception to think that our description, as a subjective action, had first depicted everything and then projected it into the painting." On the contrary, it is "through the work and only through the work" that what is portrayed in the work "arrives at its appearance" (*PLT*, pp. 35–36).

A number of important claims are being made here. It is crucial to our understanding of Heidegger's project that we perceive how, in making these claims, he is both continuing within and departing from (or better, radicalizing) a tradition established by previous philosophies of art. Most importantly, Heidegger moves away from what he and other commentators have called the "aesthetic" view of art (not to be confused with "aestheticism"), which he believes dominates all art theory and aesthetics. In the "aesthetic" view, whose genealogy is usually traced back to Kant, art is a recreation—a playfulness that contrasts with the "real" world of work. The aesthetic view denies that there is any special connection between art and truth. It is psychological rather than cognitive in its focus, for it looks at art in its relation to a feeling or state of mind (in Kant's case, the "disinterested pleasure" that art induces), and not in relation to a truth-claim. Opposed to the "aesthetic" view is the "ontological" view, which holds that art is not mere play but is rather a revelation of truth and hence of Being.[20] Obviously, Heidegger's view of art is "ontological" rather than "aesthetic" (ultimately, of course, it is "ontogenetic" as well, for his aestheticism leads him to see art not simply as revealing truth but also as creating it).

Paradoxically, then, though Heidegger articulates his conception of art within the space opened up by the Kantian critiques, he denies Kant's conception of what art is. But one should not view this as a complete break with previous aesthetics. In the first place, in suggesting that art is a "symbol of the morally good" and in putting forward the notion of the "aesthetic idea," for which "an adequate concept can never be found," Kant himself comes close to articulating an ontological view of art.[21] And in the second place, Heidegger did not have to go very far from Kant in order to find a philosopher who did articulate such a view. I refer, of course, to Hegel, whom Heidegger acknowledges as having provided "the most comprehensive reflection on the nature of art that the West possesses," the "final and greatest aesthetics in the Western tradition" ("The Origin of the Work of Art," Epilogue, *PLT*, p. 79; *NI*, pp. 100/84).

Hegel explicitly views art not as a mere recreation but rather as something that is necessary to man as man. It is necessary, he suggests, because it is one of the ways by which man comes to grasp the Absolute, that is, reality in its highest manifestation. As he points out in his *Lectures on Aesthetics*, art is often regarded as a mere appearance or illusion. But this characterization is better applied, he argues, to the entire sphere of the empirical world. For we arrive at reality only by penetrating beneath the surface play of what is immediately perceptible, thus attaining to the "universal powers" that govern the world. Art is one of the ways in which these powers are made manifest, so that, far from being appearance and nothing more, it has a "higher reality and more veritable existence" than the realities of everyday life: it functions "to unveil the truth in the form of sensuous artistic configuration."[22] This is in some ways close to Heidegger's view of art, and it is little wonder that the latter should have thought so highly of the *Lectures on Aesthetics*.

But Hegel makes a further move that holds him back from Heidegger's aestheticism. Specifically, he limits the potential truth claims of art by elevating philosophy to the highest position within the sphere of absolute knowledge. Thus, philosophy stands in judgment over art, testing its claims to be a revelation of truth and finding those claims, in each individual case, to be either warranted or unwarranted. Heidegger accepts the positive side of Hegel's account of the revelatory character of art and rejects the negative. Of all his predecessors, he is closest to Schelling, who in his *System of Transcendental Idealism* subordinates philosophy to art. But again there is a crucial difference with Heidegger, for whereas Schelling is able to assume a world that is inherently coherent, Heidegger, standing after the thought of crisis, is not. Thus, crisis separates Heidegger, as it separated Nietzsche before him, from the Romantic dispensation.

There is a further important way in which Heidegger's position differs from previous thought on the nature of art. Heidegger informs us, in his discussion of the painting of the pair of peasant shoes, that it is not van Gogh who speaks through the painting but the painting itself that speaks. Within the Romantic dispensation, and in Nietzsche insofar as he continues that dispensation, a quite different emphasis usually prevailed. Art was most often viewed in "subjectivist" terms, as an expression of the will, consciousness, or creativity of the artist. Such an emphasis is entirely antithetical to Heidegger's attempt to invest the work of art with a truth value of its own, and it is not at all surprising that Heidegger begins "The Origin of the Work of Art" with an attack on this view.

Heidegger's most sustained attack on the subjectivist view of art is to be found in the first of his lecture courses on Nietzsche, entitled "Nietzsche: The Will to Power as Art" (winter semester, 1936–37; first published in 1961). As I have already noted, Heidegger views Nietzsche as a more or less straightforward "naturalist," missing the poetic aspect of the Nietzschean text (what Blanchot calls his "écriture fragmentaire")[23] and the clearly aestheticist suggestions that Nietzsche makes. In accordance with this tendency, he sees Nietzsche as having grasped art from the point of view of the artist, a position for which, as we have seen, there is considerable textual support. Thus, he views Nietzsche's conception of art as technologistic, as a "configuration of the will to power" (*NI*, pp. 90/76; also pp. 162–163/139 and passim). From this perspective, the relation between the two thinkers is clearly one of antagonism. But when one looks at Nietzsche's other, aestheticist aspect, Heidegger appears rather as his successor than as his antagonist. In Part I, I sought to justify an aestheticist reading of Nietzsche. I shall confine myself here to pointing out the importance of the notion of crisis for the conception of the artist in both thinkers. The "death of God" is also, at the same time, the death of man, of author, and of artist. This, ultimately, is why Nietzsche is able to speak of the world as "a work of art that gives birth to itself"; this is why he is able, at the aestheticist turns in his text, to attribute to art, now taken in its broad rather than its narrow sense, a world-creating capacity. And the same denial of author and artist, which Nietzsche no more than suggests, is absolutely central for the later Heidegger.

In Heidegger's view, then, art is not subjective; it simply *is,* and questions of subjectivity and objectivity are irrelevant. Much of Heidegger's argument with Kantian and post-Kantian aesthetics is concerned with attacking what he sees as the trivialization that was initiated by Kant's insistence on discussing art in terms of the subjective powers of the mind.[24] It is necessary for Heidegger to reject a subjectivist approach to art because he wants to hold that when the artwork speaks, it does so in a nonsubjective, Being-attuned voice.

It is interesting that Blanchot, who is an important linking figure between Heidegger and the French, articulates an antisubjectivist view of art that is in some ways close to Heidegger's. In Blanchot's words, art "does not refer back immediately to someone who supposedly made it"; it has no necessary relation to a creator, an author. Blanchot admits that an object made by a factory worker also has this impersonal quality ("*il ne porte pas de nom d'auteur*"). But this sort of object "disappears entirely in its use," becoming entirely a use value, never announcing what it is but only what use it serves. The work of art, in contrast, does refer to itself, standing as an "'impersonified' reality," as something existing "beyond and before all reality."[25] Blanchot, however, is a negative Heideggerian, closely akin in his reflections on art to Foucault and especially to Derrida, and one indication of this is his notion of art as concerned not with truth but with "nontruth": art "gives voice to the unnameable, to the inhuman, to that which is without truth, justice, right"; it "escapes from the movement of the true"; it is an "exile from truth."[26]

Blanchot's anti-Heideggerian turn is telling; it indicates that we need not see Heidegger's "truth value" move as the only conclusion to be drawn from the denial of the subjectivity of art. But it is the "truth value" move that Heidegger makes. When van Gogh's painting or any other "great" work of art "speaks," it puts us in touch, according to Heidegger, with a truth that we cannot attain otherwise than through art. Indeed, as I have noted, art for Heidegger is not merely a revelation of truth (for example, the truth of a pair of shoes) but its creation. This creation, he makes clear, is a creation *ex nihilo.* As he puts it, "*art . . . is a becoming and a happening of truth.* Does truth, then, arise out of nothing? It does indeed if by nothing is meant the mere not of that which is [*das Seiende*], and if we here think of that which is as an object present in the ordinary way" (*PLT*, p. 71 [translation altered]). Here we see why Heidegger is not (as he is sometimes accused of being) a nihilist. To be sure, nihilism is the precondition for Heidegger's "thinking," which would be unthinkable without the assumption of a human world utterly voided of meaning. Heidegger's enterprise aims, however, not at confirming the void but at building over it, creating a meaning that is self-originating and self-sustaining. And the soundest metaphor that Heidegger can find for such an enterprise is the metaphor of art—an art that stands alone, in total independence of any creator.

Art and language

There is much that one could say about Heidegger's position as articulated in "The Origin of the Work of Art." Anyone who wishes to know Heidegger ought to read it, for it is clearly a nodal work in his career, yet is free of technical vocabulary and other barriers to comprehension. Moreover, it is in some ways extremely suggestive about its subject. The notion of art as a "becoming" (*Werden*) or "happening" (*Geschehen*), for example, seems peculiarly suited to the contemporary artistic world, where art is so often conceived as an event, an experience, a "happening." But a lengthy consideration of this single essay would be inappropriate here, for our concern is to come to grips with his later thought as a whole.

While Heidegger's aestheticism is clearly in place by 1936, there are nonetheless some later shifts of emphasis. Most noteworthy is the extent to which, in his subsequent writings (especially the important essay collection *On the Way to Language* [1959]), he turns his attention from "the work of art" to "language." This shift is not at all surprising, when one considers the weight that the Heidegger of 1935–36 expected the work of art to bear. The work of art, in "The Origin of the Work of Art," is in no way tied to an "empirical," "ordinary" reality. It is in no way subject to the demands of mimetic or representational truth. On the contrary, it creates truth; more than this, it creates worlds—as Heidegger puts it, "to be a work means to set up a world": *Werksein heisst: eine Welt aufstellen* (*PLT*, p. 44).

The notion of "setting up" worlds can be interpreted in a weaker and in a stronger sense. Taking it in its weaker sense, we can see that Heidegger is asserting that art serves to sensitize us to realities that we might not otherwise be aware of—as, for example, when a painting by Bridget Riley helps open us up to the play of colors. Heidegger makes the widely accepted point that the world is not immediately present to us, but requires, on the contrary, a quite staggering receptivity. This is clearly part of what he intends when he tells us that the work of art "holds open the Open of the world" (*PLT*, p. 45).

But he also has in mind a stronger sense of the "setting up" of worlds. For he by no means accepts, in all its implications, the view of art as something that sensitizes us to the experience of the "real world." Such a view implies that the "world of the work of art" is an imaginary world that gains its sensitizing power from the fact that it stands apart from the "real world" and hence provides us with an aesthetic distance from, and perspective on, that world. Heidegger's tendency, on the contrary, is to cancel out the distance between the aesthetic and the nonaesthetic. Ultimately, he holds not simply that the work of art lets us see things more clearly, but more tellingly that it lets things be: it "lets the earth be an earth" (*PLT*, p. 46). Just as the early Heidegger holds that the Newtonian laws of motion become true only with Newton (see *B&T*, p. 227), so the later Heidegger holds that the truth of the world establishes itself only in the work of art. This is why, as distinguished from Hegel, Heidegger does not see the work of art as the bearer of truth—a truth that could in principle appear in the form of a message separable from it. Instead, he sees the work of art itself as truth's "becoming" and "happening."

While this view obviously depends on Hegel's notion of the truth value of art, in its identification of art and truth it goes far beyond anything Hegel (or even Schelling) could have accepted. Notwithstanding the "raging discord" that Nietzsche saw between art and truth, one is reminded of Nietzsche, and specifically of his assertion in *The Birth of Tragedy* that "the Dionysian, measured against the Apollonian, appears as the eternal and original artistic power that calls the whole phenomenal world into existence." But this world-creating significance is a heavy burden for the work of art to bear. It is in fact a mythic significance, since it is to myth that such a power is usually attributed. Given this burden, we are not surprised to find that as he continued his pursuit of the notion of world-making, Heidegger came to focus more and more on the broader reality of language. Near the end of "The Origin of the Work of Art," he suggests that language itself, through its nominative power, "first brings beings to word and to appearance" (*PLT*, p. 73). Two identities underlie this statement: an identification of poetry as the essential form of art (an identification that is central to the Romantic conception of art); and an identification of poetry with language (so that, in Heidegger's words, "language itself is poetry in the essential sense" [*PLT*, p. 74]).

Of the three connected centers of force that are thus set up—art, poetry, and language—it is obvious which has the widest resonance and power. With his notion of *Zarathustra* as "the first language of a new series of experiences," Nietzsche broaches the idea of language as world-making—as raising us, somehow, to an entirely new level of experience. Heidegger, too, makes the "linguistic" move: indeed, this move seems to be a necessary outcome of the aestheticist position, and we shall see it coming into play again in the writings of Foucault and Derrida. But what is still very tentative in Nietzsche, and in many respects undermined by other tendencies in his thought, becomes primal and definitive in the later Heidegger, who is obsessed by language in a way that Nietzsche is not. In Heidegger's eyes, the experience with language is not merely one experience among other experiences; above all, it is not thought's experience of the particular object that we know as "language." Rather, the experience of language is thought's experience with and against itself—for language is thought, and vice versa, and this language/thought brings the whole of the human world into existence.

In "A Dialogue on Language between a Japanese and an Inquirer" (written in 1953–54 and published as part of *On the Way to Language*), Heidegger admits, however, that he has not yet found "the fitting word" (*das gemässe Wort*) for his reflection on the nature (*Wesen*) of language, and that the "prospect" of the thinking that seeks to answer to that nature "is still veiled, in all its vastness" (*OWL*, p. 8). Heidegger holds this veiling to be unavoidable; the saying of language is ultimately a *Geheimnis*, a secret or mystery that must at all costs be safeguarded. To speak *about* language, he tells us, inevitably turns language into an object, causing its essence to vanish; the point is rather to let language itself speak, and this speaking cannot occur within an investigation that seeks to be scientific in character (*OWL*, pp. 50–51). In another of the essays included in *On the Way to Language*, "Words" (first given as a lecture, in 1958), Heidegger maintains that poetry and thinking "are a distinctive Saying in that they remain delivered over to the mystery as that which is most worthy of their thinking" (*OWL*, p. 156). In view of this emphasis on language's ultimately mysterious character, it is not surprising that the task of clarifying what Heidegger actually means by language is extremely difficult—more difficult, indeed, than the clarification of any other aspect of his "way."

As one might expect, there is something systematic here, a position that has been shrewdly, or cunningly, adopted. Twice in the "Dialogue on Language," Heidegger declares that his way of thinking must be left without a name (*OWL*, pp. 29, 42). This is a scandal to the critic, for criticism is a matter of trying to find the right name for what is being criticized. In rejecting such namings, Heidegger is rejecting the critic's enterprise. From his own point of view, he is doing so with good reason, for his ultimate aim is to create a new world through the power of his word, and criticism can only serve to undermine this power. As the legends of Delphi and of the Sphinx suggest, enigma is the characteristic stance of the prophet and seer. It is the enigmatic, mysterious character of the Heideggerian text that makes it possible for his followers to attribute to his words a world-historical significance. By definition, the enigmatic—the "riddle-like" (*rätselhaft*)—resists clarification. And language is at the center of this resistance.

Consequently, in approaching Heidegger's reflections on language, we are approaching something that is almost willfully concealed—an immense and forbidding forest, a looming, veiled presence. I can promise here only to open a pathway, and a limited one at that, through these writings. Whether this way is a *Holzweg*, a blind alley, remains to be seen. I hope that it is not, and that it will bring to light some of the issues that Heidegger's reflection raises. In particular, I hope to make clear to the reader the connections that this reflection has to less difficult, less esoteric, less oracular, rather more familiar thought. To be sure, from both a Nietzschean and a Heideggerian perspective, this attempt to view the unfamiliar in terms of the familiar will be rejected, but the rejection is a risk that needs to be run. The hostility between the enigmatizing and the clarifying is deep and immediate. Unriddled, the Sphinx is deprived of her powers and the philosopher of his world-historical significance.

Language and poetry

We have seen how Heidegger's perspective changed radically as he moved beyond *Being and Time,* for only after that work did the possibility of aestheticism open up. Not surprisingly, Heidegger's views on language also changed; indeed, they did so for the second time. In his *Habilitationsschrift,* he had adhered to a Husserlian position, according to which language is a medium for conveying objective meanings. In this view, grammar has an *a priori* foundation in formal logic. The philosopher is concerned with logical, and not at all with linguistic issues. He seeks, in his work, to "bracket out" ordinary language, with all its confusions and uncertainties, and to construct an ideal language that is perfectly logical in character.[27]

In *Being and Time*, Heidegger leaves this view behind, for he now sees language in existential rather than in logical terms. Thus, in section 34 ("Being-there and Discourse. Language"), he speaks of the need to "liberate" grammar from logic (*B&T*, p. 165). Similarly, in section 18 ("Involvement and Significance; the Worldhood of the World"), he portrays Dasein as producing significations (*Bedeutungen*) in the course of its coming to understand the world with which it is involved, and on these significations the "Being of words and of language" is founded (*B&T*, p. 87). In short, he assumes a progression from Dasein's involvement in the world, to its understanding of that world, to the production of significations, to language.

It is telling that in a notation that he subsequently made opposite this latter assertion in the margin of his personal copy of *Being and Time*, Heidegger says: "Untrue. Language is not an extra storey added on top [*aufgestockt*], but on the contrary *is* the original essence of the truth as there."[28] We can readily see why he should have made such a statement, for in terms of his later perspective it is not Dasein but language that is primal. In "Language" (first given as a lecture, in 1950 and 1951), which serves as the introductory essay of *On the Way to Language*, he makes clear his intention to reflect "on language itself, and on language only." Within this perspective, it is not Dasein that speaks but language. Consequently, to reflect on language "demands that we enter into the speaking of language in order to take up our stay with language, i.e., within *its* speaking, not within our own." And this speaking, furthermore, "takes place as that which grants an abode [*Aufenthalt*] for the Being of mortals" (*PLT*, pp. 190–191).

Here is a view of language radically different from that of *Being and Time;* and it is different because, with his discovery of Nietzsche and his consequent recognition of the derelict nature of present reality, he has opened up a void that only the creative power of the word can fill. "The word alone gives Being to the thing," says Heidegger in "The Essence of Language" (given as lectures in 1957–58 and published in 1959). This applies, says Heidegger, even to such a thing as sputnik, which could never have come into existence if the word of modern technology had not ordered man to take up its challenge (*OWL*, p. 62).

The aestheticist resonances of this view are clear. They become even clearer when one notes how persistently Heidegger attempts to identify language and poetry. His reflections on language in *On the Way to Language* all hinge on a consideration of language as it is displayed in poetry. He maintains, in "The Essence of Language" and elsewhere, that language does not manifest itself "as language" in everyday speaking, where the utilitarian concern with conveying information holds sway, but does so only in poetry, where such considerations are excluded (*OWL*, p. 59). This view may be compared to the notion, common to a certain strand of post-Romantic aesthetics, that art in general and the poem in particular are self-reflexive in character—that they are concerned with their own mode of speaking rather than with the content to be spoken. Think of Mallarmé, with his conception of literature as a kind of self-contained verbal ceremony, as a "Book" whose dense suggestiveness takes the whole of discourse into itself. Think of Northrop Frye, for whom literature constitutes a verbal universe that looks inward upon itself, with the sign-value of its constituent symbols subordinated to their role as elements in a structure of interconnected motifs. Such views have their origin in a distinctly Romantic sensibility, reflecting the Romantic artist's retreat from an uncongenial world into the sheltering product of his own aesthetic creativity. Notwithstanding his denial of his own Romantic ancestry, Nietzsche's notion of the artist as one who regards as content, as "the thing itself" (*die Sache selbst*), what the nonartist regards as form fits clearly within this tradition (*WP*, §818; *KGW*, 8. Abt., 2. Bd., pp. 251–252).

Heidegger, too, has links to Romantic thought, though he seems to engage in an almost calculated concealment of the Romantic connection. Still, he is not the virulent anti-Romantic that Nietzsche is, and it is entirely in keeping with this that he should begin his essay "The Way to Language" (1959) with a quotation from Novalis's *Monologues*: "The peculiar property of language, namely that language is concerned exclusively with itself—precisely this is known to no one" (*OWL*, p. 111). Heidegger holds that poetic language, and by extension language in general, speaks in order to say nothing other than its own saying. (Compare this with the opinion of certain philosophers of art who hold that just this sort of purposeful yet purposeless saying is an essential characteristic of the work of art.) Equally indicative of an aesthetic connection is Heidegger's insistence that he does not wish to treat language as an object of scientific investigation but wishes rather to "undergo an experience" with it. (Compare this with Nietzsche's hope that we will "experience" the language of *Zarathustra*.) Here, too, the model for Heidegger's stance is aesthetic; for when we approach a work of art *qua* work of art, this is precisely what we do. We accept the work of art's assumptions, suspending, in the moment of appreciation, our disbelief. We treat fiction as if it were truth.

Also relevant is Heidegger's emphasis on mystery and enigma, which in his view are inseparable from the "Being" of language. These seem also to be inseparable from the "Being" of the work of art, for without enigma—without the establishing of a gulf between saying and meaning—how would we distinguish between a work of art and a mere statement of fact? And finally, of greatest importance, there are the notions of the abyss and of world-making, for this is the point at which Heidegger's reflection on language ceases to be merely "ontological" and becomes, instead, ontogenetic. Heidegger professes to find an abyss (*Abgrund*) in the sentence "Language speaks." But, he continues, when we fall into this abyss, "we do not go tumbling into emptiness"; on the contrary, "we fall upward, to a height. Its loftiness opens up a depth. The two span a realm in which we would like to become at home, so as to find a residence, a dwelling place for the life of man" ("Language," *PLT,* pp. 191–192). In the dereliction of the present (what Heidegger elsewhere refers to as "the age of the world's night"), man is without a dwelling place ("What are Poets For?" [written in 1946, published in 1950], *PLT,* p. 92). The task of language is to create such a dwelling place, to create a world in which man may once more live.

Heidegger's perspective, as I have here characterized it, builds on the earlier Nietzschean perspective. Both thinkers begin with an assumption of crisis. Both find in art, and ultimately in language, the means for overcoming this crisis. But Nietzsche, as we have seen, is uncertain about the new ground that he has created for himself. If he can on occasion declare that "it is enough to create new names and estimations and probabilities in order to create in the long run new 'things,'" he does not adhere steadily to such a view. Considered as an aestheticist, he is insufficiently utopian, insufficiently revolutionary in his perspective. Thus, one can read Nietzsche in nonaestheticist ways: as a pragmatist, an existentialist, a naturalist. But one can hardly read Heidegger in such ways—I mean, of course, the Heidegger of 1935 and after—for he is absolutely unequivocal about the role that language plays in constituting the world. As he puts it in "Language" (and similar statements appear repeatedly in his later writings): "In the naming, the things named are called into their thinging. Thinging, they unfold world, in which things abide and so are abiding ones" (*PLT,* pp. 199–200).

Moreover, particularly after 1945, all traces of voluntarism disappear from Heidegger's thought, so that we are not tempted, as we are with Nietzsche, to try to find our way back to the Zarathustrian creator of the new language. We move within language, as Heidegger tells us in *What Is Called Thinking?* (given as lectures in 1951–52, published in 1954; *WCT*, p. 192): it is not we who create language, but language that gives itself to us. On such grounds, there is no difference between language and reality—or, to use the Heideggerian formulation, between language and Being. Language speaks, and so does Being; Heidegger refers indiscriminately to the "Being of language" and the "language of Being." Thus, it is not a matter of a formal Apollonian language facing a disordered Dionysian reality and seeking to impart order to it (a modernist and structuralist view); rather, Dionysian and Apollonian, "nearness" and "distance," are both embodied within language itself—and within the world. We may thus say that language is both Hermetic and Orphic, creating self-referring structures of meaning at the same time that it generates, out of itself, worlds that are entirely new and unheard-of.

I do not believe that aestheticism can be logically refuted, nor, for that matter, do I believe that it can be logically established. It has the same exemption from (conventional) logical criteria that a consistent religious fideism has. Those who regard Heidegger's thought as a secularized version of religious faith are right in their assessment of him, even though they do not, to my mind, go far enough toward establishing precisely what kind of faith is here envisaged. But if aestheticism thus shares with fideism an exemption from logical criteria, it also has within itself a persistent tendency to overstep what those who do not share its perspective can only regard as its proper boundaries. In so doing, it makes statements regarding the nature of its own enterprise—and, more importantly, regarding the nature of the world—that an "ordinary" perspective is forced to reject. Aestheticism adopts the "extraordinary" perspective of unconstrained aesthetic creation and apprehension: a perspective which, as I have already noted, seeks to put us "somewhere else than we usually tend to be." From an "ordinary" point of view, this amounts to an obfuscation, concealing from us the world as it really is by substituting for that world an imagined creation. From this point of view, were aestheticism to acknowledge its creations as fictively separate from the world in which we live our lives—were it to remain, in short, within the territory of the work of art—nothing could be said against it. Alternatively, were it to retain its ontogenetic pretensions while remaining entirely silent about them, it would be equally safe from cavil.

A comparison with Wittgenstein suggests itself. While I can only touch on the affinity between Wittgenstein and Heidegger, not explore it in detail, it is clear that they confront many of the same issues and in some ways come close to each other. For example, when Wittgenstein observes, on the next-to-last page of the *Tractatus,* that "it is not *how* things are in the world that is mystical, but *that* it exists," he is making a supremely Heideggerian point. Yet, there is an important difference between the two, leading Wittgenstein away from aestheticism; for where Heidegger chooses language or poetry, Wittgenstein chooses silence. The mystical, Wittgenstein avers, "cannot be put into words," and must consequently be passed over in silence: *Wovon man nicht sprechen kann, darüber muss man schweigen.* In short, Wittgenstein has a much more explicit sense of what he calls "the limits of language" than does Heidegger. He thus turns aside, in the *Tractatus,* from the way of Heidegger, just as he also does, somewhat differently, in the later *Philosophical Investigations.*[29]

To be sure, I do not want to overemphasize this difference between the two thinkers. After all, it can be convincingly argued that Heidegger's poetry is a form of silence, and Wittgenstein's silence a form of poetry. Still, by the very fact that he opts for words rather than for silence, Heidegger exposes himself to the particular force and bias of those words. He himself seems to have glimpsed this, for he notes in "The Onto-Theo-Logical Constitution of Metaphysics" that "the difficulty lies in language. Our Western languages are languages of metaphysical thinking, each in its own way" (*I&D,* p. 73). Yet, he declines to acknowledge the applicability of this statement to his own case. More than this, in accordance with his tendency to see himself as coming out of "the tradition," with its sequence of "great dead philosophers" offering us "words of Being,"[30] rather than (more modestly) out of his own particular time and place, he fails to acknowledge that the most telling compulsions on his thought are the most immediate ones, those connected with his own experience as a German philosophy student and teacher coming to maturity in the years before, during, and after World War I.

Privileged texts

We thus return, though from a slightly different perspective, to an issue broached in Chapter 3. If Heidegger's indenture to his own cultural beginnings is clear in his articulation of the notion of crisis, it is equally clear in his choice of certain literary texts as especially significant, and in the peculiar twists that, for all his claims to have gone beyond interpretation, he gives to them. The list of poets with whom he engages in "dialogue" is quite short: the major names are Rilke, Trakl, George, and, above all, Hölderlin. One Heideggerian commentator has averred that "the preferential value judgments implicit in Heidegger's choices for exposition and illumination are less crucial than the results he obtains from these choices."[31] This is disingenuous: both the "choices for exposition" and the "results" are indicators of a certain cultural milieu, of a certain *Weltanschauung*. More specifically, they are indicators of Heidegger's indebtedness to a view of art and literature of which the members of the George circle were, in Heidegger's time, perhaps the most important proselytizers. Behind this view lies the shift evident in early twentieth-century literature (especially German literature) from the naturalistic description of social conditions to the expression of subjective and highly personal visions. "The poet" came to see himself not as a detached and objective observer of the everyday world but as a seer, shattering the bounds of quotidian experience by bringing us intimations of a deeper, more intense reality. In short, we find the emergence of a neo-Romantic orientation in literature. This new orientation took up and intensified one aspect of the Romantic heritage, and did so within the context of a bourgeois, urban, industrial, bureaucratic society that it saw as utterly common and mediocre.

It is with such a notion of poetry that the later Heidegger works, both when he refers, as he does in the middle 1930s, to the "essence" of poetry, and when, a few years later, he begins to focus on the alleged convergence of "poetry" and "thinking." But it is not every poet that satisfies Heidegger's criteria; only some do. The poets (taking that term in its broadest sense) who draw his accolades turn out to be those who champion the radically personal and who engage in, or can be interpreted as engaging in, a nostalgic withdrawal from the present. Obviously, this eliminates from consideration much of the corpus of Western literature. For example, although Heidegger professes an admiration for Homer, the *Iliad* and the *Odyssey* would nonetheless have proved highly resistant to his peculiar mode of Being-discovery or Being-invention. In the first place, the personal in Homer is unproblematic and hence unexplored. Secondly—and this follows almost necessarily—the utopian, idealistic element, whether nostalgic or imaginative, is lacking. Even more difficult would be an Heideggerian interpretation of, say, Dickens, or other modern writers of a primarily realistic or mimetic orientation. Certainly, the enterprise *could* be carried out, as a *tour de force* dependent on a judicious selection of proof texts, freely interpreted. Derrida has done as much. Heidegger, in contrast, prefers to focus on poets whom he sees as congenial to his own vision.

Heidegger's most important "choice for exposition" is Hölderlin (1770–1843), whom he comes close to deifying. Significantly, Hölderlin was "rediscovered" by George and his circle in the years immediately preceding World War I. Especially important in this rediscovery was Norbert von Hellingrath, who set about the task of bringing out a complete edition of Hölderlin's works. It is fateful that Hellingrath—to whose memory Heidegger, in 1936, would dedicate "Hölderlin and the Essence of Poetry"—was killed in battle before completing his work, for this became part of a growing myth of Hölderlin as the great hero of German nationalism. Hölderlin was first Fichteanized, then Nazified; under the Third Reich, specialists in *Germanistik* praised him for embodying the leadership principle, for recognizing an absolute division between the German race and all others, and for founding a new, German religion. This process reached its height (along with the Third Reich itself) in 1943, with the establishment of the Hölderlin Society under the patronage of Dr. Joseph Goebbels.[32] Heidegger himself, I must point out, did not take up this aspect of the Hölderlin myth: his attachment was not to the mighty fatherland but to the more intimate and personal native region, not the *Vaterland* but the *Heimat*. Instead, he emphasizes the notion of Hölderlin as seer and prophet.

In an essay of 1919, George praised Hölderlin as "the great seer of his *Volk*"—one who, in his later writings, was "the founder of a new line." Hölderlin's merit was in his rediscovery of Dionysus and Orpheus, and in his consequent championing, against factual description and a critical, skeptical tone, of the life-giving powers of the word. As the "rejuvenator of the language and thereby the rejuvenator of the soul," he stands as "the cornerstone of the imminent German future," calling (or calling forth) "the New God."[33] Heidegger's Hölderlin closely resembles George's, except that Heidegger tends to interpret Hölderlin in world-historical rather than in merely German terms. According to Heidegger, Hölderlin is "*the poet of the poet*," one who in fact establishes the essence of poetry and who thus has a greater claim on our attention than such estimable figures as Homer, Sophocles, Virgil, Dante, Shakespeare, and Goethe. For it is Hölderlin who, in establishing poetry, "first determines a new time"—the time of "the flown gods *and* of the approaching god" that, as we have seen, plays such an important role in Heidegger's reading of the present ("Hölderlin and the Essence of Poetry," *E&B*, pp. 270–271, 289). Or, as Heidegger says in "What Are Poets For?", Hölderlin is "the pre-cursor of poets in a destitute time. This is why no poet of this world era can overtake him" (*PLT*, p. 142).

Even when one acknowledges that in the second of the above quotations Heidegger is comparing Hölderlin only with other modern poets, this remains an astonishingly high assessment of one who, incapacitated by mental illness for most of his life, failed to attain, many would think, his full promise as a poet. It is part of Heidegger's neo-Romanticism that he should regard Hölderlin's madness as evidence of the depth of his vision as a seer. Hölderlin saw more clearly than his contemporaries, and was in consequence driven insane—or, as Heidegger delicately phrases it, was "received into the protection of the night of madness" (E&B, p. 282). Thus, as also happened with Nietzsche, the poet's insanity contributes to the myth of his transcendent genius. Also worth noting is how similar Heidegger's assessment of Hölderlin is to Nietzsche's assessment of Zarathustra: both figures are brought up against the great, creative figures of the past, who are found wanting.

There is no denying the existence of important affinities between the historical Hölderlin and the Hölderlin that Heidegger invents. For example, one does find in Hölderlin a sense of crisis. We have seen how the idea of an historical turning makes an appearance in Hegel; indeed, the notion seemed a plausible induction from the apparently world-shaking reality of the French Revolution and the Napoleonic conquests. With Hölderlin, however, the sense of crisis acquires a more markedly nostalgic bias than it has for Hegel. This is evident in his poem "Bread and Wine," a favorite of Heidegger's, where he evokes the "happy land of the Greeks" and regrets the passing of the thrones, temples, songs, and oracles that ruled over Greek life.[34]

Along with this sense of loss comes a diffuse and undefined but nonetheless very powerful religiosity, for Hölderlin regrets most of all the withdrawal of the Greek gods, gods who came down to men instead of keeping themselves, as the Christian god does, at a remote distance. Hölderlin's lament at this state of affairs reminds one of Hegel's discussion of the "depopulation of Heaven" in the *Phenomenology of Spirit,* except that for Hegel the death of the Greek gods—their return from the earth "into the unitary being of Zeus"—does not mark a moment of decline; instead, it marks a further advance in the self-consciousness of spirit.[35] Heidegger interprets this difference in his own way when he observes in *An Introduction to Metaphysics* that although both Hegel and Hölderlin assisted in "the rediscovery of the authentic Greek spirit" (which they were able to do, says Heidegger, because they were both under the spell of Heraclitus), Hegel "drew a line" under the Greek past, whereas Hölderlin "looked forward and opened up the way to the future" (*IM,* p. 126). This future would involve, in some way, a return to Greek experience.

Finally, with his poignant longing for the (alleged) Greek past,

Hölderlin could not help regarding the present as abandoned and derelict. "But, my friend, we have come too late," he declares; though the gods
are living, they are "over our heads ... up in a different world."[36] This
well accords with the Heideggerian vision of the present—the vision of a
purely technocratic age from which all possibility of divinity and art has
receded, yet which, in its very dereliction, offers up the promise of a radical return.

But despite the affinities, Hölderlin ought rather to be regarded as a
pretext for Heidegger's commentaries than as a text. Like Heidegger, I
shall refrain from entering the territory of "Hölderlin research."[37] I shall
merely point out that through selective quotation and through a highly
strained interpretation of Hölderlin's words, Heidegger, like George, constructs a fictional Hölderlin who is a radical intensification of certain aspects of the actual historical figure. Heidegger declares in the preface to
the fourth edition of *Illuminations of Hölderlin's Poetry* that his reflections on Hölderlin "arise out of a necessity of thinking."[38] But this seems
disingenuous. He claims to be engaging in a dialogue with the poet, but
the exchange has rather the character of a monologue. One is struck by
the implicit political radicalism, utterly ignored by Heidegger, of the
young Hölderlin's *Death of Empedocles,* whose hero sinned by profaning
the divine. As for Heidegger's notion that the apparent schizophrenia of
the older Hölderlin had some connection with his destiny as a seer, this
seems little short of mockery.

Nor is it only on Hölderlin that Heidegger practiced such reinterpreta-
tions: his writings on the pre-Socratics, for example, are said to be
marked by an even greater spirit of invention (he is helped here by the
exiguousness of the pre-Socratic texts). One could appeal, in fact, to the
work of a small army of scholars, each of whom manages to show that
Heidegger is mistaken about one or another historical text or personage.
A model in this genre is Robert Minder's devastating study of Heidegger's
treatment, in *Hebel—der Hausfreund* (1957), of the minor Alemannic
poet Johann Peter Hebel (1769–1863). Minder demonstrates that
Heidegger's account, shot through with pseudo-Wagnerian profundities
and echoing the language of various Nazi poets and publicists, completely
misconstrues the social and political—not to say literary—significance of
Hebel's work.[39]

But the most telling attack on Heidegger—and this because it comes
not from the realm of conventional scholarship but from an intellectual
confrère—is to be found in Derrida's essay "Restitutions of Truth in
Painting." Derrida starts off from a "conventional" scholarly attack on

Heidegger, an essay by Meyer Schapiro in which the renowned art historian discusses Heidegger's account of van Gogh's painting of the peasant shoes. Schapiro points out that there is nothing to suggest that the pair of shoes belongs to a peasant, let alone (as Heidegger asserts) to a peasant woman. On the contrary, the evidence indicates that the shoes in question belonged to van Gogh himself.[40] Derrida takes Schapiro to task for thinking that the shoes are "clearly" van Gogh's "own" and for assuming that they are a pair and not two odd shoes somehow thrown together. But much of the weight of his attack falls on Heidegger himself, who in Derrida's view remains attached to conceptions of property and of proximity that his own thought calls into question. Heidegger claims to have situated himself "in the nearness of the work" [*in der nähe des Werkes*], but, as Derrida points out, there are "pathetico-fantasmico-ideologico-political investments" tied up with the world that Heidegger seeks to invoke in the painting. Why should the shoes belong to peasants? Why should they not be claimed by "armed phantoms, or an immense wave of deportees trying to find again their name"? Why, indeed, should the shoes "return to" or "be attached to" anyone at all? Why not rather "the bottomless memory of a dispossession, of an expropriation, of a spoliation"? "And tons of shoes piled there, the pairs mixed up and lost" (*VenP,* esp. pp. 355, 377, 409). In short: why *this* truth—why any truth at all—from the work of art, from poetry, from language?

Subjectivity and insight

In seeking to defend Heidegger against his scholarly and antischolarly attackers, one can counter with the observation that every interpretation is subjective, and that what really matters is not the partiality of vision that this subjectivity betokens but rather the degree of insight that it can bring despite (or because of) its partiality. Certainly, there are insights to be derived from Heidegger's various encounters with works of art and literature. Steiner, for example, has suggested that Heidegger's commentaries on George's poem "Das Wort" in the essay "Words," and on Trakl's "Ein Winterabend" in "Language," are especially illuminating.[41] And even when the harmony between poem and commentary is not so evident as in these two instances, Heidegger does manage to expand our sensitivity to the works that he examines.

Our post-Romantic conception of the work of art as something that can bear a multitude of meanings runs here in Heidegger's favor. In reading Hölderlin's "Bread and Wine" or in looking at van Gogh's painting of the shoes, we are willing to go a long way in Heidegger's direction. The poem could, after all, refer to a "destitute time," in Heidegger's sense; the shoes could belong to a peasant (as Derrida points out, van Gogh sometimes did paint peasant shoes [*VenP*, p. 414]). Moreover, there is the fact that Heidegger's commentaries, whatever the degree of their plausibility or implausibility, become part of the web of associations surrounding the works on which they comment and thus add to the richness of their perception. In the wake of Duchamp, we can hardly look at the "Mona Lisa" in quite the same way we did before, nor, in the wake of Heidegger and Derrida, can we have quite the same attitude toward Hölderlin or van Gogh.

But the matter goes far beyond the question of our attitude toward works of art. At the end of the "Letter on Humanism," Heidegger succinctly characterizes the mode of thought that he wishes to practice: "It is time to break the habit of overestimating philosophy and of thereby asking too much of it. What is needed in the present world crisis is less philosophy, but more attentiveness to thinking; less literature, but more cultivation of the letter." This new thinking, he continues, thinks "more originally" than philosophy. Laying aside any claim to absolute knowledge, it engages in a more modest task—it "gathers language into simple saying [*das einfache Sagen*]." In so doing, it "lays inconspicuous furrows in language. They are still more inconspicuous than the furrows that the farmer, slow of step, draws through the field" (*HBW*, pp. 241–242).

This notion of thinking as laying "inconspicuous furrows in language" is profound and telling, for it points toward the function of art in our world. How is it that art is necessary to human beings (evoking here Hegel's notion of the necessity of art)? Let us think of our imaginary novelist. Sitting down each morning before a blank sheet of paper, he creates a new and unheard-of world, the world of the novel that he writes. For all its mysteries, this world will connect in various ways with the world we already know. If the novelist is master of his art, the world that he creates will enable us to understand matters that we did not hitherto know, or knew only dimly and inarticulately. The novelist furrows his page with language, taking what is given and out of that givenness creating something new.

But this is not all. For far from leaving language as it was, the writer adds to it new possibilities of thought and feeling and thereby opens up new experiences to those who speak it and are sensitive to its nuances. One thinks of the impact of Shakespeare and Milton on the English language, Molière's impact on the French, Luther's on the German. In each instance the language, and the minds of the language's speakers, were subtly altered.

And it can be argued that sculptors and painters and composers work the same miracle, that by the creation of new languages they open up new possibilities of experience to those who encounter their works.

It is clear that Heidegger views his enterprise on the model of the artist's. Artists do lay furrows in language: the whole interest of their work resides in this task. In *An Introduction to Metaphysics*, Heidegger tells his listeners that philosophy is "one of the few autonomous creative possibilities and at times necessities of man's historical Dasein." As such, it is "always the concern of the few. Which few? The creators, those who initiate profound transformations. It spreads only indirectly, by devious paths that can never be laid out in advance, until at last, at some future date, it sinks to the level of a commonplace; but by then it has been forgotten as original philosophy." Philosophy's task, Heidegger continues, is not to provide a foundation on which a nation can build its historical life and culture. Nor is it to act as a unifying cultural force by giving us a systematic view of the world or by laying the theoretical foundations of the sciences. Rather, philosophy should be seen as "a thinking that breaks the paths and opens the perspectives of the knowledge that sets the norms and hierarchies, of the knowledge in which and by which a people fulfills itself historically and culturally, the knowledge that kindles and necessitates all inquiries and thereby threatens all values" (*IM*, pp. 9–10). This notion of philosophers as "creators" initiating "profound transformations" by "devious paths" is strikingly akin to Nietzsche's notion of the "*artist-philosopher*." Like Nietzsche, Heidegger attributes an immense power to the poet-thinker.

And yet, there are difficulties here. We are again reminded of Shelley's characterization of poets as "the unacknowledged legislators of the world." In Shelley, however, this notion has a specificity and a restraint that we do not find in Heidegger and Nietzsche; for in the aestheticist Nietzsche and in the later Heidegger, the realm of the given, of the natural, is left out of account. Nietzsche can aver that we ourselves create "the world that concerns man"; in Heidegger, with his notion of the radical impersonality of art, "man" disappears entirely from sight, and language alone—its "shifting ground," its "billowing waters" (*WCT*, p. 192)—is left. Both thinkers engage in a *metabasis* that confuses the realm of art, where everything is indeed at the call of our creativity and our language, with the realm of what is not art. Admittedly, much of the human world *is* a human construction: the notion of the "social construction of reality" is true and important. But, read literally, Nietzsche and the later Heidegger go significantly beyond such a view. For, firstly, their notion is one of

creation rather than of construction, while, secondly, there is nothing social in what they have to say. Theirs is the vision of intellectuals who wish
to believe that words, and words alone, will make the waters part and the
ground move beneath our feet. Such will indeed happen—in the world of
art. But the intransigent world of the nonaesthetic is more than the sum of
its rhetorics.

In Nietzsche and the later Heidegger, we see a radical idealism that is
radical only in idea. Nietzsche is explicit about the subjectivity of his project: his "try me" is a "try *me*." Heidegger, a further development of aestheticism, is not. Heidegger wants us to undergo an "experience with
language"; and undergoing this experience, we will "thereupon become
transformed . . . from one day to the next or in the course of time" ("The
Essence of Language," *OWL*, p. 57). This is certainly in part right: our
use of language does alter us. But we need to ask some questions about
this experience that Heidegger does not entertain, such as "whose language?" and "to what end?" And we need to ask, moreover, what will be
transformed and what left exactly as it was before.

Of crucial importance in this regard is *Gelassenheit* (1959), a work
that epitomizes, if anything can, the Heidegger of the 1950s and 1960s.
Here he argues, more forcefully and succinctly than he does anywhere
else, that the modern age is devoid of thought. We are dominated, he
maintains, by a "calculative thinking," a thinking that is entirely technological, that concerns itself solely with the imposition of man's will upon
the world. In calculative thinking, in the hustle and bustle of the present
day, we never really think. Calculative thinking, Heidegger concedes, is
indispensable; but instead of stopping and collecting itself, it "races from
one prospect to the next." In Heidegger's eyes, it is in fact a flight from
thinking—from the recollective, meditative thinking of which he regards
himself as the spokesman. Speaking in 1955, he links this thoughtlessness
to the new and more advanced modes of communication and transportation that have now come into use and have served to uproot men in general, and Germans in particular, from their native soil. Some Germans
have been driven from their homelands; but even those who have not are

> often . . . still more homeless. . . . Hourly and daily they are chained to radio
> and television. Week after week the movies carry them off into uncommon,
> but often merely common, realms of the imagination, and give the illusion
> of a world that is no world. Picture magazines are everywhere available. All
> that with which modern techniques of communication stimulate, assail,
> and drive man—all that is already much closer to man today than his fields
> around his farmstead, closer than the sky over the earth, closer than the

change from night to day, closer than the conventions and customs of his village, than the tradition of his native world.

Man, in short, has been uprooted, and this uprootedness has taken him away from the sphere of meditative thought, of recollection ("Memorial Address," *DT,* pp. 45–49).

What, then, is to be done? Shall we root out all evidence of technology? Shall we smash our radios and television sets? Shall we abandon our automobiles and trudge to our (nonexistent) native villages, there to take up, in the traditional manner, the cultivation of the land? Not at all. For in Heidegger's view, the "forces of technology" have "moved long since beyond [man's] will and have outgrown his capacity for decision." Man did not make the forces of technology and therefore cannot destroy them. I repeat the question: what is to be done? In simplest terms, nothing at all—indeed, to *do* anything would be to fall victim to the very preoccupation with willing that has brought us to our sorry pass. Our need is rather to practice what Heidegger calls a "releasement toward things," a "*Gelassenheit zu den Dingen,*" that leaves the machinery in place. This, in Heidegger's eyes, will be quite enough, for

> we can affirm the unavoidable use of technological devices, and also deny them the right to dominate us, and so to warp, confuse, and lay waste our nature. But will not saying both yes and no in this way to technical devices make our relation to technology ambivalent and insecure? On the contrary! Our relation to technology will become wonderfully simple and relaxed. We let technical devices enter our daily life, and at the same time leave them outside, that is, let them alone, as things which are nothing absolute but remain dependent upon something higher. I would call this comportment toward technology which expresses "yes" and at the same "no," by an old word, releasement toward things. (*DT,* p. 54.)

To Heidegger's reflections here, one also has to say both a "yes" and a "no." In a literal sense, one clearly has to say "no." Stanley Rosen observes that "ontological *Gelassenheit* means an acceptance of or submission to history, now called Historicity.... The ontic consequence is to counsel resignation to whatever forces dominate in human history."[42] To be sure, one can see what is bothering Heidegger, for within a bureaucratic, technocratic culture that tends continually to separate us from the consequences of our actions, banality, in Arendt's usage of the term, is a constant threat. But Heidegger's response to the problem shares something of this same banality. It is entirely in the spirit of this response that, as we have seen, he declares in the *Der Spiegel* interview that only a god can save us: "*Nur noch ein Gott kann uns retten.*" Thus does an uncritical idealism lead to an equally uncritical positivism; thus does a thought without reality issue in a reality without a thought, a reality simply left as it is. Heidegger inculcates a quietism. This quietism is dangerous: those who think that the forces of technology lie utterly beyond human control are likely to find that this is in fact the case; those who believe that only a god can save them will likely need such salvation.

But I do not think that quietism is the main danger of Heidegger's thought. For I would argue that a Heideggerian activism risks equal danger. It is not simply a matter of rejecting the passive for the active mode. It is a matter of moving beyond Heidegger's utopian idealism toward an understanding of the forces, structures, passions, and desires at work in the real world. (Admittedly, the world in question is the "ordinary" world, not Heidegger's "extraordinary" world.) The danger, in short, lies in the tendency of Heidegger's utopianism to obscure this world, enveloping it in a utopian haze. Heidegger is a poor guide for those who want to grasp how the "ordinary" world operates. His archaizing idealism tempts one into ignoring the forms of social, economic, and political power at work within it. If this sounds like a defense of an intelligent empiricism against Heidegger's utopianism, this is indeed what it is.

Yet, on the other hand, one must also say "yes" to Heidegger. In the preface to *Identity and Difference* (1957), Heidegger himself says that "here nothing can be explained, but much may be pointed out" (*I&D*, p. 22). This suggests, in fact, a reading of Heidegger that is ironic and distanced rather than pedestrian and literal. Much of what Heidegger says can plausibly be considered to be true. For example, it surely does matter for our lives what attitude we adopt toward "technological devices" and toward technology in general. Moreover, Heidegger's vision of a completely different order—an order free from "one-dimensionality," from "banality"—is surely itself a critical instrument, something that helps us see the limitations of the society in which we live. Like all prophets, Heidegger summons us to a transformation of our way of being in the world. Such summonses are perhaps impossible to translate into literal terms. But for all that, they should not be ignored.

PART III

Michel Foucault and the Activism of Discourse

Henceforth . . . it is the world that becomes culpable (for the first time in the Western world) in relation to the work; it is now arraigned by the work, obliged to order itself by its language, compelled by it to a task of recognition, of reparation. . . .

—*Foucault*

CHAPTER 5

Foucault and Structuralism

The perspective that Nietzsche suggests and that the later Heidegger then unequivocally adopts finds further expression in the brilliant, speculative, and in some ways deeply disturbing writings of Michel Foucault (b. 1926). Foucault stands as an heir to the diverse thoughts of his two great predecessors. However much he may differ from them in detail, he accepts their fundamental assumption of cultural crisis, of a derelict present, of a nothing out of which everything must be created. The presuppositions of his historiography lie in crisis thought (in the present essay, I am much more concerned with these presuppositions than I am with the historiography itself). He actively cultivates the idea and the reality of crisis. It is his evident wish to leave the extant world in ruins. He regards himself as a critic and an ontologist, but his ontology is the ontology of his own language, and he views criticism not in the conventional sense of a project designed to bring us to the haven of understanding, but in the poststructuralist (and, I might add, etymologically defensible) sense of "to put into crisis."

There is a peculiarly morbid glee in this. One commentator has referred, in an apt image, to Foucault's *böse Blick*—his malign glance.[1] Another observes that his aim is to turn the present into a past.[2] This statement is understood in its full force only when one grasps its extremity—that it is every present, in all its aspects, that is called to judgment and condemnation: the present as such is brought under attack. With a thinker such as this, it is hardly surprising that among the things he breaks are his own rules, which he regularly (or irregularly) reformulates and then breaks again. Equally frustrating is his persistent misuse and misinterpretation of texts, including those by writers who in important respects share his own perspective.

But to accuse him, on these grounds, of intellectual irresponsibility is to miss the point, for he is not engaging (as such accusations tend to assume) in "normal" intellectual discourse. Foucault does not adhere to the normal intellectual rules because he does not want to write texts that can be neatly fitted into a preexisting genre or tradition. He does not want to write such texts because this would undermine their critical function as he conceives it. He wants his texts to go out into the world and, by the power of their rhetoric, to change it. It is not the text but the activity that is central for Foucault; the former is merely a tool. Moreover, it is a tool whose efficacy tends to be undermined by the operations of a demystifying criticism. The authority of Foucault's discourse lies in the fact that it is *not* understood—that for all its apparent concern with changing the present, the content of that change remains enigmatic. Thus, his texts can be many things to many people, appealing to all who perceive a defectiveness in the existing order.

Since Foucault claims to be articulating a rhetoric that moves out beyond the text into the complex world, it is not surprising that the task of articulating a plausible characterization of his work is difficult. What is one to do with a thinker who regards his writings as bombs directed against extant reality, who wants them to "self-destruct after use, like fireworks" (as he tells us in an interview of the mid-seventies)?[3] And yet, it is possible, I think, to lay down some markers that will guide us in our confrontation with him. Though I shall greatly qualify this notion as I proceed, I nonetheless find it useful as an initial approximation to view Foucault as a synthesis of his two critical/ontological predecessors, Heidegger and Nietzsche. Viewing him from this perspective, one sees him as lying both "between" and "beyond" Nietzsche and Heidegger. One sees him as adding to the Nietzschean affirmation and to the Heideggerian negation of that affirmation a distinctly original negation of the negation. Since in such a view Foucault ends up by reaffirming Nietzsche, it is not surprising that his Nietzscheanism turns out to be blatantly obvious. He makes no secret of this debt. He has repeatedly noted the Nietzschean precedent for what he is doing, identifying Nietzsche as the first practitioner of a form of thought that is now, after many diversions, becoming decisive. Nietzsche offers us, he suggests, both the promise and the task of a postanthropological future; he "marks the threshold beyond which contemporary philosophy can begin thinking again," and will "no doubt continue for a long while to dominate its advance" (*MC*, pp. 353/342).

Foucault's Heideggerianism, on the other hand, seems almost willfully concealed, just as Heidegger's Romanticism does. Unlike Derrida, Foucault has never invoked (indeed, rarely even mentions) Heidegger's name. Until recently, his commentators have maintained an equally deafening silence about a thinker with whom Foucault has such a strange and compelling affinity.[4] The fact that the Heideggerian elements in Foucault remain concealed is in part attributable to the complexity and concealedness of Heidegger's thought, so that Foucault's readers, even the most diligent among them, are simply not attuned to the muffled echoes of Heidegger that make themselves heard in his text.

But more importantly, the echoes *are* muffled. The relationship between the two thinkers is inherently antithetical. Heidegger, as I have suggested, is the thinker whose thought Foucault negates. Though the two remain within the same intellectual territory, with the same assumption of radical crisis, Foucault nonetheless appears in many respects to be virtually Heidegger's opposite. We have seen that Heidegger ends in a quietism, in an attitude of letting "beings" be. Foucault, in apparent contrast, is a radical activist, engaging in what seems to be an unending attack on the world as it is; he is, or appears to be, a revolutionary. To shift the focus slightly, Heidegger seems fascinated by the nostalgic side of Nietzsche, turning toward an ideal past that remains hidden in the dark mists of pre-Socratic time, whereas Foucault embraces the imaginative side, seeking to discover or invent a "mythos of the future." Of course, we have already observed that this division between the imaginative and the nostalgic is by no means absolute, for Heidegger's ideal past presents itself to us as a future, while Foucault's "future thought" (*MC,* pp. 398/386) turns out, in some undefined way, to have the aspect of a return. Nor is this surprising, for the ideal past and the ideal future have in common an immense hostility to the present order.

An intellectual milieu

Yet, it is also necessary to point out that some important new preoccupations, absent from or only dimly suggested by Nietzsche and Heidegger, come into play in Foucault. Thus, it is not entirely fair to consider Foucault as merely the third moment in a Nietzschean-Heideggerian dialectic. To a large extent, these new preoccupations have their matrix in French, and more specifically in Parisian intellectual life in the period following World War II. Were this an "influence" study, I would be concerned with exploring this milieu in detail. But my aim here is less to explain how our protagonists arrived at their ideas than it is to display these ideas (however they were arrived at), to lay bare the underlying assumptions, to point out the affinities with other, more familiar thought, to account for rhetorical impact, and finally to criticize—in the conventional sense. In influence studies, one runs the risk of becoming so caught up in the pursuit of connections that one fails to articulate an independent critical perspective, so that the historian's role completely overshadows the role of critic.

Moreover, Nietzsche, Heidegger, Foucault, and Derrida are all highly original thinkers. With such thinkers, one is constantly reminded how the whole tenor of the ideas being appropriated is altered in that very appropriation. This is perhaps most obvious in the relationship between Nietzsche and the Romantics. Though Nietzsche clearly takes over certain Romantic themes and motifs, it is equally clear that he is no Romantic. Foucault, too, appropriates and transforms. A detailed rendering of the intellectual context within which he emerged would undoubtedly help us to understand more fully certain features of his career. We would better see, for example, how it was possible for him to develop his distinctive, highly bravura, intellectual style; we would better see how this style was able to find a receptive audience. We would better understand, too, his relationship to other intellectuals in the same milieu, for we would have some sense of how they represent different developments of a shared intellectual tradition. But to describe and analyze Foucault's intellectual milieu is not to understand his work, which has a structure and rationale of its own. Even less is it to criticize that work, for criticism and the cataloguing of influence are two quite different things.

Nonetheless, we cannot avoid confronting certain aspects of this milieu. (As we shall see, it is a milieu that is important for Derrida as well, and I shall have more to say about it in Part IV.) Firstly, there is the impact of Hegel on French intellectuals in the period 1945–60. In this regard, one person was of special importance for Foucault: Jean Hyppolite (1907–68), his philosophy teacher at the *lycée* Henri IV and later at the Sorbonne. Hyppolite did more than any other figure (with the possible exception of Alexandre Kojève) to introduce a serious consideration of Hegel into French philosophy. His celebrated translation of the *Phenomenology* (published in 1939–41) and his monumental commentary on it (published in 1947) made Hegel accessible to the French. These works did so, moreover, at a time when the political impact of Marxism provided an impetus for studying Marx's Hegelian roots. Both Hyppolite and Kojève insisted on Hegel's decisive importance for modern thought. One can plausibly view Foucault's enterprise as an attempt to escape from Hegel; indeed, in his 1970 inaugural lecture at the Collège de France, *The Order of Discourse* (published in 1971), Foucault presents this as an important theme in his work (*OD*, p. 74).

The need to escape from Hegel presupposes a prior entrapment. The entrapment was partly a consequence of Hyppolite's activities. Foucault declares in *The Order of Discourse* that it was Hyppolite who gave us "this Hegelian presence" (*OD*, p. 76). In his eulogy for Hyppolite, delivered in 1969, he speaks more generally, declaring that "all the problems which are ours . . . it was he who established them for us."[5]

Secondly, it is also necessary to note the impact that the writings of Husserl and Heidegger had on French philosophers in this period. Contact with these two figures was frequently indirect, for the original texts were more often than not untranslated. Sometimes, as was the case with the Husserl manuscripts at Louvain, they were not conveniently available even in the original German. If anything, however, inaccessibility increased their prestige, and at the same time freed their French interpreters to engage in creative transformations of them.[6]

Admittedly, Foucault has frequently denied that he is a philosopher. He has gone so far as to suggest that he has "never concerned" himself with the subject.[7] But we shouldn't take these denials entirely at face value. It is quite true that he is usually not interested in working out in detail the philosophical background or implications of the notions that he advances. In consequence, to readers looking for this sort of analysis he is often sorely disappointing. His various statements on language, for example, seem at first glance philosophically promising. But when one tries to put them together, no coherent view emerges—no attempt to define the phenomenon "language" (in this respect, he closely resembles Nietzsche). Yet, philosophical resonances are there, even if usually hidden. After doing his *classe de philo* under a teacher so impressive as Hyppolite and then taking his first degree in philosophy, he could hardly be expected to shake off all such imprints on his thought. It is thus not surprising that his *Madness and Unreason: History of Madness in the Classical Age* should read like an oddly inverted Hegelian *Geistesgeschichte*. Nor is it surprising that in *The Order of Things: An Archaeology of the Human Sciences* he should comment extensively on what he sees as the state of philosophy in our time. These comments are all but incomprehensible unless one understands the decisive importance that a select group of philosophers—of which the most important figures are Descartes, Kant, Hegel, Husserl, and Heidegger—have for him; while the appeal that he makes to Nietzsche is in turn conditioned by his sense of the presence of these thinkers. In short, there is a "myth of the tradition" in Foucault. The tradition in question comes to him out of his early training within a philosophical milieu where these figures were considered important and other figures were either seen as unimportant or not thought about at all.

But we ought not confine ourselves, in this brief look at the intellectual milieu out of which Foucault emerged, to the domain of philosophy. We are told by a writer who seems well-informed on such matters that Foucault's friends, in the late 1940s and early '50s, were painters, writers, and musicians rather than philosophers.[8] This makes sense, for it is evident that the literary and artistic avant-garde has had a profound impact on Foucault's work. The figure who comes first to mind is Antonin Artaud (1896–1948), the actor, dramaturge, and poet. Artaud, who was himself confined for long periods as a patient in mental institutions, insisted on the affinity between genius and madness, situating himself among the company of other geniuses who had gone mad: Hölderlin, Nerval, Nietzsche, van Gogh. These names—and Artaud's—appear repeatedly in *History of Madness.* And yet, Artaud does not see the madman as bringing liberation. If the madman is the bearer of a subversive wisdom, he is also society's victim, one who cannot possibly escape from the oppression that society visits on him. This sense of the necessarily incomplete nature of subversion is central for Foucault as well. By its very existence, the excluded group (the insane, homosexuals, criminals) tends to subvert the extant social order. Yet, despite this, it cannot provide the nucleus for a future regenerate order. There is no ultimate social and political truth, no possibility of a final end to repression. Consciousness, in both Artaud and Foucault, is *in extremis,* and the condition is a permanent one. All one can do is struggle against this condition, engaging in a continual guerrilla warfare, in a political theater of cruelty directed against the existing order.

A second figure, hardly less important for Foucault, is Georges Bataille (1897–1962), whom Foucault has characterized as "one of the most important writers of his century."[9] This was a view generally shared by the French anti-Hegelians of the late 1960s and early '70s. Philippe Sollers, for example, remarked in 1972 that "our whole epoch is worked over by Artaud, by Bataille."[10] Educated at the École des Chartes, archivist at the Bibliothèque nationale, Bataille was a voraciously curious intellectual. Early in his career, he discovered Nietzsche, Hegel, and Heidegger, and he was connected with the Surrealists and other artistic and literary movements. Most of his writings touching on philosophy were directed against what he saw as the totalizing and normalizing tendencies of the Hegelian dialectic. An auditor at Kojève's influential lectures on Hegel in the 1930s, Bataille intensified Kojève's notion of the "violence" of the dialectic to such an extent that the dialectic itself was shaken apart. Against Hegel's "philosophy of absolute knowledge," he articulated a "philosophy of nonknowledge" that subjected the very idea of dialectical unity to attack. In this "philosophy," the notions of exhaustion, excess, limit, transgression, and play (in part borrowed from anthropologists' writings on the potlatch and on the incest taboo) were given prominence. Bataille's speculations appealed immensely to Foucault, evidently because they connected with his own interest in abnormality and exclusion.[11] Artaud and Bataille, along with a number of other writers of a similarly "excessive" character, gave Foucault the possibility of a rhetoric distinctly different from the earlier rhetorics of Nietzsche and Heidegger, a new, sophistic rhetoric in which the denial of truth, the awareness of transgression, the shock of perversity, and the proliferation of language are endlessly celebrated.

Finally, another aspect of Foucault's intellectual milieu having a significant impact on his writing was structuralism, which in various diverse forms (articulated by Claude Lévi-Strauss, Jacques Lacan, Roland Barthes, and Louis Althusser) began to take hold of the Parisian intellectual scene around 1960. These structuralisms (for there are other kinds as well) can be most succinctly characterized as attempts to move the center of intellectual concern away from the speaking subject and toward the structure of the language being spoken. But there were different ways of making this move, embodying intentions that were often opposed to one another. Hence, the "structuralist" label has been applied to intellectual commodities that differ radically in character. Part of my task in Part III will be to show in precisely what senses Foucault may and may not be regarded as a structuralist.

Foucault himself has vehemently denied that his work has any connection with structuralism. An especially irritable outburst occurs in the foreword to the English edition of *The Order of Things*, where he complains that "in France, certain half-witted 'commentators' persist in labelling me a 'structuralist.' I have been unable to get it into their tiny minds that I have used none of the methods, concepts, or key terms that characterize structural analysis" (*MC*, pp. —/xiv).

As we shall see, it is true that Foucault was never a structuralist in any narrow sense of the term. But in a broader sense, he certainly was—even though there was always a fundamentally antistructuralist element in his thought as well. (I here identify structuralism with the Apollonian, an identification that I shall explore shortly.)

Moreover, one is constantly struck by the "receptivity" of Foucault's writings, by which I mean their tendency to take up and exploit terminologies and preoccupations of the moment (a feature that has done much to ensure his continuing popularity). In the early and middle 1960s, structuralism was one such preoccupation. It is not at all surprising that in his writings of that period he uses a terminology that suggests a structuralist concern. In both *History of Madness* and *Birth of the Clinic,* he says that he is carrying out a "structural study" (*HF1,* p. vii/—*; *NC,* pp. xv/xix). In both works, he says that he is engaged in a search for the "fundamental structures of experience" (*HF1,* p. 633/—; *HF2,* p. 548; *NC,* pp. 201/ 199). And though *The Order of Things* differs in some important respects from these earlier works, it, too, is articulated in such a way as to suggest that some variety of structuralism is being deployed. It is quite true that in his subsequent writings all hints of structuralism disappear. But his en- counter with structuralism was an important part of his intellectual ca- reer in the 1960s. Moreover, this encounter casts a good deal of light on his relation to Nietzsche and Derrida.

History and crisis

What I have said so far indicates clearly enough that the lability of the Parisian intellectual scene is reproduced and even intensified in Foucault's own very diverse writings. How, then, are we to approach these writings? Obviously, one cannot write *finis* to the work of someone who is still very much alive† and may well continue to occupy the intellectual scene for years to come. Nonetheless, viewing Foucault from the standpoint of a still uncompleted present, we can tentatively see his work as falling into three more or less well-defined stages. It would be false to say that these stages are absolutely divided from one another. Rather, they are the prod- uct of several overlapping trajectories. A particular notion or preoccupa- tion makes its first appearance, is worked out in detail, and is finally aban-

---

*This characterization of Foucault's project does not appear in the English translation of *History of Madness,* which is a much-abridged version of the original.

†On June 25, 1984, while this book was in press, Michel Foucault died. He was fifty- seven years old.

doned, or at any rate assumes a position of lesser importance—yet remains apt to be resurrected later in some widely different context.

Foucault's first work of major interest is his *History of Madness* (1961). Very striking in this book is his concern with making madness speak again, with reawakening a contact with the "experience of madness" that the science of psychiatry (he says) has unfortunately cut off. *Birth of the Clinic: An Archaeology of Medical Perception* [*du regard médical*] (1963) is in many ways an addendum to *History of Madness*. It seeks to do for clinical medicine what the earlier work had already done, on a larger scale, for psychiatry. At the same time, it points forward, in its emphasis on "space" and on "the gaze" (*le regard*), to *The Order of Things* (1966) and to *The Archaeology of Knowledge* (1969).

In these latter works, the encounter with structuralism becomes important—all the more so because the notion of experience drops out of the picture, to be replaced by a concern with "language" or "discourse." In *History of Madness*, Foucault was able to talk about engaging in the "archaeology of a silence," for he still assumed that "experience" can exist independently of language (*HF1*, pp. ii/xi). In *The Order of Things* and *The Archaeology of Knowledge*, he no longer finds such a project intelligible. Hence, he turns in these works from the "structures of experience" to the structures of language. In *Michel Foucault: Beyond Structuralism and Hermeneutics*, Dreyfus and Rabinow refer to Foucault's writings of this period under the heading "the illusion of autonomous discourse."[12] I link this "illusion" to the aestheticism of Nietzsche and the later Heidegger.

Finally, there are Foucault's writings of the 1970s. Useful as an introductory statement is *The Order of Discourse* (1971). More important are *Discipline and Punish: The Birth of the Prison* (1975) and *The Will to Knowledge: History of Sexuality*, vol. 1 (1976). I find two conflicting tendencies in these writings. *Discipline and Punish* shows a concern with institutions—a concern that takes Foucault away from the discursive focus of his writings of 1963–69 and opens up real possibilities for a rapprochement with conventional historiography. On the other hand, in *The Will to Knowledge*, the focus on discourse is just as pervasive, and just as suggestive of "autonomy," as in the writings of the earlier period. In the present essay, I propose to emphasize what is still within the orbit of the "aestheticist" Nietzsche and Heidegger; correspondingly, I shall not pay much attention to the other possibilities that Foucault's recent work suggests. To be specific, I propose to view Foucault's preoccupation with "power" in these writings as a reprise of Nietzsche's notion of the will to power. This power manifests itself in a discourse through which it arbitrarily, and for its own purposes, engages in the invention of "truth." The relevant connection here is with the Nietzsche of "On Truth and Lie," with all its implications of discursive autonomy.

Foucault claims emphatically that his writings are either works of history *tout court* or else methodological treatises whose purpose is to make possible the writing of works of history.[13] But it must be understood that Foucault's "histories" are only arguably "about" the past. Ostensibly, his project is to describe the mechanisms of order and exclusion that have operated within European society since the sixteenth century, and above all since the late eighteenth century. In a motif that recalls Bataille's reflections on Hegel, Foucault sees a conflict in history between "the Same" and "the Other." Every "Same" needs an "Other" against which it can define itself, just as (in Kojève's exegesis of Hegel) every "master" needs a "slave."[14] When such an "Other" is absent, it must be invented. In *History of Madness*, Foucault recounts the story of how society, deprived of an excluded class by the disappearance of leprosy at the end of the Middle Ages, turned its attentions to the insane, whom it enclosed in mental asylums and subjected to the alienating objectivity of modern psychiatry. In *Birth of the Clinic*, he deals with the emergence of clinical medicine, which he sees as having placed bodily illness under the same sort of objectifying gaze. In *Discipline and Punish*, it is crime that now finds itself under the all-seeing eye, with criminals put under observation in prisons in the same way that the insane were placed under observation in mental hospitals and the organically ill in hospitals. And in *The Order of Things*, Foucault concentrates not on mechanisms of exclusion but on the oppressive "Same"—that is, on the modes of thought and discourse that the dominant order created for itself.

But the claim of these works to be "historical" is ambiguous. Admittedly, many of Foucault's readers do see his works as providing representations of the past. On the one hand, his more naive enthusiasts take these accounts of order and exclusion as accurate representations. On the other hand, his more naive opponents take these accounts as inaccurate representations. Thus, the conventionally historical objection to Foucault has the following form: Foucault is wrong about A, wrong about B, wrong about C, . . . and so on, with A, B, and C each standing for discrete aspects of the reality of the past. To be sure, many conventional historians have found Foucault's works brilliantly suggestive. It is clear that he has an almost unerring instinct for ferreting out important but neglected historical problems. But suggestiveness is one thing and accurate representation another—as his less naive followers are perfectly willing to concede. For the fact is that he rejects the regulative idea of conventional historiography, to present the past *wie es eigentlich gewesen ist.* Alternatively, he has maintained that he is engaged in writing "the history of the present" (*SP,* pp. 35/30–31). But even this statement cannot be taken at face value, for he seems as uninterested in representing the present as he is in representing the past. Rather, his prime concern seems to be in mounting a series of attacks against the existing order of things.

This radical hostility toward the existing order brings us to the notion of crisis in Foucault. The presence of the crisis notion in Foucault's historiography is indicated most clearly by his well-known penchant for seeing history as broken by a series of ruptures or discontinuities. This motif is already in place in *History of Madness* (*HF1,* p. 131/—; *HF2,* p. 120). But it will be better known to the average reader of Foucault through its appearance in *The Order of Things.* Here Foucault insists that the "mutation" from one "*episteme*" to the next is so radical as to be inexplicable. Elements of continuity, though not necessarily denied, are largely left out of Foucault's successive still photographs of the past. The usual explanation for this focus on discontinuity, in *The Order of Things* and in some of Foucault's subsequent works, is that he is trying to "destroy the privilege of the subject." This is true enough, but will perhaps be better understood if it is put in more specific terms: what he is actually doing is declaring his independence from Hegel—thereby showing, for all those declarations, how important a role Hegel plays in his thought. Hegel the dialectician sought to encompass the universe within the movement of the rational mind. Foucault the antidialectician challenges the Hegelian *homo dialecticus* ("La Folie, l'absence d'oeuvre," *HF2,* p. 576). Instead, he champions an antitotalizing thought that explicitly rejects any notion of a "world spirit" or even of a "European mind." Foucault here sees himself as following in the wake of Nietzsche, whose thought he rightly interprets as existing under the Zarathustrian sign of rupture ("Theatrum Philosophicum" [1970], *LCMP,* p. 195). Note, too, the affinity with Heidegger's notion, articulated in "The Onto-Theo-Logical Constitution of Metaphysics," of coming to grips with difference as difference, rather than trying to enclose it within identity (*I&D,* p. 47). There are clear echoes of this theme in *The Order of Things.*

It would be a mistake, however, to view Foucault's attack on continuity and his espousal of radical breaks in history as simply a conflict between the claims of totality and the claims of otherness. For the theme of breaks is also connected, as in Nietzsche and Heidegger, to the conception of the present as derelict. It is a sense of alienation from the present that underlies the rejection of representation: to "re-present" a reality is seen as, *ipso facto,* to legitimize it. We have seen how Nietzsche and Heidegger also turn aside from representation. Significantly, in both writers this move gets connected with an attack on conventional historiography. Thus, in "The Uses and Disadvantages of History," Nietzsche maintains that the only valuable historiography is one that seeks to provide life-enhancing myths, with any representational function subordinated to this more vital task. He uses a musical analogy here—the analogy, that is, of the least representational of all the arts. The real value of the historian's work, he asserts, lies "in its taking a familiar, perhaps commonplace theme, an everyday melody, and composing inspired variations on it, enhancing it, elevating it to a comprehensive symbol, and thus disclosing in the original theme a whole world of profundity, power, and beauty."[15] Nietzsche's rejection of representation in history is of a piece with his rejection of the *stilo rappresentativo* in opera, his rejection of naturalism in drama, and his rejection of the truth-conveying function of language (*BT,* chaps. 11, 19; *NBW,* pp. 69–75, 113–121; "On Truth and Lie," throughout). In short, we find Nietzsche arguing (though admittedly with some hesitancies) for the rejection of history as representation and its re-creation as literature, as poetry, as myth.

In Heidegger the hesitations disappear, and historiography in its conventional, representational sense is portrayed as unequivocally oppressive. Thus, Heidegger declares in "Overcoming Metaphysics" that if we were to construct a history of Being in accord with "*historiographical* representational thinking," this would simply confirm the oblivion of Being in the modern age (*EP,* pp. 92–93). In "The Anaximander Fragment," he is rather more illuminating on the question of precisely why this is so, for he here tells us that "all historiography predicts what is to come from images of the past determined by the present. It systematically destroys the future and our historic relation to the advent of destiny" (*EGT,* p. 17). Here we see that Heidegger's attack on conventional historiography is not simply an irritated reflex on his part toward all those conventional historians (historians of literature, historians of philosophy) who have challenged his textual interpretations. It arises rather from his fundamental conviction that the present is derelict in character.

This conviction leads in Heidegger to a radical passivity, to the notion that we ought to let beings be. Heidegger's position has political implications, though it denies its own political nature, for it amounts to nothing less than an acceptance—indeed, a confirmation—of the existing social and political order. But this is not the only option that a prophet of extremity can take up. A sense of crisis can lead one to wash one's hands of action, on the grounds that every action will become part of the present's degradation. But it can also translate itself into an unending action, whose point is not to bring into being a new present but rather to undermine any and all extant orders, past, present, and future. It is this option of radical criticism that Foucault chooses. In a 1976 lecture, he speaks of engaging in a kind of guerrilla warfare against the existing system. This warfare is carried out by "subjugated knowledges" undertaking "dispersed and discontinuous offensives." "Global, *totalitarian theories*" are to be viewed with suspicion, for they have an "inhibiting effect" on such struggles ("Two Lectures," *P/K*, p. 80). Here Foucault is speaking the language of precisely this sort of radical activism. For the point is that there will always be subjugated knowledges. Foucault's identification is not with any particular subjugated knowledge but with subjugated knowledge as such.

It is not at all surprising that Foucault should have taken up such a position, for the whole logic of his work, from *History of Madness* onward, points toward such an activism—just as the logic of Heidegger's work points toward a pure, atheoretical contemplation. Foucault views all claims to knowledge as irremediably tied up with the exercise of power. There is no such thing as an "objective" knowledge, no possibility of retreating into the Cartesian *poêle*. Any claims to objective knowledge, to valid theory, are merely attempts to exercise power of one sort or another. The corollary of this is that theory has no status as theory; on the contrary, it is nothing other than practice. As Foucault puts it in a 1972 conversation with Gilles Deleuze, "theory does not express, translate, or serve to apply practice: it *is* practice" (*LCMP*, p. 208).

On these grounds, one might expect Foucault to engage in a "theoretical practice" (cf. Althusser) designed to advance the interests of some particular class or group within society. But he does not do so. This is partly because there is no group with which he can "identify" himself, for every group is part of the degraded order that he seeks to destroy. But there is more to his position than this, for his failure to adopt an Althusserian or, more generally, Marxist strategy derives ultimately from his rejection of theory itself. In a 1971 interview with a group of radical *lycéens*, he advises: "Reject all theory and all forms of general discourse. This need for theory is still part of the system we reject" ("Revolutionary Action: 'Until Now,' " *LCMP*, p. 231). Finally, on the broadest level of significance, Foucault's rejection of theory (and his rejection of representation—for theory is merely a peculiarly stylized type of representation) can be connected to his rejection of a whole visual, or ocular, metaphor of understanding: as we shall see, this is central to his movement beyond "structuralism."

Superficially, Foucault's activism may seem to have an affinity with praxis in the Marxian sense. It is therefore important to point out how much more radical Foucault's position is than Marx's. In the *Theses on Feuerbach*, Marx does not argue, as Foucault does, for the collapse of theory into practice. Rather, he argues for the close collaboration of the two. Were one to misinterpret Marx on this point—and he has sometimes been so misinterpreted—one would come very close to the perspective embodied by Foucault. For example, it is sometimes assumed that in the eleventh thesis Marx says that philosophers, having hitherto interpreted the world, should now seek to change it. But Marx says no such thing. What he actually says is that "the philosophers have only *interpreted* the world, in various ways; the point is to *change* it": "Die Philosophen haben die Welt nur verschieden *interpretiert,* es kommt drauf an, sie zu *verändern*." There is an hiatus in Marx between the interpretation of the world and its transformation. It is this hiatus that Foucault denies. In so doing, he shows that, epistemologically, his more proper affinity is not with Marx but rather with those various other philosophers—including Wittgenstein and Dewey, as well as Nietzsche, Heidegger, and Derrida—who have sought to call into question the visual metaphor of understanding.[16]

In view of his rejection of the present in all its forms, and his related rejection of the visual, representational metaphor, Foucault is perhaps best regarded as the exponent of an unaccustomed form of utopianism. I have used the term *utopian* before, in relation to both Nietzsche and Heidegger. It is essential that I say something about this term now, especially since the utopian moment is much more obvious in Foucault than it is in either of his predecessors. By *utopian* I mean an orientation that carries idealism, in Berki's sense, to the furthest degree. The idealist thinkers whom Berki discusses all contain residues of "realism"; they "can at the end always be revealed to 'stand for' something, some definite norm or principle or arrangement."[17] The radical idealists with whom I am concerned here cannot be pinned down in this way. It is notorious that, despite major efforts, commentators have been unable to provide satisfactory ideological analyses of Nietzsche and Heidegger, and it is a foregone conclusion that the same difficulty would arise should similar attempts be made with Foucault. Yet, at the same time, utopianism in the sense in which I use the term ought not to be confused with utopianism in Mannheim's sense, which is explicitly contrasted with ideology.[18] Though Mannheim's discussion of "the utopian mentality" does connect in some ways with what we are considering here, his concept of utopianism is far too broad for our purposes. Better is Berki's characterization of utopianism as an "ideal that is incapable of realization."[19] Yet, even Berki's formulation is not extreme enough to suit the thinkers with whom we are here concerned. For the utopianism of Nietzsche, Heidegger, and Foucault is not only incapable of realization, it is incapable even of being described. It is a "that of which we cannot speak." Alternatively, it is something around which we must speak interminably, precisely because we can never connect with it. When Heidegger suggests in "The Thinker as Poet" that *Denken* tends to appear in the guise of "the utopism of a half-poetic intellect," it is this difficulty of expression that he surely has in mind (*PLT*, p. 12).

Foucault's utopianism, because it is wedded to the activist ideal of change, in some ways resembles previous utopianisms of a socialist or anarchistic type. One thinks, for example, of Fourier. And yet, Foucault is radically different from Fourier, for he puts forward no vision of happiness or liberation. As Foucault says in the final sentence of *The Will to Knowledge*: "Irony of this apparatus: it makes us believe that it is a matter of our 'liberation' " (*VS*, pp. 211/159 [translation altered]). (Foucault is speaking here of the "apparatus of sexuality" that in his view has come to dominate our lives—or, more accurately, our discourse—since the nineteenth century.) Foucault's position is clear: in matters not only of sexuality but of everything else, there is no liberation, no "other community" (*VS*, pp. 15/8 [translation altered]) where we can be free. Indeed, not only does his utopianism present no vision of liberation; it has no positive content whatsoever. He perhaps best defines this position in "A Preface to Transgression." Evoking Bataille, he here speaks of a "philosophy of nonpositive affirmation" whose sole aim is to "contest" the existing order. "Contestation," according to Foucault, "does not imply a generalized negation, but an affirmation that affirms nothing, a radical break of transitivity; . . . to contest is to proceed until one reaches the empty core where being achieves its limit and where the limit defines being" (*LCMP*, pp. 35–36).

In short, Foucault opposes the existing order of things, strategically attacking it at what he believes to be its weakest points. But he does so in the name of no other order that he intends or hopes will replace what exists. Order itself is brought before the bar. It is brought before the bar because every order is necessarily extant—even if only in thought—and hence participates in the corruption of all that is present. As Foucault says in his interview with the *lycéens*, "to imagine another system is to extend

our participation in the present system" (*LCMP*, p. 230). Or as he puts
in the more authoritative *Order of Things,* thought "cannot help but lit
erate and enslave" (*MC*, pp. 339/328). Putting a plausible gloss on thi:
we may suggest that thought first liberates, then (as it becomes part of
new, oppressive order) serves to enslave. Given the enslaving tendencies c
all thought, all interpretation, all discourse, and all language, one is ir
finitely justified in opposing these orders. One does this not in the name c
a better order, but because opposition is the only choice, aside from absc
lute passivity, that one has. Foucault thus opts for a peculiar brand c
permanent revolution—permanent because it seeks to realize no image c
an ideal society.

Foucault's progress: phenomenology

I propose to consider in roughly chronological order the main texts tha
Foucault has written. In this way, we shall be able to see how a perception c
crisis, and a commitment to the activism of discourse, have manifeste
themselves over the course of his career. Not incidentally, we shall also gai
some sense of how stimulating and provocative a writer he can be. After all
we ought to be interested in Foucault not because he happens to be on
exemplar of a perspective that is also to be found in certain other thinker:
but because the things he says are interesting and important. My portraya
of Foucault as the third moment in an anti-Hegelian dialectic (whose fourtl
moment is the deconstructive criticism of Derrida) is an heuristic fiction, on
that aims to help the puzzled reader come to grips with what Foucault anc
related writers are doing. Thus, the focus must be on the writings them
selves, or at any rate on such of the writings as can be made to tell a
interesting story. And for the most part, Foucault's writings do tell an inter
esting story. Though we may not agree with the vision Foucault puts for
ward, there is no doubt that his work has both a critical and an historica
importance. Certainly, the more imaginative philosophers and historian:
have found him suggestive and thought-provoking, if sometimes als(
wrongheaded or just plain mistaken. As for the assumption of crisis, whil(
we may deny the reality of a crisis in the sense and to the degree tha
Foucault perceives one, we can hardly deny that our period is one of grea
uncertainty. Hegel to the contrary, we find it difficult to see ourselves a:
participants in a teleology. On the most concrete level, the radically un
founded character of the age seems demonstrated by the possibility of it:
own immediate destruction. In such a universe, it simply cannot be taker
for granted that Foucault is wrong.

Essential to Foucault's first major work, *History of Madness,* is the notion of experience. Time and again in *History of Madness,* he refers to "the experience of madness."[20] He contends that the concept of mental illness, invented by psychiatry and psychology at the beginning of the nineteenth century, has wiped out our contact with this experience. "Mental illness" takes as a given the separation of reason from unreason: the separation, that is, of reasoning subject from insane object. By accepting—or rather, in Foucault's view, by constituting—this division, it causes the experience of madness to be obscured; it "thrusts into oblivion all those stammered, imperfect words without fixed syntax in which the exchange between madness and reason was made" (*HF1,* pp. x/—).

According to Foucault, psychiatry (and the closely allied discipline of clinical medicine, dealt with in *Birth of the Clinic*) claimed to be unconditionally faithful to the actual content of experience. The new psychiatrists and clinicians of the early nineteenth century saw themselves as bringing nothing to the objects they observed other than a trained and neutral eye. This claim, Foucault holds, was false. His intention in writing *History of Madness* is to demonstrate its falsity by going back behind psychological and psychiatric perception. Thus, he tells us that "we must try to return, in history, to that zero point in the course of madness at which madness is an undifferentiated experience, a not yet divided experience of division itself"; he tells us, too, that it is his intention to write a history "not of psychiatry" but rather "of madness itself, in its most vibrant state, before being captured by knowledge" (*HF1,* pp. i, vii/ix,—).

Foucault's concern here is as much with present-day psychiatry and psychology as it is with their nineteenth-century forms; for in his view, contemporary medicine still operates within the framework established by Pinel, Tuke, and other heroes of medical and psychiatric science. It is by no means irrelevant to note, in this regard, that after obtaining his *license de philosophie* at the Sorbonne in 1948, he went on to obtain a *license de psychologie* (1950) and then a *diplôme de psycho-pathologie* (1952). Moreover, we are told that in the early 1950s he spent "long periods of time observing psychiatric practice in mental hospitals."[21] It is clear that in the course of these studies and observations, he conceived an intense hatred for what he saw. Some of this animus is well conveyed in an essay of his published in 1957 in a volume in which a number of young French *savants,* most of them, like Foucault, recent graduates of the École Normale Supérieure, discuss the current states of their various disciplines.

As his contribution to this critical effort, Foucault attacks contemporary psychology. He assails it for what he sees as its peculiar combination of scientific pretension and theoretical blindness. As Foucault portrays it—and his portrait is a convincing one—psychology in France in the 1950s was utterly certain of its own objectivity and utterly committed to a positivistic methodology in which measuring, counting, and calculating took pride of place. Yet, for all its pretension, it was cut off from practice, for it had no social function: in particular, there were very few posts for practicing psychologists in the society at large. Because nothing else was available to them, persons with diplomas in psychology had no other recourse than to apply for grants to do research. Not surprisingly, much of the resulting work was incredibly vapid and inane. In Foucault's view, practical circumstance and theoretical blindness went hand in hand. It was virtually impossible to "practice" psychology, and this had an effect on the kind of research that was done. Separated from practice, psychological research "necessarily allows itself to be led by the myth of exteriority, of the indifferent gaze, of the nonparticipating spectator." Falling victim to this myth, it forgets "the negativity of man"; it fails to grasp its true vocation, which is to explore the infernal regions of the human psyche.[22]

The 1957 essay gives us some sense of what must have been a harsh confrontation between the young Foucault and his would-be scientific mentors. Two earlier writings, both published in 1954, help make clear the philosophical, as distinguished from the clinical, background to his concern in *History of Madness* with getting at the experience of madness. I am referring to his first book, *Mental Illness and Personality*, and to the long introduction that he provided for the French translation of the essay "Dream and Existence," by the Swiss existential psychiatrist Ludwig Binswanger (1881–1966). These writings show the connection between Foucault's preoccupation with the experience of madness and the phenomenologists' preoccupation with getting back to "the thing itself." (Admittedly, Foucault demonstrates an openness to unorthodox experience, to an "*étrangeté légitime*" [*HF1*, p. xi/—], that is quite absent from mainstream phenomenology.) From the point of view of the present study, this connection is extremely interesting. Most importantly, we can note a close affinity between the early Foucault and the early Heidegger, for Heidegger's most pervasive concern in *Being and Time* is precisely with circumventing, by means of a "phenomenological seeing," the subject/object dichotomy. We are not wrong, I think, in viewing this concern as an important precondition for the aestheticist move—the move toward the notion of an art or discourse that encloses within itself all those oppositions, such as the opposition between subject and object, that we conventionally see as existing in reality. Nor are we wrong in seeing an affinity between the phenomenologists' attack on the subject/object dichotomy and the "radical reflection on language" that Nietzsche articulated in the 1880s.

But the lines between Foucault and phenomenology can be drawn more tightly than this. Binswanger, the founder of *Daseinanalyse*, or existential analysis, was himself profoundly influenced by *Being and Time*. And it is clear that in 1954 Foucault was very much interested in Binswanger's work. His introduction to "Dream and Existence" is a substantial, if somewhat undisciplined piece; and he also promises that in a subsequent work he will "seek to situate existential analysis within the development of contemporary reflection on man."[23] In commenting on "Dream and Existence," Foucault emphasizes, among other things, Binswanger's preoccupation with uncovering the "structures of existence";[24] a similar preoccupation pervades both *History of Madness* and *Birth of the Clinic*.

For Binswanger and for phenomenological psychology in general, the uncovering of these structures involved an attempt to go beyond the subject/object distinction. In his chapter on "Illness and Existence" in *Mental Illness and Personality*, Foucault deals explicitly with this theme. "Naturalistic analysis," says Foucault, establishes a distance between the doctor and the patient, with the latter treated as if he were a natural object, a "thing" totally separate from the consciousness that observes him. Phenomenological psychology, on the other hand, seeks to place itself at the center of the experience of mental illness, attempting, through intuition, to enter into the consciousness of the ill person. It aims to see the world with the eyes of the ill person himself; the truth it seeks belongs not to the order of objectivity but to that of intersubjectivity.[25] (Note the easy move to intersubjectivity; Foucault here eludes one of the great difficulties of phenomenology.)

Obviously, such a conception of the relation between doctor and patient has radical implications, for it implies a coming together of the two, with the latter accorded the same status as the former. It invites, in short, an attack on the privileged status that psychiatry and psychology see themselves as having. Indeed, it invites an attack on the notion of mental illness itself, a move that Foucault finally makes in *History of Madness*. If Foucault in the 1950s was not yet willing to do away with that notion, we can nonetheless see how his early preoccupation with phenomenology points toward such an outcome. In this regard, it is interesting to note the affinities between Foucault and the British antipsychiatrist R. D. Laing. Laing's *Divided Self: A Study of Sanity and Madness* (1960) emerged out of the tradition of existential analysis in rather the same way as did *His-*

tory of Madness.[26] Laing and his colleagues were among the first in the English-speaking world to draw attention to Foucault's work; and given the common background, it is not surprising that this should have been so. If Foucault came to a radical attack on psychiatry earlier than Laing did, this is perhaps an indication of the fact that Foucault's radicalism was also nurtured by traditions other than phenomenology: most obviously, it was nurtured by Nietzsche, Artaud, Bataille, and others in the avant-garde literary and philosophical fold.

Beyond phenomenology: the structuralism of the sign

In both *History of Madness* and *Birth of the Clinic,* the concern, derived from phenomenology, with searching out the "structures of experience" remains of paramount importance. As Foucault puts it in the former work, he is interested neither in giving a chronicle of discoveries nor in writing a history of ideas. Rather, by following "the sequence of the fundamental structures of experience," he hopes to provide a history of "that which has made possible the very appearance of a psychology" (*HF1*, p. 633/—; *HF2*, p. 548). In *Birth of the Clinic,* this characterization of his work is pervasive: here the formation of clinical medicine is seen as "merely one of the more visible witnesses to . . . changes in the fundamental structures of experience" (*NC,* pp. 201/199).

When one turns to Foucault's works of after 1963, however, one is struck by the total disappearance of the concept "experience." To be sure, in *The Order of Things* he is not explicit about this shift, and the word *experience* does appear at least once in the book, in a reference to "modern experience" (*MC,* pp. 338/327). But the experience in question is completely linguistic, an immersion in a language or discourse that is taken as primary. There is no question of trying to get down to a prelinguistic level, to an originality that precedes its own expression. This shift is brought out very clearly in *The Archaeology of Knowledge,* where Foucault attacks *History of Madness* for having accorded "far too great a place, and a very enigmatic one too, to what I called an 'experience'" (*AS,* pp. 26–27/16 [translation altered]). Explicitly repudiating certain of his statements in the original preface to *History of Madness* (which he was to omit from the 1972 edition), he tells us that "there can be no question of interpreting discourse with a view to writing a history of the referent. . . . We are not trying to reconstitute what madness itself might be, in the form in which it first presented itself to some primitive, fundamental, deaf, scarcely articulated experience." On the contrary, he now defines his task as "to substitute for the enigmatic treasure of 'things' anterior to discourse the regular formation of objects that emerge only in discourse." Moreover, he rejects the whole phenomenological thematic of seeking an immediate grasp of the object; in his words, the "history of discursive objects" in which he is engaged ends up by suppressing "the stage of 'things themselves'" (AS, pp. 64–65/47–48).

In this movement from a seeking out of "the thing itself" to a total repudiation of that notion, one sees at work the antidialectical dialectic that is so important within aestheticism. For aestheticism is characterized by a continual movement between two poles, the Dionysian pole of immediacy and the Apollonian pole of dream and illusion—with the character of dream and illusion imputed, as we have seen, to logic itself. The search for immediacy ends in the denial of the independent existence of that entity with which immediate contact is sought. All such entities are reconstructed or reinvented on the level of language itself: this is the background to Foucault's "illusion of autonomous discourse." The object, as something independent of the subject, is destroyed, and the destruction of the object is accompanied by the destruction of the subject as well. Thus, in *The Archaeology of Knowledge*, Foucault is bothered not only by the fact that *History of Madness* fell victim to the notion of "the thing itself" but also by its implicit admission, thereby, of an "anonymous and general subject of history" (AS, pp. 27/16). The suppression of "the thing itself," then, also implies the suppression of the subject that experiences "the thing itself." This subject must be "anonymous" and "general" because it claims to see "the thing" as it really is, independent of all identifiable perspectives.

In thus suppressing the subject, Foucault moves into the much disputed territory of structuralism. Admittedly, already in *History of Madness* and *Birth of the Clinic* he had suggested, as we have seen, that he was engaged in a "structural study" of madness and of clinical medicine, respectively (HF1, p. vii/—; NC, pp. xv/xix). And there was much in these works that did seem "structuralist" in orientation. Note, for example, Foucault's concern in *History of Madness* with uncovering the "obstinate murmur" of a language (that of madness) that would "speak *all by itself*—without speaking subject and without listener, heaped upon itself, knotted at its throat, dissolving before having attained any formulation and returning soundlessly to the silence from which it was never able to get away" (HF1, p. vi/—). This notion of a language that speaks by itself, independently of speaker and listener, already suggests a structuralist position. But only in *The Order of Things,* where Foucault's celebrated *epi-stemes* function as just such a subjectless, objectless, all-embracing language, does the structuralist concern come entirely to the fore. Here, finally, both subject and object disappear; here, finally, the world is conceived as nothing other than language.

For purposes of giving a preliminary characterization of Foucault's position in the early and middle 1960s, it is perhaps sufficient to see his version of "structuralism" as essentially an attack on the Cartesian cogito and on its contemporary successor, the phenomenological subject.[27] Viewed in this way, Foucault can be seen as continuing the later Heidegger's attack on the whole tradition of Western science and technology.[28] But such a characterization, while adequate *en gros,* will not do when it is a matter of trying to work out in detail his intellectual trajectory and the relation of that trajectory to what lay outside it. I have already noted that Foucault has consistently denied that he was ever a structuralist. But what, exactly, does this denial mean? Unfortunately, the word *structuralism* has been endowed with so many meanings that it can hardly be said to have a meaning at all. Obviously, it is a question here of determining in precisely what senses Foucault was and was not a structuralist, a task that forces us to substitute, for the broad connotative penumbra surrounding that word, the rigors of definition.

Certainly, those who in the middle and late 1960s began to label Foucault a structuralist did seem to have good reasons for doing so. Thus, it is well known that structuralism is intimately tied up with language; and when one looks at Foucault's text, one sees that he, too, is deeply concerned with language. Indeed, Foucault's reflections on language form the underlying theme of *The Order of Things.* It is well known that structuralism, in its search for a stable object of investigation, concentrates on language (*langue*) rather than on the human speaker, and Foucault's attack on subjectivism and anthropologism did seem to fit within this framework. It is well known that structuralism is synchronic rather than diachronic in orientation, and this is apparently paralleled by Foucault's preference for discontinuity in history and by his refusal to explain the transitions or "mutations" leading from one *episteme* to the next. It is well known that structuralist analyses are articulated in terms of "binary opposition"; and when one looks at Foucault, one finds, or seems to find, a massive and all-embracing opposition between "the Same," dealt with in *The Order of Things,* and "the Other," dealt with in *History of Madness* and *Birth of the Clinic.* And finally, it is well known that structuralism focuses on the concept of the sign; and when one looks at Foucault's text, one finds a pervasive interest in signs and their permutations. Witness, for example, the chapter on "Signs and Cases" in *Birth of the Clinic* (*NC,* pp. 87–105/88–106); witness also the close relationship between significatory change and epistemic change in *The Order of Things* (see, most importantly, *MC,* pp. 57–58/42–43).

But these parallels, which in the wake of the publication of *The Order of Things* became journalistic commonplaces, betrayed a serious failure to attend to what Foucault was actually saying. It is little wonder that, confronted in the late 1960s by a concerted attempt to confine him in a box marked "structuralism," he should have reacted with angry repudiations of a term that he himself had used to characterize his work. Yet, for all his denials, Foucault in the 1960s remained in an important sense a structuralist. In arguing this, I have something more specific in mind, however, than the gross parallels mentioned above. Of course, one can "slice" almost any synthetic concept in a variety of ways, for articulate general concepts tend to be articulated at more than one point. But for our present purposes—and without denying the possibility of other analyses—I wish to distinguish between a narrower "structuralism of the sign" and a broader "structuralism of structure," each of which may in turn be construed in both a strict and a loose sense. The structuralism of the sign has its conceptual origins in Saussure's *Course in General Linguistics,* and more specifically in Saussure's definition of the sign as a union of signifier and signified. But the import of Saussurean structuralism can be variously interpreted. Some analysts of the concept of structuralism adhere to a relatively strict, "linguistic" definition of the term, restricting it to intellectual enterprises conforming rather closely to the outlines of Saussurean and post-Saussurean linguistics. Other analysts adhere to a looser, "semiological" definition. They link the term not to linguistics but to Saussure's proposal for a science of semiology that would concern itself with the study of "the life of signs within social life."[29]

Perhaps the most rigorous attempt to see structuralism in a strict, linguistic sense is to be found in Philip Pettit's *The Concept of Structuralism: A Critical Analysis.*[30] Structuralism, Pettit asserts, involves an attempt to extend certain Saussurean and post-Saussurean analytical procedures beyond linguistics, applying them to such areas as literary criticism, art criticism, social psychology, social anthropology, and the analysis of "customary arts" like fashion and cuisine. All analysts of the structuralism of the sign would agree with Pettit up to this point. But Pettit interprets the structuralist model of language narrowly, arguing that anyone who is extending this model beyond linguistics may think of doing so in terms of three, and only three, analogies: structural phonology (as in Jakobson), generative syntax (as in Chomsky), and differential semantics (as proposed by Pettit himself).[31] Each of these analogies, Pettit argues, requires that the nonlinguistic object being analyzed contain some element that corresponds to the sentence in language. But since none of the nonlinguistic objects upon which structural analysis has been attempted contains such an element, Pettit concludes that the structuralist model, though it may have some heuristic value in fields outside linguistics, does not in any proper sense "fit" any of those fields.

Though Pettit mentions Foucault only in passing,[32] preferring to concentrate his attentions on Lévi-Strauss, there is never any doubt that Foucault does not conform to the kind of strict Saussurean model that Pettit articulates. For the parallels, mentioned above, between Foucault's work and structuralism in its Saussurean sense turn out on further examination to be almost entirely specious. True, Foucault's reflection on language is an extremely important part of his work. But this reflection owes far more to Mallarmé (mediated through Blanchot and other French literary critics) than it does to Saussure; nor should we forget to mention, on matters of language, Nietzsche and Heidegger, who largely inspire this interpretation of Mallarmé.[32] It is true that Foucault attacks subjectivism and anthropologism. This is bound up, however, not with Saussure's elimination of the individual speaker from the purview of linguistics, but rather (as we are beginning to see) with a radical attack on phenomenology. Foucault's debt, here, is not to Saussure but to Nietzsche, interpreted in the light of the later Heidegger's attack on the subjectivistic "humanism" of the modern age (see, for example, "The Age of the World Picture," QT, p. 133). Thus, Foucault sees Nietzsche as having been the first to awaken us from "the anthropological sleep," the first to tear us free from "the anthropological field" (MC, pp. 351–354/340–343; see also pp. 317–318/306–307 and 332/322). It is true that Foucault has tended to emphasize the discontinuous in history, and that this has sometimes made it appear that he is engaging in something that resembles, in its temporal orientation, Saussure's synchronic linguistics. But once again the appearance is entirely deceptive, for the metaphysical (or antimetaphysical) intentions that underlie this emphasis turn out to be entirely absent from Saussure. As for his alleged interest in binary opposition, it is true that at a certain moment in his career Foucault was attracted by the idea of constructing "a whole series of binary divisions which in their own way would have cashed in on the great division 'reason-unreason' that I had tried to reconstitute with regard to madness" ("The History of Sexuality" [interview with Lucette Finas, 1977], *P/K,* p. 185 [translation altered]). But this idea was never really worked out, remaining an entirely subsidiary theme in his *oeuvre* as a whole.

We are left, then, with our final parallel, the fact that the concept of the sign, which is centrally important for Saussure and on which basis he wanted to construct a semiology, also functioned as an important concept for Foucault at this stage in his career. We are thus led from the strict, linguistic reading of the structuralism of the sign to the looser semiological reading. Many of those who have called themselves structuralists have been far more interested in the science whose outlines Saussure did not articulate than in the science whose outlines he actually did articulate. Indeed, in recognition of this, Pettit admits the rough interchangeability of the terms "semiology" and "structuralism," even though he goes on to discuss structuralism in terms of a strictly linguistic model.[34]

But other analysts, in their attempts to define the limits of structuralism, have taken Saussure's semiological intentions more seriously. One such commentator was the philosopher François Wahl, who, in an important essay on structuralism and philosophy (included in the volume *What Is Structuralism?*), attempted to come to grips with the structuralist phenomenon. Like Pettit, Wahl identifies structuralism and semiology, asserting that "under the name of structuralism are grouped the sciences of the sign, of systems of signs."[35] But unlike Pettit, he does not go on to assert that the practice of a science of signs requires a strict conformity between the structure of the object being analyzed and the structure of language. On the contrary, he is willing to allow the possibility of structural analysis wherever the object being analyzed passes through a structuring linguistic grid. Thus, he tells us that "the most diverse facts of anthropology" can be the object of structural analysis, "but only insofar as they pass through the facts of language—that they are caught within the institution of a system of the type *Signifier/signified* and lend themselves to a communicative network—and that they receive from this their structure."[36] In short, structuralism, for Wahl, deals with structures; but it deals with structures only insofar as they have acquired their structure from their passage through a system of signs.

For Wahl, then, the sign is the absolutely critical defining element in structuralism: where the sign is, there also is structuralism, regardless of the absence of such linguistic elements as the sentence. In attempting to distinguish what is "not yet" structuralism from what is "no longer" structuralism, Wahl tells us that "wherever the sign is not yet conceived as being in an absolutely fundamental position, thought has not yet taken note of structuralism. Wherever the primacy of the sign is disputed, wherever the sign is destroyed or deconstructed, thought is no longer in the orbit of structuralism."[37] In this reading of structuralism, where does Foucault stand?

Since Wahl's account of Foucault's relationship to structuralism is based on a reading of *The Order of Things,* a brief summary of the general thesis of that work is required. The book is set within the context and between the limits of an event stunning in its gratuitousness—namely, the presence, retreat, and return of language (for the outlines of this theme, see *MC,* pp. 57–59, 314–318, 394–398/42–44, 303–307, 382–387). The central protagonist of *The Order of Things* is "language." Foucault means language not in the ordinary sense of the word, but rather in its Mallarméan, Nietzschean, and, as we are able to see (though Foucault does not mention his name in this context), Heideggerian sense. He means, that is, language insofar as it has an autonomous and self-referring, yet expansive and world-creating existence—in short, language as the ontogenetic work of art.

The mirror image of language, which appears when language disappears and disappears when language appears, is discourse. Again, Foucault employs the word *discourse* in a special sense, derived from the epistemological and linguistic reflections of the Idéologues, Condillac, and Locke. Discourse, for Foucault, is language from which all self-reference, all inner play, all metaphorical distortion are eliminated. The sole function of discourse is to serve as a transparent representation of things and ideas standing outside it.[38] Hence, language and discourse are totally antithetical. In language, the "direction of meaning" is entirely inward, for language recognizes itself as the world; in discourse, it is entirely outward, for discourse recognizes itself only as representing the world.[39] Where "language" disappears, as Foucault argues it did at the beginning of the seventeenth century, all that remains of language is "its function as representation: its nature and its virtues as *discourse*" (*MC,* pp. 95–96/81). Conversely, when language returns—and Foucault asserts that it returned at the end of the eighteenth century, though it has not yet regained its unity—then discourse disappears (*MC,* pp. 314–315, 397/303–304, 385–386).[40]

Foucault's account of the disappearance and return of language is closely connected with an account of signs and signification. This is especially true of his account of the disappearance of language, which he relates to a fundamental change, at the beginning of the seventeenth century, in the structure of the sign. From the Stoics to the Renaissance, the system of signs in the Western world was, Foucault asserts, a "ternary" one. In this system, signifier and signified were linked together by a "conjuncture"—specifically, by a relationship of resemblance of one sort or another. But at the beginning of the seventeenth century, the system of signs became "binary," with a purely arbitrary relationship between signifier and signified coming to prevail. It was this change, Foucault holds, that signaled the disappearance of language and its replacement by a supposedly transparent discourse (*MC*, pp. 57–58, 42–45/42–43, 27–30).

Unfortunately, quite apart from the question of the historical accuracy of what Foucault here argues (and I am not directly concerned in this essay with whether Foucault is right or wrong in what he says about the past), his account of signs and signification remains unclear, even after one has gone to the considerable effort of learning his somewhat idiosyncratic terminology and of grasping the architectonics of the book. The locus of the problem is to be found in his failure to explain clearly his distinction between representation and signification. Representation, he argues, is characteristic of the classical *episteme* of the seventeenth and eighteenth centuries; signification is characteristic of the modern *episteme* that began in the late eighteenth century and that is now, he suggests, on the verge of its demise. Yet, he never tells us what the distinction between representation and signification is. Nor does he make fully clear the implications of this distinction for the concept of the sign, which remains binary in structure throughout the classical and modern *epistemes*. The drift of Foucault's account suggests that he sees the two concepts as variants of each other, since both exist under the aegis of the binary sign and in an economy in which "language" either does not exist (representation) or exists in a fragmentary state only (signification).[41] But they are incompatible variants, for if Foucault does not tell us precisely what distinguishes the two, he does tell us that the "universal extension of the sign within the field of representation precludes even the possibility of a theory of signification" (*MC*, pp. 79–80/65).

In considering the question whether Foucault is a structuralist, Wahl concentrates on what he sees as the inadequacies in Foucault's account of representation and signification. In the first place, Wahl distinguishes—and distinguishes clearly—between the two. He holds that whereas representation involves a "doubling," within the order of language, of what is outside language, signification involves not doubling but difference, with the meaning of the sign being determined—in classic Saussurean terms—by the difference between it and all other signs.[42] With signification, then, language constitutes a coherent structure in which an alteration in one signifying element will necessarily alter, through the play of difference, every other signifying element. With representation, on the other hand, the structure of language is merely a repetition of the structure of "reality." Laying great stress on a passage in which Foucault suggests that "the binary theory of the sign" and "a general theory of representation" are linked together in an inextricable relation that "probably extends up to our own time" (*MC*, pp. 81/67), Wahl attacks Foucault for failing to see that representation and signification are mutually exclusive, and especially for failing to grasp the fundamentally differential nature of the sign. Because Foucault had failed to grasp this, he had also failed, according to Wahl, to grasp the fundamentally systematic structure of language:

> To persist in thinking of the sign within representation is not only to forbid oneself the means of reinstating the formal organization that constitutes the semiological edifice as such: . . . it is in truth to *resist* this organization, in practice to *contradict* it and from that point on to deny the sign, at the very moment that one seems ready to accord to it its founding place. . . . The "primacy of representation" is the negation of the sign—because the sign . . . entails the denunciation of representation.

In consequence, Foucault remains, according to Wahl, "on this side of the sign, on this side of discourse, on this side of structure."[43] Foucault is thus to be counted among those who have "not yet" arrived at structuralism.

There is ample reason for agreeing with Wahl that Foucault is not a structuralist in Wahl's definition of the term. But the problem is not that Foucault is not yet a structuralist in this sense; it is rather that he is "no longer" a structuralist—that he lies beyond, and not short of, the structuralism of the sign. For Wahl's treatment of Foucault fails to recognize that Foucault does indeed hold representation and signification to be incompatible. Moreover, while Foucault never raises the issue of "difference" in its Saussurean sense, his evocations of the post-Classical fragmentation of language are a clear indication of his belief that the structure of things no longer establishes, as in representation, the structure of language. Besides, elsewhere in his discussion of Foucault, Wahl gives a reading of *The Order of Things* that, if it were correct, could certainly be taken as placing Foucault under the rubric of the structuralism of the sign. This reading suggests not that Foucault was not yet a structuralist but that he was a structuralist without knowing it.

In Wahl's reading, Foucault leaves the concept of the sign—which Wahl defines, following Barthes, who follows Saussure, as a *relatio* between two *relata*—"curiously in the shadows," even though, over the length of *The Order of Things,* this concept is shown to be the element that governs the epistemic mutations.[44] The configuration of knowledge that makes up any given *episteme* necessarily implies, Wahl argues, a whole series of interrelations. Each figure within the grid of a configuration, he asserts, functions as the representative of other elements and at the same time as the representative of the configuration in general. On account of these mutual relations, "the episteme, like every order, envelops a semiology."[45] Within any given *episteme*, the relations, and hence the signs, are of a given type. As long as the *relationes* between the *relata* retain the same nature, the *episteme* remains the same. Thus, Marx remains within the same *episteme* as Ricardo because, however much he attacks Ricardo's bourgeois presuppositions, he maintains the same relationship between "the surface circulation of values" manifested by the movement of commodities and "the profound, unrepresentable fact of the activity that produces them: labor."[46] But when the nature of the relationship between the *relata* changes, then the *episteme* changes: "The edifices of knowledge topple...and there is a change of episteme ...when the assigned relation of the sign to what it signifies changes: when 'to signify' no longer signifies the same thing."[47]

If we were to accept this reading of Foucault, we would have to acknowledge that he indeed conforms to the structuralism of the sign in its loose sense; for here the sign does appear to be in "an absolutely fundamental position," even though Wahl is right in pointing out that Foucault makes no use of the Saussurean conception of difference. But this reading is in my view an incorrect one, for it falls prey to a misleading metaphor of depth, of which I shall have more to say below. It is only because Wahl sees the concept of the *episteme* in terms of depth, order, and firm foundations that he is able to give a semiological reading of Foucault, holding that the Foucauldian *episteme* "envelops" a semiology. I here touch on Foucault's Dionysian antistructuralism, and more specifically on the fact that for Foucault there are no firm foundations, no original or transcendental signified to which all signifiers can ultimately refer.[48] And given the absence of a signified, there can be no sign. The *episteme* stands, in short, beyond the firmly founded world presupposed by the Saussurean conception of the sign. It belongs rather to the radically unfounded, post-Saussurean world of Heidegger and Nietzsche—though in 1966 Foucault had not yet worked out the implications of such a stance.

The structuralism of structure: Western metaphysics

But structuralism need not be confined to a linguistic or semiological sense, for one can detach it from any indenture to the sign, taking structure itself to be its defining feature. Both Pettit and Wahl recognize the possibility of a "structuralism of structure," even though they reject such a definition for the purposes of their own analyses. Pettit tells us that "I give quite a specific sense to 'structuralism': unlike some commentators, I do not take it to embrace every science ... which claims to investigate 'structures.'"[49] Wahl, for his part, evokes Lévi-Strauss, who would take as the object of the structural sciences "whatever has the character of a 'system,' that is, any ensemble in which one element cannot be modified without bringing about a modification of all the others." As Wahl points out, such a definition would mean that "everything that touches on the idea of structure ... would fall under the rubric of structuralism."[50] Where, then, does Foucault stand in relation to "structuralism" when we broaden the idea of structuralism to take in "everything that touches on the idea of structure"?

The answer to this question depends, of course, on how this structuralism of structure is defined, for the structuralism of the structure, like the structuralism of the sign, can be taken in both a strict and a loose sense. One example of a strict construing of the structuralism of structure is provided by Jean Piaget in his book *Structuralism.*[51] Whereas Pettit and Wahl base their analyses of structuralism on linguistics and semiology respectively, Piaget bases his analysis on a congeries of sciences, including not only linguistics but also mathematics, physics, biology, psychology, and anthropology. The effect of this broadening of the field is to rob the sign of any decisive role within the concept of structuralism. In contrast to Pettit and Wahl, Piaget makes no reference to the sign in his definition of structuralism. For Piaget, structuralism is concerned with structure, and a structure is a "system of transformations." Included within Piaget's definition of structure are three ideas. In the first place, for Piaget a structure is not a mere aggregate; it is not an accidental collection of elements and their properties. Rather, it is a whole whose elements are subordinate to laws, in terms of which the structure qua whole or system is defined. In the second place, a structure is subject to transformations, brought about by the play of its governing laws. And finally, a structure is self-regulating—that is, the transformational laws of the structure "never yield results external to the system nor employ elements that are external to it."[52] In short, a structure necessarily entails self-maintenance and closure: it operates according to its own inner system of laws, a system of laws that never transforms the system into something other than what it is.

Piaget pursues this definition of structure through a wide variety of sciences. He claims to show that the definition is applicable to "groups" and "parent structures" in mathematics, to organisms in biology, to perceptual totalities in psychology, to kinship groups in anthropology, and so on. In each of the fields he examines, he is able to find without much difficulty investigators who have adhered to a basically "structuralist" methodology. But when—at the end of the book—he finally turns to Foucault, he is unable to find structuralism in the Piagetian sense. Piaget tells us that Foucault's concept of the *episteme* seems at first glance to be a promisingly structuralist notion, for it suggests the discovery of "strictly epistemological structures that would show how the fundamental principles of the science of a given period are connected with one another." Unfortunately, however, Foucault is simply not scientific enough in his approach to carry out this program. He does not develop an appropriate methodology for his enterprise. For example, instead of inquiring into the criteria for determining when a new *episteme* can be said to have come into existence, or those for judging the validity or invalidity of alternative interpretations in the history of science, he relies on "intuition and . . . speculative improvisation."[53] His *epistemes* turn out to be idiosyncratic inventions rather than a genuine attempt to discover the epistemological foundations of the history of science. He has "no canon for the selection of an *episteme*'s characteristics; important ones are omitted and the choice between alternative ones is arbitrary."[54] His *epistemes,* in consequence, are not systems of transformation at all. His structuralism, which in Piaget's view retains all the negative features of structuralism (such as the devaluation of history and genesis, contempt for functional considerations) without its positive features, can justly be called a "structuralism without structures."[55]

There can be no doubt that if we take structuralism, as Piaget does, to be essentially a form of scientific methodology, then Foucault is not a structuralist. But the structuralism of structure can be defined in a much looser sense, a sense that is at bottom metaphysical rather than scientific. It can be defined, that is, in the sense that Derrida proposes, as the Apollonian element in the Nietzschean conflict between Apollo and Dionysus. As we have seen, Nietzsche maintained in *The Birth of Tragedy* that Greek culture at its height was the product of a peculiar and delicate union of the calm, clear, lucent spirit of Apollo and the frenzied, extravagant, ecstatic spirit of Dionysus. The Apollonian spirit is the spirit of temperance, moderation, and justice, a spirit that demands the strict observance of the limits of the individual, of the *principium individuationis*. The Dionysian spirit is the spirit of *hubris,* of mystical jubilation, of the shattering of the *principium individuationis* in a savage and ritual unity.

As might be supposed, the Apollonian and the Dionysian spirits differ radically in their attitude toward forms: the Apollonian spirit teaches the acceptance and retention of forms, while the Dionysian spirit teaches their destruction and recreation. As Nietzsche puts it, speaking of the Greek experience, "Apollo wants to grant repose to individual beings ... by drawing boundaries between them and by again and again calling them to mind as the most sacred laws of the world, with his demands for self-knowledge and measure." But, Nietzsche continues, "lest this Apollonian tendency congeal the form to Egyptian rigidity and coldness, ... the high tide of the Dionysian destroyed from time to time all those little circles in which the one-sidedly Apollonian 'will' had sought to confine the Hellenic spirit" (*BT,* chap. 9; *NBW,* p. 72; see also *BT,* chaps. 21 and 25; *NBW,* pp. 128 and 143). Nor is it only a question of Greek culture, for every culture, if it is to be truly creative, requires the presence of these two spirits, the form-creating and the form-destroying.

Nietzsche held that all primitive peoples are endowed with Dionysian energies; but because the Greeks had, in addition, the Olympian figure of Apollo, they had been protected from Dionysian barbarism. The crude and uncouth Dionysian power was now sublimated into culture—indeed, into the greatest culture that the world had ever seen. But with Socrates this vital collaboration between the Apollonian and the Dionysian, which found its archetypal manifestation in the tragic myth, was broken. For— to recur to our earlier discussion of this—Socrates was the great exemplar of "theoretical man," of the man who believes that "thought, using the thread of causation, can penetrate the deepest abysses of being" (*BT,* chap. 15; *NBW,* p. 95). Theoretical man is deeply suspicious of the irrational sources of being, of knowledge, and of creativity, holding that culture must be based on conscious intelligence rather than on instinct. Hence, he has a great faith in science, in "the god of machines and crucibles," in "the powers of the spirits of nature recognized and employed in the service of a higher form of egotism" (*BT,* chap. 17; *NBW,* p. 109). Hence, too, he opposes the irrational powers of Dionysian art, believing as he does that the beautiful and the reasonable should be made to coincide. The whole of Western culture is caught, Nietzsche argues, within the net of this theoreticism, this rationalism, this scientism; from the time of Socrates onward, the man of theory has been the ideal of Western thought.

But if Nietzsche holds that ever since the great age of Greek tragedy the logic of Socrates has dominated Western culture, he also holds that this logic is always on the brink of its own collapse. For logic has its outer limits, its margins beyond which it cannot move, and it also has an inner core that it cannot grasp. Science cannot extend itself indefinitely, but rather "speeds irresistibly toward its limits," where it "suffers ship-wreck"; logic, reaching these boundary points, "coils up . . . and bites its own tail" (*BT*, chap. 15; *NBW*, pp. 97–98). But the man of theory, be-cause he believes that "a culture based on the principles of science must be destroyed when it begins to grow *illogical*," refuses to recognize the nec-essarily illogical accompaniment of logic (*BT*, chap. 18; *NBW*, p. 113). Nietzsche and, even more, Derrida see their task as that of alerting West-ern man to what they allege to be the ultimate illogicality of Western culture. Indeed, taken together, Derrida's works constitute a single, con-certed attack on "logocentrism," on what he regards as the blindly logical orientation of Western thought.

I cannot deal here with Derrida's variations on this Nietzschean theme. Suffice it to say that Derrida sees structuralism, in the sense of Apollonian formalism, as intimately tied up with the whole of "logocentric" culture. The most obvious indication of this relationship is to be found, Derrida contends, in the metaphorical biases and determinations of structuralism. In the first place, structuralism in the Derridean sense is biased toward— or determined by—a metaphoric of light. It is this metaphoric that links Apollo—the sun god; the god of light; the "shining one," as Nietzsche calls him; the god who stands over "the Apollonian art of sculpture," as opposed to "the nonimagistic, Dionysian art of music"—to what Nietz-sche refers to as "the one great Cyclops eye of Socrates" (*BT*, chaps. 1, 14; *NBW*, pp. 35, 89). It is in Plato, Nietzsche tells us, that we see most clearly the "enormous driving-wheel of logical Socratism" (*BT*, chap. 13; *NBW*, pp. 88–89). And it is no accident, Derrida holds (repeating a Heideg-gerian motif), that the whole of Platonic philosophy is based on the oppo-sition of light and dark, of which the myth of the cave is only the most obvious indication.

Nor, says Derrida, is it accidental that nearly all our expressions for thought are connected with visual metaphors. Thus, "theory" comes from the word *theoria,* meaning a looking at, a contemplation; "idea" comes from *eidein,* meaning "to see." Derrida goes so far as to maintain (in his 1963 essay "Force and Signification") that this "metaphor of dark-ness and light (of self-revelation and self-concealment)" is "the founding metaphor of Western philosophy as metaphysics." From Plato onward, Derrida claims, Western philosophy has been indentured to a heliocentric metaphysics that has subjected Dionysian force to Apollonian form. Force, according to Derrida, cannot be thought in terms of *eidos,* that is, in terms of "the form which is visible to the metaphorical eye," for to grasp "the structure of a becoming, the form of a force," is already to destroy their quality as becoming and as force. Indeed, in Derrida's eyes the whole project of understanding, of the search for meaning (*sens*), is thoroughly Apollonian in nature, for understanding requires "the repose of the beginning and the end, the peacefulness of a spectacle, horizon or face" (*E&D*, pp. 44–45/26–27).

Derrida maintains that the entity he calls "modern structuralism" is an integral part of this larger Apollonian project. Modern structuralism grew up in the shadow of phenomenology. According to Derrida, phenomenology lacks any concept that would permit it to conceive of intensity or force. This inability to conceive of force has been carried over into modern structuralism, which is biased toward—or determined by—a force-excluding metaphoric of space that in its form and in its implications is closely connected to the central philosophical metaphor of light. As Derrida points out, the notion of structure "refers only to space, geometric or morphological space, the order of forms and sites" (*E&D*, pp. 28/15). The very idea of a center or of an end, without which structure cannot be thought, is an exclusion of Dionysian revel. In Derrida's words, "the concept of centered structure is in fact the concept of a play based on a fundamental ground, a play constituted on the basis of a fundamental immobility and a reassuring certitude, which itself is beyond the reach of play" (*E&D*, pp. 410/279). Modern structuralism, then, is only the most recent manifestation of the persistent Apollonianism of Western philosophy.

It is hardly necessary to point out that Derrida's thesis (if it is a thesis) or his position (if it is a position) deserves a considerable effort of exegesis and criticism. Moreover, as I have already argued, the Apollonian/Dionysian distinction itself is questionable, having a dubious conceptual validity. But it does have an aesthetic validity. It brings to consciousness a number of polarities that actually do exist in art and in our experience of it, and for this reason it is of some use here. For Foucault's project *is*, essentially, an aesthetic one. Moreover, it is a project that fits into the same aesthetic universe from which the Apollonian/Dionysian opposition arises. I decline to ask the potentially destructive question, "Is there any logical basis for the distinction between the Apollonian and the Dionysian?," for the answer is a foregone conclusion. I propose rather to ask, in an entirely heuristic spirit, the potentially illuminating question, "Was the Foucault whom we are here considering—the Foucault of the early and middle 1960s—a structuralist in the metaphysical, or antimetaphysical, sense proposed by Derrida?"

The answer to this question is to be found in an examination of the metaphoric of Foucault's works of this period. More specifically, it is to be found in an examination of the works that in Derrida's sense of the term are most "structuralist," namely, *Birth of the Clinic* and *The Order of Things* (here the former book, which in other respects seems more akin to *History of Madness*, points forward to the book that followed it). In both books, we discover precisely the sort of metaphoric that Derrida argues is central to the "adventure of the gaze" that in his account constitutes structuralism (*E&D*, pp. 9/3 [translation altered]). For both are dominated by the theme of looking at space, and hence by a visual and spatial metaphoric. The theme of "the gaze" does make a passing appearance in *History of Madness* (*HF1*, pp. 614, 620/ —; *HF2*, pp. 532, 537), but in *Birth of the Clinic* it becomes absolutely central. Thus, the work bears the subtitle "An Archaeology of the Medical Gaze," and begins with the announcement that "this book is about space, about language, and about death; it is about the act of seeing, the gaze" (*NC*, pp. v/ix). This statement is amply confirmed in the rest of the book, in which vision, visibility, invisibility, and space are obsessively recurring motifs. I cite, for example, the following passage from the conclusion, in which Foucault looks back on the book as a whole:

> This book...concerns one of those periods that mark an ineradicable chronological threshold: the period in which illness, counter-nature, death, in short, the whole dark underside of disease came to light, at the same time illuminating and eliminating itself like night, in the deep, visible, solid, enclosed, but accessible space of the human body. What was fundamentally invisible is suddenly offered to the brightness of the gaze;...doctors... approach the subject of their experience with the purity of an unprejudiced gaze;...the forms of visibility...have changed;...the abyss beneath illness has...emerged into the light of language. (*NC*, pp. 197/195.)

Though in *The Order of Things* the metaphoric tends, as in "Las Meninas," to shift from the gaze observing to the space observed, it is just as obsessive as in *Birth of the Clinic*. To enter into the world of *The Order of Things* is to enter into a world whose fundamental metaphor is the metaphor of arrangement in space. It is to enter into a world that is strangely silent and unmoving, into a frozen world of penetrating glances and arrested gestures. A cursory examination of the preface to *The Order of Things* is enough to impress upon the reader the prominence of this metaphoric. Foucault asks us, for example, where the strange typologies given in Borges's Chinese encyclopedia could be juxtaposed, except in the "non-place of language," in the "unthinkable space" that language spreads before us (*MC*, pp. 8/xvii). He talks about "the common space in which encounters are possible" (*MC*, pp. 8/xvi); about "the table upon which...language has intersected space" (*MC*, pp. 9/xvii); about the "space of order" within which knowledge was constituted (*MC*, pp. 13/xxii); about the "space of knowledge" (*MC*, pp. 13/xxii); not to mention the evocation of such spatial and visual figures as the "relation of contained to container" (*MC*, pp. 8/xvii); and "sites" (*MC*, pp. 9/xvii); and "the already 'encoded' eye," that is forcibly confined by "linguistic, perceptual, and practical grids" (*MC*, pp. 12/xx–xxi). This metaphoric, with its visual and spatial bias, dominates the whole of *The Order of Things*, from the initial analysis of "Las Meninas" to the terminal evocation of the erasure of man.

Foucault thus portrays for us—without, I would argue, being fully conscious of what he is doing—a lucent, Apollonian world. In short, he conforms, in *Birth of the Clinic* and, above all, in *The Order of Things*, to structuralism in the Derridean sense; he is, in Derridean terms, in complicity—albeit a complicity that is entirely unintended—with the very "logocentric" culture whose claim to absolute validity he wishes to contest. His radical rejection of that culture is not yet radical enough. To be sure, Derrida himself is less than explicit in applying his critique of "logocentrism" to the works of Foucault. He comes closest to this in his 1963 critique of *History of Madness*, entitled "Cogito and the History of Madness." Here he holds that Foucault is trapped in logocentrism. Though Foucault claims to have written a history of "madness itself...before being captured by knowledge," his claim is unjustified, since he is no more able than anyone else to escape from the language of reason: "All our European languages, the language of everything that has participated, from near or far, in the adventure of Western reason—all this is the immense delegation of the project defined by Foucault under the rubric of the capture or objectification of madness. *Nothing* within this language, and *no one* among those who speak it, can escape the historical guilt...which Foucault apparently wishes to put on trial" (*E&D*, pp. 58/35).

In the same essay, Derrida also claims to detect in Foucault a "structuralist totalitarianism" that attempts "an act of enclosure of the Cogito similar to the violences of the classical age" (*E&D*, pp. 88/57 [translation altered]). Derrida has never engaged in any formal and explicit critique of Foucault's more obviously "structuralist" works. Virtually his only comment in this direction occurs in a 1966 essay on the structuralism of Lévi-

Strauss, where he observes that "the movement of any archaeology" is in complicity with the attempt to "center" structure, with the attempt to place structure upon a foundation that is itself out of play (*E&D*, pp. 410/ 279). Nonetheless, despite the lack of explicit connection, the applicability of the Derridean critique of structuralism to Foucault's work of the early and middle 1960s is clear. François Wahl was right in observing in *What Is Structuralism?* that "the schema of structuralism that Derrida attacks is more or less the same as the one to which Foucault adheres."[56]

CHAPTER 6

Beyond Structuralism

In discussing Foucault's movement beyond the phenomenologically tinged perspective of *History of Madness,* I have already had occasion to refer to *The Archaeology of Knowledge.* But there is yet another standpoint from which we can approach the latter work—namely, the standpoint of its critique of *The Order of Things:* for if it still retains a close affinity with the earlier book, it constitutes at the same time a significant revision of the position that is maintained there.

At the end of *History of Madness,* in what is perhaps the book's most apocalyptic passage, Foucault speaks of the relationship between "madness" and "the work" (*oeuvre*). Invoking the names of those geniuses who went mad—Hölderlin and Nerval, and (touching us more closely) Nietzsche, van Gogh, and Artaud—he sees the work as interrupted by madness, and thus rendered incomplete; but at the same time, by its very madness, it "opens a void, a moment of silence, a question without answer, provokes a breach without reconciliation where the world is forced to question itself" (*HF1,* pp. 643/288; *HF2,* p. 556). Foucault is here suggesting a kind of anti-Heideggerian Heideggerianism, though Heidegger's name is nowhere mentioned in *History of Madness.* For, firstly, Foucault is putting forward a notion of radical crisis. Though he never explains precisely how this is so, he is convinced that the great artistic works of madness call our world into question. This world, he holds, seeks to measure and justify madness via the science of psychology, while at the same time, and on another level, it seeks to measure itself against the unmeasured works of Nietzsche, van Gogh, and Artaud; yet, there is nothing to assure the world that these works of madness provide any justification for its existence. To put it bluntly: the world is radically without ground; we know this because the mad poets tell us so.

Foucault's position, so far, is indistinguishable from that of the later Heidegger, who invokes Hölderlin as his great example of the mad genius. But, secondly, while both the early Foucault and the later Heidegger emphasize the work of art, in Heidegger this emphasis is connected with a "truth value" claim that Foucault never makes. In Foucault, as in Nietzsche, art is a matter not of truth but of lie. The work of art establishes a vision, but the vision is conceded to be a creative falsification. Moreover, whereas Heidegger sees the work of art as existing in harmony with the world that it sets up, a world that it seeks to keep in force through its consecrations and praisings, in Foucault the relationship between work and world is quite the contrary. In Foucault's words: "Henceforth, and through the mediation of madness, it is the world that becomes culpable in relation to the work: it is now arraigned by the work, obliged to order itself by its language, compelled by it to a task of recognition, of reparation" (HF1, pp. 643/288 [translation altered]; HF2, p. 556). On the one hand, we find an acquiescence; on the other hand, a radical hostility. But both positions are aesthetic in their focus. Both postulate the ontogenetic work of art, whether that work carries truth or invents lies, whether that work stands with the world or against it.

There is an important difference, however, between the perspective that Foucault articulates in The Archaeology of Knowledge and his perspective in History of Madness, for in the later book the notion of "the work" disappears. In consequence, there might seem to be no justification for referring to Foucault's stance as an "aestheticism." But this is misleading, for what Foucault leaves behind is not aestheticism as such but only the Romantic lyricism and sense of nostalgia of his previous writings. This lyricism is already present in his writings of the 1950s. Note, for instance, the appeal in Mental Illness and Personality to intuition, as distinguished from analytical understanding. Note, in his introduction to Binswanger's "Dream and Existence," the emphasis on "oneiric" experience—that is, on the experience of dreams. Note, in the 1957 essay on contemporary psychology, the call for a descent into the "infernal" depths of the human psyche. All these motifs have close affinities with the Romantic valuation of intuition, dream, and the infernal regions.

The affinities continue in History of Madness, in Birth of the Clinic, and even, to a certain extent, in The Order of Things. Especially in History of Madness, one discerns a sense of longing for something that Foucault sees as having once existed but now is long past—namely, the immediate experience of madness. Significantly, Foucault suggests in the preface to *History of Madness* that between madness and reason "there is no common language; or rather there is *no longer* any common language" (*HF1*, p. ii/—[my italics]). In the seventeenth century, he maintains, madness was interned. Enclosed within a quasi-objectivity, it "ceased to be an experience in the adventure of all human reason." As a result, it could "no longer animate the secret life of the spirit, nor accompany it with its constant threat. It is put at a distance;—at a distance that is not only symbolized but really assured on the surface of social space by the enclosures of the houses of internment" (*HF1*, pp. 128–129/—; *HF2*, p. 118).

Though in an attenuated form, the same motif recurs in *Birth of the Clinic*, for here too there is a sense of longing, a sense that something original has been lost. As Foucault puts it in the preface to this work, "it may well be that we belong to an age of criticism whose lack of a primary philosophy reminds us at every moment of its reign and its fatality: an age of intelligence that keeps us irremediably at a distance from an original language" (*NC*, pp. xi–xii/xv). Both works, moreover, have a strongly lyrical aspect. This is most evident in Foucault's appeals to what he calls the "lyric experience of madness," by which he seems to mean the experience of madness as it manifests itself in the writings of the mad poets (see, for example, *HF1*, pp. 620–621/—; *HF2*, pp. 537–538; *NC*, pp. 200/198). To be sure, there is already something decidedly unlyrical in Foucault's insistence that madness interrupts the work, reducing it to silence. Already, in these works, one finds a crisis orientation. Foucault is thus linked to his Romantic predecessors, yet at the same time divided from them. He observes, toward the end of *History of Madness,* that in Romantic poetry madness is seen to speak "the language of the great return"—the language of "final end" and of "absolute recommencement" (*HF1*, p. 619/—; *HF2*, pp. 536–537). But Foucault's conception of crisis and return explicitly involves, as the Romantic conception did not, a radical break between these two moments, and hence a radical denial of the notion of return as involving the recovery of something that is simply *there*, waiting for us to pick it up again.

Depth and interpretation

Evident in *The Archaeology of Knowledge* is the utter disappearance of any such nostalgic and lyrical suggestions. Even as late as *The Order of Things*, these suggestions still play a significant role in Foucault's thinking, as is shown by the importance in that work of the notion of a return of language. In *The Archaeology of Knowledge,* both the work of art and "language" drop entirely out of sight, to be replaced by "discourse." This shift to discourse involves a full acceptance, on Foucault's part, of the interpretive consequences of the notion of crisis, with its devaluation of all ideas of presence. The key statement of this notion in *The Archaeology of Knowledge* is perhaps that passage where he declares his intention to "dispense with 'things,'" to "'depresentify' them," to "substitute for the enigmatic treasure of 'things' anterior to discourse, the regular formation of objects that emerge only in discourse" (*AS,* pp. 65/47). Translated into Nietzschean terms, this passage can be rendered as "there are no facts, only interpretations."

Foucault's confrontation with the problems of meaning and interpretation began long before the appearance of *The Archaeology of Knowledge.* This is most clearly shown by his essay "Nietzsche, Marx, Freud," delivered as a lecture in 1964, though published only in 1967. Until the advent of postmodernism, it was customary to read Nietzsche, Marx, and Freud on the model of "depth" interpretation—that is, on the model of a search for "deep structures." It was customary, in short, to read these thinkers as engaging in an attempt to find the will to power underlying the moral ideal, the social force underlying the ideological fetish, the latent wish underlying the manifest dream. But this is not the way that Foucault reads them. He refuses to see them as having founded a system of interpretation that would link a deceptive superstructure to the firm and comforting reality of a "base." True, he does assert that Nietzsche, Marx, and Freud added the dimension of depth to the field of interpretation. But this depth must be understood, he maintains, not in the comforting terms of "interiority" but rather in the disturbing terms of "exteriority."[1]

Foucault understands by "exteriority" not an illegitimate separation of subject and object (the meaning that the term has in *Mental Illness and Personality*) but rather a rejection of firm foundations. In pursuing their descending course, Nietzsche, Marx, and Freud had discovered, according to Foucault, that there is no solid and objective truth that can serve as a point of termination, no final signified in which all signifiers find their culmination. They had discovered, in short, that every *interpretandum* is always already an *interpretans.* Interpretation does not illuminate some "thing" that passively allows itself to be interpreted, but rather seizes upon an interpretation already in place, "which it must upset, overturn, shatter with hammer blows."[2] Thus, Foucault contends that in interpreting the history of productive relations, Marx was not interpreting a *thing,* an extra-interpretive entity, but rather something that was already an interpretation. Similarly, under the symptoms that his patients exhibited, Freud discovered not the concrete, historical reality of traumas but rather anxiety-charged phantasms, which were already interpretations of historical reality. And finally, above all, Nietzsche demonstrated through his analysis of language that there is no original signified; for words, which are always invented by the higher classes, do not indicate a signified but rather impose an interpretation. In consequence, depth itself, now reconstituted as "an absolutely superficial secret,"[3] is shown to be a deception, and the task of interpretation, which would otherwise have ended in the discovery of a foundation, becomes an infinite task of self-reflection.

We can detect, here, a modification in Foucault's project: a turning away from discourse conceived as a system of signs pointing outward or downward to a referent, to a discourse that would systematically form the objects of which it speaks. Foucault already acknowledges this modification in his project in *Birth of the Clinic*. In the preface to this work, he rejects the strategy of depth interpretation, which he here refers to under the name of "commentary." As he defines it, commentary "questions discourse as to what it says and intended to say; it tries to uncover that deeper meaning of speech that enables it to achieve an identity with itself, supposedly nearer to its essential truth" (*NC*, pp. xii/xvi). He goes on to assert that this activity conceals a strange attitude toward language—an attitude that admits by definition an excess of the signified over the signifier, since it holds that it is possible, through depth analysis, to read the signified within the signifier's gaps. To speak about the thought of others, Foucault observes, has traditionally been to analyze and bring to light the signified. But, he asks, "is it necessary to treat the signified only as a content?" Is it not possible, he further asks, "to undertake a structural analysis of the signified that would evade the fate of commentary by leaving signified and signifier in their original adequacy of one to the other?"

Were one to do this, Foucault suggests, one would treat the semantic elements of a statement not as "autonomous nuclei of multiple significations" but rather as "functional segments, gradually coming together to form a system." In such an approach, the meaning (*sens*) of a proposition would be defined not by the intentions embodied within it but rather by "the difference that it articulates upon other real or possible statements that are contemporary to it or to which it is opposed in the linear series of time" (*NC*, pp. xiii/xvii [translation altered]). For all its difficulties, this is a telling and important statement. It reveals the kinship between Foucault's mode of interpretation and the widely diffused postmodernist notion of the superficiality of art (a point that I shall develop in discussing

Derrida). Postmodernism teaches us to look at the work of art not in order to discern a meaning that lies beneath it but rather to enjoy it for what it is, with nothing concealed, no intention to be discovered, only the infinite play of the work itself. Foucault takes this conception of art and transposes it to the realm of historical and philosophical interpretation. He thus opposes modernist interpreters, whose hallmark is a systematic distinction between depths and surfaces, and who perpetually engage in "commentary" in Foucault's sense.

In *Birth of the Clinic,* the principle of exteriority is largely confined to the preface, for the work as a whole is concerned, as we have seen, with unveiling a "structure of experience" that until now has remained hidden. And even Foucault's next major work, *The Order of Things,* is still only an imperfect exemplification of this new mode of interpretation. To be sure, in *The Order of Things* Foucault sees his task as entailing not an attempt to get down to the true, inarticulate reality of the past, but rather an analysis of sets of discourses. Yet, his commitment to the principle of exteriority remains inconsistent, for he continues to conceive his enterprise in terms of the visual and spatial metaphoric that I evoked in Chapter 5.

Most importantly, *The Order of Things* is replete with images of depth and firm foundation. These images suggest, with great insistence, that despite his apparent adherence to the principle of exteriority, Foucault is still involved in depth interpretation, still involved in the attempt to move from what is visible and superficial to what is invisible, profound, and certain. Thus, he speaks of "the *fundamental* codes of a culture" and of an "order that manifests itself *in depth*" (*MC,* pp. 11/xx). He tells us that "it is *on the basis of* this order, taken as a firm *foundation,* that general theories as to the ordering of things . . . are constructed" (*MC,* pp. 12/ xxi). He tells us that a culture "finds itself faced with the fact that there exists, *below the level of* its spontaneous orders, things that are in themselves capable of being ordered, that belong to a certain unspoken order" (*MC,* pp. 12/xx). He tells us that "what I am attempting to bring to light is the epistemological field, the *episteme* in which knowledge . . . *grounds* its positivity and thereby manifests a history which is not that of its growing perfection, but rather that of its conditions of possibility" (*MC,* pp. 13/xxii; my italics in all quotations). And finally, his predilection for images of depth is revealed by his use, throughout the work, of geological metaphors; for although he is ostensibly engaged in an "archaeological" investigation, the archaeological metaphor, with its distant and ambiguous connotations of depth, tends to give way to geological metaphors, with their unequivocal connotations of depth. Thus, we find him speaking of erosion (*MC,* pp. 64/50), of shocks (*MC,* pp. 229/217), of strata (*MC,* pp. 233/221), and of "our silent and naively immobile ground . . . that is once more stirring under our feet" (*MC,* pp. 16/xxiv).

If we are to read Foucault's "archaeology" according to these images of depth, then the task of the historian, for Foucault, must be seen as an attempt to approach the past through the strategy of a "symptomatic" reading. The historian attempts, that is, to discover what the manifest discourse of men "really" means, a task that is accomplished by finding, in its gaps and silences, symptoms of the latent discourse underlying and determining it. Of course, one must be careful to note that since Foucault rejects, as subjectivist, the unities of the book, the *oeuvre,* and the author,[4] one is concerned here not with the discourse of individuals but with the discourse of entire periods—not with what Ricardo, or Lamarck, or Bopp really meant or intended, but with the underlying meaning of the *episteme* itself. In this reading of Foucault, the task of the historian-archaeologist is to ground the signifier in the signified; the historian-archaeologist is seen as attempting to bring "a plethora of signifying elements" into relation with a "single 'signified.'" In this way, "one substitutes for the diversity of the thing said a sort of great, uniform text, which has never before been articulated, and which reveals for the first time what men 'really meant'" (*AS,* pp. 155/118). This "uniform text," this "single 'signified,'" this latent, underlying meaning to which all superficial discourse is linked, is nothing other than the *episteme.*

Such, at any rate, is one way of reading *The Order of Things.* But this reading of the work, however convincing it might seem at first glance, does not conform to Foucault's own reading as articulated in *The Archaeology of Knowledge.* For in *The Archaeology of Knowledge,* which he implies was written partly in order to repair "the absence of methodological sign-posting" in *The Order of Things* (*AS,* pp. 27/16), he asserts that it was not his intention that the *episteme* should be taken as a "basic" or "fundamental" category underlying the intellectual productions of a given historical period. He argues that his procedure in *The Order of Things* was not "totalitarian." He was not trying to show that "from a certain moment and for a certain time" everyone thought in the same way; he was not trying to show that beneath surface oppositions "everyone accepted a number of fundamental theses" (*AS,* pp. 193–198/148–151). Most of Foucault's readers had seen the classical *episteme,* for example, as an attempt to characterize the whole of seventeenth- and eighteenth-century thought. There is a great deal in the text of *The Order of Things* to support such an interpretation. For instance, Foucault explicitly says that "in any given culture and at any given moment, there is always only one *episteme* that defines the conditions of possibility of all knowledge" (*MC*, pp. 179/168).

In *The Archaeology of Knowledge*, however, Foucault asserts that the classical *episteme* as portrayed in *The Order of Things* was "closely confined to the triad being studied"—that is, to natural history, general grammar, and the analysis of wealth—and is valid "only in the domain specified." This triad is "only one of the describable groups; other groups would yield different results" (*AS*, pp. 207–208/158–159). Significantly, Foucault no longer uses the term *episteme* at all. Instead, he employs such expressions as "discursive formation" and "discursive regularity," expressions that give no suggestion of a distinction of depth. For Foucault's rejection of images of depth is now unequivocal. He explicitly sets aside the geological analogy (*AS*, pp. 173/131). He tells us that "we do not seek below what is manifest the half silent murmur of another discourse"— that it is not a question of finding "a secret discourse, animating the manifest discourse from within" (*AS*, pp. 40–42/28–29). And he distinguishes between analysis and interpretation, telling us that the "analysis of statements . . . avoids all interpretation" (*AS*, pp. 143/109). To put this in another way, analysis avoids all attempts to move from the manifest to the latent, from the statement to the intention. In thus refusing to repeat in the opposite direction the work of expression, it finally escapes, according to Foucault, from the domination of the subject, of the cogito.

The parody of method

We thus turn definitively from *The Order of Things* to *The Archaeology of Knowledge*, perhaps the most consistently misread of all Foucault's writings. It is usually viewed almost in positivistic terms, as the work in which Foucault finally gives us an account of the methodology underlying his various researches. True, Foucault does tell us, as early as *The Order of Things*, that the aim of his next work will be to consider "the problems of method" raised by archaeology (*MC*, pp. 13*n*/xxii*n*). But to take this methodological concern at face value—as is usually done—is to miss entirely what the book is about. One notes a peculiar unimaginativeness in many of Foucault's readers, that they seek to constrain within the boundaries of methodology something so obviously antimethodological.[5]

Part of the difficulty, here, is that many of Foucault's readers simply have not grasped that his statements are in fact counterstatements, and that they need, as it were, to be bounced against their prompting texts if they are to make any sense. In this particular instance, it has not been understood that *The Archaeology of Knowledge* is a parody.[6] Parody's effect depends heavily on a knowledge of the texts being parodized. "*Incipit parodia*," says Nietzsche in the preface to the second edition (1887) of *The Gay Science:* "Parody begins" (*GS,* Preface, §1). This could well stand as a motto for the writings not only of Nietzsche but of Foucault and Derrida as well. And it is no accident that this is so, for when one sees oneself as coming at the end of an oppressive tradition, parody becomes an important genre—a defensive and even a liberating tactic. Readers ignorant of the major texts in the tradition that Foucault is attacking, or even those who, though aware of those texts, remain inappropriately literal-minded, are doomed to misconstrue *The Archaeology of Knowledge* entirely. Moreover, Foucault never bothers to tell us that the book is a parody. It is little wonder, then, that though a few commentators hailed *The Archaeology of Knowledge* as a work of the utmost importance, the more general reaction was, and to a large extent continues to be, one of sheer puzzlement. Viewed in nonparodistic terms, *The Archaeology of Knowledge* is indeed a puzzle. The reader who fails to see the parody is unlikely to get much out of it.

What, then, is going on in *The Archaeology of Knowledge?* Basically, like Heidegger before him, Foucault is attacking Cartesianism. In the present context, Cartesianism must be understood in the broadest possible sense, as the whole subjectivist emphasis that allegedly underlies modern science and technology. The connection that *The Archaeology of Knowledge* bears to Descartes will probably be more immediately perspicuous and convincing to the reader than its connection to Heidegger. This is partly because Descartes's writings, having been so fully absorbed by our culture, will be more familiar than those of Heidegger, and partly because it is Descartes, not Heidegger, who is being parodied. For *The Archaeology of Knowledge* is a parodic repetition of the *Discourse on Method,* that great monument of Western cultural history (for obvious reasons, this monument looms even larger in France than it does elsewhere).

One needs little wit to see that the book has all the trappings of its predecessor of 1637. In the first place, like its Cartesian original, it advertises itself as a methodological treatise, as a work that deals with "methodological problems" and puts forward a new "method of analysis," relegating "questions of procedure" to later empirical studies (*AS,* pp. 19–20, 26, 31/ 10–11, 16, 21). In the second place, it begins with a methodical doubt, with an apparent refusal to accept as true anything that is not known to be so.

More specifically, it begins with a refusal to accept as valid the various sorts of unity and continuity to which we usually accede unquestioningly (*AS,* pp. 31–33, 44, 105/21, 31, 79). In the third place, it proceeds by the formulation of definitions, by the throwing up of hypotheses, by the suggestion of possible directions of research, by the pointing out of consequences, and by the discovery of rules (as can be seen by examining any page in Parts II and III of the book). Fourth and last, it ends by turning to "possible domains of application" within which archaeological analysis can be put to use and against which the "descriptive efficacy" of "the notions that I have tried to define" can be measured (*AS,* pp. 177/135).

The Archaeology of Knowledge is a parody of its Cartesian predecessor rather than a dialectical fulfillment or a mere imitation, for when one looks at it closely its supposed "method" turns out to be disturbingly elusive. Most importantly, it is extremely difficult to give any determinate content to the major concepts of archaeology, whose apparently rigorous definitions turn out to be almost infinitely elastic. This applies above all to the notion of discourse (see Chapter 5, note 38), which defines the framework within which the "archaeology of knowledge" operates. It also applies to the various other concepts that litter the book's pages—such as the discursive formation, the rules of formation, the statement (*énoncé*), the historical *a priori,* and the archive. Closely connected with this difficulty is the astonishing frequency with which Foucault uses "neither/nor" constructions at crucial points in his argument (see, for example, *AS,* pp. 74, 84, 93, 100/55, 63, 70, 75; but several dozen instances could be listed). Insofar as *The Archaeology of Knowledge* can be said to have a general thesis, I take it to be that the uncovering of the "archive"—which Foucault defines as "the first law of what can be said, the system that governs the appearance of statements as unique events" (*AS,* pp. 170/ 129)—can be carried out only by an analysis that is concerned neither with the internal play of signifiers, as are the practitioners of (Mallarméan) literature, nor with the external reference of signifieds, as are the practitioners of (conventional) historiography. But what the uncovering of the archive *is* concerned with (since it is concerned neither with words nor with things) is never made clear (for relevant discussions, see esp. *AS,* pp. 64–67, 82–84, 130–131, 143–144, 145–146/47–49, 62–63, 99, 109, 111). To be sure, many of Foucault's less imaginative apologists have managed to ignore the disturbingly unmethodical aspects of *The Archaeology of Knowledge* and have instead insisted on treating it as a discourse on method pure and simple. But it is difficult to see how such an interpretation can be sustained.

The problems that Foucault's interpreters have had with *The Archaeology of Knowledge* can be attributed in part to their unfamiliarity with the precedent for Foucault's project in the later Heidegger. Admittedly, *The Archaeology of Knowledge* is notably different, in style and approach, both from *Being and Time* and from Heidegger's later writings. But there is a close kinship between the two writers. This is perhaps most clearly seen if one bears in mind those writings in which Heidegger turns his attention to "technology." In *The Archaeology of Knowledge*, Foucault attacks "the twin figures of anthropology and humanism" (*AS*, pp. 22/12). There is much that enters into this preoccupation of Foucault's, including, not least, Nietzsche's notion that "man" is something not to be preserved but to be overcome (*TZ*, Pt. IV, "Of the Higher Man," §§3, 5, 6). But Foucault's preoccupation is more properly Heideggerian than Nietzschean. One is reminded especially of Heidegger's "Age of the World Picture," where "anthropology" and "humanism" are linked to the Cartesian interpretation of man as subject. Moreover, Heidegger declares that "anthropology" is unable to rise up against Descartes, let alone overcome him, thus implying a need to go beyond what anthropology has to offer (*QT*, esp. pp. 133, 140).

Along this same line, recall Heidegger's opposition to conventional historiography. He sees this historiography as something that "projects and objectifies the past in the sense of an explicable and surveyable nexus of actions and consequences," giving us a fixed "picture" of the past in the same way that natural science gives us a "picture" of nature ("The Age of the World Picture," *QT*, p. 123; also "Science and Reflection," *QT*, p. 175). This notion connects with important aspects of Foucault's historiographical project. Note, for example, his refusal in *The Order of Things* to deal with "actions" and "consequences" in the past. Note, too, how in *The Archaeology of Knowledge* he criticizes his earlier writings for purporting to give a portrait of specific periods. These writings aspired, in other words, to turn the past into a visible object viewed by a seeing subject—"the world conceived and grasped as picture," as Heidegger puts it (*QT*, p. 129).

Finally, there is the question of methodology. In "The Age of the World Picture" and other related essays, Heidegger argues that science—including, explicitly, the science of history—develops a methodology peculiar to it, which determines and circumscribes, and is in turn determined and circumscribed by, "the results that it obtains" (*QT*, p. 123). By implication, one needs to break out of this methodology, moving on to something not limited by the Cartesian starting point of modern science. Foucault's obvious attempt to constitute, in *The Archaeology of Knowledge*, a species of antimethodology must be seen as an attempt to respond to this presumed need.

Aware of the affinities with the later Heidegger, we are not surprised to find that *The Archaeology of Knowledge* develops and extends Foucault's aestheticism. For all its quasi-scientific manner, the work is an attack on science, on the whole idea of an objective knowing. As Foucault observes in its final chapter, "I have never presented archaeology as a science, nor even as the first foundations of a future science" (*AS*, pp. 269/206 [translation altered]). Rather, he is concerned with an essentially Dionysian project—that of smashing science altogether. This, surely, is the point of his grotesque parodying of an Apollonian scientific formalism—his "cautious" and "stumbling" affectation of scientific humility, his articulation of principles "so obscure that it has taken hundreds of pages to elucidate them," his creation of a "bizarre machinery" and his development of a "strange arsenal," and his determined pursuit of a thesis that he admits is "difficult to sustain" (*AS*, pp. 27, 177, 144/17, 135, 109). To take such statements at face value is to miss what is going on. Foucault is engaged in undermining a whole structure of thinking, a whole approach toward "reality" that he sees as oppressively uncreative. By focusing on "discourse" as the final end of his analysis, he aims to bypass this rigidifying mind-set, much as Nietzsche sought to do in declaring reality itself to be a human creation.

Admittedly, in some ways the label "aestheticism" is a misnomer when applied to Foucault's position as he develops it in *The Archaeology of Knowledge* and subsequent works. As I have noted, there is no longer any emphasis in these writings on the work of art (as one finds in *History of Madness*) or even on "language" (as one finds in *The Order of Things*). Another label, emphasizing Foucault's emphasis on discourse, might perhaps be preferable. Nonetheless, the aesthetic underpinnings of Foucault's notion of discourse are, to my mind, clear. Consider, for example, his assertion that in "archaeological" analysis "one is not seeking . . . to pass from the text to thought, from talk to silence, from the exterior to the interior, from spatial dispersion to the pure recollection of the moment, from superficiality to profound unity. *One remains within the dimension of discourse*" (*AS*, pp. 101/76 [my italics]). This is an immensely important statement. Moreover, it is a statement that makes sense only when it is seen for what it is: the articulation of a postmodernist sensibility, wherein art is art and nothing else, wherein, for example, *Finnegans Wake* is *Finnegans Wake* and not the representation of something outside *Finnegans Wake*. When Foucault says that the "groups of discourse" with which he deals in *The Order of Things* are "not the expression of a world-view that has been coined in the form of words, nor the hypocritical trans-lation of an interest masquerading under the pretext of a theory," he is approaching past texts in the same spirit with which we approach *Finne-gans Wake,* or *The Sound and the Fury,* or "Blue Poles" (*AS,* pp. 92/69). When he says that the "archive" is "the law of what can be said, the system that governs the appearance of statements as unique events," the word *event* needs to be understood in its aesthetic rather than in its con-ventionally historical sense (*AS,* pp. 170/129).

Similarly, his notion of the "materiality" of discourse (*AS,* pp. 138/105) ought to be understood in light of the material *thereness* of the work of art rather than as an expression of a Marxian historical materialism (for there is a crucial difference between Marx and Foucault: the former is afflicted with a desire for objective truth; the latter is not). The same applies to the notion that archaeology transforms "documents" into "monuments," treating its source texts not as "a sign of something else," as "an element that ought to be transparent," but rather as something that has its own inherently interesting volume (*AS,* pp. 182/138–139). Similarly, the notion of the "indefinite, repetitive, prolific domain of discourse," of its "great surface," has obvious aesthetic resonances (*AS,* pp. 94, 105/71, 79).

Genealogy

Yet, for all its importance in articulating the implications of an aes-theticist apprehension of discourse, *The Archaeology of Knowledge* puts forward a position that Foucault was soon to leave behind. To be sure, Foucault rejects, in *The Archaeology of Knowledge,* all images of depth. But despite this, he still remains caught up within a spatial metaphoric— a metaphoric that, in Derrida's terms, is force-excluding. The "great sur-face of discourse" is still a surface, a plane that we observe even though we no longer try to see behind or below it. At the same time, however, the work also points forward to Foucault's writings of the 1970s, for along with the rhetoric of space there is also, in the book, a rhetoric of practice. Thus, Foucault characterizes discourse as "a practice that has its own forms of sequence and succession" (*AS,* pp. 221/169), and he refers time and again to "discursive strategies" and "discursive practice" (for exam-ples, see the index to the English translation).

In the writings that come after *The Archaeology of Knowledge,* Foucault abandons the lingering theoreticism of that work. In a move that I have already referred to, he adopts instead a radical activism within which theoretical activity is seen as having an entirely practical significance. That is to say, theory does not simply "analyze" or "describe" reality; far more importantly, it seems to articulate strategies by which what is extant may perpetually be overcome. This shift toward a notion of discourse as praxis can be linked to the events of 1968 in France, and to the reaction that those events occasioned among the avant-garde Parisian intellectual community. Certainly, in the wake of 1968, there was an audience for a philosopher willing to move in the direction of a new and exciting practice. But at the same time, the shift was, in view of positions that Foucault had taken up as early as 1961, a logical one.

As we have seen, in his critique of *History of Madness* Derrida points out that Foucault is, by his own argument, trapped within "logocentrism," within the general historical guilt borne by Western language. For whatever his claims to be resurrecting the silent language of an oppressed madness, Foucault continues to speak the language of the very reason that carried out the oppression in the first place. In short, he is still caught within the all-powerful order that he is seeking to evade. Thus, the radicalism of Foucault's critique of psychiatry is called into question. Given the character of Western reason, does it suffice, Derrida asks, "to stack the tools of psychiatry neatly inside a tightly closed workshop, in order to return to innocence and to end all complicity with the rational or political order which keeps madness captive? The psychiatrist is but the delegate of this order, one delegate among others" (*E&D*, pp. 57–58/35).

Derrida's characteristic response to the historical guilt that in his view inevitably accompanies Western reason is to engage in a play with the text. But why should we follow Derrida? The dereliction of the present, which Nietzsche, Heidegger, Derrida, and Foucault all point to, leads as well to radical activism as it does to the nostalgic passivity of Heidegger or to the almost indefinable stance of Derrida. It is a strategy of absolute praxis—understood in a political and not merely in a textual sense—that Foucault, in the period after the publication of *The Archaeology of Knowledge,* definitively adopts. This transition in Foucault's work, which can be situated in the years from 1970 to 1972, brought an abandonment of the entire "bizarre machinery" of *The Archaeology of Knowledge.*

Foucault's turn to radical activism is closely tied up with his discovery of the rhetorical possibilities offered by the thought of Nietzsche. Significantly, after 1970 Foucault characterizes his work not as "archaeology" but as "genealogy" (on those rare occasions when he recurs to the former term, he very clearly fits "archaeology" within a "genealogical" framework [see, for example, "Two Lectures," *P/K,* p. 85]). So far as I know, Foucault's first reference to the affinity between his own work and the historico-critical project of Nietzschean genealogy occurs in an interview of 1967, in which he declares that archaeology "owes more to Nietzschean genealogy than to structuralism properly so called."[7] But it was only after the publication of *The Archaeology of Knowledge* that he began to insist on the Nietzsche connection. In his next major book, *Discipline and Punish* (1975), he never uses the term "archaeology." Instead, he characterizes this study as "a correlative history of the modern soul and of a new power to judge; a genealogy of the present scientifico-legal complex from which the power to punish derives its bases, justifications and rules, from which it extends its effects and by which it masks its exorbitant singularity" (*SP,* pp. 27/23). And in a 1975 interview in which he comments on *Discipline and Punish,* he tells us that "if I wanted to be pretentious, I would use 'the genealogy of morals' as the general title of what I am doing" ("Prison Talk" [interview with J.-J. Brochier], *P/K,* p. 53).

With this genealogical turn, Foucault also comes (as one might expect) to acknowledge the fictional character of his historical writings. In 1967, to be sure, he had ventured to suggest that *The Order of Things* was "purely and simply a 'fiction.'" But at the time he had not bothered to follow up on this suggestion, which conflicted so radically with his quasi-scientific pretensions of that period. Indeed, the point was immediately vitiated by his assertion that the fiction had not been invented by Foucault, but was an expression of the relationship between the epistemological configuration of our own epoch and the "whole mass of statements" emanating from the past.[8]

By way of contrast, in 1977 another interviewer evoked the following response from Foucault:

> As for the problem of fiction, it is for me a very important problem; I am well aware that I have never written anything but fictions. I do not mean to go so far as to say that fictions are beyond truth [*hors vérité*]. It seems to me that it is possible to make fiction work inside of truth, to induce truthful effects with a fictional discourse, and to operate in such a manner that the discourse of truth gives rise to, "manufactures," something that does not yet exist, that is, "fictions" it. One "fictions" history on the basis of a political reality that makes it true, one "fictions" a politics not yet in existence on the basis of an historical truth. ("The History of Sexuality" [Finas interview], *P/K,* p. 193 [translation altered].)

Foucault's histories, then, are fictions. They are explicitly not representations of the literal truth concerning the past. They do not aim to portray the past "as it actually was." On the contrary, they have a mythmaking function. Foucault accepts, in his later writings, Nietzsche's notion of history as something that propagates, or at any rate ought to propagate, myths that will be useful in the present. And he turns, too, to a criticism of "the effects of a power which the West since Medieval times has attributed to science and has reserved for those engaged in scientific discourse" ("Two Lectures," *P/K*, p. 85).

Useful myths, for Foucault, are those that will disorder order, those that will break up what is extant, those that will turn the present into a past. The process is an unending one, for every future present will likewise come under the hammer of Foucault's disordering rhetoric. Foucault makes this absolutely clear in another interview of 1977, this one with Bernard-Henri Lévy. Lévy suggests that after we have reversed the terms in which we speak of sex, abandoning the notion that power is negative and that once it is demolished fulfillment will be ours, there will then come "the time to stop, the moment to reflect and to regain an equilibrium." Foucault replies: "On the contrary. What must follow is the moment of new mobility and new displacement, for these reversals of 'for' and 'against' are quickly blocked off."[9] If *Waiting for Godot* is an appropriate allegory of Heidegger's project, then one can imagine an allegory of Foucault's project entitled *Running after Godot*—it being understood that Godot will not allow himself to be caught, if he exists at all.

In his essay "Nietzsche, Genealogy, History," which appeared in 1971 in a volume of essays dedicated to the memory of Jean Hyppolite, Foucault articulates a justification for this new, fictionizing emphasis in his work. Distilling the essence of lectures that he had earlier given at the new, Vincennes campus of the University of Paris, this is the first significant writing of his to postdate the May 1968 explosion: *The Archaeology of Knowledge*, though it appeared in print only in 1969, was completed before the events of 1968.[10] It is not, I think, wrong to see the essay as a response to those events, an attempt to reproduce on the level of discourse what had been attempted and thwarted on the level of politics.

Foucault articulates, in this essay, the notion of an historiography that "disturbs what was previously considered immobile; . . . fragments what was thought unified; . . . shows the heterogeneity of what was imagined consistent with itself" (*LCMP*, p. 147). In so doing, it affirms knowledge "as perspective," aiming not at "objective" truth but rather at a particular impact on its readers. It thus functions as "effective history" (*wirkliche Historie*), breaking up a present order that has hitherto enjoyed the advantage of an assumed historical legitimacy. As Foucault puts it, history becomes "effective" when it "introduces discontinuity into our very being," when it "deprives the self of the reassuring stability of life and nature" (*LCMP*, p. 154). Such a history is in all respects opposed to the extant order; it is "parodic, directed against reality, dissociative, directed against identity, . . . sacrificial, directed against truth" (*LCMP*, p. 160).

With regard to this final, sacrificial function, Foucault insists particularly on the notion of a "will to knowledge" that arbitrarily establishes its own "truth." Such a "truth" is violent and coercive in character. In Foucault's words, "knowledge does not slowly detach itself from its empirical roots, the initial needs from which it arose, to become pure speculation subject only to the demands of reason; . . . rather, it creates a progressive enslavement to its instinctive violence" (*LCMP*, pp. 162–164). This applies as much to "genealogical" knowledge as it does to the various forms of conventional knowledge that genealogical knowledge opposes.

As these comments suggest, Foucault's turn to genealogy brings with it a much more explicit articulation of the agonistic character of his enterprise. This comes out clearly in his inaugural lecture as Professor of the History of Systems of Thought, delivered, as I have noted, in December 1970 and published the following year. Here the notion of an enclosure within discourse is absolutely decisive. Indeed, Foucault begins by regretting that he is obliged to take speech. He wishes rather that speech might have taken hold of him—that instead of being one from whom discourse comes, he might not rather be "at the hazard of its unrolling, a slender gap, the point of its possible disappearance" (*OD*, pp. 7–8). But perhaps most significant in *The Order of Discourse* is his stress on power and struggle. Whereas in *The Archaeology of Knowledge* discourse was envisaged in Apollonian terms, as a kind of plane surface that one seeks to order or disorder, it is now seen as "that for which, that by which one struggles, the power that one seeks to seize" (*OD*, p. 12).

In *Michel Foucault: Beyond Structuralism and Hermeneutics,* Dreyfus and Rabinow suggest that while Foucault in the 1960s was caught within "the illusion of autonomous discourse" (or, in my terminology, within aestheticism), in the 1970s he works himself free from this enclosure, turning now to a "genealogy of the modern individual" that strives to articulate an "interpretive analytics of power, truth, and the body." In Dreyfus and Rabinow's view, whereas in his writings of 1963–69 Foucault dwelt almost exclusively on "linguistic practices," in his post-1969 writings he now deals with "the social practices that formed both institutions and discourse."[11]

To what extent is this interpretation of Foucault's writings of the 1970s borne out by the texts themselves? As I noted earlier, I see conflicting tendencies in these writings, which are probably too close to us to allow any firm articulation of their direction and significance. On the one hand, much of *Discipline and Punish* suggests a focus on actual social practices. There is no doubt that this work diverges in an important way from the notion of discourse as primary exemplified in *Birth of the Clinic* and *The Order of Things* and justified in *The Archaeology of Knowledge*. Largely because Foucault does strive in *Discipline and Punish* to confront, in some manner, actual social institutions, the book has proved to be of much greater interest to conventional historians than any of his other works. In spite of the lacunae that they have discerned in its evidential bases, and the flaws that they have uncovered in its movement from evidence to generalization, it has nonetheless had an important impact on conventional historiographical writing and research.[12] But on the other hand, in *The Will to Knowledge* the focus on discourse is pervasive, while even in *Discipline and Punish* there are problems with the notion of power that cast doubt on the concreteness of Foucault's concern with social practices.

Discourse

Let us first consider the question of discourse. *The Will to Knowledge* claims to be an introduction to a history of sexuality, but it all but identifies the history of sexuality with the history of discourses *about* sexuality. Time and again, Foucault implies that in discussing such discourses he is discussing sexuality as it actually operates within society. Note, firstly, the major thesis of the book—namely, its denial of what Foucault calls the "repression hypothesis." According to the repression hypothesis, sexuality has been repressed in the modern world. Foucault declares that the repression hypothesis—which he holds to be the usual view—is wrong: sexuality has not been repressed in the modern world but has rather proliferated. As he puts it, "sexuality . . . has been expanding at an increasing rate since the seventeenth century" (*VS*, pp. 146/110). But what sort of evidence does he present for this conclusion? In briefest terms: none. Instead, he leaps from the fact that discourses about sexuality have proliferated to the assertion that sexuality has proliferated. He declares that our age "initiated sexual heterogeneities" (*VS*, pp. 51/37), when his evidence indicates only that our age initiated the discussion of such heterogeneities (an important innovation, no doubt, but not to be confused with the innovation of the "heterogeneities" themselves). He tells us that in the nineteenth century a host of new "personages" made their appearance: "the nervous woman, the frigid wife, the indifferent mother, . . . the impotent,

sadistic, perverse husband, the hysterical or neurasthenic girl, the preco-
cious and already exhausted child, and the young homosexual who rejects
marriage or neglects his wife" (*VS*, pp. 146/110). Again, he says more
than he ought to, for his evidence indicates only that these personages
appeared in a certain nineteenth-century discourse, not that they were
new elements in the social landscape. (Of course, they *may* have been new
elements in the social landscape, but the point is that Foucault's evidence
gives us no reason for believing so.) Finally, "sexuality," in Foucault's perspective, is presented as an "historical apparatus" (*dispositif*) arising
from discourse about sexuality, for what is involved in the discourse about
sexuality, according to Foucault, is "the very production of sexuality"
(*VS*, pp. 139/105 [translation altered]).

In such formulations, discourse seems as autonomous as ever. I detect
here a conscious political strategy on Foucault's part. Crucial for understanding this strategy is "Nietzsche, Genealogy, History," with its postulating of a rancorous, creative, destructive "will to knowledge." Pursuing
this notion of a will to knowledge, in his writings of the 1970s Foucault
abandons the notion of "space"—even the entirely superficial space of an
"order of discourse." Instead, he portrays discourse as something that
goes out to do battle. Consider, for example, *I, Pierre Rivière, having
slaughtered my mother, my sister, and my brother,* the chronicle of a
young Norman peasant who in 1835 murdered most of his family with a
pruning hook. Foucault tells us in his introduction to this work that the
documents of the case reveal "a strange contest, a confrontation, a power
relation, a battle *among discourses and through discourses*" [my ital-
ics].[13] It is not that elements *outside* "discourse" seek to seize control of it
or redefine its terms; rather, the whole of the battle is seen as taking place
within discourse itself. Effectively, Foucault is viewing the world as if it
were discourse. This is a significant move, for if the world is discursive,
then the whole of the extant order is discursive; and if the whole of the
extant order is discursive, then it is obviously susceptible to discursive
attack. What prevents us from replacing the reigning discourse with another discourse? What privilege could the reigning discourse possibly
have? For example, if the present mode of sexuality is a discursive product, why not discursively produce another mode of sexuality? In the
reigning discourse, homosexuality is subjected to exclusion; Foucault's
strategy is designed, among other things, to show the absolutely arbitrary
character of that exclusion. The power of a subversive discourse is mag-
nified by its defining as purely discursive that which it seeks to oppose.

To be sure, when the present order is overturned and the subversive discourse becomes the reigning one, it, too, will be subject to discursive attack. But this is exactly what Foucault wants: as a thinker of crisis, he is implicitly committed to the notion that the reigning order, whatever its nature, is degraded. One can thus imagine him turning against the discourse of homosexuality if that discourse becomes dominant, for far from ushering in the millenium, any such rise to dominance will merely provide the occasion for erecting new systems of exclusion. It is thus not surprising that Foucault's attitude toward the various so-called "action groups" with which he has been associated is peculiarly double-edged and ironical. He is willing to ally himself with these groups insofar as they are able to mount challenges to the existing order, attacking that order at one or another of its weak points. But insofar as they are committed to establishing new, allegedly liberating orders, he remains highly suspicious of them. For what Foucault has articulated is an instrument of systematic suspicion toward any order whatsoever—an analytical weapon that can be used against any and all "discursive productions," even those with which Foucault has for the moment aligned himself.

There is something obviously self-interested in this redefinition of the universe as a realm of discourse. Let us consider again Foucault's intellectual milieu—which is, in fact, the milieu of intellectuals, intellectuals who take it as self-evident that they have a crucially important political role to play. Descombes notes, in his history of recent French philosophy, that the staking out of a political position has been so important to philosophers in France that the "definitive meaning" of even the most abstruse epistemological or metaphysical problems is not considered settled until its implications for the next elections, or for the attitude of the Communist Party, have been disclosed.[14] In short, it is assumed that the intellectual has a political role to play as an intellectual, distinct from his status as person and citizen; and it is assumed, too, that all his intellectual work will have some sort of political significance.

Given these assumptions, the question of the political role of the intellectual becomes a standing problem. Not surprisingly, it is a problem that Foucault has addressed on a number of occasions; one notes especially the long discussion of the issue at the end of his 1977 interview with Fontana and Pasquino, and his March 1972 conversation with Gilles Deleuze on the same subject ("Truth and Power," *P/K*, pp. 126–133; *LCMP*, pp. 205–217). Many French intellectuals of the generation prior to Foucault's considered the political role of the intellectual to be unambiguous: the intellectual was "the clear, individual figure of a universality whose obscure, collective form is embodied in the proletariat" (*P/K*, p. 126). But for Foucault this peculiar form of Kantian theoretical universalism obviously will not do. We all know that intellectuals have a political role to play—but what is it? The advantage, here, of a discursive redefinition of reality is clear; for discourse is a matter, finally, of words, and words are the peculiar concern of intellectuals. Hence, the political importance that Foucault attributes to Nietzsche (*P/K,* p. 133). If politics is finally a matter of discourse, then intellectuals become our true politicians.

Power

In the reading of Foucault put forward by Dreyfus and Rabinow, Foucault in his writings postdating 1968–69 is seen as coming to focus on the exercise of power within modern society. To be sure, Foucault had touched on this subject in his earlier writings, but only in his writings of the 1970s did he come to deal with it in an adequate fashion. As Foucault puts it in "Truth and Power," in the earlier writings he had "not yet properly isolated" the "central problem of power" (*P/K,* p. 113). But with his 1970s writings, Dreyfus and Rabinow suggest, "the problem of power had been well-located indeed."[15]

But to what extent *does* Foucault "well locate" the problem of power in his more recent writings? Looking at *Discipline and Punish,* one is struck by the peculiar elusiveness of Foucault's analyses. Frank Lentricchia notes that power, in Foucault's social theory, "tends to occupy the 'anonymous' place which classical treatises in metaphysics reserved for substance: without location, identity, or boundaries, it is everywhere and nowhere at the same time." It resembles in its ubiquity the God of theism. Unlike that God, however, it has "no predominant direction, no predominant point of departure, no predominant point of terminus." Indeed, in its imperviousness it resembles "some Eastern metaphysical force that ensnares us all."[16] The historian Jacques Léonard makes a similar point, noting how vague Foucault is when it comes to specifying exactly who is exercising the power that is so ubiquitous in *Discipline and Punish.* Foucault manages to evade the question of agency in a number of ways: for example, by making liberal use of reflexive verbs, infinitives, and the impersonal French *on*—the anonymous "one"; by speaking of strategy, tactics, and the like without indicating whose strategy or tactics it is; and by telling us that such and such an historical reality "can be viewed as" having such and such a significance, with the question of whether this was its significance for the historical actors themselves not really confronted.[17]

The same anonymity surrounds the related conception of "biopower" in *The Will to Knowledge* (*VS*, pp. 177–211/135–159).

What, then, are we to make of Foucault's concern with power? I would suggest that this concern can only really be confronted if one looks at it in the light of Foucault's relation to Nietzsche. Foucault's turn to genealogy marks a turn, too, to a Nietzschean conception of power. Looking back in the middle 1970s on his work of the 1960s, Foucault judges his earlier conception of power to be inadequate, because entirely negative in character (as he suggests in his 1977 interview with Lucette Finas, *P/K*, pp. 183–184). Power, in such a work as *History of Madness*, was an entity whose importance was to be found in the fact that it "excludes," "represses," "censors," "abstracts," "masks," and "conceals." In his writings of the 1970s, on the other hand, Foucault asserts that power is not a negative but a positive phenomenon: "Power produces; it produces reality; it produces domains of objects and rituals of truth" (*SP*, pp. 196/194). *Discipline and Punish* eloquently testifies to this new attitude toward power, for a central contention in this work is that the social role of the prison was not to repress delinquency but to create it. By thus manufacturing a threat to social stability, the prison provided a rationale for the construction of the vast apparatus of control and discipline that now dominates bourgeois society. This "productive" conception of power is even more firmly embodied in *The Will to Knowledge,* which Foucault designated, soon after its publication, as the first book in which he *really* liberates himself from the search for "things themselves in their primitive vivacity," the first book in which he *fully* frees himself from the idea that power is "bad, ugly, poor, sterile, monotonous, and dead."[18]

There need be no mystery where Foucault's assertion of the productivity of power comes from or to what internal dynamic it responds—for commitment to the productivity of power is the supremely Dionysian insight, well known to "that Dionysian monster," Zarathustra. In asserting that power is a creative force, Foucault distances himself from the structuralism of his earlier work, in which the excluded, the repressed, the censored, the abstracted, the masked, the hidden was alone "in play" (*en jeu*), and power—that is, the center from which these operations were created—was *hors jeu.* That is to say, he rejects Apollonian formalism for a position that is now explicitly poststructuralist (the antiformalistic theme is especially obvious in "Nietzsche, Genealogy, History" [*LCMP*, pp. 142, 144, 146, 147, 152]).[19]

Foucault's rebellion against structuralism in its Apollonian sense brings with it an alteration in his attitude toward the visual and spatial metaphoric with which Apollonian structuralism is so closely connected. A major part of Foucault's concern, now, is to bring to the bar of judgment what he had hitherto accepted as a given. Especially in *Discipline and Punish*, the theme of visibility is utterly pervasive. Useful here is a comparison with *Birth of the Clinic*, the "archaeological" work with which *Discipline and Punish* has the closest affinities. As we have seen, the earlier book is replete with visual and spatial metaphors. Indeed, the work is constructed around the concept of the *regard médical*—the "medical gaze." But Foucault in no way attacks these metaphors: his concern is the less revolutionary one of outlining the field of knowledge that these metaphors allegedly constituted. In *Discipline and Punish*, by way of contrast, the whole notion of a visual and spatial metaphoric is subjected to a penetrating examination. Visibility itself, in the form of Bentham's project for a "panoptic" prison, is brought into question. According to Foucault, the "major effect" of the Panopticon was "to induce in the inmate a state of conscious and permanent visibility that assures the automatic functioning of power." The aim was "so to arrange things that the surveillance is permanent in its effects, even if it is discontinuous in its action; that the perfection of power should tend to render its actual exercise unnecessary; that this architectural apparatus should be a machine for creating and sustaining a power relation independent of the person who exercises it; in brief, that the inmates should be caught in a power situation of which they are themselves the bearers" (*SP*, pp. 202–203/201).

Nor is Foucault's argument confined to the prison. On the contrary, it is his contention that we are *all* caught within disciplinary systems—systems of *micro-pouvoirs*. These systems, he asserts, exist throughout bourgeois society and control our behavior without our knowing it. Their functioning is dependent on a regime of observation, surveillance, and inspection similar to Bentham's Panopticon, even though less obvious in its workings. The whole exercise of discipline within modern society presupposes, according to Foucault, "a mechanism that coerces through the play of the glance [*par le jeu du regard*]" (*SP*, pp. 173/170 [translation altered]). This disciplinary power "is exercised through its invisibility"; yet, at the same time, it "imposes on those whom it subjects a principle of compulsory visibility" (*SP*, pp. 189/187). In a 1977 interview, Foucault goes on to link the Benthamite project with Rousseau's dream "of a transparent society, visible and legible in each of its parts"—the dream "of there no longer existing any zones of darkness, zones established by the privileges of royal power or the prerogatives of some corporation" ("The

Eye of Power," *P/K*, p. 152). In an important sense, Foucault engages in a reversal of Rousseau, viewing as insidious and threatening what Rousseau saw as desirable.

At this point, we arrive at the essential core of Foucault's historiographical project (insofar as it can be said to have an "essential core"); for, as his abandonment of the notion of the gaze suggests, he is now concerned not with the Apollonian portrayal of a dead past—a past that, as far as we are concerned, exists in a state of "Egyptian rigidity"—but rather with what he sees as the active play of forces in the present. Such, at any rate, is his persistent claim.

To be sure, Foucault has always written with the aim of revolutionizing, or destroying, the present: as early as *History of Madness,* he had this obvious present end in view. But there was a tendency, in his earlier work, for much of this to be obscured. This was particularly so in *The Archaeology of Knowledge,* which in its very parody of science became caught up in a kind of theoreticism of its own. With his genealogical turn, however, there was no mistaking the direction of his project. In a 1971 interview, he informs us that "it is a question, basically, of presenting a critique of our own time, based upon retrospective analyses"; and he goes on to explain that "what I am trying to do is grasp the implicit systems which determine our most familiar behavior without our knowing it. I am trying to find their origin, to show their formation, the constraint they impose upon us; I am therefore trying to place myself at a distance from them and to show how one could escape." For Foucault, it is now explicitly a question of shaking things up, of putting "into play," or risking, "the systems that quietly order us about."[20] In a 1975 interview, he emphasizes even more strongly the total insertion of his works into the context of a present struggle: "Writing interests me only insofar as it enlists itself into the reality of a contest, as an instrument of tactics, of illumination. I would like my books to be, as it were, lancets, or Molotov cocktails, or minefields; I would like them to self-destruct after use, like fireworks." It is necessary, Foucault asserts, for historical analysis to be a real part of "political struggle"—not that it attempts to give such struggles a "guiding thread" or a "theoretical apparatus," but rather that it "constitutes" their "possible strategies."[21] It is in *Discipline and Punish* that this concern first comes fully into play. He tells us in this work that "I have learnt not so much from history as from the present" that "punishment in general and the prison in particular belong to a political technology of the body." He goes on to say that it is of the prison in its actuality "that I would like to write the history," an enterprise that he characterizes not as "writing a history of the past in terms of the present," but as "writing the history of the present" (*SP*, pp. 35/30–31).

Yet, the rhetorical component in this "history of the present" is so pervasive that it is very difficult to see how, even in its own terms, it can claim to be a "history of the present" at all. We have already seen that Foucault views genealogy as directed against the notions of an "objective" reality, an "objective" identity, and an "objective" truth—for he sees these notions as confirming the extant order. Indeed, in his conversion of Nietzsche's monumental, antiquarian, and critical modes of history into his own parodistic, dissociative, and sacrificial modes, he leaves out of play—as he himself points out—the appeal that the early Nietzsche still makes to "the affirmative and creative powers of life" (*LCMP*, p. 164). Against the will to knowledge that has allegedly dominated our perception up to now, he deploys a will of his own—a will to creative opinion.

We can most conveniently approach the ambiguities in this position by looking at Foucault's double claim, which I have already noted, that "one 'fictions' history on the basis of a political reality that makes it true, one 'fictions' a politics not yet in existence on the basis of a historical truth" (*P/K*, p. 193). This statement marks an odd interplay between truth and lie: a lying history is legitimized by the existence of a "true" political reality; a lying politics is legitimized by the existence of a "true" history. To expand on this: what makes "true" a representationally inadequate account of, for example, prisons is the truth that we do live in a disciplinary society. In consequence, despite its inadequacies or even its outright falsehoods, such an account is justified insofar as it enables us to see more clearly the reality of this disciplinary society. In other words, it can be argued that Foucault is engaging in a legitimate rhetorical tactic, telling us lies about the past in order to open our eyes to the reality of the present.

In this argument, the only difference between Foucault and more conventional scholars is that Foucault is far more open in acknowledging what he is doing. And indeed, the rhetorician has long enjoyed a place within society: sometimes an honored place. If that place is not very honored today, this is perhaps a reflection of our own intellectual confusions. As Richard Weaver puts it in *The Ethics of Rhetoric*, rhetoricians are often accused of indulging in "exaggerations." But, says Weaver, "the exaggeration which [the true] rhetorician employs is not caricature but prophecy; and it would be a fair formulation to say that true rhetoric is concerned with the potency of things. The literalist . . . is troubled by its failure to conform to a present reality. What he fails to appreciate is that potentiality is a mode of existence, and that all prophecy is about the tendency of things."[22]

Weaver's argument could well serve as a defense of Foucault against all those conventional historians and philosophers who object to him on literalistic grounds, pointing out that he is wrong about *A,* wrong about *B,* wrong about *C,* has an error in logic with regard to *D,* and so on. These objections may be entirely correct, but at the same time they utterly miss the point. For whatever his tactical claims to be a mere diagnostician (claims that Nietzsche, for equally tactical reasons, also made), Foucault's enterprise is clearly a prophetic one. He is simply not interested in logical or historical correctness, or at any rate not in logical or historical correctness for its own sake. Rather, he is interested in changing the way things are. Sometimes logical and historical correctness may contribute to this aim, but it is equally plausible that they may not. Those who refuse to countenance this latter possibility simply do not understand how the world operates.

But this is not to exempt Foucault from criticism, for his claims are infinitely more radical than those of Weaver's "true rhetorician." The "true rhetorician," in Weaver's reading, admits the legitimacy of a counterpart to rhetoric—namely, dialectic. Dialectic is here defined in the Aristotelian rather than in the Hegelian sense as (in Weaver's words) "a method of investigation whose object is the establishment of truth about doubtful propositions."[23] In contrast, by his exclusion of representation, Foucault excludes the establishment of truth in this sense. Foucault speaks not of truth but of "truth," understanding this term in the same way that Nietzsche understands it in "On Truth and Lie." Thus, we can call into question, as having a rhetorical significance and no other kind, Foucault's claim that he is engaged in "fictioning" a history "on the basis of a political reality that makes it true." In Foucault's own terms, this claim is a lie, for Foucault has already excluded from consideration any notion of "political reality" (let alone political reality considered as a "basis" or "starting point") separable from rhetoric itself. We may admit that there can be a sense of liberation in opting for the free play of the interpretation of interpretation as against the circumscribed work of the interpretation of things—particularly when it is a matter of confronting a stifling and unimaginative scholarship. But surely this sense of liberation is in an important way deceptive. Foucault postulates a present reality on the basis of which we attribute truth to a "fictioned" history, but this present reality is itself a fiction. It follows that he is not in the proper sense a radical, for he fails to touch the roots; his "fictioning" of the past is at the same time a fictioning, and a mythifying, of the present.

Let me emphasize that I am not arguing against Foucault's political stance *in toto*. As a matter of fact, his political pronouncements are often appealingly modest, open, and undoctrinaire, and his interventions shrewdly, subtly, and intelligently carried out. The last French intellectual to play a role comparable to Foucault's was Sartre, and it is worth comparing the very different political postures of the two writers. Richard Rorty has noted that "Foucault's attempt to get philosophy and politics together is much more wary, complicated and generally intelligent than Sartre's."[24] This is in part the consequence of a philosophical position that requires Foucault to be highly circumspect in his political commitments. From the Foucauldian perspective, political action is a matter not of "engagement in" but rather of "experience with."[25] Moreover, Foucault is much more conscious than Sartre ever was of the oppressive potential that rests in every state, in every mass movement. Recall that amazing statement with which Sartre opens *Situations III*: "We were never more free than under the German occupation."[26] And compare this with Foucault's memories of the occupation, as recounted in a 1981 interview: "I have very early memories of an absolutely threatening world, which could crush us. To have lived as an adolescent in a situation that had to end, that had to lead to another world, for better or worse, was to have the impression of spending one's entire childhood in the night, waiting for dawn. That prospect of another world marked the people of my generation, and we have carried with us, perhaps to excess, a dream of Apocalypse."[27]

I *am* arguing, however, against naive readings of Foucault. For example, there is a temptation to derive from Foucault's history of the prison true propositions regarding the actual institution within society that we know as the prison. But it is an error to try to derive from Foucault such propositions as, for example, "the prison exists in order to foster delinquency and thus to provide a rationale for strengthening the instruments of repression." Rather, what one can usefully find in Foucault's writings on the prison are suggestions, pregnant hints for further work and investigation, perspectives that, pursued and tested, may allow us to see more clearly the world in which we live—and may perhaps help us in any attempts to alter that world. Foucault is best treated as an animator—not as an authority. And it ought to be remembered, too, that underlying his work is the assumption of crisis. Confronted by the presumed crisis, Foucault adopts an activist stance—a commitment to a *truly* permanent revolution, the exact counterpart to Heidegger's passivity. This commitment comes out very clearly in his writings of 1978–79 on Iran, in which we find him reaffirming his faith in revolt in the face of the atrocities of the new regime. As Foucault puts it, "there are revolts and that is a fact. It is through revolt that subjectivity (not that of great men but that of whomever) introduces itself into history and gives it the breath of life."[28] This evocation of revolt is entirely in character for Foucault. The question remains, however, whether the "dream of Apocalypse" that Foucault puts before us is really one we want to make our own.

To sum up: Foucault's writings have a potential utility, helping us to see the world in ways that we might not have thought of otherwise. But they also have a potential danger—namely, that the visions and prophecies that they contain will conceal from us an "ordinary" world very different from the world of Foucault's invention. This "ordinary" world is the world of natural and social human needs and of commonplace, rather than of miraculously creative, work. Indeed, Foucault's own rhetorical strategy caters to such a misreading; for if he can on occasion admit the fictional character of his supposed histories, to do so consistently (to declare, for example, that he is really engaged in the writing of novels, and that his works are not histories at all) would entirely deprive these works of the rhetorical force that he seeks to give them. For rhetorical reasons, he must continually balance on the edges of a positivism. In consequence, it is all too easy to take his writings literally, to read him in the mode of "is" rather than in the mode of "as if."

Power and discourse

Still, it is tempting to see Foucault's concern with "power" as indicating an attempt on his part to go outside the framework of discourse. Foucault himself underwrites such an interpretation of his recent work. For example, in an interview given soon after the publication of *The Will to Knowledge*, he discusses the new notion of the "apparatus" (*dispositif*) that he deploys in *Discipline and Punish* and *The Will to Knowledge*. He tells us that the *episteme* was "a specifically *discursive* apparatus," whereas the apparatus in its general form "is both discursive and non-discursive" ("The Confession of the Flesh," *P/K*, p. 197). Certainly, in his later work Foucault does deal, or at least claims to deal, with what he calls "effects of power"—and hence, it would seem, with a world outside that of discourse (*SP*, pp. 219/217; *VS*, pp. 20/11).

But it is important to understand precisely where these "effects of power" come from and what they entail. In *The Will to Knowledge*,

Foucault informs us of his intention to advance toward an "'analytic' of power." Such an "analytic" would define "the specific domain formed by relations of power," and would establish "the instruments that allow its analysis" (*VS*, pp. 109/82). This all sounds very sociological, as if Foucault were concerned with analyzing the actual exercise of institutional and personal power within society. Yet, Foucault's "analytic" of power turns out on close examination to be highly elusive. It seems to bear approximately the same relation to the exercise of power within the social order as Heidegger's reflections on "technology" bear to actual technology. This amounts to saying that Foucault's "analytic" ought to be read in ironic rather than in literalistic terms. It may certainly suggest to conventional historians, sociologists, and anthropologists ideas capable of animating their researches. But it is not itself worthy of our literal belief, for the whole question of its representational truth is not so much left in abeyance (this would be to underrate the imperiousness of the gesture) as ordered off the stage forever.

The elusive character of the analytic becomes especially clear when one tries to pin down what, exactly, Foucault *means* by power. In a 1975 interview, he tells us that

> nothing is more material, physical, corporal than the exercise of power. . . .
> From the eighteenth to the early twentieth century I think it was believed
> that the investment of the body by power had to be heavy, ponderous, metic-
> ulous and constant. Hence those formidable disciplinary regimes in the
> schools, hospitals, barracks, factories, cities, lodgings, families. And then,
> starting in the 1960s, it began to be realized that such a cumbersome form
> of power was no longer as indispensable as had been thought and that in-
> dustrial societies could content themselves with a much looser form of
> power over the body. Then it was discovered that control of sexuality could
> be attenuated and given new forms. One needs to study what kind of body
> the current society needs. ("Body/Power," *P/K*, pp. 57–58.)

This is very suggestive: one could imagine a series of illuminating historical studies dealing with the issues that Foucault here raises. But Foucault himself manages to muddy the waters. Thus, he writes in *The Will to Knowledge* of the "omnipresence of power: not because it has the privilege of consolidating everything under its invincible unity, but because it produces itself at every moment, at every point, or rather in every relation of one point to another. Power is everywhere" (*VS*, pp. 122/93 [translation altered]). Yet, he also says, in a conversation in which he comments on *The Will to Knowledge*, that "power in the substantive sense, *'le' pouvoir*, doesn't exist. . . . The idea that there is either located at—or emanating from—a given point something which is a 'power' seems to me to be based on a misguided analysis. . . . In reality power means relations, a more-or-less organized, hierarchical, co-ordinating cluster of relations" ("The Confessions of the Flesh," *P/K*, p. 198). Power, then, is everywhere. But it cannot be found anywhere in particular, since it does not exist in the substantive, "essentialist" sense at all—that is to say, there is no thing, power.

The difficulties are further increased when one takes into account the ubiquitous relation that Foucault seeks to establish between power and knowledge. As he puts it in *Discipline and Punish* (he makes the same point repeatedly elsewhere):

> power produces knowledge [*savoir*]; . . . power and knowledge directly im-
> ply one another; . . . there is no power relation without the correlative con-
> stitution of a field of knowledge [*savoir*], nor any knowledge that does not
> presuppose and constitute at the same time power relations. These "power-
> knowledge relations" are to be analyzed . . . not on the basis of a subject of
> knowledge who is or is not free in relation to the power system, but, on the
> contrary, the subject who knows, the objects to be known and the modali-
> ties of knowledge must be regarded as so many effects of these fundamental
> implications of power-knowledge and their historical transformations. In
> short, it is not the activity of the subject of knowledge that produces a
> corpus of knowledge, useful or resistant to power, but power-knowledge,
> the processes and struggles that traverse it and of which it is made up, that
> determines the forms and possible domains of knowledge [*connaissance*].
> (*SP*, pp. 32/27–28.)

I quote rather extensively because the difficulties that these passages raise are crucially important for Foucault's later work. Some of Foucault's commentators, pointing in particular to the role played by the notions of "materiality" and "power" in this work, have been inclined to connect his analytic of power with the historical materialism of Marx. But any such connection has to be extremely tenuous, for Foucault's insistence on a unified "power-knowledge" radically separates his position from Marx's. As I noted above, Marx is committed to the notion of objective science (or is a victim of the "will to truth," to put it in Foucauldian terms). Foucault, on the other hand, holds that there is no such thing as objective science. In Foucault's perspective, every "science" is in fact an "ideology," not in the strict sense of its being a reflection of the interests of some particular class but in the broader sense that it is irremediably caught up within relations of power (for Foucault on "ideology" in the strict sense, see "Truth and Power," *P/K,* p. 118). This is not Marx's position: Marx repeatedly insists that an objective view of social reality is indeed possible. Whereas Marx insists that his analysis of capitalism is scientific, Foucault declares that his genealogies are "anti-sciences" ("Two Lectures," *P/K*, p.83).

My point here is only to draw attention to this difference between Marx and Foucault, not to explore all the complexities involved in a confrontation between the "power-knowledge" model and the "science versus ideology"model. What does seem clear, however, is that Foucault's denial of the objectivity of science cannot be logically refuted: having adopted the language of power-knowledge, he has taken up residence within a self-consistent rhetoric. And looking at things from the other direction, the notion of an objective science—to which many others besides Marx have adhered—cannot be convincingly established for those who have rejected the language within which this notion exists. At best, lacunae within each language can be pointed out; each language speaks about certain things while failing to speak about certain other things. This is evident in, among other places, Foucault's analytic of power, for Foucault consistently evades any attempt to pin down this power in a socially and institutionally specific way. As one perceptive questioner pointed out, in discussion with Foucault, "perhaps there is a problem when one is dealing not with the 'theoretical' but with the 'practical' field. Given that there are relations of forces, and struggles, the question inevitably arises of who is doing the struggling against whom? Here you can't escape the question of the subject, or the *subjects*" ("The Confession of the Flesh," *P/K*, p. 207). Not surprisingly, the same questioner remained unconvinced by Foucault's assertions that the notion of "apparatus" allowed him to get at "a 'non-discursive' domain" (*P/K*, p. 197).

Foucault sidesteps this and similar objections, even while conceding their force. In view of his own conception of what he is doing, this evasion makes sense. If the "object" is created by an elusive power, if knowledge is the product of power rather than power the product of knowledge (as has been held since the seventeenth century), if everything is a lie designed to aid the continuing struggle against the extant order, then it simply does not matter who, objectively, is struggling against whom. Foucault gives not an "analytic" but rather a "rhetoric" of power—or, perhaps better, a vision of power as rhetoric. As he puts it in *The Order of Discourse*, "we must conceive discourse as a violence that we do to things" (*OD*, p.55). All discourse, Foucault holds, is "violent"; there is no "genuine" discourse, no rhetoric capable of conveying "the truth," of showing us "the thing itself." Though it is possible that a world exists outside the world of our rhetoric, we can never communicate this world (one sees here the *re-*

ductio ad absurdum, or perhaps the full logical development, of Kant). Hence, the notion of a power other than the power of our own language is, in Foucault's perspective, irrelevant; power, like everything else, necessarily remains an elusive, ungraspable entity.

As these reflections suggest, it is not to Marx but to Nietzsche that Foucault's concern with power needs to be connected. Foucault's "power" is not an historical or sociological concept, though it may have its historical or sociological uses. Rather, it is a reworking of Nietzsche's "will to power." But what is "the will to power"? Symptomatically, the notion remains highly indeterminate in character. We know that the will to power is a positively charged entity, so that when Foucault declares power to be creative rather than repressive he is following Nietzsche. But *what* "the will to power" is—what "will" is, what "power" is, how they are related—remains in darkness.

In his attempts to rationalize Nietzsche, Walter Kaufmann found the will to power a special stumbling block. Evoking Nietzsche's definition of the will to power as "self-overcoming," he notes that "it is far from plain what exactly is meant by self-overcoming"; he also notes that it is not evident how one is to gauge degrees of power.[29] Surveying Nietzsche's attempts to explain all human behavior in terms of the will to power, he observes that "one may doubt the cogency of Nietzsche's argument in places."[30] He points out that in Nietzsche's view the will to power is "always at war with itself."[31] He admits that, though "power is something specific for Nietzsche: self-overcoming," it is also "an elastic term."[32] Thus, Kaufmann helps us to see that there are all kinds of nagging contradictions in Nietzsche's account of the will to power. These contradictions are repeated, *mutatis mutandis,* in Foucault.

But we have not yet fathomed the full extent of the difficulty that Nietzsche and Foucault raise for us. As Kaufmann points out, Nietzsche considers the will to power an absolutely universal principle, to which even the search for truth is subject. But what is Nietzsche's project if not the articulation of a truth—namely, the truth that all truth is subject to the will to power? Kaufmann observes that "by including truth within the confines of this theory of the will to power, [Nietzsche] has perhaps called in a Trojan Horse that threatens his entire philosophy with ruin."[33] The same objection—if objection it is—applies to Foucault. Foucault tells us that there is no such thing as a "genuine" rhetoric, that all rhetorics are subject to the play of power, that all rhetorics are coercive. But he does so in a rhetoric that by this very argument cannot be genuine. Why, then, should we believe Foucault? All Cretans are liars. Or are they? We can hardly be sure. The move that seemed to get us outside discourse finishes by enclosing us even more deeply within it.

Sex, sexuality, and the body

This enclosure within discourse is closely tied up with Foucault's simultaneously critical and prophetic intentions and with the rejection of conventional theory that underpins those intentions. In *The Order of Things*, speaking of the role that "thought" plays within "modern experience," Foucault tells us that

> what is essential is that thought, both for itself and in the density of its workings, should be both knowledge and a modification of what it knows, reflection and a transformation of the mode of being of that on which it reflects. Whatever it touches it immediately causes to move: ... modern thought, from its inception and in its very density, is a certain mode of action.... Thought ... is no longer theoretical. As soon as it functions it offends or reconciles, attracts or repels, breaks, dissociates, unites or reunites; it cannot help but liberate and enslave. (*MC*, 338/327–328.)

In the language of *The Archaeology of Knowledge* and the works that followed it, "thought" becomes "discourse"; it is discourse that makes and unmakes our world. As we have seen, this notion of the ontological, or more properly the ontogenetic, function of discourse has a strategic potential: it opens up a space within which the bearer of discourse can act—as he hopes—to change the world. Foucault has remarked that some of those who read his earlier books thought that he was trying to show how we are all trapped within fixed, unchangeable structures, missing his real aim, that of showing how even those things that seem most deeply rooted are "due to historical phenomena" and "can be changed."[34] By viewing the world as if it were discourse, against which one then sets one's own competing, questioning, undermining discourse, one destroys all its apparent solidity, everything within it that seeks to impose itself on us as a given, as something that must simply be accepted.

Admittedly, in much of his 1970s work, Foucault focuses on the relations between "power" and "the body." This confrontation might seem as nondiscursive as one could possibly imagine. For example, in *Discipline and Punish* Foucault has a great deal to say about the torture of bodies in premodern criminal punishment and about the *dressage* of bodies in military drill and in reform schools (*SP*, esp. pp. 9–35, 137–196/3–31, 135–194). But Foucault's notion of "the body" is rather less concrete than one might think. It is significant that his first reference to "the body" occurs in

"Nietzsche, Genealogy, History," where he defines it as "the inscribed surface of events (traced by language and dissolved by ideas), the locus of a dissociated Self (adopting the illusion of a substantial unity), and a volume in perpetual disintegration" (*LCMP*, p.148). This is hardly the way we usually think of bodies, our own or others'.

Similarly, in *The Will to Knowledge* the body, in its literal sense, plays no role whatsoever, though one might think that "sex" and "sexuality" are even more "corporal" in character than are discipline and punishment. But as Foucault explains near the beginning of the book, he is concerned with "the 'putting into discourse' of sex." This leaves aside the question of whether the discursive productions that thus emerge formulate the "truth of sex," or alternatively are "lies destined to hide [sex] from view." The aim of the analysis is rather to discern "the 'will to knowledge'" that serves simultaneously as the "support" and as the "instrument" of these discursive productions (*VS*, pp. 20/11–12 [translation altered]). Admittedly, Foucault does distinguish between "sex" and "sexuality," and one might be tempted to interpret sexuality as discourse about sex, and sex as "the thing itself." But this will not do. Commenting on *The Will to Knowledge* shortly after its publication, Foucault tells us that in an earlier draft he took "sex" as "a pre-given datum," with "sexuality" figuring as "a sort of simultaneously discursive and institutional formation which came to graft itself on to sex, to overlay it and perhaps finally to obscure it." But he eventually decided that this was not very satisfactory, and instead hypothesized that sex is produced by "the apparatus of sexuality." To sum up: discourse about sexuality produces sexuality; the ensemble of discourses about sexuality constitutes the apparatus of sexuality; the apparatus of sexuality produces sex. This is why Foucault is able to say—in a statement that must have momentarily stunned his listeners—that sexuality has existed only since the eighteenth century and sex only since the nineteenth century. Of course, certain things did take place in previous centuries, but that was a matter of "the flesh," not of sex or sexuality ("The Confession of the Flesh" [1977], *P/K*, pp. 210–211).

Though *The Will to Knowledge* seems to me decidedly inferior to most of Foucault's other books, there is a point to his paradoxical, but far from stupid, proceedings here. In brief, Foucault is articulating an antinaturalism. He is trying, for all his references to "the body," to demolish any connection between sex (or sexuality) and a presumed natural substratum. He is trying to rid us of the idea of nature as norm. Thus, he says that we ought not to conceive of sexuality "as a kind of natural given that power tries to hold in check, or as an obscure domain which knowledge tries gradually to uncover." On the contrary, it is "the name that can be given to an historical apparatus: not the reality of something lying underneath, over which one maintains a difficult hold, but a great surface network where the stimulation of bodies, the intensification of pleasures, the incitement to discourse, the formation of sciences [*connaissances*], the reinforcement of controls and of resistances, are linked to one another, in accordance with a few main strategies of knowledge [*savoir*] and power" (*VS*, pp. 139–140/105–106 [translation altered]). This theme of the sundering of sexuality from nature goes back to *History of Madness*, where it appears in connection with Foucault's discussion of the Marquis de Sade. Sade has frequently been interpreted as a naturalist, that is, as one who argues for the free expression of natural desire. But as Foucault points out, Sade's position vis-à-vis nature is not so simple as this, for in various of his writings Sade envisages a society that will have dismissed nature. Such a society would reject all notions of natural liberty and natural equality in favor of "the sovereign rigor of subjectivity" (*HF1*, pp. 638–639/—; *HF2*, pp. 252–253). Significantly, Sade reappears, in precisely the same context, in *The Will to Knowledge* (*VS*, pp. 196/149).[35]

But from our point of view (and this will come as no surprise), Foucault's crucial connection as antinaturalist is with Nietzsche. We have seen how, exploiting notions of aesthetic creativity, Nietzsche views nature as an invention of human subjectivity. It is entirely in keeping with this aestheticist perspective that he should move from a definable anthropology to an undefinable superanthropology, for in making this move he transcends the limiting effects of the notion of human nature. So also with Foucault: his attacks on "humanism" and "anthropologism" need to be viewed as attacks on the constraints that he, too, sees such notions as imposing. Foucault's position thus differs radically from that of Marcuse and other lyrical and existential Marxists of the 1960s, who wanted to get back to a true, authentic, social order in which our polymorphously perverse drives, our joyfully pleasurable instincts, would finally be able to express themselves freely. Unlike these writers, Foucault finds no beach underneath the paving stones, no "natural" order at all.[36] There is only the certainty of successive regimes of power. Each of these regimes is made to be attacked, for each participates in the perpetual crisis of the present.

I am well aware that Foucault would deny much of what I have said about the assumptions underlying his writings: the effect of his work, after all, depends heavily on these assumptions being kept in the background. I am equally aware that my account of these assumptions and my portrayal of his trajectory from the 1950s to the middle 1970s are perhaps in some ways an overschematization of writings that have often tended to be diffuse, temporary, tactical, and local in character. We ought to have learned by now that the writings of such figures as Nietzsche, Foucault, Heidegger, and Derrida are intended to be provocative rather than pro-grammatic, therapeutic rather than constructive. In this respect, they touch such other figures, less committed to the notion of crisis but equally committed to a therapeutic conception of thought, as Wittgenstein and Dewey.[37] Foucault's texts clearly do not stand alone. Rather, they must be contrasted with, bounced off, and thrown against what we already know—or think we know. They do not constitute a "method" or "sys-tem." Indeed, the whole notion of a "system" is anathema to Foucault; for him, as for Nietzsche, "the will to a system is a lack of integrity" (TI, "Maxims and Arrows," §26).

Foucault's rejection of system might lead us to regard him as an anar-chist, though his anarchism is one that does not assume, as the classic anarchisms do, an underlying order that needs only to be expressed for harmony to prevail. (Note, too, how these "classic" anarchisms are in fact romantic—as Hayden White points out.[38] Thus, we perceive one more problematic connection back to Romanticism.) In Foucault's work, there is no natural order, no possible harmony. Here his postmodernist sensibility is manifest, for central to postmodernism is a disabused atti-tude toward any "given" order. If Foucault attempts an aesthetic recrea-tion of the world, he also knows that the recreation is itself doomed to be undermined. There results from this a willful sense of movement. At the end of the introduction to The Archaeology of Knowledge, an imaginary questioner asks Foucault whether he is quite sure of what he is saying, whether he is going to shift his position yet again: "Are you already pre-paring the way out that will enable you in your next book to spring up somewhere else and declare as you're now doing: no, no, I'm not where you are lying in wait for me, but over here, laughing at you?" To which Foucault replies that this is indeed the case, that he is preparing a laby-rinth "in which I can lose myself and appear at last to eyes that I will never have to meet again. I am no doubt not the only one who writes in order to have no face. Do not ask me who I am and do not ask me to remain the same: leave it to our bureaucrats and our police to see that our papers are in order" (AS, pp. 28/17).

In short, Foucault does not so much have a "position" as a number of successive positions—and we cannot be sure how his future positions will be related to those that he has already articulated. Thus, the Foucauldian trajectory that I have attempted to describe ought to be regarded as peculiarly tentative and hypothetical. There is nothing to prevent Foucault from moving off in a different direction in the future. Still, most of his work to date is best summed up under the dual headings of utopianism and crisis. He is clearly an enemy of the dominant, Western tradition. A major problem with his attack on the tradition, however, is his inability to specify what we have outside it. At times he appeals to the sophists, whose "explosive laughter . . . tears through the mask of Socrates" ("Theatrum Philosophicum" [1970], *LCMP*, p. 196); he has also appealed to "the East" (*HF1*, p. iv/—). But these appeals remain peculiarly empty and abstract. It may well be that "the West"—whatever that is—is all we have. For all its apparent activism, in the face of this emptiness Foucault's stance risks dissolving into a kind of postethical, aesthetic, Warholian laughter. "Not by wrath does one kill but by laughter. Come, let us kill the spirit of gravity!" says Nietzsche/Zarathustra. Whatever the spirit of gravity, gravity itself is surely less easily killed than this.

Moreover, there is an odd contradiction between this laughter and the gravity of the crisis notion—a contradiction that shows up in the former's forced, almost hysterical quality. I shall deal in some detail with crisis in my discussion of Derrida. Suffice it to say here that though crisis is a widely accepted cliché, its wide acceptance by no means establishes its truth. In a peculiar way, the crisis assumption is merely the reverse image of nineteenth-century historicism, for it presupposes a developing "tradition" that is now in crisis. Obviously, crisis is a metaphor—and it depends on a prior, enabling metaphor. The question is not simply whether the crisis metaphor is in some sense "correct," though certainly this is an important part of the story. The question is also whether, now that historicism is no longer an intellectual position that is seriously maintained, it has any illuminative power left. Still, there is much that we can learn from Foucault. By the very fact that his writings cut across accepted categories, generating a tension with analyses of a more conventional kind, they are not only intriguing but also sharply illuminating.

PART IV

On the Meaning of Jacques Derrida

There is nothing outside of the text.

—*Derrida*

CHAPTER 7

The Deconstruction of Crisis

To interpret the writings of Jacques Derrida (b. 1930) is already to engage in an act of violence, for Derrida contends that his writings are meaningless—that they are, in the literal sense of the word, nonsensical. At any rate, this is what Derrida appears to be contending. But perhaps I have gotten it wrong. Perhaps it is the matter of *risk* that most interests Derrida. As he tells us in a 1967 interview, *"je me risque à ne rien-vouloir-dire."* With typically Derridean ambiguity, this can be translated either as "I am taking the risk of not wishing to say anything" or as "I am taking the risk of not meaning anything" (*POS,* pp. 24/14 [translation altered]). No wonder it seems especially difficult to come to grips with Derrida's enterprise. "I asked you where to begin, and you have led me into a labyrinth," the interviewer observed in some frustration (*POS,* pp. 13/4). And the labyrinth has now become far more complex and ramified than it was in 1967. One is reminded of an Escher print.

Let's shift analogies. (Derrida is such an elusive figure that only by analogy to what is less elusive will we be able to get a handle on him.) Imagine Derrida as a modern Penelope, unraveling by night what he weaves by day—or rather, raveling and unraveling at the same time, as he waits for a Ulysses who will never come home. (What is not accidental about my choice of words here is that *ravel* means both "to ravel" and to "unravel"—leaving to my reader what *unravel* means.) Distinctions are grandly postulated, yet simultaneously undermined: in a single movement posed, exposed, deposed, reposed—laid to rest in their very postulation. Yet, Derrida manages to spin out page after page as if he were somehow committed to these distinctions.

It is no accident that at crucial points he will move into the interroga-
tive or suppositional modes, thus distancing himself from his text and
destroying the apparently declarative force of what he is saying. In many
of his writings, he seems to be presenting a "thesis," a "position." But one
looks again, and sees that there is no "thesis," no "position" at all. This is
different from what we found in considering Foucault, for the problem
with Foucault is not the absence of positions but their rapid succession.
With Derrida, on the other hand, one finds an anti-ocular, antispatial
stance so radical that all positions seem to be wiped away as soon as they
become visible. One is left with a structure of words haunted by the
merest ghost of meaning—the wraith, as we shall see, of Hegel's Time-
Spook. Derrida's corpus has all the solidity of a house of cards waiting to
be blown down, yet remains arrogant in its sheer virtuosity. To attempt to
isolate a Derridean position or articulate a Derridean thesis is to misun-
derstand the character of Derrida's enterprise. And yet, at least from the
perspective of intellectual history, it is virtually impossible to get anything
out of Derrida without engaging in such misinterpretations. I readily admit that my view of Derrida is one view among others. I hope, however,
that my readers will find it useful in making sense of the truly formidable
body of writing that Derrida has produced.

Since Derrida seems intent on destroying the very notion of sense, my
aim here is profoundly un-Derridean. Yet, this infidelity is more Derridean than it might seem at first glance. For Derrida is a supreme ironist:
undoubtedly the most accomplished ironist of our age. (He is also a parodist, but more about that later.) In a work that is still one of the most
telling studies of irony we have, Kierkegaard shrewdly notes that the
ironist "must always be understood at a distance."[1] In other words, we
ought not to view the ironist from three inches away. We must not allow
ourselves to become too caught up in the individual brushstrokes. We
must rather step back, in a sense other than Heidegger's. We must open
ourselves up to the effect of the canvas as a whole. To be sure, each brush-
stroke contributes to this effect, but only indirectly, through our "reading" it in relation to something larger. It is the same with Derrida. It is not
his single, literal statements that matter but their role within a larger project. Derrida's single, literal statements are often impossible to decipher.
His masterpiece, *Glas,* is a mere blur when viewed too closely. But the
larger project embodies a coherent perspective, even if that perspective,
being ironical in an extreme sense, rejects the notion of coherence. Of
course, we can detect a like irony in Derrida's precursors—especially in
Foucault. But Derrida's irony is far more radical than theirs, for whereas

Nietzsche, Heidegger, and Foucault reject the extant world but hew to ideal, utopian alternatives (whether nostalgic or imaginative), Derrida seems to reject the alternatives as well.

Why Derrida?

One of the most striking features of much modernist and postmodernist literature is its inaccessibility at first reading. One thinks of *Ulysses* or (even more formidably) of *Finnegans Wake,* or of that great American lyric masterpiece *Gravity's Rainbow.* Derrida shares this inaccessibility: he is unquestionably a difficult writer. This raises the question why we should want to subject ourselves to Derrida's difficulty, why we should want to engage in the considerable and not altogether pleasant effort of reading and interpreting him. There are at least two good reasons for doing so. Firstly, despite his difficulty, Derrida does afford some pleasure. Kierkegaard remarks that "as there is something forbidding about irony, so also it has some extraordinarily seductive and enchanting moments."[2] This could almost have been written about Derrida. His work is certainly forbidding—but also, if one is patient enough, if one allows the text to work its peculiar magic, it is capable of generating (as Geoffrey Hartman suggests) a serene hilarity.[3] Secondly, his writings have an exemplary significance. The "play of ironic seriousness"[4] that we find in Derrida renders explicit and obvious an attitude pervasive in modernist and especially in postmodernist art. Thus, his writings can help us come to grips with a large part of twentieth-century aesthetic consciousness. They can help us come to grips, that is, with certain assumptions pervasive in works of art in our time.

Obviously, I hold no brief for modernism and postmodernism. And I do not wish to suggest that because modernism and postmodernism have been on the cutting edge in the making of art in our century we ought to be modernists and postmodernists. I impute no necessity to these aesthetic orientations. In fact, we are free to choose from the whole panoply of previous art what we want and like. But whether we like them or not, modernism and postmodernism are important aspects of our historical and intellectual experience. Especially in Chapter 8, I shall show how these are not only aesthetic categories. On the contrary, the underlying assumptions of modernism, and to a lesser extent those of postmodernism, are influential in areas of thought that we do not usually think of in such terms. They have been carried over into other, putatively nonaesthetic reaches of our intellectual culture. Consequently, the historical crit-

icism of modernism and postmodernism is an important matter. And
Derrida helps open the way to such a criticism.

In other words, I am convinced that Derrida can and ought to be
viewed in a wider perspective than the one he is usually accorded. Often,
he provokes sheer puzzlement in his readers, leading to his quick rejection
as someone utterly nonsensical and therefore not worth considering. But
even among those who do pay attention to him, one detects a certain
narrowness of range. Briefly, Derrida has become a figure of some interest
to a small collection of avant-garde intellectuals. Most of these are literary
critics. It should not be imagined, however, that all literary critics are
interested in Derrida. Rather, this interest is pretty much confined to a
small faction of literary critics—the faction of "poststructuralist" or "de-
constructionist" critics.[5] But the faction is a vigorous one, and as a result
of its activities Derrida has become the central figure in a storm of controversy that rages over the ivied halls of American literary criticism. This
tempest has generated a large and growing literature, all of it concerned
with the question of how literary texts ought to be interpreted. More dis-
tantly, it is concerned with how we ought to live our lives, but this issue
tends to be covered over by the debate over literary interpretation.

I am not directly interested here in this controversy. Still, it does connect with issues important in the present work, and a brief look at it is
necessary. Suffice it to say that certain influential literary critics, including
Harold Bloom, Paul de Man, Geoffrey Hartman, and J. Hillis Miller, have
taken up modes of literary interpretation that owe much to Derrida's example. The defining feature of this group (insofar as it can be said to have
a defining feature) is its conviction that interpretation is really only a variety of misinterpretation. Thus, the quality of an interpretation of a literary text cannot properly be judged on the basis of whether it is "correct"
or "incorrect." What counts, rather, is the technical skill or verbal brilliance with which the interpretation is put forward, and its aptness for
generating further interpretations that in their turn can be seen to be tech-
nically skillful or verbally brilliant. On the other side, many critics have
attacked this orientation, arguing that there is indeed some standard of
critical value lying outside the sphere of literary interpretation itself.
There are disagreements as to what this standard is, but these disagreements pale before the conviction that there *is* a standard.

The resulting debate is the locus of virtually all the interesting theoretical discussion in American literary criticism today.[6] Since I am an historian rather than a literary critic, my preoccupations are very different
from those of most participants in the debate. For example, I have no

special interest in an alleged "crisis in criticism."[7] I am not immediately concerned with how literary texts ought to be interpreted or with what younger literary critics ought to be doing these days. I am interested almost solely in the historical and theoretical significance of the issues raised in the debate, and hardly at all in their implications for the practice of criticism.

In briefest terms, the debate is important here because it connects with an extremely important ontological question: what is a work of art? Derrida's writings can be seen as an important exploration of this question. We all live in a post-Kantian world, and in the shadow of Kant's distinction (elaborated on and turned into a "problem" by his Romantic successors) between the theoretical, the practical, and the aesthetic. Out of this distinction comes the dualism between theory and practice which Foucault, most obviously among our four thinkers, seeks to call into question. (Of course, attacks on the theory/practice distinction are by no means restricted to Foucault. On the contrary, they have been a widespread theme in twentieth-century intellectual life.) Also out of this distinction comes a dualism between the aesthetic and the nonaesthetic, which Derrida, among our four thinkers, is especially concerned with attacking. Such a dualism is crucial to the work of such modernists as Yeats, Pound, and Eliot, for an important aspect of modernism, as we shall see, is its attempt to play off the "anironic" possibilities that it sees as embodied (however tenuously) in art against ironic, degraded reality.[8] The same dualism runs through the work of the so-called "new critics," who are now widely acknowledged to have been systematizers of modernism, and is also to be found in such an apparently antimodernist and anti–new critic as Northrop Frye.

Postmodernism, in contrast, has consistently called into question the distinction between "art" and "reality." Works of art in the postmodern mode demonstrate an ontological concern, continually asking what it is to be a sculpture, a play, a novel, a painting. In this sense, postmodernism is anti-Kantian—though in a peculiar way it is dependent on the very position that it seeks to undermine. Derrida, I shall argue, is not a postmodernist. But he nonetheless has close affinities with the whole postmodern trend in contemporary art. And one mark of this affinity is that he, too, systematically calls into question the Kantian distinction between the aesthetic and the nonaesthetic.

In writing the *Critique of Judgment,* with its postulation of art as the sphere of "purposiveness without purpose," Kant founded the philosophy of art. In setting up (or appearing to set up) a separate sphere for the aesthetic, he opened up an intellectual space for the vast Romantic and post-Romantic expansion of art and for the claims of that art to an autonomous status. A great deal of the most acclaimed art in the modern period has been caught up in the exploration of specifically aesthetic problems—problems that, in a broad sense, we can regard as formal in character. The "aesthetic" or noncognitive view of art that we can trace back to the *Critique of Judgment* well accords with these developments. As Karsten Harries points out, the "aesthetic" view much more accurately reflects the activity of modern artists than does Hegel's "ontological," or cognitive view.[9] Of course, it must be said that to a certain extent this notion of a division between the aesthetic and the nonaesthetic and between aesthetic value and truth value is a distortion of Kant's actual position. Kant himself subordinated the beautiful in art to the beautiful in nature, and emphasized, too, a moral element in art. It is thus a mistake to regard his view of art as simply "aesthetic," or to see him as unequivocally asserting art's autonomy. Still, the *Critique of Judgment* did point in these directions, and the direction was taken up by Kant's successors, beginning with Schiller. A separate sphere was carved out for art; a division between the aesthetic and the nonaesthetic was established and canonized.

It is within the context of this division that one needs to view Nietzsche. Recall how Nietzsche uses the notion of art in both a narrow and a wide sense. There exist artists of art; there also exist artists of politics, science, and religion. This view is best regarded as a reactive response to the Kantian division between the aesthetic and the real. Recognizing, with Nietzsche, the affinity between aesthetic creativity and creativity in its more "serious" senses, we are forced to acknowledge that the distinction between "art" and "reality" conceals as much as it reveals. The distinction is inadequate because the "reality" within which we live is itself partly the product of our art/interpretation/language. When Shelley observes in his "Defence of Poetry" that poets are "the unacknowledged legislators of the world," he is drawing attention to the fact that artists have a hand in the construction of our reality. This holds true for artists in the narrow sense, which is what Shelley had in mind; it holds *a fortiori* for artists in the broad sense, the creators of our "metaphysics, religion, moralities, science."

Moreover, the makers of art, of whatever kind, are themselves imbedded in a society; almost unconsciously, they bring to their art that society's assumptions. To view art otherwise than as (in part) a social product is to misperceive its character: an obvious comment, perhaps, but one that we still ought to attend to. Two misperceptions are possible. One misperception sees art as simply an internal play of formal possibilities:

the "aesthetic" view. The other sees it as a source of privileged truth: the "ontological" view, with its commitment to the "truth of the work of art." Frequently the two views subsist together, so that what is initially presented as a self-contained aesthetic universe, with a "direction of meaning" that is entirely inward, is ultimately endowed with cognitive authority.[10] Part of Derrida's value is that he so radically undermines the Kantian distinction between art and reality that we can no longer view it in any way except ironically. He shows us that it is not a matter of opting either for "realism" against "aestheticism" or for "aestheticism" against "realism." It is a matter, rather, of calling into question the initial distinction upon which such a choice is founded.

Kant is important for the prophets of extremity because his dualisms create a serious intellectual problem (even as they try to solve earlier problems), while by appearing to postulate a separate aesthetic realm he suggests a solution to that problem. Obviously, this solution—the reinterpretation of knowledge as a form of aesthetic fiction or creativity— is central to the work of these writers. But as we have also seen, aestheticism has a precondition in the idea of crisis. The notion that the present is null opens the way to an aesthetic recreation. The world's giving birth to itself as a work of art presupposes that its present existence is derelict, that it indeed needs to be reborn. The alienation of Nietzsche, Heidegger, and Foucault from "the modern age" is beyond question: in one way or another, they all want to make a leap into a utopia that radically negates this reality. Radical dereliction and radical utopianism go together. Art best exercises its *ex nihilo* creativity where there is a nullity out of which this creation can emerge.

But if nihilism is the precondition for aestheticism, what are the preconditions for nihilism? Nihilism, I wish to argue, becomes a problem only within the context of an historicist reading of history. In *History, Man, and Reason*, Maurice Mandelbaum defines *historicism* as "the belief that an adequate understanding of the nature of any phenomenon and an adequate assessment of its value are to be gained through considering it in terms of the place which it occupied and the role which it played within a process of development."[11] In a sense akin to but much broader than Mandelbaum's, I here use "historicism" to denote *any* attribution of directionality to history, whether or not that directionality is seen in specifically developmental terms. In its original and still decisive meaning, *crisis* denotes a turning, a point of decision. The word was initially applied to the course of a disease to indicate its turning point, at which "an important development or change takes place which is decisive for recovery or death" (*Oxford English Dictionary,* s.v. "crisis"). Unless history has a direction of some sort to change or continue or lose in aimless wandering, it cannot have a "crisis." Yet, the notion that history *has* directionality (or even *is* directionality) is questionable, and Derrida manages to show us just how questionable it is. In so doing, he radically undermines crisis thought.

In my interpretation of Derrida, which is by no means the only one possible and which may be sharply contradicted by some, we find in his writings a double deconstruction: deconstruction of the aesthetic, and deconstruction of "crisis." (As we shall see, this can be viewed as amounting to a deconstruction of Kant and Hegel, respectively.) The notion of a radical crisis in the affairs of men is one of the great clichés—perhaps the greatest—of modernist and postmodernist thought. Modernism and postmodernism are absolute in their conviction of the reality of the crisis; this conviction lies at the foundation of the various world-views, the various approaches to life or art, that they propose. And these world-views, these approaches, are highly charged by aesthetic categories. Nietzsche, Heidegger, and Foucault give us the most radical examples of this type of thought, but in so doing they merely express in an extreme form notions that in less radical versions pervade recent intellectual life. As for Derrida, he can be regarded as both an aestheticist and a parodist of aestheticism. His quintessentially aestheticist statement, "*il n'y a pas de hors-texte*" (*GRAM,* pp. 227/158), can be translated as "there is nothing outside of the text," but it can equally well be translated (meaninglessly) as "there is no inset plate." Indeed, at one point Derrida tells us that "there is only *hors-texte*" (*DISS,* pp. 50/43 [translation altered]). Every stance that Derrida articulates has both its "pro" and its "anti" aspects; every position that he adopts is immediately rendered nugatory. If Derrida is an aestheticist, he is also an antiaestheticist. I prefer to focus here on the latter figure, the Derrida who criticizes and undermines the strand of thought that I have been concerned to point out in this study.

I find warrant for this preference in the fact that Derrida is in at least one respect strikingly different from his predecessors. In neither Nietzsche nor Heidegger is there the slightest trace of the comic (nor, for that matter, is Foucault a comic writer). Nietzsche's attempts at the comic are far too strained and nervous to be in the least degree successful. Heidegger, perpetually meditating on the departure of the gods and on the unlikelihood of their return, wraps himself in a somber, unending gloom. Foucault's laughter (so far, at any rate) is bitter and hysterical rather than comic. The absence of the comic from these writers is not at all surprising, for the comic imagination requires a measure of acceptance and toleration—stances not prominent in Nietzsche, Heidegger, or Foucault. Though I am concerned here with the comic rather than with the generic entity of comedy, it is nonetheless worth pointing out how far comedy is from a crisis mentality. Comedy's theme, as Frye (following Hegel) reminds us, is the integration of society.[12] Hence, it withers when the universe is seen as irremediably crisis-ridden. (So too does its opposite, tragedy. Those critics like Nietzsche or, more derivatively, George Steiner, who have reflected on the decline of tragedy draw attention to this incompatibility.)[13]

But what of Derrida? Much of his writing is as devoid of the comic as the writings of his predecessors. From the very beginning of his career, there was clearly a wit at work, but a clever rather than a comic one. The laughter that he evokes in his 1967 essay on Bataille and Hegel, "From Restricted to General Economy," is still the laughter of Nietzsche and Foucault, too hemmed in by the oppressive presence of the dialectic to be truly comic (*E&D*, pp. 369–407/251–277). This changes, however, in his more recent writings. I am thinking especially of the brilliantly funny epistolary novel, "Sendings" (*"Envois"*), which prefaces his most recent major work, *The Postcard from Socrates to Freud and Beyond* (1980). Geoffrey Hartman has suggested that there is "little humor and mother wit in Derrida,"[14] but this is surely true only up to the monumental deconstruction of Hegel that Derrida carries out in *Glas* (1974). After *Glas* ("death knell"), fun again wakes. Laughter is no longer reduced.[15] Comic catharsis once more becomes possible, for Derrida's is a postethical, aesthetic laughter that knows the limits of the thought of crisis and of the aestheticist stance that rises up on the basis of that thought. Whether Derrida's recovery of the comic will persist remains, of course, to be seen. There is no telling what he will do next; he can disconfirm our views at any moment. But the fact that he is able to be funny at all clearly marks his departure from the prophecy of extremity as Nietzsche, Heidegger, and Foucault have articulated it.

Four Thinkers: Nietzsche, Heidegger, Foucault, Hegel

Two largely different contexts seem relevant to our understanding of Derrida: the context marked out by Nietzsche, Heidegger, and Foucault, and that marked out by French intellectual life (or rather, by a certain segment of that life) from the late 1950s to the present. On the one hand, we can see Derrida developing and criticizing the aestheticist position worked out by his three forerunners. On the other hand, we can see him responding to a contemporaneous intellectual environment. Almost all his texts are more or less direct responses to a text or texts that he has been reading, and these "provoking" texts—the "pre-texts" for his own textual enterprise—have usually come to him out of a certain French intellectual scene. We need to look at both contexts if we are to get some sense of how Derrida's astounding enterprise got off the ground and how his texts might profitably be read.

Nietzsche, Heidegger, and Foucault are all present in Derrida. And so is Hegel (or "Hegel"), with his negative relationship to aestheticism, his status as the authority figure against whom the thinkers of crisis rebel. What is more, Derrida refers to these figures within the context of precisely those problems—of interpretation, of the relation of subject and object, of crisis, of the concealing power of tradition—that are crucial for aestheticism. Take, for example, Derrida's assertion in *Of Grammatology* that

> Nietzsche, far from remaining *simply* (with Hegel and as Heidegger wished) *within* metaphysics, contributed a great deal to the liberation of the signifier from its dependence or derivation with respect to the logos and the related concept of truth or the primary signified, in whatever sense that is understood. Reading, and therefore writing, the text were for Nietzsche "originary" operations . . . with regard to a sense that they do not first have to transcribe or discover, which would not therefore be a truth signified in the original element and presence of the logos. (*GRAM*, pp. 31–32/19.)

It is perhaps an understatement to say that there are difficulties in this passage. In the first place, it is written in that terrible Derridean jargon, so off-putting to most readers. Secondly (though this does not appear in the translation), the original French is written in the conditional mode. The effect of this is to cast into doubt the extent to which Derrida himself is committed to what he is saying. Yet, despite the difficulties, we can attribute to this statement a meaning that is fairly clear, and to which we must assume that Derrida is in some sense committed—for without such a commitment, his enterprise would indeed be incomprehensible.

Briefly, Derrida puts forward an interpretation of Nietzsche that (as I have argued) is importantly correct—even though in Derrida's perspective questions of correctness and incorrectness presumably have no place. Derrida sees Nietzsche as a crisis thinker: as someone who is no longer within the tradition (though, in a characteristically Derridean touch, Derrida must also hold that Nietzsche is not outside the tradition either, that somehow he moves along the margins of a tradition from which he cannot entirely escape). And how did Nietzsche manage to put himself, if not outside the tradition, at least on its margins? He did so by making the aestheticist move. The notion of "the liberation of the signifier," as we can now see, is aestheticist in character. There is the idea, here, of a text liberated from its formerly subordinate status with regard to Truth, with regard to the "original" or "transcendental" signified. This is why reading and writing become "originary" operations: they involve not the "discovery" of truth but its invention. The text is endowed with the attributes of the work of art as conceived in post-Romantic aesthetics. Derrida himself makes the aesthetic connection, particularly in his essay *Spurs: Nietzsche's Styles* (1978), where we find him discussing at some length a number of those passages in which Nietzsche is most explicit about the artistic character of his own philosophy (see, e.g., *SPURS*, pp. 45–47, 75–77).

If Nietzsche's presence in Derrida is clear, Heidegger's is overwhelming. Derrida refers in his essay "Différance" (1968) to "Heidegger's uncircumventable meditation" (*MARGES*, pp. 22/22). He has been known to remark in conversation that he eats, sleeps, and breathes Heidegger, or words to that effect. As he puts it in *Positions,* "Heidegger's text is extremely important to me, . . . it constitutes a novel, irreversible advance all of whose critical resources we are far from having exploited" (*POS,* pp. 73/54). But Derrida is by no stretch of the imagination a Heideggerian. On the contrary, he has been Heidegger's most patient and most severe critic. As he says, also in *Positions,* "I sometimes have the feeling that the Heideggerian problematic is the most 'profound' and 'powerful' defense of what I attempt to put into question under the rubric of the *thought of presence*" (*POS,* pp. 75/55).

What accounts for Derrida's preoccupation with Heidegger? The answer lies partly in the fact that Heidegger has been an important preoccupation among post–World War II French philosophers generally. Given Derrida's presence (however marginal) within this community, he could hardly have avoided dealing with Heidegger. Moreover, Heidegger is such a gnomic and complex writer that he easily provides a starting point for the ironic play of interpretation that Derrida so much cultivates. But the most profound impulse for Derrida's continuing confrontation with Heidegger seems rather to lie in his consciousness of the moral ambiguities of Heidegger's career. These ambiguities (I here speculate) led Derrida to question certain prominent tendencies in Heidegger's thought—most importantly, the nostalgic tendency. Derrida persistently attacks Heidegger's use of nostalgic motifs.

Note, for example, the following passage in "Différance," where Derrida plays Heidegger off against Nietzsche: "There will be no unique name, even if it were the name of Being. And we must think this without *nostalgia;* that is, outside of the myth of a purely maternal or paternal language, a lost native country of thought. On the contrary, we must *affirm* this, in the sense in which Nietzsche puts affirmation into play, in a certain laughter and a certain step of the dance" (*MARGES,* pp. 29/27). Heidegger's "destruction" aims at discovering "the proper word and the unique name." Derrida is concerned not with "proper" names but with "improper" ones—as Rudolf Kuenzli points out.[16] Heidegger envisages destroying a tradition in order to get back to an original, unconcealed meaning. In Derrida the "destruction" becomes a "deconstruction," a simultaneous smashing down and building up, with no privilege granted to the origin and with the tradition retained, though not in an historicist form. It is part of Derrida's deconstructive genius that he draws one of his most insistent metaphors for deconstruction, the writing down and subsequent erasure of all words and concepts, from Heidegger himself: specifically, from *The Question of Being,* where Heidegger suggests that "Being" ought to be written crossed out (see *QB,* pp. 80–83). In fact, Derrida's project would have been all but inconceivable without the later Heidegger.

Foucault's presence in Derrida is far less imposing than that of Nietzsche or Heidegger. But he is there nonetheless. This is not surprising. Like Foucault, Derrida studied at the École Normale Supérieure; like him, he studied under Jean Hyppolite. Derrida is only four years younger than Foucault, and the intellectual situations that confronted the two were not remarkably different: there is no question of any intellectual revolution (so frequent in French intellectual life) separating them. Indeed, for a time Derrida was willing to admit a formidable community of interest with Foucault. At the beginning of his 1963 critique of *History of Madness,* he tells us that he had "formerly had the good fortune to study under Michel Foucault" and that he still retained "the consciousness of an admiring and grateful disciple" (*E&D,* pp. 51/31). It is clear, however, that Derrida soon embarked on a course very different from the one followed by his former teacher. Since 1963, Derrida has written almost nothing about Foucault, but we can easily infer where the divergence lies.

Contrary to what some have held, it lies not in Derrida's entrapment in the "text," as distinguished from Foucault's concern with the broader field of "history" (see Foucault, *HF2,* pp. 602–603). It lies rather in their different patternings of the historical process. For Foucault gives an apocalyptic reading of history, whereas Derrida undermines such a reading. Speaking of Foucault's *History of Madness,* Derrida declares that "nowhere else and never before has the concept of *crisis* been able to enrich and reassemble all its potentialities, all the energy of its meaning as much, perhaps, as in Michel Foucault's book" (*E&D*, pp. 96/62). Derrida is entirely right about the crisis-ridden character of *History of Madness*, and the same rhetoric of crisis persists in Foucault's later texts as well. In Derrida, crisis is almost always brought into play in order to be undermined. He makes no ringing claims to have detected earthquakes in the offing or the imminent wiping out of man. Foucault seeks to build a politics (or metapolitics) of crisis. Derrida's real interest, especially in his later work, seems to be in opening us up to the hermeneutical possibilities of the written word—using the term "hermeneutical" in Rorty's rather than in Schleiermacher's sense, as a continuing conversation rather than as the unveiling of definitive truth. And beyond this, Derrida engages in a sustained attempt to criticize the notion of crisis, to show the limitations of the crisis view.

This takes us to the figure who makes possible the thought of crisis, Hegel. "Hegelianism" is Derrida's most persistent target, the object of a special "deceleration."[17] In his essay of 1967 on Bataille and Hegel, Derrida portrays Hegelianism as an insidious and all-embracing threat: "Misconstrued, treated lightly, Hegelianism only extends its historical domination, finally unfolding its immense enveloping resources without obstacle. Hegelian self-evidence seems lighter than ever at the moment when it finally bears down with its full weight" (*E&D*, pp. 369/251). Derrida engages in an oddly ironic attack on the dialectic—oddly ironic because, unlike Foucault (see *OD*, p. 74), he sees no possibility of ever "escaping" from Hegel. Derrida's position (insofar as it can be called a position) is that every attempt to state a truth is already a reintegration into the dialectic. Thus, he refers "to Hegel, who is always right as soon as one opens one's mouth in order to articulate meaning" (*E&D*, pp. 386/ 263). Foucault, for example, attempted to state the truth of madness, but in the very act of employing a language he subjected madness to the power of reason. And a similar fate, it seems, will await every attempt to establish a countertruth to the dialectic, for every countertruth will be engulfed by the dialectic's devouring maw.

Derrida's own anti-Hegelian strategy might be characterized as a perpetual withholding operation. In his 1967 *Positions* interview, he declares that all his texts to date "are doubtless the interminable preface to another text that one day I would like to have the force to write, or still the epigraph to another that I would never have the audacity to write" (*POS*, pp. 13–14/5). Similarly, in *Postcard* we find a preface almost as long as the rest of the book; he describes it as "the preface of a book that I have not written" (*CARTE,* pp. 7/—). All Derrida's texts are prefatory; none comes to a disclosure of the truth. To imagine a nonprefatory Derrida would be to imagine another, entirely different writer. Here is part of the secret of Derrida's awe-inspiring productivity, for the task of writing, in Derrida's view, is not to say something—to make a point and be done with it. On the contrary, the writing is its own justification. A logorrhea results, an immense outpouring of words around an unsayable center. As so often in Derrida, one is reminded of Wittgenstein—the Wittgenstein not of the *Tractatus,* with that final lapse into silence, but of the *Philosophical Investigations.* The image of the journey is decisive for this work. Wittgenstein's journey, like that of Derrida, is not the teleological quest of Hegel, whose turnings all point toward a rational end. Instead, it is a dogged and aimless crisscrossing of territory—the journey of a mapmaker or land-surveyor, not of a traveler from one place to another.[18] One is reminded, too, of the later Heidegger, with his *Holzwege,* his "*chemins qui ne mènent nulle part,*" and also of that side of Freud that seeks to make analysis interminable.

These interminable prefaces do not *escape* from the movement of the dialectic, but neither do they fall victim to it. At the beginning of the *Phenomenology of Spirit,* Hegel avers that the preface "cannot be accepted as the way in which to expound philosophical truth."[19] Derrida's whole corpus can be seen as a commentary on this observation. As we all know, Hegel did write a preface to the *Phenomenology,* a text that sought to recapitulate his system as a whole. For Derrida, the notion of recapitulation will not do. Rather, in the preface to *Dissemination* ("Outside the Book: Prefaces"), he characterizes the preface as "another text entirely" that is at the same time the "double" of the main text (*DISS,* pp. 35/28). This notion of "doubling" is already familiar to us. For there is one literary genre that "doubles" in precisely the way that Derrida sees the preface as doubling the book—namely, parody. In a peculiarly heightened form, parody, as we shall see, is central to Derrida's work.

The rule of four

In the preface to *Dissemination,* Derrida also tells us that "the written preface ... becomes ... a fourth text" (*DISS,* pp. 33/27). I read this as meaning that the preface exceeds the three terms of the dialectic: position, negation, and negation of the negation (this last becoming a new position, a new thesis). It is in his failure to "state a truth," to "get to the point"—his failure to write the book that he is interminably prefacing—

that Derrida evades the maw of the dialectic. A key term in Derrida is "dissemination." He sometimes renders this as "dissemenation," the falling of seed on barren ground, which contrasts with the dialectic's infinite production of new meanings. In short, dissemination is a kind of anti-dialectic, going against the dialectical rule of three, against the "ternary rhythm" of Hegelian philosophy (*VenP*, p. 32). As Derrida says in the following obscure but still decodable passage:

> Dissemination *displaces* the three of onto-theology along the angle of a certain re-ployment. A Crisis of *versus:* these marks can no longer be summed up or "decided" according to the two of binary opposition, nor sublated into the three of speculative dialectic (for example, "differance," "gramme," "trace," "broach/breach" [*entame*], "de-limitation," "pharmakon," "supplement," "hymen," "mark-march-margin," and several others; since the movement of these marks transmits itself to all writing and therefore cannot be enclosed within any finite taxonomy, still less in any lexicon as such), they *destroy* the trinitary horizon. Destroy it textually: these are marks of dissemination (and not of polysemy) because they cannot at any *point* be pinned by the concept or by the holder of a signified. They "add" to it the more or the less of a fourth term. (*DISS,* pp. 32/25 [translation altered].)

Whatever its difficulty, this is an important passage, for the destruction of the "trinitary horizon" is an obsessive and recurrent theme in Derrida's writing. (Note that the "trinitary horizon" can also be read as a reference to Christianity, a point that I shall develop later on.) Perhaps I ought to cross out the word *theme*, for it is distinctly un-Derridean to have anything like a "theme" at all. Better is the word *motif,* with its stronger artistic and literary connotations. Derrida himself speaks of "paren-thèmes,"[20] within which we can read "anthems," thus suggesting a musical analogy that ties in nicely with the notion of a motif. Note, too, the joke hidden in Derrida's assertion that the "marks of dissemination" do not allow themselves "at any point to be pinned." To any French-speaker, this brings to mind the expression *tiré à quatre épingles,* literally, "pinned at four corners," which means dapper, spic and span, "just so." Derrida here suggests a departure from logical tidiness: the image is of someone with his hair unbrushed and his tie askew, rattling the cups at the dean's tea party (but remember: he *does* attend).

So, slouching onto the scene comes the Derridean four, which is the "four" not of "four square" but of a dialectical triangle opened to form a fourth side, a disreputable, upsetting four, one that absolutely refuses to behave. The possibility of a fourth moment of the dialectic destroys the whole dialectical machine. (One could imagine a fifth, sixth, or seventh moment, perhaps in the form of Derrida's epigones, but such further moments would bring nothing new, for it is the fourth moment that blows the dialectic apart.) The fourth moment of the dialectic is the deconstructive moment: position, negation, negation of the negation, deconstruction (or: Nietzsche, Heidegger, Foucault, Derrida).

Thus, Derrida engages in a fore-thinking, or four-thinking, that is explicitly directed against the three-thinking of Hegel.[21] This is why he continually plays on the number four. Note the untranslatable series *écart, carré, carrure, carte, charte, quatre* that he introduces in *Positions* and plays on in many subsequent works (*POS*, pp. 58/42). (The series may be translated literally as "divergence, square, breadth, card, chart, four," all supposedly derived from the Latin *quartus.*) Note his reference to the *quadrature,* or squaring, of the text (*DISS*, pp. 332/299). Note his assertion that the "fourth surface" (of the exploded Hegelian triangle) dismantles the "'Platonic' order of presence" (*DISS*, pp. 360/324; also pp. 50/43). Note his references to crossroads (*carrefour, quadrifurcus*), to the Pythagorean tetractys $(1 + 2 + 3 + 4)$, to fourfold roots, to squares and cubes, and to the four volumes of the Book (*DISS*, pp. 386, 387, 407, 340/347, 348, 366, 306). Note his concern with the problem of the *cadre,* or frame, which usually has four sides (*DISS*, pp. 329–333/296–300; *VenP,* pp. 21–168). Note his play on *écarté* and *écartement* in *Spurs* (*SPURS,* pp. 48, 50). Note his interest in Valerio Adami's "Concerto for four hands" (*VenP,* pp. 177, 200). Note the four hypotheses in the preface to *Truth in Painting,* and the recurrence of the number four throughout that work (*VenP,* e.g., pp. 5, 8, 9, 10, 14, 15, 16, 64, 74, 80, 87, 88, 90).

But there is more. See especially the play on four in the essay "The Purveyor of Truth," where Derrida discusses Lacan's discussion of the fate of the letter in Poe's story "The Purloined Letter." Derrida holds, against both Lacan and the detective, Dupin, that "the text escapes on a fourth side the eyes of both Dupin and the psychoanalyst"—that it "implies at least a fourth avenue for appeal that escapes and manages the escape of the letter of the text from the decoder, the purveyor of truth." Derrida continues: "at the very moment when Dupin and the Seminar find the letter, when they find its proper place and course, when they believe the letter is at one place or another as if on a map [*carte*], a place on a map as if on the woman's body, they no longer see the map itself: not the map described by the text at one moment or another but the map that the text 'is,' that it describes, 'itself,' like the four-way divergence [*l'écart du quatre*] with no promise of topos or truth" (*CARTE,* pp. 471–472/65).

The repetition of *carte,* which can mean both map and card, leads us to the "play" of cards (*le jeu de cartes*—which stands in opposition to *le jeu Descartes* that has dominated modern Western history). Think of the antidialectical character of the whole business of card games: four suits, four unnumbered cards—ace, king, queen, joker. Derrida, the antidialectician, is obviously the joker; in fact, on occasion he identifies himself as such (*ni roi, ni valet, mais joker*). In "Purveyor of Truth," we find a game of checkers in which "the pieces are reduced to four kings" (*CARTE*, pp. 515/103). And further: "four kings, hence four queens, four police prefects, four ministers, four analysts Dupin, four narrators, four readers, four kings, etc., all more insightful and more foolish than the others, more powerful and more powerless" (*CARTE*, pp. 522/111). And the four female private detectives (counting Farrah Fawcett) in "Charlie's Angels" (*CARTE*, p. 263/—). What began, perhaps seriously, as an attack on Hegel takes on a life of its own; the play of four becomes genuinely fascinating, quite independently of its initial function as an anti-Hegelian weapon.

Postmodern Paris: philosophy

But what of the other context that we have chosen to consider—not aestheticism and its forerunners but Paris and its enthusiasms? As I have noted, Derrida largely shares this context with Foucault. Nonetheless, there are some striking differences. Firstly, Foucault gave up the academic study of philosophy in the late 1940s, turning to psychology instead. By way of contrast, Derrida remained (however tenuously) within philosophy: he now holds a position in the history of philosophy at the École Normale. We have seen how Foucault's engagement with phenomenological psychology had a considerable impact on his early writings, and how even as late as *The Archaeology of Knowledge* (1969) he was still trying to free himself from phenomenological notions that, from his point of view, had covertly insinuated themselves into his writing. His slowness in confronting these notions was perhaps a consequence of his relative lack of interest in specifically philosophical problems or texts. Derrida, on the other hand, was deeply concerned with philosophical issues. In his early work, he came to grips with certain conceptual problems arising out of phenomenology—above all, the problems of historicity and of identity or intersubjectivity. These are problems that phenomenology tends to accentuate. By the same token, it has had great difficulty coming to terms with them, to such a degree that one is tempted to suggest that they are insoluble within a phenomenological framework.

Secondly, while both Foucault and Derrida stand as champions of "alterity," or otherness, against the supposed domination of the mainstream Western tradition, the locus of their respective alterities has been very different. In his opposition to the domineering tendencies of Western reason, Foucault has concentrated on the oppression (in his terms, the production) of the sick, the insane, criminals, and sexual "deviants." Derrida's concern with alterity, on the other hand, has been much less concrete in character, much less a matter of identifiable social groups being oppressed (or produced). His concern is much more clearly focused on the exclusion of deviant modes of thought. Of course, I am oversimplifying here. For in the first place, in such an important work as *The Order of Things*, Foucault makes no reference whatsoever to social groups, but focuses entirely on systems of thought. And in the second place, there is one telling exception to Derrida's relative lack of interest in social groups. At this point, it seems appropriate to introduce what might seem a purely personal indication—namely, that Derrida was born into a Sephardic Jewish family living in El Biar, a suburb of Algiers (Derrida himself lets us see bits and pieces of this background in some of his more recent writings, especially "Sendings"). Presumably as a consequence of this background, he has shown a persistent fascination with Judaism and with the problem of its relation to a predominantly Greek and Christian culture. This fascination, I shall argue, is important for understanding the depth, rigor, and passion of the attack that he launches on the Western tradition.

One is struck, when one attempts to say something about Derrida's relation to post–World War II French intellectual life, by the discontinuity between his style of intellectual activity and the styles of those figures who seem, in one way or another, to have influenced him. This partly explains why I am more concerned with drawing out Derrida's relation to Nietzsche, Heidegger, and Foucault than with trying to establish his connections to writers and philosophers who belong to his more immediate intellectual milieu (Foucault, of course, does belong to this milieu, but that is not why I have chosen to deal with him in the present book). And yet, despite the general difficulty of establishing connections, various figures prominent in French intellectual life in the 1950s and early '60s, and various problems that were being debated within that context, are important for understanding Derrida's enterprise. While it sometimes seems very difficult to discern how Derrida came to respond to those problems in the highly idiosyncratic and original way that he did, on the other hand it is clear that without the milieu he could not have responded to them at all.

Remember that I am interested in making some sense of Derrida; I am not interested in presenting an intellectual history of post–World War II France. Moreover, I concede that this context, and all the other contexts that I have articulated in this study, are in an important sense fabrications. They are contexts that I have constructed in the course of trying to understand the figures with whom I am concerned. But let me point out that all contexts are constructed; none is simply given—a lesson that Burckhardt long ago taught us. This applies as much to the notion of "French intellectual life after 1945" as it does to the dominant constructions of this study, aestheticism and the prophecy of extremity. For in fact there is no single thing that we can designate as "French intellectual life." Instead, one finds a multiplicity of disorganized, competing strands. How we decide to organize these strands depends on what we are interested in doing. Since I am concerned here with understanding Derrida—and with understanding him in a particular way, more related to aestheticism and the prophecy of extremity than to postwar French intellectual life—I must confine myself to drawing the reader's attention to a few persons and preoccupations that seem to connect in a more or less coherent manner with his writing.

Derrida's departure from mainstream French philosophy is most clearly announced in his style, which almost from the very beginning was "literary" in bearing. Admittedly, French phenomenologists were not averse to literary media—note Gabriel Marcel's direct adoption of the diary form, and Sartre's indirect use of it in *Nausea*.[22] But it is still disconcerting to find Derrida frivolously quoting Joyce and Poe in the midst of his meticulous and almost self-consciously rigorous analyses of what appear at first glance to be highly technical problems in Husserl's phenomenology (*ORGEO*, pp. 104–106/102–104; *VP*, pp. i/1). Nonetheless, philosophy did give Derrida his initial problems. He observes in *Positions* that his major concern in the early 1960s was with investigating "the textual systematics of Hegel, Husserl, and Heidegger" (*POS*, pp. 114/109). It is not at all surprising that he should have chosen to investigate these philosophers in particular. We have seen how important Hegel was for French philosophers in the period 1945–60, and the widespread influence of phenomenology meant that Husserl and Heidegger were of similar moment. Indeed, Vincent Descombes refers to this as the period of "the three H's."[23] The prominent role that a confrontation with these three figures plays in Derrida's work by no means indicates that he sees them as "objectively" more important than any others, for his stance excludes any notion of objectivity. Rather, his preoccupation with Hegel,

Husserl, and Heidegger is indicative of the rhetorical situation within which he found himself. This situation in large measure dictated to him the figures and problems with which he was to deal.

In his early writings, Derrida was concerned much more directly with Husserl than with Hegel or Heidegger. (Once more, as with Heidegger and Foucault, an initial engagement with phenomenology appears almost as a precondition for the aestheticist move.)[24] But Derrida's deconstruction of Husserl would have been all but inconceivable without his own very deep engagement with the other two figures. Think, for example, of Heidegger's critique in *Being and Time* of the notion of knowledge as an objective seeing, the notion of an *intuitus* that in his view has "guided all interpretation of knowledge from the beginning of Greek ontology until today" (*B&T*, p. 358). Much of Derrida's discussion of Husserl, especially in *Speech and Phenomena* (1967), involves an undermining of Husserl's unquestioning commitment to the visual, theoretical understanding, to the supposed light of immediate intuition. As we shall see, this Heideggerian theme was especially stressed by the French phenomenologist Emmanuel Levinas. It is perhaps possible that Derrida could have launched his attack on Husserl without the previous examples of Heidegger and Levinas, but I do not find it likely.

The interest in Hegel brought to French philosophy in this period a concern with history. Hegel's importance was all the greater because, before Althusser's separation of the two, he was seen as laying the groundwork for Marx. Sensitized to history by the massive congruence of Hegel and Marx, French phenomenologists approached Husserl in the hope of deriving from him a phenomenology of history. This was an important concern of Merleau-Ponty, who, as professor of philosophy at the Collège de France from 1952 until his premature death in 1961, played an influential role in French philosophy at the time. Significantly, it was also a major concern in Derrida's early work, which in this respect connects with what mainstream French phenomenologists were thinking about. His first public paper, given at a conference in 1959 and later included (in revised form) in *Writing and Difference,* deals with the relation between "genesis" and "structure" in Husserl's phenomenology. It focuses attention on the difficulty Husserl had in explaining the genesis—that is, the histories—of the static "eidetic" structures that he sought to isolate in his work. And the first of Derrida's writings to appear in print, his long introduction to Husserl's essay "The Origin of Geometry," likewise deals with the problem of how history is to be understood phenomenologically.

It was not only the *understanding* of history that was a preoccupation in French philosophy at the time, but also the possibility of its *end*. This preoccupation took various forms and had various sources. Hegel was important here as well. We have seen how Hegel's notion of the end of philosophy was transformed, in certain circles, into the notion of the end of history itself: a not implausible transformation if one was willing to identify *Geist* with what philosophers thought (as, for example, some of the Young Hegelians were all too willing to do in the middle 1840s). In France, Kojève's account of the supposed end of history in Hegel was immensely influential.[25] So too, toward the end of this period, were the evocations of the end of philosophy in the writings of the later Heidegger (for an example that postdates the 1945–60 period, see Heidegger's essay "The End of Philosophy and the Task of Thinking," first published in 1966 [available in *HBW*]).

The notion of end is closely tied up with that of crisis. Every end need not be a crisis, for it is possible to imagine a smooth transition to something new. But smooth transitions have not been characteristic of thought in our century. It is thus not surprising that one finds an apocalyptic tone being adopted by many French philosophers in this period. As Descombes points out, "at the beginning of the sixties there was much talk concerning the 'end of philosophy.' It was thought that the Western *ratio*, its resources exhausted, was nearing the end of its run."[26] Notions of an end or crisis show up all over the philosophical scene. Note Jean Wahl's *Toward the End of Ontology* (1956); it seems likely that both the work and the writer had some impact on Derrida.[27] Note, too, the presence of the crisis notion in Merleau-Ponty's posthumously published work *The Visible and the Invisible,* with its accompanying "working notes" (1964).[28] Again, one suspects that Derrida was in some measure "influenced" by Merleau-Ponty, though evidence for any such influence is slight (Foucault's work of the 1960s, especially *The Order of Things,* also shows some intriguing parallels with Merleau-Ponty).

What is important, however, is not any specific influence but simply the fact that the notion of crisis was widely mooted in French philosophical circles at the time. In *The Order of Things,* Foucault suggests that "if the discovery of the Return is indeed the end of philosophy, then the end of man, for its part, is the return of the beginning of philosophy" (*MC,* pp. 353/342). This has a lyric suggestiveness and a Nietzschean affirmative quality to it not to be found in Wahl or Merleau-Ponty. But its relatedness to the philosophical discussion of the time is manifest. And Derrida, more than Foucault, was intimately familiar with the milieu within which these things were being said.

Postmodern Paris: literature

It is clear that the philosophical milieu provided Derrida with the initial grist for his milling. The manner of that milling, however, came largely from elsewhere. Derrida's textual derring-do finds no parallel in any other French philosopher. But it does find a parallel in the literary and artistic avant-garde, especially in those figures whom we can in one way or another link to postmodernism. And in fact Derrida has shown a long and continuing interest in various avant-garde literary and artistic figures. He seems especially interested in those who can be interpreted as challenging what he sees as the dominant Western commitment to representation. In his writings of the 1960s and early '70s, he devoted a great deal of attention to Artaud, Bataille, Sollers, and, above all, Mallarmé; more recently he has turned to Ponge and to a succession of graphic artists. Instead of attempting to create the illusion of an external world, as writers in a more realist tradition do, these figures engage in a species of textual play—one that seeks to question the very category of "literature" itself. Derrida explains his interest in their work in his 1971 *Positions* interview:

> it is incontestable that certain texts classed as "literary" have seemed to me to operate breaches or infractions at the most advanced points.... Why? At least for the reason that induces us to suspect the denomination "literature," and which subjects the concept to belles-lettres, to the arts, to poetry, to rhetoric, and to philosophy. These texts operate, in their very movement, the demonstration and practical deconstruction of the *representation* of what was done with literature, it being well understood that long before these "modern texts" a certain "literary" practice was able to operate against this model, against this representation. But it is on the basis of these last texts, on the basis of the general configuration to be remarked in them, that one can best reread, without retrospective teleology, the law of the previous fissures. (*POS*, pp. 93–94/69.)

In Chapter 8, I shall pursue this literary and aesthetic connection further. My concern here is simply to explore, in some degree, the background to Derrida's interest in aesthetic (or antiaesthetic) matters. A good place to begin is with the novelist and critic Maurice Blanchot, who can be seen as in some ways providing a theoretical (or antitheoretical?) foundation (antifoundation?) for Derrida. I have referred to Blanchot previously on a number of occasions. This was no accident, for Blanchot's perspective is very close to that of aestheticism. I have noted that he is a negative Heideggerian, for while he insists, like Heidegger, on the "impersonality" of art, he at the same time rejects the notion that art has "truth value." Art, in Blanchot's view, "hides itself from signification, designating that region where nothing lives, where that which has taken place has however not taken place, where that which begins again has never yet begun, a place of the most dangerous indecision." Separated from the world, where "truth has its foundation and basis," it "represents originally the foreboding and scandal of absolute error." It suggests, indeed, that the "nontrue" might be "an essential form of authenticity."[29]

Closely related to this distinction between the "truth" of the world and the "nontruth" of art is Blanchot's distinction between two kinds of language. Blanchot here appeals to Mallarmé's assertion that there is a "double state of language, on the one hand raw or immediate, on the other essential." "Raw" language—*parole brute*—is concerned with "the reality of things." Narrating, teaching, describing, it gives us things in their presence—that is, it "represents" them, in Blanchot's view. Since the aim of *parole brute* is to put us into a direct relationship with things, language as language remains silent; beings speak, not language. *Parole brute* functions as one instrument in a world full of instruments; it connects us with the life of the world and with the ends governing that life.

Parole essentielle, on the other hand, distances us from things, making them disappear. It is "always allusive, it suggests, it evokes." It is not a language of the real but rather "of the unreal, fictive and delivering us up to fiction." Whereas *parole brute* strives to efface itself as language and to become a pure representation of things, *parole essentielle* seeks to impose itself—though in imposing itself it imposes nothing outside itself. *Parole essentielle* is not, says Blanchot, the language of thought, for the language of thought "still refers us to a world." It is rather the language of poetry—in which, according to Blanchot, "beings and their preoccupations, their projects, their activity" become silent. In the language of poetry, it is language itself that speaks: "language assumes its full importance; it becomes what is essential; it speaks *as* essential, and that is why the speech that is entrusted to the poet can be said to be *parole essentielle.* This means first of all that words, taking the initiative, must not serve to designate some thing or to give voice to some one, but that they have their ends in themselves."[30]

This account of art and literature expresses a postmodern sensibility (I concede that postmodernists will reject the notion of expression). In his insistence on seeing art and literature as absolutely cut off from the world, Blanchot is reproducing the sense of crisis or division that is fundamental to both modernism and postmodernism. Unlike the modernist, however, the postmodernist does not countenance the reconstituting of truth on the level of literature. Rather, he holds (see, for example, Borges) that fiction is merely fiction. Characteristically, the postmodernist extends the notion of fictionality to the world in general. Alan Wilde rightly points out that the "anironic" impulse to be found in literary modernism—that is, the impulse to create an appearance of order to counterbalance chaotic reality—disappears from postmodernism.[31] Blanchot's view of art is undeniably postmodern; indeed, it is much more faithfully postmodern than Heidegger's, which in many ways it closely resembles. Blanchot's notion of the impersonality of art, for example, is paralleled by Heidegger's conviction that it is not man but language that speaks (*die Sprache spricht*). But note how there is still a hint of the anironic in Heidegger, in his sometime tendency to see art, or language, or the nostalgic world of ancient Greece as a refuge against the ironic, unhoming, fragmenting character of modern technology. There is nothing of the anironic in Blanchot, as his unequivocal rejection of the "truth value" notion clearly indicates.

I am not sure of the extent to which Derrida was "influenced" by Blanchot, though there is evidence to suggest that the influence was significant.[32] Again, however, it is affinity rather than influence that counts. To be sure, stylistically Blanchot and Derrida are very different, since Blanchot's writing has a surface clarity to it that one does not find in Derrida. But whatever the differences of style, both writers manifest a great openness and sensitivity to postmodernism in art and literature. This is to be seen partly in Derrida's preference for postmodern artists (e.g., Magritte, Adami, Titus-Carmel) over modernist ones—his favoring of figures who are unequivocally ironic, even parodic in spirit, with no longing for the anironic moment.[33] And it is to be seen even more tellingly in the "artistic," "literary" character of his own enterprise. Postmodernist intellectuals reject what modernist intellectuals still accept—namely, the notion of science as a haven or refuge, as an anironic protection (however uncertain) against the irony of existence (I develop this point later, in relation to modernist and postmodernist interpretations of Freud). Thus, they no longer take seriously the distinction between scientific discourse and nonscientific discourse, or between criticism and art.

Blanchot's criticism, for example, is not radically divergent from his fictions, nor his fictions from his criticism. And with Derrida, too, criticism and creation are intertwined. This is most evident in his masterpiece, *Glas,* a work that needs to be seen rather than summarized. Though supposedly a commentary on Hegel and Jean Genet (an outrageous juxtaposition if there ever was one), it says nothing—in the usual sense of commentary—about these two writers. Instead, by typographical stratagems, by extensive quotation, by the chopping up of passages, by recourse to dictionary definitions, and by word play of various kinds, Derrida creates a literary-philosophical *collage.* To attempt to read it as philosophical or critical commentary is silly. One must read it, rather, as a work of art—and more specifically as a postmodern work of art, designed not to reconstitute an order (however provisional) in the mind of the reader/viewer but rather to generate an infinite free association. Admittedly, Derrida challenges the assumption of crisis that underlies postmodernism—as we shall see. But this is no denial of the postmodern impulse in his work.

Derrida's affinities with Blanchot are perhaps most obvious in his essay "The Double Session," first published in 1970 and included in the collection *Dissemination* (1972). This essay ties together a number of important strands in Derrida's work. In it he discusses, among other things, a short text of Mallarmé's entitled "Mimicry." According to Derrida, the Mallarméan mime "represents nothing, imitates nothing, does not have to conform to any prior referent with the aim of achieving adequation or verisimilitude" (*DISS,* pp. 233/205). Thus, the mime manages to occupy a position outside, or at least on the edges, of the "logocentric" Western tradition. According to Blanchot, *parole essentielle* is allusive, suggestive, evocative. But as Derrida has it, the allusion is to nothing: "the mime's operation does allude, but alludes to nothing, alludes without breaking the mirror, without reaching beyond the looking-glass." Miming "reflects no reality; it produces mere 'reality-effects' [*'effets de réalité'*]." It "will prove to be inaccessible, otherwise than by simulacrum, just like the dreamt-of *simplicity* of the supreme spasm or of the hymen" (*DISS,* pp. 234/206). Or, in language that is perhaps a little clearer, "the referent is lifted, but reference remains; what is left is only the writing of dreams, a fiction that is not imaginary, mimicry without imitation, without verisimilitude, without truth or falsity. . . . There remain only traces, foretellings, recallings, fore-blows and after-blows which no present will have preceded or followed and which cannot be arranged on a line" (*DISS,* pp. 239/211 [translation altered]).

Derrida is here describing a literature of crisis—a literature, moreover, that marks out its absolute alienation from the extant world by refusing in any way to repeat, to "re-present" it. This is why imitation, verisimilitude, truth, and falsity are all excluded. Obviously, such a literature is supremely ironical—and not only in the simple sense of saying one thing but meaning another, but also in the heightened sense of saying one thing and meaning, or "wishing to say," nothing at all. Such an irony inevitably takes parody as its most important resource. As Derrida says in his essay on Bataille and Hegel: when faced by the all-encompassing dialectical maw, we must "redouble language and have recourse to ruses, to stratagems, to simulacra" (*E&D*, pp. 386/263). "The Double Session" is a sustained reflection on this business. Derrida's "double science" is parodic. Nor is it surprising that Derrida should turn so resolutely in this direction, for we have seen how parody also plays a role in his predecessors.

As Margaret A. Rose puts it, "parody, as the criticism of a prevailing manner of thought, does not aim to be soothing, but to disturb preconceptions and prejudices."[34] While one could conceive of a parody that would confine its disturbances to literary history, I am inclined to believe that its broader tendency is toward disturbing the whole prevailing order. Hence, in view of his disinclination for upsetting the reigning powers, it is not surprising that of our four prophets of extremity Heidegger is the least parodic—unless, of course, one chooses (as Robert Minder has done) to regard much of his later work as an unwitting parody of the very worst in German poetry.[35] But if Heidegger is at most an unconscious parodist, Nietzsche and Foucault are both consciously so, as *Thus Spoke Zarathustra* and *The Archaeology of Knowledge* well indicate. Derrida, for his part, carries the business of parody one step further, parodying logocentrism (as Nietzsche parodies Christianity and Foucault Cartesianism) but also parodying his own parody.

Parody is a difficult genre; "self-parody" (to use Richard Poirier's term)[36] even more so. Tremendous demands are made on the reader. Familiarity with the parodized texts is assumed, but on top of this one must be able to detect the most minute tonal variations in the parodist's text. Without great sensitivity and erudition, one misses much of what is going on. Indeed, to read Derrida properly, one would have to be his twin, in which case one's reading would at the same time be a writing—but a double writing, as in Borges's story. Yet, Derrida seeks, in his writings, to deconstruct the notion of identity. To read him properly, in short, would require that one possess the very thing that he wishes to attack. This amounts to saying that none of us can hope to fulfill the conditions for reading him properly. But even badly perceived, there is a suggestive richness in his interplay of parodies, which perhaps explains the addictive effect that the reading of his texts can have.

The fate of writing

I have not yet unveiled any Derridean thesis. This should not be thought surprising, for part of Derrida's point, if it can be said to be a point, is that the very desire for a thesis needs to be attacked. This puts me in an odd position as a reader of Derrida. For I am seeking something more than an appreciation of the richness of the Derridean text—that is, its appreciation as a work of art. Rather, as an historian of ideas, I seek an intellectual content in Derrida's work, which I can then examine, question, "place" within a context, and discuss in relation to the other ideas that I have been considering in this book. In Derridean terms, this can only be regarded as an illegitimate attempt to appropriate what cannot be appropriated. As Derrida puts it in an essay on Mallarmé, "a text is made in order to dispense with references."[37] By this he means to exclude all appeals to authors, to contexts, or to "the thing itself" ("the thing itself always escapes," he says at the end of *Speech and Phenomena* [*V&P*, pp. 117/104]). And he also means to exclude an appeal to theses, for theses are irremediably Hegelian in character, and set one on the road to entrapment in the dialectic.

Perhaps it suffices to say that Derrida puts forward something resembling a thesis, at least in his writings up to *Glas*. This thesis seems to have just about disappeared from the more recent writings, at least as something "seriously" put forward. At most it is a vehicle for the burlesquing slanders that Derrida directs against Socrates and Plato in *Postcard*. But I know that it sticks in the minds of most people who have had any encounter with Derrida as an important aspect of his enterprise. It is obsessively present in Derrida's three books of 1967: *Speech and Phenomena*; *Writing and Difference* (especially the last five essays); and *Of Grammatology* (especially Part I). And it is rehearsed, from different perspectives, in the three books of 1972: *Margins of Philosophy*; *Dissemination*; and *Positions*. Briefly, Derrida's "thesis" (this inaccuracy seems necessary) is that over the course of Western history writing has been "abased" in favor of speech (see, e.g., *POS*, pp. 72/53). Speech stands for immediacy—or more precisely for intelligibility, for the possibility of contact with Truth, with the "transcendental signified." Writing stands for a peculiar kind of secondariness—one that recognizes that secondariness is all we have. The Western tradition, says Derrida, has looked down upon writing; as he puts it in *Of Grammatology*, "writing, the sensible inscription, has always been considered by Western tradition as the body and matter external to the spirit, to breath, to speech, and to the logos" (*GRAM*, pp. 52/35).

Derrida's "grammatological" thesis seems, then, to be a shorthand method of condemning the Western tradition for its commitment to the ultimate possibility of literal truth. Ironically, such is Derrida's incredible display of erudition in advancing this thesis that many of his readers interpret him as arguing for its literal truth. But clearly this is not his intention, at least insofar as we can claim to know that intention. In his essay "Violence and Metaphysics," originally published in 1964, he declares that "the limit between violence and nonviolence is perhaps not between speech and writing but within each of them" (*E&D*, pp. 151/102). And in his essay on Bataille and Hegel, he speaks of two forms of writing, one sovereign and the other servile (*E&D*, pp. 385–396/262–270). In short, the whole opposition between speech and writing is itself deconstructed. Derrida engages in a parodistically scholarly *tour de force*, trying with all the resources available to him to make the implausible look plausible. And then, in a move that we shall see him make again, he wipes out the very distinction that he has tried so hard to establish.

The speech/writing opposition is by no means foreign to the previous literature. The decisive reference for Derrida is Plato's *Phaedrus*. He refers frequently to this work in the course of his various "grammatological" writings, and discusses it in detail in his hilarious essay "Plato's Pharmacy," originally published in 1968 and included in *Dissemination*. *Phaedrus* embodies the classic Platonic attack on rhetoric; this, certainly, has been its major interest for subsequent readers.[38] It is characteristic of Derrida, however, that he no more identifies himself with rhetoric than he does with dialectic. He is highly suspicious of "the categories of classical rhetoric" and is not about to play rhetoric off against its long-standing enemy (*DISS*, pp. 296/264; see also "White Mythology" in *MARGES*). To put this in other terms, Derrida's opposition to the "Western tradition" is so radical and unyielding that even the sophists, those great practitioners and teachers of rhetoric, come under his attack.

Instead of focusing on the rhetoric/dialectic conflict in the *Phaedrus*, Derrida directs his attention to Socrates' attack, near the end of the dialogue, on writing. Writing, Socrates here maintains, is only an image of living speech; speech is far preferable to it. Writing weakens the memory. Writings get out of the hands of the writer and come to be misinterpreted. Writings should serve only as a reminder to the reader of truths that he already understands (*Phaedrus*, 274c–276e). Derrida sees this Socratic rejection of writing as dominating the entire subsequent history of the West. As he says, rather complexly, in *Of Grammatology*, "the system of 'hearing (understanding)-oneself-speak' through the phonic substance— which *presents itself* as the nonexterior, nonmundane, therefore nonempirical or noncontingent *signifier*—has necessarily dominated the history of the world during an entire epoch" (*GRAM*, pp. 17/7–8). Speech is presence; writing, the denial of presence. Whereas the voice goes out immediately into the world and disappears immediately upon its being said, writing is a mediate form, separating itself from its origin and preserving itself even in the absence of that origin. In Derrida's words, writing is "a mediation and the departure of the logos from itself. . . . Writing is the dissimulation of the natural, primary, and immediate presence of sense to the soul within the logos" (*GRAM*, pp. 55/37).

Most readers of the *Phaedrus* pass very quickly over the few lines in which Socrates attacks writing. One who did not was Blanchot, who commented on this passage in an essay on René Char first published in 1953. Blanchot again provides a plausible approach to Derrida. As Blanchot explains it, Socrates objects to the written word because it "gives voice to absent being, like the divine voice of the oracle, where the god himself is never present in his words, it being only his absence which speaks. And like writing, the oracle refuses to justify, explain, or defend itself; there is no argument with writing, any more than with the god. Socrates remains nonplussed by this speaking silence."[39] Behind Blanchot's focusing on this passage lies something very close to a Heideggerian concern with the work of art. For Socrates' dismissive view of writing parallels his equally dismissive view of art. According to Blanchot, Socrates is dismayed by the silence of writing, which is similar to the silence of art. In Blanchot's words, this is

> a majestic silence, a stubborn dumbness, essentially inhuman, informing art with the awe of sacred forces, forces which, by means of their fear and horror, open man's mind to strange regions. There could be nothing more striking than this shock, this uneasiness which the silence of art inspires in the lover of the spoken word, the faithful upholder of the honor of living speech; which is nothing but a semblance, a thing which speaks truth and yet with nothing but a void behind it, no possibility of discussion, so that in it the truth has nothing with which to confirm itself, appears without support, is only a scandalous semblance of truth, an image, and by its imagery and seeming draws away truth into depths where there is neither truth nor meaning, not even error.[40]

In Heidegger's view, "language speaks"—that is, language *itself* speaks, without the presence of an author. It is precisely this notion of the independence, of the *impersonality* of language and art that Blanchot sees Socrates as attacking. And it is significant, moreover, that these reflections occur in the context of an essay on René Char, whose poetry exemplifies the view that art is not the conveying of a meaning that would somehow be separable from the art but is rather (to use Heidegger's phrase) "a simple Saying." (Heidegger's liking for Char's work is well known, and one can easily understand the basis for this affinity.) Blanchot quotes a saying of Heraclitus that he finds significant for understanding Char's poetry: "The Lord whose oracle is at Delphi neither expresses nor conceals but indicates." This, precisely, is Blanchot's—and Char's, and Heidegger's—view of art: "saying nothing, hiding nothing, opening a space, opening it to whoever opens himself to its access." As Blanchot points out, Socrates makes a "reasonable" demand. He does not want "a language which says nothing, and behind which nothing conceals itself." He wants instead "a word of certainty, vouched for by a living presence, an exchangeable word, made for that purpose."[41] With all its reasonableness—the same reasonableness detected and excoriated by Nietzsche— this demand amounts to a denial of art.

Blanchot's celebration of Char's poetry, which he sees as opposing the logical mentality of Socrates and Plato, foreshadows Derrida's celebration of postmodern art and literature. The question of fiction is here crucial. The fourth moment of the dialectic is quite obviously a fictional moment. As Derrida says in "Outside the Book": "the beyond of the whole, another name for the text insofar as it resists all ontology . . . is not a *primum movens*. Nevertheless . . . it imprints upon the whole a movement of fiction" (*DISS*, pp. 65/57). But not all fiction qualifies for this anti-ontological role; only a certain type of fiction. Nor is Derrida backward about naming names. In *Positions,* as we have seen, he discusses Artaud, Bataille, Mallarmé, and Sollers. Not only do their texts call "literature" into question, however; they also "seemed to me to mark and to organize a structure of resistance to the philosophical conceptuality that allegedly dominated or comprehended them, whether directly, or whether through categories derived from this philosophical basis, the categories of traditional aesthetics, rhetoric, or criticism" (*POS*, pp. 93–94/69 [translation altered]). Derrida contrasts these writers—all antimimetic in orientation, all concerned with the "play" of language itself—with what he sees as the oppressive Platonic commitment to the immediacy of intuition.

This contrast is direct and explicit. In "The Double Session," for example, Derrida plays various of Mallarmé's texts off against a passage from Plato's *Philebus*. And in "Dissemination," the title essay of the book, he contrasts Philippe Sollers's avant-garde novel *Numbers* with the *Republic*. Thus, he asks us to imagine Plato's cave not simply overthrown by some philosophical move-ment but transformed in its entirety into a circumscribed area contained within another—an absolutely other—structure, an incommensurably, unpredictably more complicated machine. Imagine that mirrors would not be *in* the world, simply, included in the totality of all *onta* and their images, but that things "present," on the contrary, would be in *them.* Imagine that mirrors (shadows, reflections, phantasms, etc.) would no longer be *com-prehended* within the structure of the ontology and myth of the cave . . . but would rather envelop it in its entirety, producing here or there a particular, extremely determinate effect. The whole hierarchy described in the *Repub-lic,* in its cave and in its line, would once again find itself at stake and in question in the theater of *Numbers. (DISS,* pp. 360/324.)

With the possible exception of Mallarmé, the figures whom Derrida mentions as exemplifying an anti-ontological stance won't mean much to English readers. Nonetheless, readers unfamiliar with French literature can find meaningful examples elsewhere: in Duchamp's urinal, in Magritte's punning paintings and drawings, in the writings of James Joyce. The affini-ties with Joyce are perhaps most worth exploiting, for Joyce's work is widely known and appreciated. Fans of Joyce will have a sense of *déjà vu* in con-templating Derrida. It is *Finnegans Wake* that seems relevant here, much more than *Ulysses* (*Dubliners* occupies a different sphere altogether). As S. L. Goldberg points out, Joyce was deeply concerned in *Ulysses* with re-storing art to "its context in experience," with holding to the "here and now."[42] This contrasts with Derrida, who explicitly rejects the notion of the "here and now"; note, above all, his sustained attack on Husserl's concep-tion of the "living present." But in *Finnegans Wake* we find a very different Joyce, one much closer to Derrida. Goldberg suggests unsympathetically (though admittedly with some tentativeness) that the later Joyce is "so im-patient to discover high metaphysical significances that he disdains the hu-man and *dramatic* meaning of what is before him, the 'natural' or 'literal' level of human experience."[43] A sympathetic reading would hold that it is precisely the notions of naturalness and literality that Joyce *wants* to call into question—that these notions are used much too unthinkingly and that we, as readers and actors, need to be made aware of their questionable character. One might characterize this as a conflict between epistemology and hermeneutics, to borrow Rorty's distinction. According to Rorty, we are epistemological "where we understand perfectly well what is happen-ing but want to codify it in order to extend, or strengthen, or teach, or 'ground' it." We are hermeneutical where "we do not understand what is happening but are honest enough to admit it."[44]

Obviously, there is one situation where hermeneutics beats epistemology hands down—that of crisis. For in crisis we indeed do not understand what is happening: we sense a turning but do not know where the turning will end. Otherwise there would be no crisis. Crisis underpins and, in its own way, justifies such a work as *Finnegans Wake*. And crisis is crucial for Derrida as well. Little wonder, then, that we should find telling marks of affinity between Derrida and the later Joyce. When Derrida writes of a mimicry "without imitation, without verisimilitude, without truth or falsity," in which one finds only "traces, foretellings, recallings, fore-blows and after-blows which no present will have preceded or followed," he could hardly have given us a better description of *Finnegans Wake*. And what is *Glas*—that is, *Death Knell*—but the *Finnegans Wake* of philosophy? Derrida himself recognizes the affinity. In his recent "Sendings," we find him beginning to wake to the *Wake*. Shaun the postman becomes Derrida's *facteur* (factor, purveyor, postman) of truth, while Joyce's Babel references—especially his evocation of the "babbling pumpt of platinism"—become yet another indication of the hostility between Platonic presence and the text that refuses to conform to this present. Not surprisingly, Joyce's grave in Zurich receives an obligatory visit (*CARTE*, pp. 154–155, 161, 257/—).

Fictionality and crisis

But if we adopt a hermeneutical stance, in Rorty's sense—a sense that seems applicable to Derrida—what happens to crisis? Note the paradox. The hermeneut tells us that there is nothing outside of the text, that interpretation is an endless play that connects with no extra-interpretive referent. Yet, implicitly or explicitly, he also justifies his hermeneutic enterprise on the grounds that we are in crisis. But how does he know that we are in crisis? In *Of Grammatology*, in the course of a discussion of "my principles of reading," Derrida tells us that "reading... cannot legitimately transgress the text toward something other than it, toward a referent (a reality that is metaphysical, historical, psychobiographical, etc.) or toward a signified outside the text whose content could take place, could have taken place outside of language, that is to say, in the sense that we give here to that word, outside of writing in general" (*GRAM*, pp. 227/ 158). In short, there is no such thing as a theme. But if there is no such thing as a theme, what is one to make of the crisis notion? After all, insofar as Derrida is a postmodernist his position seems predicated on the notion of crisis. What becomes of this crisis when he denies that we can possibly know that such a thing as a crisis can take place outside the confines of the text?

As the shrewdest of our writers—the deconstructive angel of contemporary thought—Derrida is entirely aware of the problem. And his response to it is to write in a strangely weighty mode of fiction. He cannot be a critic in the usual sense, articulating a discourse that claims to deal in truth. Nor can he be a writer of fictions in the usual sense, for (as we shall see more fully later on) he rejects the Kantian notion that aesthetic fiction is something separable from the serious truth of science. Instead, he walks a line between the two, writing in a genre (or anti-genre) that is oddly mixed. Thus, he can speak with some insistence of the situation of crisis in which literature finds itself from Mallarmé onward (*DISS*, pp. 267, 275, 309–317/237, 244, 277–286), but we are never entirely sure to what extent he actually believes that such a crisis prevails. It is perhaps best to say that he writes *as if* literature has entered into crisis. He seeks, in those of his writings that connect most insistently with literary criticism, to work out the implications of such a crisis, whether the crisis exists or not. It is this working out of implications that is perhaps the most interesting part of Derrida's enterprise, at least of his enterprise as a literary critic. According to Derrida, Mallarmé's *crise de vers* "shakes up [*sollicite*] the very bases of literature, depriving it, in its play, of any foundation outside itself. Literature is at once reassured and threatened by the fact of depending only on itself, standing in the air, all alone, separated from being" (*DISS*, pp. 312/280 [translation altered]). And the *crise de vers* means that thematic criticism—that is, criticism in its traditional sense—is obsolete. At any rate, it has failed to come to terms with its own presuppositions. These presuppositions are firmly rooted in the belief that the world is not in crisis, that a fundamental order prevails therein.

Yet, Derrida's enterprise goes far beyond the territory of literary criticism. In "The Double Session" and elsewhere, he argues that literary criticism in its traditional forms is only a stalking horse for the dominant Western commitment to presence. It is this commitment that is his main target. Note his rhetorical question: "Wouldn't 'literary criticism' as such be part of what we have called the *ontological* interpretation of mimesis or of metaphysical mimetologism?" (*DISS*, pp. 275–276/245). The language is pure jargon, but the meaning seems clear enough. Derrida wishes to say that "traditional" literary criticism has treated literature under the category of "presence," thus subjecting it to "Western philosophy." He wishes to say that it has ignored or repressed those aspects of the literary enterprise, and of "Western" experience, that do not accord with present-ist, mimetological, ontological, metaphysical assumptions. According to Derrida, "traditional" criticism always seeks a theme that is outside the text. It seeks "to determine a meaning through a text, to pronounce a decision upon it, to decide that this or that *is* a meaning and that it is meaningful, to say that this meaning is posed, posable, or transposable as such: a theme" (*DISS,* pp. 276/245). Theme is here conceived as "a nu-clear unit of meaning, posed there before the gaze, present outside of its signifier and referring only to itself, in the last analysis, even though its identity as a signified is carved out of the horizon of an infinite perspec-tive" (*DISS,* pp. 281–282/250 [translation altered]).

For example, the phenomenological critic Jean-Pierre Richard argued that Mallarmé's literary adventure is centered on the themes of the "blank" and the "fold." Derrida argues that these themes deconstruct themselves: that there is no clear truth or meaning in Mallarmé. Richard took the "blank" and the "fold" as the nodal points of two chains of polysemic association in Mallarmé's text. Derrida holds that Mallarmé gives us not polysemy but "dissemination"—that is, a complete dispersal of meaning—for in Derrida's view, Mallarmé refers to nothing outside the text to which meaning or truth can be attributed, or to which can be given the grand characterization of a theme. There is no "parousia of meaning" in Mallarmé. Mallarmé's concern, Derrida maintains, is not with the revelation of truth but with the operation of writing. He makes no attempt to unveil truth, but seeks only to constitute "textual traces" to which no definitive meanings can be given (*DISS,* pp. 293–294/261–262).

If there is a crisis in literature, there is also, Derrida seems to suggest, a crisis in the Western tradition as a whole. In Derrida's perspective, it is ultimately this crisis that makes untenable the kind of position that Rich-ard adheres to. But in view of what I have so far said about Derrida's fictionality, it is not surprising that his evocations of this crisis are pecu-liarly strained. The tension is especially evident in *Of Grammatology,* the work in which Derrida comes closest to articulating a sustained historical argument. The logic of his stance and the sensitivity of his intelligence oblige Derrida to say simultaneously that there is a crisis and that there is not a crisis. The more obviously struck note is that there *is* a crisis; one often feels a continuity with the writings of Foucault. And yet, the crisis theme is consistently counterpointed and undermined.

Take, for example, Derrida's claim in the "Exergue" to *Of Grammato-logy* that we can glimpse the "closure" (but not the "end") of "an his-

torico-metaphysical epoch" (*GRAM*, pp. 14/4). The first chapter is entitled "The End of the Book and the Beginning of Writing," which seems to
suggest a movement from one to the other, thus a crisis of the book.[45]
Note, too, the following passage: "By a slow movement whose necessity
is hardly perceptible, everything that for at least some twenty centuries
tended toward and finally succeeded in being gathered under the name of
language is beginning to let itself be transferred to, or at least summarized
under, the name of writing" (*GRAM*, pp. 15–16/6). And a little later, we
read (in a passage that deserves to be quoted *in extenso*) that

> it is therefore as if what we call language could have been in its origin and in
> its end only a moment, an essential but determined mode, a phenomenon,
> an aspect, a species of writing. And as if it had succeeded in making us
> forget this, and *in wilfully misleading us,* only in the course of an adventure:
> as that adventure itself. . . . It merges with the history that has associated
> technics and logocentric metaphysics for nearly three millennia. And it
> now seems to be approaching what is really its own *exhaustion*; under the
> circumstances—and this is no more than one example among others—of
> this death of the civilization of the book, of which so much is said and
> which manifests itself particularly through a convulsive proliferation of li-
> braries. All appearances to the contrary, this death of the book undoubtedly
> announces . . . nothing but a death of speech (of a *so-called* full speech) and
> a new mutation in the history of writing, in history as writing. Announces it
> at a distance of a few centuries. It is on that scale that we must reckon it
> here, being careful not to neglect the quality of a very heterogeneous histor-
> ical duration: the acceleration is such, and such its qualitative meaning,
> that one would be equally wrong in making a careful evaluation according
> to past rhythms. (*GRAM*, pp. 18/8.)

I feel obliged to quote extensively because only by doing so can I hope
to convey some feeling for the peculiarity of Derrida's position. We find
him writing of apocalypse in a strangely backtracking way. "Closure"
rather than "crisis" or "end"; "as if" rather than "is." Derrida clearly
feels uneasy about the whole crisis notion. The apparent seriousness with
which he pursues a notion so uneasily held makes *Of Grammatology* an
utterly bizarre work. The evocations of crisis remind one of Foucault, and
yet the tone is very different, for in Foucault the apocalypticism is unequivocal and unrestrained. For example, there is nothing in Derrida's corpus to match the last few paragraphs of *The Order of Things*, where the
death of the modern *episteme* is gleefully proclaimed. Derrida's "mutation"—the death of the book and of full speech, and their replacement,
presumably, by writing—is announced "at a distance of a few centuries,"
which obviously calls into question its immediate, crisis character. We

seem to be reading a parody, not of conventional, "Cartesian" scholarship (though this certainly is part of what Derrida parodizes in *Of Grammatology*) but of crisis thought itself. Think of Nietzsche's proclamation: "What I relate is the history of the next two centuries" (*WP*, Preface, §2). It is this kind of confident apocalypticism—invented by Nietzsche and run into the ground by Foucault—that Derrida makes fun of. To be sure, there are other ways of making sense of *Of Grammatology:* for example, treating it as simply a more uncompromising attack on phenomenology and structuralism than that launched by Foucault. But any such reading would miss the point if it failed to take account of the multiple parodies of the work. *Incipit parodia?* Then let the parodist be parodized.

Crisis and tradition

I have already noted that a precondition for the crisis view is the notion that history has directionality. Without the assumption that history is directional or linear in character, crisis would be inconceivable. The prophets of extremity are, in Rorty's sense of the term, "therapeutic" thinkers. They force us to question our own assumptions and thus help us to understand better what we believe and do not believe. But one thing remains therapeutically unexamined and untreated: the notion of crisis itself. Moreover, we should not think that the categories *modernism* and *postmodernism,* with their underlying assumption of crisis, apply only to art and literature. It is true that artists and fiction-writers have played a major role in dramatizing notions of crisis, break, discontinuity, and separation in our century. But these terms are also applicable in a more broadly intellectual sense, including, for example, existentialism, phenomenology, structuralism, poststructuralism, and the more radical of the postpositivistic philosophies of science. Looking at individuals, such names as Yeats, Pound, Eliot, Tzara, Kafka, Cioran, Pynchon, Barth, Barthelme, Arendt, Voegelin, Leo Strauss, Sartre, Lévi-Strauss, Althusser, Barthes, Kuhn, and Feyerabend come to mind. Nietzsche, Heidegger, and Foucault are merely the most extreme and forthright exponents of a view that enjoys wide currency.

I hardly need, at this stage, to rehearse the presence of crisis in these three writers. One thinks of Nietzsche's evocation of the death of God and especially of his declaration, in *Ecce Homo,* that "one day my name will be associated with the memory of something tremendous—a crisis without equal on earth, the most profound collision of conscience, a decision that was conjured up *against* everything that had been believed, demanded, hallowed so far. I am no man, I am dynamite" (*EH*, "Why I am a Destiny," §8). One thinks, too, of Heidegger's assertions from 1933 onward of a spiritual crisis in the modern world, and of Foucault's cataclysmic "mutations."

But I do need to point out the extent to which these assertions of crisis coexist with a deep interest in history—though "history" needs to be understood here in a special sense. At least superficially, this interest is most evident in Foucault. Foucault claims emphatically to be an historian, and in such writings as *The Archaeology of Knowledge* and "Nietzsche, Genealogy, History" he has reflected on the meaning of the historiographical enterprise. It appears, too, in Nietzsche's reflection on "The Uses and Disadvantages of History," and his persistent criticism of "modern historiography" for claiming to be a "mirror" of events—for falling victim to "the dangerous old conceptual fiction" of a "pure, will-less, painless, timeless knowing subject" (*GM*, 3rd Essay, §§12, 26; *NBW*, pp. 555, 593). And it also shows in Heidegger's emphasis toward the end of *Being and Time* on "historicity" (*Geschichtlichkeit*), as well as his later attacks on conventional, "representational" historiography (see, e.g., *EP*, p. 93, and *EGT*, pp. 17, 57).

Why is this preoccupation with history and its perception shared by these writers? Is this not strange, for shouldn't their commitments to the notion of a break with the past lead them to remain utterly indifferent to history, let alone historiography? How does this preoccupation connect with their similarly shared notion of crisis?

The answer is clear. Since it is only within the context of a certain view of history—a linear or directional view—that the crisis notion makes sense, it is to be expected that crisis thinkers should expend some effort articulating such a view. I suggested earlier that the crisis notion embodies a metaphor of turning. But this depends on another metaphor, that of linearity. The linearity metaphor has in the past had wide allegiance. As Maurice Mandelbaum makes clear, it was especially influential in the nineteenth century, in the form of a developmental view of history. Mandelbaum shows that "historicism" (in his sense, tied to the notion of development) was the closest thing to a unifying notion beneath the diverse schools of thought in this period.[46] As Mandelbaum also points out, historicism has lost its grip on more recent thought. This is partly because of purely intellectual developments, such as the wide diffusion of the view that laws simply describe events rather than govern them, a shift implying that there was "no longer reason to suppose that history necessarily followed a definite, determined course." The decline of historicism is also attributable to historical events, especially the experience of World War I and subsequent social and political upheavals, which undermined the nineteenth-century faith in progress and thus destroyed what had become, by late in that century, a crucial underpinning of historicist doctrine.[47]

We have already seen, in considering the background to Heidegger, what this undermining of historicism amounted to: it amounted to an assertion of the thought of crisis. Nineteenth-century historicism gave way to the twentieth-century crisis commitment. But there is a deep paradox here. Historicism has disappeared from the mainstream of contemporary thought, yet modernism and postmodernism, in both their narrowly aesthetic and their broadly intellectual senses, are centrally defined by adherence to a notion that itself makes sense only on the assumption that historicism is true. In short: the convincing power of the crisis notion depends on one's prior belief in the linear or directional character of history, yet the whole point of the crisis notion is to undermine any such belief. By and large, the notion of the linear character of history *has* been undermined. Historicism in Mandelbaum's sense—that is, an historicism that sees the linearity of history in developmental, progressivist terms—has been explicitly rejected by twentieth-century thinkers. Historicism in the broader sense—that is, historicism as *any* view that holds history to be linear—is almost never seriously articulated. Thus, crisis serves as a therapeutic antidote to another notion that no thinker worth taking seriously has adhered to for at least the last sixty years.

As a matter of historical fact, the notion of crisis to which our prophets of extremity adhere was the product of a brilliant intellectual move by Nietzsche. Historicism rejected the concept of absolute value. But it retained its own absolute—namely, the historical process itself, in terms of which all particular values were to be understood and judged. Nietzsche de-absolutized this absolute by using against it the same intellectual solvent that historicism had applied to all realities but one. Thus, Nietzsche saw history not as "an organic adaptation to new conditions" but as a (largely arbitrary) set of breaks, leaps, and compulsions: in a word, of crises (*GM*, 2nd Essay, §17). But all this depends on the existence of something to be broken, leapt over, and compelled. We can see why there is a close relation between taking Hegel seriously and taking Nietzsche seriously, for whether and to what extent Hegel was an idealist, he was undeniably an historicist. In fact, his relationship to the historicist tradition is paradigmatic.[48]

Gilles Deleuze observes in *Nietzsche and Philosophy* that "there is no possible compromise between Hegel and Nietzsche."[49] Yet, by the same

token, without Hegel (or similar advocates of continuity) there could have
been no Nietzsche. For the crisis notion is essentially *reactive* in character.[50] In postulating various breaks, leaps, mutations, and divine deaths, it
is reacting against an implied assumption of continuity over time. The
whole post-Nietzschean notion of belatedness is historicism's offspring.
Heidegger, for example, can suggest that we are "latecomers in a history
now racing toward its end" only insofar as he is still under the historicist
spell ("The Anaximander Fragment," *EGT,* p. 16). Paradoxically, then, in
attacking assumptions of development or continuity over time, the
thought of crisis destroys the very ground on which it rests. The more
successful its attack, the more completely it undermines its own reason
for existing.

This is one of the two crucially important points that Derrida makes in
his writing. In Derrida the thought of crisis finally undermines itself, for
Derrida turns his critical attentions to the whole notion of history as linear (what Foucault calls "the linear series of time" [*NC,* pp. xiii/xvii]).
This is pervasive in his various examinations of Husserl, whose teleological view of history he persistently exposes (see, e.g., "Genesis and Structure," *E&D,* pp. 232, 247–251/157, 165–168). In his deconstruction of
Foucault's *History of Madness,* this preoccupation likewise appears, for
Derrida makes a direct connection between Foucault's idea of a "crisis" or
"decision" constituting madness and the notion that makes this decision
possible—namely, "historicism" in our sense. As he puts it, "a doctrine
of *tradition* . . . seems to be the prerequisite implied by Foucault's enterprise." For in postulating a rising up of madness, Foucault tends to accept
as a given the unity of that against which it rises. In Derrida's words, "the
attempt to write the history of the decision, division, difference runs the
risk of construing the division as an event or a structure subsequent to the
unity of an original presence, thereby confirming metaphysics in its fundamental operation" (*E&D,* pp. 65/40–41). Derrida shrewdly notes the
implicit presence of Hegel in *History of Madness,* notwithstanding the
"absence of any precise reference" to this thinker. And he declares that
"the concept of history has always been a rational one. It is the meaning of
'history' . . . that should have been questioned first" (*E&D,* pp. 59/36).

It is precisely the notion of history as an ordered line of presents—
history with a capital *H*—that Derrida criticizes in *Of Grammatology.*
He tells us in his preface that he wants reading to free itself "from the
classical categories of history" (*GRAM,* pp. 7/lxxxix). In one of the most
interesting passages of the book, he declares that "the word *history* has
no doubt always been associated with a linear scheme of the unfolding of

presence, where the line relates the final presence to the originary presence according to the straight line or the circle" (*GRAM*, pp. 127/85; also
POS, pp. 77–78/56–57, and *DISS*, pp. 209/183–184). There is a certain
provinciality in this assertion, since history most assuredly has not always
been conceived in this way. But it has been so conceived in the prophecy of
extremity and in historicism. Thus, if we pay proper attention to the context to which this statement is applicable, we can see that Derrida is right.
And he is also right when he declares that "the enigmatic model of the *line*
is . . . the very thing that philosophy could not see when it had its eyes open
on the interior of its own history" (*GRAM*, pp. 128/86). Derrida seeks to
expose this dependence on the model of linearity. Thus, he sees through
the myth of the tradition that animates and makes possible the prophecy
of extremity. Seeing through the myth of the tradition, he undermines the
crisis view. The knell of historicism is also the knell of crisis.

To be sure, Derrida should not be seen as absolutely breaking from his
predecessors. When Nietzsche turns his attentions away from the horrors
of the existing order and contemplates instead the transfigured order that
will succeed it, he suggests an attitude in which History is not felt as
burdensome—the attitude of active nihilism. Similarly, when Foucault
turns aside from his rhetoric of permanent revolution, he sounds surprisingly like a conventional historian, for whom crisis does not figure. Even
The Order of Things, which is in some ways his richest, most impressive
work to date, can be read in a way that undermines the notion of crisis.
For one can see the *epistemes* not as succeeding each other in a linear
movement but rather as existing without any reference to each other
whatsoever. In this reading, an *episteme* simply is, in the way that a work
of art is. One follows its rules and plays its game, without thought to its
possible end, without reference to the possibility that its dominant categories might be erased "like a face drawn in sand at the edge of the sea"
(*MC*, pp. 398/387). Finally, the later Heidegger's notion of *Gelassenheit*
tends to cast into oblivion those notions of destiny, History, and crisis
upon which his project is constructed. In a sense, then, Derrida is merely
making explicit what is still inchoate and tentative in the thought of
Nietzsche, Heidegger, and Foucault. But in so doing, he deconstructs the
prophecy of extremity itself.

CHAPTER 8

The Deconstruction of Art

Derrida's deconstruction of art—that is, his deconstruction of a whole philosophy, of a whole ideology that has grown up around art—runs parallel to his deconstruction of tradition and crisis. Derrida is deeply engaged with questions of art and literature. Looking at his first-published collection of essays, *Writing and Difference,* we see that five of its eleven essays deal with what seem to be aesthetic or literary topics. The first essay, "Force and Signification," is a critique of the "structuralist" (and modernist) literary criticism of Jean Rousset; two essays deal with the work of Antonin Artaud; and two essays are appreciations of the poetry of Edmond Jabès. As for his 1972 collection, *Dissemination,* we have already seen how deeply involved it is with Mallarmé and other figures of similar orientation. Even in his other essay collection of that year, *Margins of Philosophy,* which as its title suggests is primarily concerned with philosophical texts, we find one essay on Paul Valéry. In *Glas* he deals extensively with the writings of Jean Genet, while in *Truth in Painting* (1978) he reflects on various recent and contemporary painters.

Of course, in one way or another, Nietzsche, Heidegger, and Foucault were also concerned with art and literature. Derrida's concern, however, is considerably more immediate and (especially in his recent works) more aesthetically engaged than that of his predecessors. Remember how Nietzsche was for the most part concerned with art in the "broad" rather than in the "narrow" sense. He showed little interest in the artists of art; his real interest was in the illusionistic creators of cultural mythologies— the makers of "metaphysics, religion, moralities, science." (It was in this guise that he conceived of Wagner. This was the worst of all possible perspectives on Wagner, and largely accounts for the depth of Nietzsche's disappointment with him, the bitterness of his sense of betrayal.)

As for Heidegger, in his later writings he commented on the work of such artists and poets as van Gogh, Rilke, and Hölderlin. Nothing equivalent is to be found in Nietzsche. But again, this concern is so closely tied up with Heidegger's reflections on larger, "onto-theological" matters that we are in little danger of mistaking what he says about, for example, Hölderlin, for a contribution to literary criticism. Indeed, Heidegger explicitly denies that he is doing literary criticism.[1]

With Foucault, to be sure, the matter stands a little differently, for he has written two books that we can plausibly view as works of literary or aesthetic criticism: his 1963 book on Raymond Roussel, and his commentary of 1973 on Magritte.[2] Yet, both these works seem out of place when one attempts to view them in the light of his corpus as a whole. It is no accident that I did not find occasion to mention them in the previous essay. This is not to say that I find them uninteresting: the commentary on Magritte is especially revealing for anyone concerned with Foucault's aestheticist background. But it is difficult to know how to discuss it in relation to such works as *The Order of Things, The Archaeology of Knowledge,* or *Discipline and Punish.*

Derrida presents us with no such problem. Indeed, the problem is quite the reverse, for the aesthetic strand in Derrida is so prominent that in considering his second deconstruction we might well be inclined to confine ourselves to a reflection on art and aesthetics alone. In short: Derrida as artist and as literary critic—a formula that is all the more tempting when we see that literary critics are so prominent among those who have engaged themselves with his work. What we seem to find in Derrida is a postmodernist polemic against modernism in art and criticism. Derrida's reading of Jean Genet in *Glas* can be seen as paradigmatic of this. Derrida's Genet, articulated in part against the Genet of Sartre (see *GLAS,* pp. 36–37), takes on a decidedly postmodern cast. In Sartre's interpretation, Genet is an existentialist, proudly asserting his own identity against a hostile world—the figure whom Sartre praises for inventing "the homosexual *subject*" and for attaining "that absolute consciousness which approves of itself and chooses itself."[3] (Note the modernist dualism here, the opposition between hard-won identity and threatening reality.) Derrida's Genet, in contrast, calls into question the very notion of identity, holding identity as nothing and the play of the text as everything. In *Literature and Evil,* Georges Bataille observed that "Genet, the writer, has neither the power to communicate with his readers nor the intention of doing so."

In Bataille's eyes, this invalidated Genet's work.[4] Derrida turns Bataille's accusation into a celebration. Thus, he emphasizes the intertwined motifs in Genet's work, the tendency of plot to become absorbed into all-inclusive metaphor. The whole of Derrida's critical work can similarly be seen as an attack on aesthetic modernism carried out from the standpoint of aesthetic postmodernism.

At the same time, however, the tendency of postmodernism is toward breaking down not only dualisms within art but also the fundamental dualism upon which the notion of an aesthetic realm rests, the distinction between the aesthetic and the nonaesthetic, between art and reality. This has been evident for some time in the art world itself—as documented in, for example, Harold Rosenberg's *The De-definition of Art*.[5] Derrida can be seen as providing the intellectual or philosophical complement to such aesthetic developments as Duchamp's urinal/fountain and Christo's monumental sculptures. It is in consequence a mistake to view Derrida as a figure whose significance is restricted to art and to the criticism of art.

Two different but equivalent misreadings are possible here. One misreading involves a rigid compartmentalization of Derrida's work. It is possible to see Derrida as producing three different types of texts. Certain of his works can be read as philosophical commentary or as literary criticism of a relatively conventional sort: these works are written "in the style of commentary," as he says at one point (*E&D*, pp. 114–115/84). To be sure, after his introduction to Husserl's "Origin of Geometry," none of these texts really *is* conventional, for they all seek to break out from the usual confines of theoretical or critical discourse. Still, in such works as *Speech and Phenomena*, with its patient unraveling of Husserl's assumptions regarding language, Derrida at least makes a show of conformity to the usual scholarly rules. Another, rather small group of texts constitute interventions on political and institutional questions mostly having to do with the French educational system. I am thinking here of Derrida's essay "Where Does a Teaching Body Begin and How Does It End?" and of his several contributions to the collection *Who's Afraid of Philosophy?*[6] Finally, there are other texts—and these seem to be gaining in weight and importance as Derrida pursues his career—that are unclassifiable in either scholarly or political terms, but appear instead to be peculiarly graphic works of art. *Glas* is the most imposing example of such a text.[7]

One is tempted, when faced by such a bewildering variety of writings as those that Derrida has produced, to consider each type in isolation. Thus, one would read his "scholarly" texts as if they were concerned only with resolving specific philosophical or textual problems, his "political" texts as if they were concerned only with intervening in favor of such-and-such a political position, and his "aesthetic" texts as if they were concerned only with generating a high intellectual pleasure in the reader. But this is to miss a decisive aspect of Derrida's project. In Derrida's eyes, there can be no such thing as a strictly scholarly, political, or aesthetic problem—a conclusion that follows from his own attempts to undermine the Kantian distinction between the theoretical, the practical, and the aesthetic.

Note that the distinction between Derrida's conventionally scholarly works, his political interventions, and his basically unclassifiable works of postmodern art corresponds to this Kantian distinction. We are thus not surprised to find Derrida arguing that his seemingly conventional commentaries are already engaged in political issues and already break the normal scholarly rules, that his political interventions are intimately connected with the apparently philosophical attack on "logocentrism" that dominates his commentaries, and that a work like *Glas,* for all its air of being a postmodern work of art, is both scholarly and political in character.[8] He is certainly right in these observations: it is only as a ladder to be kicked down that I pass on to the reader the distinction between these three sorts of texts. The distinction is useful in giving us a rough framework for coming to grips with the various parts of Derrida's corpus, but none of his works in fact fit comfortably into any one category. Some fit rather less comfortably than others. *Of Grammatology,* for example, is already a scholarly work of art, a sustained parody of conventional scholarly production even if not quite a self-parody like *Glas.* Similarly, it is difficult to classify the essays included in *Dissemination,* a collection that is far more excessive in content and appearance than the other essay collections, *Writing and Difference* and *Margins of Philosophy.*

The second and rather more sophisticated misreading involves not compartmentalization but aestheticization. It involves, that is, interpreting the whole of Derrida's corpus in aesthetic terms. Certainly, his work is powerfully aesthetic in both its sources and its range. What one can perceive only dimly in Foucault is glaringly obvious in Derrida. His writings would have been utterly inconceivable were it not for the kind of self-questioning in which many of the most influential twentieth-century artists and writers have engaged. It is in consequence tempting to see *Glas* as a French equivalent to *Finnegans Wake,* or "Sendings" as the latest incarnation of the epistolary novel. Yet, this doesn't quite work either. Thus, *Glas* belongs to no recognizable aesthetic genre or type. I am aware of no other work that proceeds as it does, as a bifold commentary on such an odd couple as Hegel and Genet. And "Sendings" has features that separate it from the genre of the epistolary novel. One could imagine reading it in tandem with John Barth's *Letters,* but there is much in Derrida's work that has no equivalent in Barth's. For if "Sendings" is an epistolary novel, it is also an attack on another odd couple, Socrates and Plato, about whom Derrida makes some frankly scurrilous observations, like a twentieth-century Rabelais. To attack Socrates and Plato is already to speak philosophy. And if "Sendings" can be read as an attack on philosophy's founding figures, it can equally well be read as an attack on its would-be destroyer, the all-constructing Heidegger. Specifically, Derrida seems to be concerned with undermining that offspring of historicism, Heidegger's *Geschick* ("destiny"). Note the affinity between *Geschick* and *schicken* ("to send"), and the relation of the English "destiny" to "destination," as in the destination of a letter. A philosophical subtext is at work in "Sendings"—and in everything Derrida has written. The presence of this subtext calls into question the category "art," just as the aesthetic subtext in his primarily "philosophical" writings calls into question the category "philosophy."

Some have suggested that Derrida's project aims at purging pathos from literature, through a demonstration that pathos, too, is "figurative, ironic or aesthetic."[9] I find no pathos in the coldly lucid deconstructive criticism of Paul de Man. But I do find a pathos—at least the remnants of a pathos—in Derrida. For Derrida's radical irony, immense in both its hostility and its ambivalence, is recognizably dependent on the historical existence of a tradition that lends it pathos. This tradition is intertwined with that of the logocentric, phonocentric West, to such an extent that the two now seem almost inseparable. Yet, it suffices to give Derrida a position, if not outside the "Western" tradition, at least on its margins, from which his irony can work.

This "other" tradition is Judaism, understood in a decidedly unethnic and unreligious sense. Derrida conceives of Judaism as an historical reality, but also as a symbol or token of marginality. The idea of crisis, which Derrida so strangely hangs onto even as he destroys its foundations, derives its poignancy in Derrida's writings from certain well-known events of our century. Though it is never present in any vulgar way (on the one occasion that he addresses it directly, he allows a poet to speak for him), it is nonetheless clear that Derrida writes in the shadow of the Holocaust. Derrida's appeal to Judaism as a marginal tradition, present within the interstices and along the edges of the "Western" tradition, gives to his writings a much greater sense of alienation from that tradition than one finds in Nietzsche and Heidegger. If his predecessors can appeal to the pre-Socratics and sophists, Derrida cannot—for these, too, are part of the tradition that he wishes to attack. Neither Nietzsche nor Heidegger is a thinker of marginality. Neither writer concerns himself with what is marginal to society, politics, or thought. Derrida's confrontation with Heidegger is especially sharp, for in Derrida's eyes the German philosopher embodies some of the most questionable aspects of the mainstream tradition. Closer to Derrida is Foucault, for whom homosexuality plays something of the same marginal role that Judaism does for Derrida.

In raising the question of Judaism, I am evoking a problem of vast historical dimensions, which I shall not be able to deal with adequately in the present essay. Let me emphasize, too, that Derrida does not address the "thematics of the Jew" (*GRAM*, p. —/317, note 1 [Spivak]) in primarily literal terms. Instead, he moves between "the too warm flesh of the literal event" and "the cold skin of the concept" (*E&D*, pp. 113/75). We thus risk skewing our understanding of his work by dwelling too explicitly on this theme. The "thematics of the Jew" most often appears in Derrida in sublimated or disguised form. Judaism is a hidden center and motivation for other issues that might at first glance seem to be entirely unrelated to it. Four issues, to which I link four names, seem particularly important here, and will govern my reflections in this chapter. First, there is the question of the "other," raised in its most obvious and compelling form by the unorthodox French phenomenologist Emmanuel Levinas. Second, there is the question of "writing," or of secondariness, which we can link to the poet Edmond Jabès. Third, there is the question of "interpretation," for which Freud can serve as a convenient cipher. And fourth, there is the question of "art," linked to Kant.

These four issues are closely interconnected; they also connect back to the Romantic and Kantian roots of aestheticism. Firstly, the question of the "other" involves a rejection of the Romantic quest for unity and self-identity. It is no accident that many of those literary critics most closely associated with Derrida began their careers as students of Romanticism, for the Romantic notion of an unmediated vision, often seen as involving a circuitous journey back to primal unity, tends to generate its own opposite, the ironic conviction that unity is impossible, that the division into "same" and "other" is a fatal necessity. To be sure, Derrida himself came out of phenomenology, not out of Romantic literary criticism: but phenomenology's search for "the thing itself" implicitly involved a theory of identity, the notion of an unfissured phenomenological self capable of attaining the immediacy of intuition that Husserl so much valued. Secondly, the question of writing assumes its great importance for Derrida because the perceived impossibility of immediate vision means that the mediate, fallen, divided form of writing is all that we have. Thirdly, there is the question of interpretation—the whole *process* of writing, which in view of the inaccessibility of any ultimate *interpretandum* becomes an end in itself. Finally, the question of art assumes *its* importance when we come to see the fallen character of writing and interpretation not as defects but as opportunities. Writing and interpretation come to be valued not because they can reveal to us the light of truth but because they are themselves truth. Thus, they have a "purposiveness without purpose" analogous to that which Kant found in aesthetic objects. Derrida's move beyond Kant is to argue that "purposiveness without purpose" pervades all we do. His move beyond Hegel and Heidegger is to substitute an explicit irony for their conviction that in one way or another art gives us access to the truth of Being.

Levinas and the pursuit of the "other"

I have already noted the degree to which Derrida's radical irony makes problematic the approach to his writings that I am attempting here. As Northrop Frye points out, the ironic attitude is one from which "all assertive elements, implied or expressed, are eliminated."[10] In a writer so manifestly ironic as Derrida, ideas tend to be reduced to oblivion: a difficult situation for the historian of ideas. In consequence, it is frequently illuminating to approach Derrida via other writers, not so self-withholding as he. This is why I have dwelt at some length on Blanchot, and it seems equally useful to consider Levinas, Jabès, Freud, and Kant, with all of whom Derrida comes into important contact.

Levinas is the focus of by far the longest essay in *Writing and Difference,* "Violence and Metaphysics: An Essay on the Thought of Emmanuel Levinas." As I have said before, I am not ultimately concerned in this study with ferreting out lines of influence. I am convinced of the relative unimportance of constructing a linear series, *A* influencing *B* influencing *C*: to this extent, I am committed to the structuralist and poststructuralist notion of the discontinuity of history. Much more interesting than influence are the strange affinities and telling differences between thinkers, whether or not they can be shown to have "borrowed" from one another. But having said this, I am still tempted to characterize Levinas's relation to Derrida in terms of influence.

Derrida does engage in a radical critique of Levinas. Moreover, his whole tone is very different from Levinas's: an ironic seriousness in the one writer, a direct earnestness, with religious overtones, in the other. Yet, a number of themes or motifs prominent in Derrida might almost be read as elaborations of points earlier made by Levinas. In consequence, it is hard to avoid seeing Levinas's work as an important intellectual resource for the younger philosopher. In rather the same way, we were led to see Blanchot as contributing to Derrida (interestingly enough, there are important ties between Levinas and Blanchot, as Derrida points out [E&D, pp. 152/103]).[11] Admittedly, Derrida also borrows from other French philosophers, and his discussion of Levinas is carried out against the background of the phenomenological tradition as a whole, with its massive indebtedness to Husserl and Heidegger. But there are elements in Levinas's thought that one does not find elsewhere, and these seem important for Derrida.

Who, then, is Emmanuel Levinas? From our perspective, it is perhaps best to regard him as a relentless critic of phenomenological orthodoxy— Derrida's true forerunner in this calling. Born in 1905, he studied under Husserl and Heidegger in Freiburg in 1928–29. His *Theory of Intuition in Husserl's Phenomenology*, published in 1930, was one of the first books on phenomenology to appear in France. In this work, Levinas calls into question Husserl's unswerving allegiance to the visual metaphors of theory and intuition. In short, he anticipates the attack that Derrida would later launch on the metaphoric of vision, on the "ocular metaphor" of understanding. Levinas does see Husserl's work as constituting a significant advance in philosophy. Levinas was never to abandon his commitment to what he conceived to be the Husserlian method, the method of an "intentional" analysis aimed at uncovering the "unsuspected horizons" of reality.[12] Nonetheless, it is quite clear even in this early book that Levinas disagrees with Husserl on a fundamental point.

We can trace this disagreement to the impact of Heidegger. As Levinas remarks in the introduction to *The Theory of Intuition*, "we shall not fear to take into account problems raised by other philosophers, by students of Husserl, and, in particular, by Martin Heidegger, whose influence on this book will often be felt."[13] Still rather tentative in his criticism, Levinas suggests that Husserl "may have been wrong in seeing the concrete world as a world of objects that are primarily perceived. Is our main attitude toward reality that of theoretical contemplation? Is not the world presented in its very being as a center of action, as a field of activity or of *care*—to speak the language of Martin Heidegger?"[14] In thus drawing attention to the implications of the whole "intuitional," that is, visual focus in Husserl, Levinas sketches out a point that would be central to Derrida's *Speech and Phenomena*. To be sure, there are other aspects of

Speech and Phenomena not present in *The Theory of Intuition*: notably the contrast between voice and writing and the attack on Husserl's belief in the possibility of a neutral language. But the crucially important anti-ocular motif certainly is present.

Levinas was not to become a Heideggerian, however, for his initial attraction to Heidegger ultimately turned to disenchantment. His first major attempt to articulate his own independent philosophical position, *Existence and Existents,* appeared in 1947. It is not incidental to mention that Levinas was in a prisoner-of-war camp in Germany during the war and partly wrote the book there. He now asserts that "if at the beginning our reflections are in large measure inspired by the philosophy of Martin Heidegger, . . . they are also governed by a profound need to leave the climate of that philosophy."[15] Levinas's subsequent philosophical writings can be interpreted as an attempt to "go beyond" Heidegger: they thus anticipate Derrida's efforts in that direction. Levinas's fundamental argument against Heidegger is that his distinction between Being and beings, and the alleged priority of the former to the latter, is a manifestation of the most vicious of all tyrannies, that of the "same" over the "other." In Levinas's view, Heidegger's thought had its origins in a primal peasant mentality, a mentality suspicious of all outsiders and determined, through a pre-technological power of possession, to make everything its own. As Levinas puts it in his most important book, *Totality and Infinity* (1961):

> Ontology as first philosophy is a philosophy of power. . . . Even though it opposes the technological passion issued forth from the forgetting of Being hidden by the existent [i.e., *étant*, "being"], Heideggerian ontology, which subordinates the relationship with the Other to the relation with Being in general, remains under obedience to the anonymous, and leads inevitably to another power, to imperialist domination, to tyranny. Tyranny is not the pure and simple extension of technology to reified men. Its origin lies back in the pagan "moods," in the enrootedness in the soil, in the adoration that enslaved men can devote to their masters.[16]

Indeed, argues Levinas, the tyranny of the same over the other characterizes the entire history of "Western philosophy." In Levinas's view, "Western philosophy has most often been an ontology: a reduction of the other to the same."[17] He concedes that Western philosophy has maintained a distinction between the "one" and the "other." But he holds that this distinction has acted as an exclusion of the other, since in his view it rests on the presumption that there is a single, discriminating consciousness that makes the distinction. It has compromised the "alterity" of the other, enclosing it within an other-denying totality. An alterity that can be thought—that can be apprehended by Reason—is not an alterity at all. As Derrida puts it, summarizing Levinas's position, "the infinitely-other cannot be bound by a concept, cannot be thought on the basis of a horizon; for a horizon is always a horizon of the same, the elementary unity within which eruptions and surprises are always welcomed by understanding and recognized" (*E&D*, pp. 141/95).

Evoking the maieutic, Levinas maintains that the central teaching of Socrates was "to receive nothing of the Other but what is in me, as though from all eternity I was in possession of what comes to me from the outside." In short, Socrates' central teaching was the "primacy of the same."[18] This teaching has subsequently been repeated by all the great figures in the history of philosophy. Of most immediate relevance for Levinas is its repetition by Husserl and by Heidegger. Speaking of Husserl, Levinas tells us that "phenomenological mediation follows another route, where the 'ontological imperialism' is yet more visible. It is the Being of the existent that is the *medium* of truth. . . . Since Husserl the whole of phenomenology is the promotion of the idea of *horizon,* which for it plays a role equivalent to that of the *concept* in classical idealism: the existent arises upon a ground that extends beyond it, as the individual arises from the concept."[19] And similarly with Heidegger: "To affirm the priority of *Being* over the *existent* is to already decide the essence of philosophy: it is to subordinate the relation with *someone,* who is a being, (the ethical relation) to a relation with the *Being of the existent,* which, impersonal, permits the apprehension, the domination of the existent (a relationship of knowing)."[20] Or again, still on Heidegger: "The relation with Being that is enacted as ontology consists in neutralizing the existent in order to comprehend or grasp it. It is hence not a relation with the other as such but the reduction of the other to the same."[21]

The breadth of Levinas's attack on Western philosophy suggests that he sees himself as standing outside the philosophical tradition. And indeed, though he employs a philosophical language and method, the dominant preoccupation of his thought arises within the perspective of a certain kind of Judaism. This comes out very clearly in his essay "Judaism and the Present Time," first published in 1960. The distinguishing feature of Western civilization, Levinas here asserts, has been the advance of reason: "Despite the violence and madness that play before our eyes, we are living at the hour of philosophy. Men are sustained in their activity by the certainty of being right [literally: of having reason], of finding themselves in accord with the calculable forces that actually move things, of moving in the *direction* [*sens*: also, of course, 'meaning'] of history." But this advance in rationality is dangerous, for if the worldwide industrial society that is coming into being promises to suppress the contradictions that tear humanity apart, it promises at the same time to suppress the inner soul of man. "Reason," Levinas maintains, "is rising like a fantastic sun that renders transparent the opacity of creatures. Men who have lost their shadows! Nothing is capable any longer either of absorbing or of reflecting this light, which abolishes the very core of beings."

This development, Levinas argues, is especially dangerous to Judaism. For Judaism is an essentially ethical religion, offering no transcendental rewards. In consequence, it is utterly dependent for its persistence on the preservation of precisely that interiority which the advance of reason aims to destroy.[22] To Western philosophy, Levinas opposes eschatology—a "messianic eschatology," as Derrida calls it (*E&D*, pp. 123/83). In Levinas's words, eschatology "institutes a relation with being *beyond the totality* or beyond history." Eschatology is "a relationship with *a surplus always exterior to the totality*," a relationship that he expresses with the concept of "infinity."[23] Although he finds the locus of eschatology in our relationship with the other person, his "eschatological vision" does not oppose totality in the name of any personal egotism. On the contrary, always present in Levinas is the infinite, God. In Derrida's formulation, "the other is the other only if his alterity is absolutely irreducible, that is, infinitely irreducible; and the infinitely Other can only be Infinity" (*E&D*, pp. 154/104). Indeed, as Derrida points out, Levinas *needs* God, lest the violence against the other that Levinas perceives in Western philosophy make its appearance, in an even more virulent form, in the conflict of irreconcilable alterities (*E&D*, pp. 158/107).

Greek/Jew/Jew/Greek

In his commentary on Levinas, Derrida concentrates on this conflict between an eschatological Judaism and a totalizing, Greek philosophy. In fact, the whole commentary centers on the Greek/Jew, Hebraism/Hellenism, Jerusalem/Athens opposition. In Derrida's interpretation, Levinas's thought "summons us to a dislocation of the Greek logos, to a dislocation of our identity, and perhaps of identity in general; it summons us to depart from the Greek site and perhaps from every site in general, and to move toward what is no longer a source or a site (too welcoming to the gods) but toward an *exhalation,* toward a prophetic speech already emitted not only nearer to the source than Plato or the pre-Socratics, but inside the Greek origin, close to the other of the Greek" (*E&D*, pp. 122/82). But whereas Levinas sees Western philosophy as unequivocally committed to the same as against the other, Derrida maintains that the Greek tradition, far from being a tradition of pure identity, is already permeated by the alterity that, on an explicit level, it seems to deny.

Such, at any rate, is what Derrida argues in the course of his critique of Levinas's critique of "those two Greeks," Husserl and Heidegger (*E&D*, pp. 123/83). Where Levinas attacks Husserl for treating the other as a mere *alter ego* and thus reducing its infinite alterity, Derrida maintains that "the themes of nonpresence" work over phenomenology unceasingly, however much it might appear to be a metaphysics of presence (*E&D*, pp. 178/121). This point is central for "Violence and Metaphysics"; and central, also, for *Speech and Phenomena*. Derrida seeks to show that Husserl himself concedes the impossibility of knowing, of "thematizing," the other. Where Levinas argues that phenomenology perpetrates a violence against the other, Derrida holds that it respects the other, indeed that it is "respect itself" (*E&D*, pp. 178/121). Similarly, where Levinas attacks Heidegger for asserting the primacy of Being over beings and thus subjecting alterity to totality and ethics to ontology, Derrida argues that Heidegger's "Being" is not "the lord of beings," a higher sort of being, an exercise of power, or an instance of "ethical violence" (*E&D*, pp. 200–203/136–138). Nor is Being in any way caught within a relation of knowledge, for, like the "other," it is "refractory to the category" (*E&D*, pp. 206/140). In consequence, Being "is not at all the accomplice of the totality, whether of the finite totality (the violent totality of which Levinas speaks) or of an infinite totality. The notion of totality is always related to the existent [i.e., to beings]. It is always a 'metaphysical' or 'theological' notion, and the notions of finite and infinite take on meaning in relation to it" (*E&D*, pp. 207/141).

Derrida thus deconstructs Levinas's account of Western philosophy. He also deconstructs Levinas's conception of a Hebraism that would stand in opposition to Western philosophy. In brief, he argues that if Western philosophy is "always already" fissured by alterity, then by the same token Hebraism is corrupted by the totalitarian violence that it seeks to evade. This is so, Derrida argues, because from the moment that the Hebraic alterity begins to speak, it finds itself within the realm of the logos, within the realm of rational discourse: eschatology, after all, is eschato-*logy*. Levinas argues that if intuitive contact with the other is violent, discourse with the other is nonviolent. For Derrida, in contrast, "all discourse essentially retains within it space and the Same," and this means that discourse is "originally violent" (*E&D*, pp. 171/116).

Hence, where Levinas presents himself as an apologist for a pristine Judaism, Derrida can do nothing more than point out the impossibility of such a Judaism, the inevitable complicity of Judaism with the totality it seeks to oppose. In Derrida's words, "if one calls this experience of the infinitely other Judaism, . . . one must reflect upon the necessity in which this experience finds itself, the injunction by which it is ordered to occur as logos, and to reawaken the Greek in the autistic syntax of its own dream" (*E&D*, pp. 226/152). To translate: occuring as logos, Judaism is necessarily Greek. Derrida introduces "Violence and Metaphysics" with an epigraph from Arnold's *Culture and Anarchy:* "Hebraism and Hellenism—between these two points of influence moves our world. At one time it feels more powerfully the attraction of one of them, at another time of the other; and it ought to be, though it never is, evenly and happily balanced between them." He closes, however, with a quotation from *Ulysses:* "Jewgreek is greekjew. Extremes meet."[24]

Derrida is thus engaged in an attempt to "erase" the distinction between Hebraism and Hellenism—as he erases *all* the distinctions that he entertains in his work. But the distinction still remains visible under its erasure (to use one of Derrida's favorite images), and its presence is essential to understanding Derrida's project. To be sure, while Levinas speaks (or claims to speak) eschatologically—that is, outside the Hellenic tradition—the same cannot be said of Derrida. But this betokens a concealment rather than an absence—a concealment carried out for strategic reasons. Derrida refers in "Violence and Metaphysics" to the necessity of "lodging oneself within traditional conceptuality in order to destroy it" (*E&D*, pp. 165/111). In another passage, he declares that "Levinas exhorts us to a second parricide. The Greek father who still holds us under his sway must be killed; and this is what a Greek—Plato—could never resolve to do, deferring the act into a hallucinatory murder. . . . But will a non-Greek ever succeed in doing what a Greek in this case could not do, except by disguising himself as a Greek, by *speaking* Greek, by feigning to speak Greek in order to get near the king?" (*E&D*, pp. 132–133/89).

This is one of the most revealing statements in the whole Derrida corpus. Admittedly, it is with some trepidation that I seek to attribute a meaning to a body of writing held by its author to be meaningless. But remember that the author in question also denies that authors ought to have any special privilege in the interpretation of texts. Moreover, other

readers, too, have felt the Hebraic element to be crucial to Derrida's project. In *Saving the Text,* Geoffrey Hartman characterizes Derrida as "Hebrew rather than Hellene: aniconic yet intensely graphic."[25] Another recent critic, Harold Bloom, suggests in his *Map of Misreading* that Derrida
substitutes the Hebrew *davhar,* with its connection to the act and marks
of writing, for the ethereal Greek *logos.*[26] Explicit, illuminating, and ad-
mirably concise on the Hebraic element in Derrida is the critic G. Douglas
Atkins, who sees Derrida and his allies as engaged in a systematic project
of dehellenization, an attack on the values of clarity, transparency, and
intellectual mastery that are so deeply imbedded within Western consciousness. As Atkins points out, Derrida suggests for many of his readers
(among these the most sophisticated) "a way beyond modern subjectivism, nihilism, and belief in the autonomous consciousness."[27]

Of course, we may agree or disagree with Derrida's "way"; we may even
feel that his problem is not our problem, that we do not need a way beyond
positions to which we have never adhered. But whatever the case, it is
grossly unfair to accuse Derrida of giving birth to monsters when these
monsters were manifestly present long before he appeared on the scene,
and when his aim is in fact to deal with them in some coherent manner, to
slay them or at least to hold them at bay. In the preface to his *Contribution
to the Critique of Political Economy* (1859), Marx, showing himself to be a
true son of Hegel, avers that "mankind always sets itself only such problems as it can solve." What problems, one wonders, did mankind set itself in
the Holocaust—in the various Holocausts—of this century? In the light of
such events, so difficult to reconcile with what Western reason thinks about
itself, Derrida's project acquires a kind of justification. I am not making the
facile observation that Western reason was powerless to prevent Auschwitz.
Though ostensibly broached as a *mea culpa,* this observation flatters the
egos of humanists, for it suggests that humanists had the power to avert the
catastrophe but unfortunately failed to exercise it in this instance. Even
worse, the playing off of Auschwitz against Western reason has the perverse
effect of elevating thugs and bureaucrats to the status of Overmen. Even less
am I making the move to the East that often follows this. I am merely pointing out that in light of what has happened, there is a certain fittingness in
what Derrida does, a truth in the risks he takes.

Moreover, though he follows in the wake of Nietzsche and Heidegger,
he is infinitely more self-critical than either—having obviously benefited
from the intervening historical experience. He is likewise more self-
critical than Foucault, who, however impressive he may be as an un-
earther of forgotten historical realities, seems philosophically to be the

least impressive, the least original, of the four. I am well aware that any praise of Derrida is bound to seem folly to the Greeks. But we are almost certainly more Greek than we ought to be. Derrida's enterprise is perhaps best seen as a clearing-out operation, intended to free a space for the active power of creation in a world that in an illusory way has grown old. Part of Derrida's merit (see Chapter 7) is to show that the notion of history growing old *is* an illusion: that history is not History, not a burden lying upon our shoulders (as Nietzsche, still in this respect too Greek, thought). Recall that Greek thought had no room for *ex nihilo* creation, but instead insisted that "nothing can arise from what does not exist." From the perspective of Greek (and Roman) thinkers, the idea of creation *ex nihilo* was totally absurd. This was an idea that arose within the Hebraic (and Christian) world of thought—possibly a product of the doctrine of bodily resurrection, adhered to by some Jews and by all Christians, except for a few heretics.[28] Whereas we know of no Greek or Roman thinker who asserted the notion of creation *ex nihilo,* from the thirteenth century onward no Jewish thinker so much as acknowledged that any other view might be legitimate.

But if Derrida's contrast between Hebraism and Hellenism is in some ways illuminating, we must also remember its limitations. Note, in particular, the ambiguous status of Christianity. As that disabused Christian, Matthew Arnold, well understood, Christianity has both Hebraic and Hellenic aspects. This tends to be concealed in Derrida's formulation of the Hellenic/Hebraic contrast. Derrida makes much in *Glas* of the opposition that Hegel postulates between Judaism and Christianity (see *GLAS,* pp. 41–107). He pays special attention to an early, posthumously published essay of Hegel's, "The Spirit of Christianity and Its Fate" (written in 1798–99), in which Hegel interprets Christianity as a dialectical transcendence of Judaism.[29]

Judaism is the villain of the piece, its rigid, ungainly moralism standing in contrast to the beauty that animates Greek religion and the love animating Christianity. In Derrida's reading of Hegel, the Jews are excluded from the dialectic. They are the slaves of an invisible God rather than the loving followers of an incarnate one, and between them and their sovereign no legal or rational mediation is possible (*GLAS,* p. 64). Derrida's characterization of Hegel's characterization of the Jew is unequivocal: "The Jew falls back again. He signifies that which does not let itself be raised up . . . to the level of the *Begriff.* He retains, draws down the *Aufhebung* toward the earth" (*GLAS,* p. 66).

If Judaism rejects the dialectic, Christianity, by way of contrast, is the

Vorstellung, the representation or foreplacing, of the absolute knowledge that comes to fruition in philosophy. Hegel considers Christianity to be "a naturally speculative religion." Thus, "the Hegelian dialectic, the mother of criticism, is first of all a daughter: of Christianity, in any case of Christian theology" (*GLAS,* pp. 40, 227). As Derrida points out, Hegel's reading of Christianity is skewed in a Greek, that is, philosophical direction; it is telling, for example, that Hegel is mainly interested in John, the most Greek of the four Gospels (*GLAS,* p. 88).

There is an irony here, however, for Derrida's reading of Western consciousness on the model of the opposition between Greek and Jew is equally skewed. As a therapeutic thinker, Derrida reacts to (and against) Hegel; and since Hegel tends to move Christianity in a Greek direction, this opens the way for a contrast between Hellenism and Hebraism untroubled by Christianity's ambiguous status. But one can equally well postulate a reading of Western consciousness on the model of the opposition between Greek and Judaeo-Christian. Such a reading brings out of the texts with which we (and Derrida) are concerned certain tensions that Derrida's reading tends to obscure.

Take Heidegger, for example. The German philosopher shows little or no attraction to Hebraism in Derrida's sense. In contrast, he manifests a persistent attraction to Greece. Thus, Levinas and others have criticized him for ignoring the Hebraic roots of Western culture in favor of the Greek roots. But we must not forget the other element in the equation, Christianity. If Heidegger's thought is Greek, it is also importantly marked by Christian motifs. Löwith informs us that in the early 1920s Heidegger saw himself as a "Christian theologian."[30] Heidegger's Christianity, moreover, was anything but Greek. Despite his Catholic upbringing, he was attracted to the writings of the young Luther, with his rigorous faith, his scorn for the "natural reason" of the scholastics, and his condemnation of the writings of the "pagan master Aristotle."[31] Hegel attempted to syncretize the Hebraic and the Hellenic; in the course of doing so, he hellenized Christianity. Heidegger's Christianity, on the other hand, is heavily dependent on a theological tradition that sought to bring it back to its primitive, that is, Hebraic roots.[32]

Insofar as he is a Greek, Heidegger is committed to the dominance, to the persistence, to the continuing presence of Being: his Being is the everpresent Greek Being, not the created Judaic and Christian Being. In short, the world is there; it exists. We as Dasein are engaged in an attempt to come to grips with thereness, with Being standing other and apart from us. As a Greek, then, Heidegger adheres to the fundamentally Hellenic view that the work of art is a revelation of Being, of a truth that is already present. Art allows things to manifest the truth that is within them. But there is another side to Heidegger: the side that wants to see Being and truth as *created*. This creation is carried out not by man but by the work of art: "to be a work means to set up a world": *Werksein heisst: eine Welt aufstellen* (*PLT*, p. 44). In the Judaic and Christian view, *Gottsein heisst: eine Welt aufstellen*. Coming out of the Greek tradition, Heidegger divinizes a persistent Being; coming out of the Judaic and Christian traditions, he divinizes the creative work of art.

Think also of the pathos and the passion of Heidegger's nostalgia for the Greek origin. As a Greek, Heidegger dreams a return to the pre-Socratic Greeks. As a Christian, of the seed of Abraham, he knows return to be impossible. Ulysses, paradigm of the Greeks and figure of the Hegelian circle of knowledge, returns to Ithaca; Abraham, in contrast, leaves his country forever for an unknown land, forbidding his son's return to the point of departure (*E&D*, pp. 228n/320, note 92). Thus, Heidegger displays a monumental, though deeply hidden tension between the Hellenic and the Hebraic. This tension is perhaps one of the most important reasons for the overwhelming fascination of his thought.[33]

Nor is it only in Heidegger that this tension between Greek and Jew(Christian) shows itself, for the span of the *Spannung* stretches also to Nietzsche. Strange, perhaps, to say this of a thinker so explicitly pro-Greek and anti-Christian. But think of the parallels between the Zarathustrian myth and the Christian myth that I noted toward the end of Chapter 2. Consider the title of *Ecce Homo*. Think of Nietzsche's statement that eventually university chairs will be set aside for interpreting *Zarathustra* (*EH*, "Why I Write Such Good Books," §1). Think of *The Anti-Christ*, where Nietzsche makes clear the resemblance between the mythmaking projects of Jesus and Zarathustra (*AC*, §32). And think, above all, of Nietzsche's radically "creationist," ontogenetic view of art and language—as in his assertion that "it is enough to create new names and estimations and probabilities in order to create in the long run new 'things'" (*GS*, §58).

What is this but the creating word of the Judaeo-Christian God, brought down to earth? Apollo and Dionysus, those two Greeks, are ultimately insufficient to embrace the perspective that Nietzsche invents for us. On the contrary, this pastor's son tries to save Christianity even as he destroys it, imputing to the Overman those qualities that he is no longer willing to see embodied in the Godhead. He thus remains a secret Christian: like Heidegger, a post-Christian rather than an anti-Christian. It is one of Derrida's great merits that he helps us to see this, just as he helps us to see that the Nietzschean thought of crisis is bound up in the very historicism that it seeks to overcome. Certain critics make much of the "blinded insight" to be found in literary texts.[34] This phenomenon seems to be especially evident in a particular kind of literary text: that articulated under the sign of crisis. Certainly, the blindness and simultaneous insight of Nietzsche are strikingly evident.

Jabès and writing

If God is dead, then we all live in secondariness: such is the position that Nietzsche suggests and that Derrida is most explicit in working out. The name of this secondariness, as we have seen, is writing. Derrida finds a model for such a writing within Judaism—and specifically within Kabbalism. "Kabbalah" means something handed down by tradition, but Derrida does not identify traditionality with orthodoxy (E&D, pp. 112/74). On the contrary, it is precisely the unorthodox character of the Kabbalah that he exploits. The Kabbalists—especially the later, Lurianic Kabbalists—were rebels against orthodox scholasticism. To the learned labor of the Talmudic scholars, they opposed the exegetical stratagem of gematria, in which a word or group of words is explained "according to the numerical value of the letters," or in which other letters are substituted "in accordance with a set system."[35] Through such manipulation, they were able to make a given text mean anything at all. Thus (though they would not have admitted this), the priority of Text over interpretation was nullified; text was reduced to pretext. In his own "method" of dealing with texts, Derrida stands as a successor to the Kabbalah, with one crucially important difference: for where the Kabbalists sought, through the manipulation of words and letters, to find a path back through the ten Sefirot (or emanations) to God, Derrida takes the manipulation of words and letters as something close to an end in itself. In short, for Derrida there is nothing beyond the letter, no primal voice speaking a long-concealed truth: polysemy gives way to dissemination (see, e.g., DISS, pp. 382–383/ 344–345).

In his Kabbalah and Criticism, Harold Bloom honors the Kabbalists for their interpretive audacity and extravagance, and insists on Kabbalism's affinities with recent French literary criticism.[36] There are, it seems, good historical grounds for these affinities. A line in Gravity's Rainbow conveys something of the spirit of this connection: "yes and now what if we—all right, say we are supposed to be the Kabbalists out here, say that's our real

Destiny, to be the scholar-magicians of the Zone, with somewhere in it a Text, to be picked to pieces, annotated, explicated, and masturbated till it's all squeezed limp of its last drop."[37] The Kabbalists—especially those coming after the expulsion of the Jews from Spain—were writing at a time of crisis for European Judaism; their interpretive extravagance can be seen as a refuge and source of hope for people who had very little else to hope for. Postmodernism, too, is articulated within the context of difficult times. Thus, *Gravity's Rainbow* is a monumental reflection on "the Zone," by which Pynchon means American and world history after World War II. One is reminded also of Nietzsche's confrontation with nihilism, Heidegger's confrontation with modern technology, and Foucault's confrontation with humanism.[38] For Derrida it is the Holocaust, both in its immediate and in an extended, metaphorical sense, that is the most striking manifestation of the horror that he sees lurking within modern history.

As I noted above, Derrida holds back from speaking directly of the Holocaust. In this he accords with those modern critics who have seen it as an event so terrible that it exhausts the powers of language.[39] And yet, it *is* present in his work. One notes his discussion of holocaustic gifts and sacrifices in *Glas* (*GLAS*, pp. 267–272). One notes his exploration in *Truth in Painting* of the ideological resonances of Heideggerian nostalgia as displayed in Heidegger's commentary on van Gogh (*VenP*, esp. pp. 355, 377, 420). One notes, too, the glimpses of the life of a Jewish schoolboy living in Algiers during World War II that we are given in "Sendings" (*CARTE*, esp. p. 97/—). But perhaps the most revealing of his texts in this regard are two brief essays of the 1960s, "Edmond Jabès and the Question of the Book" (1964) and "Ellipse" (1967). Both essays deal with the poetry of Edmond Jabès (born 1912 in Cairo). Jabès's most striking work is his multivolume prose poem *The Book of Questions*, published between 1963 and 1973. In his first three volumes (*The Book of Questions*; *The Book of Yukel*; and *The Return of the Book*), Jabès recounts the story of two victims of the Holocaust, Yukel and Sarah. In the last four volumes (*Jaël*; *Elya*; *Aely*; and *El, or The Last Book*), he turns aside from this pair, but the consciousness of what happened to them still haunts the poem.

What particularly attracts Derrida is the immense significance that Jabès accords to the act and fact of writing. Indeed, Jabès identifies writing with Judaism. As Derrida puts it in "Edmond Jabès and the Question of the Book," Jabès is concerned with "a certain Judaism, as a birth and passion of writing" (*E&D*, pp. 99/64). In the universe of Jabès's poem, "the Jew" is defined by his homelessness, by his utter lack of a *patrie*. Lacking a homeland, he makes a homeland of his own through writing, for it is only in the book, and in the written law that the book contains, that Israel can be found: "Israel . . . is the book which, without seeing it, we write from country to country."[40] Time and again in *The Book of Questions,* the theme of writing recurs: "You are the one who writes and the one who is written," Jabès tells us in the epigraph to his first volume; "Man is a written bond and place"; "the house is in the book"; "you will follow the book, whose every page is an abyss where the wing shines with the name"; "the Jewish world is based on written law, on a logic of words one cannot deny. . . . The Jew's fatherland is a sacred text amid the commentaries that it has given rise to"; "I talked to you about the difficulty of being Jewish, which is the same as the difficulty of writing. For Judaism and writing are but the same waiting, the same hope, the same wearing out."[41]

It is true that Derrida has written relatively little about Jabès—in contrast to the outpouring of words that we find in his commentaries on other writers. But despite their brevity, Derrida's two essays on Jabès are highly revealing. They are revealing because in one respect they differ from all the other commentaries that Derrida has written. In brief, they do not "deconstruct." Derrida's usual tactic as a commentator is to point out the supposed contradictions within the texts upon which he comments, contradictions which he then associates with the fissured structure of Western philosophy. Such, for example, is the procedure he adopts in his commentary on Levinas. But the two essays on Jabès are an exception, for they are cast exclusively in the mode of appreciation. Indeed, Derrida suggests that "the organized power of the song keeps itself beyond the reach of commentary, in *The Book of Questions.*" His own commentary, he says, is a "pitiful graffiti" added to "an immense poem." He likewise suggests that the power of Jabès's song is "already betrayed by quotation" and that the most one can do in approaching it is "to question oneself as to its origin" (*E&D,* pp. 110–111/73–74 [translation altered]).

All of this suggests that we also stand close to the origin of Derrida's text. According to Derrida, Jabès's poem is born of "an extraordinary confluence . . . in which is recalled, conjoined, and condensed the suffering, the millennial reflection of a people." There is a "pain" whose "past and continuity coincide with those of writing"; a "destiny that summons the Jew, placing him between the voice and the cipher," causing him to weep for his lost voice "with tears as black as the trace of ink" (*E&D,* pp. 110/73). One suspects that the same confluence, the same destiny, is decisive for Derrida. At any rate, whatever Derrida's intentions in constructing his own immense corpus, I find it in some ways satisfying to see it as if it, too, arises from this experience of extremity. The risks that Derrida takes as a writer seem at least partly comprehensible when viewed from this perspective. "A poem always runs the risk of being meaningless, and would be nothing without this risk" (*E&D*, pp. 111/74). So observes Derrida of Jabès, but the same observation could be made of Derrida as well. The shock of separation, the unbridgeable distance between origin and end—these join Jabès, Derrida, and Judaism. "Within original aphasia, when the voice of the god or the poet is missing, one must be satisfied with the vicars of speech that are the cry and writing," writes Derrida (*E&D*, pp. 110/73). It is no accident that he places "the Nazi repetition" alongside "the poetic revolution of our century" (*E&D*, pp. 110/73 [translation altered]).[42]

Viewed in a longer historical perspective, the labyrinthine text that is Derrida's can be seen as having its precursor in the labyrinthine wanderings of the Jew. Derrida writes in "Ellipse" that "the labyrinth . . . is an abyss; we plunge into the horizontality of a pure surface, which itself represents itself from detour to detour" (*E&D*, pp. 105/69). In short, there is nothing outside the labyrinth, nothing above or below it. The horizontality of the labyrinth parallels the horizontality of so much of postmodern art—including the arts of Foucault and Derrida. And this art, which does not return to a beginning and which has neither subject nor object, goes by the name of writing. The encyclopedic, that is, circular Book gives way to the post-Nietzschean figure of the ellipse—the ellipse of writing that lacks the center of a meaning. As Derrida puts it at the beginning of "Ellipse": "The question of writing could be opened only if the book was closed. The joyous wandering of the *graphein* then became wandering without return" (*E&D*, pp. 429/294). Insofar as it is possible in such a universe to speak of "identification," Derrida identifies himself with the "Judaic anxiety" that he finds in Jabès. "Judaism" is in this instance an unhappy consciousness that refuses to see itself as merely a moment within the Hegelian dialectic (*E&D*, pp. 104,114/68–69, 76). Derrida ends each of these essays with a quotation from an imaginary rabbi: Reb Rida closes off "Edmond Jabès and the Question of the Book"; Reb Derissa closes off "Ellipse." In short, he signs himself, anagrammatically, Rabbi Derrida.

Two figures, then, are important for Derrida's reflections: the poet and the rabbi. And each has his own way of looking at the world, his own mode of interpretation. In Derrida's words:

> The necessity of commentary, like poetic necessity, is the very form of exiled speech. In the beginning is hermeneutics. But the *shared* necessity of exegesis, the interpretive imperative, is interpreted differently by the rabbi and the poet. The difference between the horizon of the original text and exegetic writing makes the difference between the rabbi and the poet irreducible. . . . The original opening of interpretation essentially signifies that there will always be rabbis and poets. And two interpretations of interpretation. (*E&D*, pp. 102–103/67.)

"Rabbinical" interpretation is the sort practiced by Talmudic scholars, who keep a clear separation between Scripture and Midrash, granting an unequivocal priority to the former and regarding the latter as a secondary working out and expansion of the Sacred Text. "Poetic" interpretation, the sort practiced by Jabès, is a very different enterprise. Here the distinction between "original text" and "exegetical writing" is blurred if not eliminated, with interpretation itself serving as an "original text." Jabès underscores this point with his imaginary rabbis, whose sayings pepper the first three volumes of *The Book of Questions*. Thus, the text to be interpreted becomes, in this instance, the product of its own supposed exegesis. Interpretation becomes "literature," in the sense intended by, for example, Mallarmé and Frye. It becomes an end in itself, no longer seeking justification in its attempt to reveal the meaning hidden in an "original text"—which is why a poem "always runs the risk of being meaningless, and would be nothing without this risk."

Freud, modernism, postmodernism

Derrida's distinction between two interpretations of interpretation readily connects with two interpretations of Freud. I justify my appeal to Freud firstly on grounds of his considerable presence in Derrida's text. Noteworthy in this regard are his essay "Freud and the Scene of Writing," first published in 1966 and reprinted in *Writing and Difference* in the following year; "The Purveyor of Truth," first published in 1975 and reprinted in *Postcard;* "Fors," which serves as the preface to a study of Freud's "Wolf-Man" by the French poet-psychoanalyst Nicolas Abraham and his collaborator Maria Torok, published in 1976;[43] and a long essay "To speculate—on 'Freud,'" appearing in *Postcard*. I also justify my appeal to Freud on grounds of his massive presence in recent and contemporary Western thought. Clearly, he is present in more ways and has penetrated more milieus than have Nietzsche, Heidegger, Foucault, Derrida.

Freud always saw himself as (among other things) a careful man of science, and hence he might seem very distant from the antiscientism of Nietzsche and his successors. Yet, there are important affinities between Freud and the prophets of extremity. Note, for example, the way in which Freud calls into question the notion of a "natural" morality, as Nietzsche did before him. Indeed, one commentator, Lorin Anderson, argues convincingly that Freud was a secret disciple of Nietzsche—one who furtively translated Nietzsche's poetic language back into the scientific language from which Nietzsche had been trying to escape.[44] Note, too, how in one way or another all these thinkers are concerned with subjectivity and its problems. This is a particularly important theme for Nietzsche, Freud, and Heidegger, all of whom turn their gaze toward a self, psyche, or Dasein that undermines the Cartesian cogito (by the time Foucault and Derrida began to write, the point was too obvious to need much elaboration).[45] Note, finally, the character of Freud's cultural impact. Freud portrayed himself as a scientist, but he is better seen as one of the prime mythopoeic thinkers of our age. In their useful study of the scientific "credibility" of Freud's work, Fisher and Greenberg point out that the question of the scientific validity of Freud's findings was long overshadowed by their "spectacular mind-expanding nature." As they put it, "it was as if a new psychological world had been discovered; people were fascinated with the novelty of its sights, rather than their reality."[46] When we grasp that Freud was a mythmaker, putting forward not simply a psychology but a new and comprehensive vision of culture, we are better able to see his affinity with Nietzsche and his successors.

This is not to say, however, that Freud can be regarded as a postmodernist. Both Nietzsche and Freud put forward myths of culture, but the myths in question are very different. The Nietzschean myth, with its unrestrained creative egoism, we have already examined. In contrast, the Freudian myth inculcates a disabused attitude toward life, a prudent restraint of wish and passion. It presents itself as a strategy for coming to terms with the contradictions in our lives and with the persistent uncertainty of fulfillment. In its own way, it is a recipe for living—a recipe accepted and indeed championed by many sophisticated intellectuals in our century. "I have not the courage to rise up before my fellow-men as a prophet, and I bow to their reproach that I can offer them no consolation," says Freud at the end of *Civilization and Its Discontents*.[47] Offering us no respite from the pains of existence, he counsels us merely to bear with them. There is a fundamental ambivalence here. Radical commitment and abject surrender are alike rejected in favor of an attitude of tense uncertainty. Modernist Freudian intellectuals—and most Freudian intellectuals *are* modernists—see this attitude as an exemplary response to the strains of contemporary life. By way of contrast, postmodern intellectuals (who for the most part lack the fidelity that would permit us to call them Freudians) oppose the notion that Freud ought to be read as a guide to the modern perplexed. They are attracted to his writings not because they see a recipe for living presented therein, but because they see a virtuoso pursuit of interpretation. To borrow Barthes's phrase, they see Freud as giving us, in purer form than almost any other writer, the "pleasure of the text."[48] A Freudian intellectual like Richard Wollheim can maintain that undergoing psychoanalysis is a "necessary qualification" for writing about Freud or about psychoanalysis because he takes Freud seriously as a guide to life.[49] Derrida has no such conviction.

Let us look again at the distinction between "rabbinical" and "poetic" interpretation. This is really a distinction between interpretation as an attempt to find rest in "the thing itself" (however tenuous that thing may be) and interpretation as a self-justifying aesthetic play. This distinction finds its parallel in the two different modes of interpreting Freud that I have just adumbrated—the modernist and the postmodernist. As Alan Wilde points out, modernism and postmodernism are united by a common assumption of crisis. They differ, however, in their response to this presumed crisis. Modernism counterposes to crisis an "anironic vision of oneness or fusion." Yet, contrary to what some critics have said, it does not have any great confidence in this anironic moment; it sees art "as, at best, an ambiguous breakwater against the turbid flow of life." In short, it adopts an ironic attitude toward the possibilities of order suggested by the anironic moment. Wilde dubs this form of irony, which stands above both fragmentation and order and holds both equally in view, "absolute" irony. In contrast, postmodernism, as I have already noted, articulates no anironic moment, for it is convinced of the inability of art and literature to provide even the most tenuous vision of an ordered universe. Here we see what Wilde calls a "suspensive" irony, in which "an indecision about the meanings or relations of things is matched by a willingness to live with uncertainty, to tolerate and, in some cases, to welcome a world seen as random and multiple, even, at times, absurd."[50]

Wilde confines himself to modernism and postmodernism in their strictly literary and aesthetic senses, and it is in fact the case that this is the way in which these terms are usually employed. But as I have pointed out, they can legitimately be extended far beyond the realm of art. An astonishingly broad range of twentieth-century thought is preoccupied by crisis, break, rupture, discontinuity, separation. True, these themes have been presented most vividly by artists and imaginative writers, but they are hardly less evident elsewhere. In a broad sense, then, much of twentieth-century thought is modernist or postmodernist in persuasion, since it accepts the fundamental modernist and postmodernist assumption of crisis. Not surprisingly, this applies to the Freudian strand in recent and contemporary thought, just as it does to many other strands. Remembering modernism's oscillation between the crisis moment and the anironic moment, we can see why the majority of Freudian intellectuals fit under this rubric. The Freudian "analytic attitude" seeks to give us the detachment that we allegedly need if we are to survive in a modern, crisis-ridden civilization. The "analytic attitude" corresponds to Wilde's absolute irony: here one looks down with cold lucidity on the possibilities both of order and of disorder in life. Those other commentators, most of them coming out of the context of French poststructuralist thought, who read Freud as an exemplary interpreter and who do not take seriously his supposed value for living, are articulating a postmodern interpretation of Freud.

The modernist Freud will be most familiar from the works of Philip Rieff, especially his *Freud: The Mind of the Moralist,* first published in 1959.[51] This is a brilliant, deeply stimulating book, to which one returns again and again. Rieff sees Freud as *the* moralist of the modern age. In Rieff's view, Freud articulates a morality for a new character type that is coming to dominance, the type of "psychological man." Psychological man, says Rieff, is "a child not of nature but of technology." He lives "by the ideal of insight—practical, experimental insight leading to the mastery of his own personality." Rejecting the prophetic egoism of Western politics and of Protestant Christianity, which "laid down the lines along which the world was to be transformed," he is "intent upon the conquest of his inner life." Turning away from the Occidental ideal of saving others, he embraces "the Oriental ideal of salvation through self-contemplative manipulation." Viewing the reason of the political man and the conscience of the religious man as inadequate guides to the complexities of life, he lives beyond both; while at the same time, "aware at last that he is chronically ill," he finds himself unable to accept the optimism that characterizes economic man. Yet, he does not engage in "the ancient quest . . . for a healing doctrine," for he is also aware that every cure will only expose him to a new illness, that every salvation is only provisional.[52] Rieff portrays Freud as the great theorist and exponent of this new character ideal: in Rieff's words, "Freud speaks for the modern individual, elaborating his sense of separateness from the world and from even the most beloved objects in it."[53]

Rieff's "psychological man" could equally well be designated "modernist man," for he embodies in his life and personality that balance of crisis and restraint that is the central theme of modernist art and literature. The assumption of crisis is fundamental not only to Rieff's portrayal of psychological man but also to his whole account of Freud and his significance. This assumption is implicit in *Freud: The Mind of the Moralist*, but entirely explicit in *The Triumph of the Therapeutic*, his subsequent and far more adventurous book on Freud. In this later work, Rieff argues at length that psychological man is the one plausible character type for a privatized, bureaucratized, and de-committed world. He suggests, too, that in his refusal to seek any kind of ultimate salvation, psychological man represents a "sharp and probably irreparable break in the continuity of Western culture."[54] As for Freud himself, he "has systematized our unbelief; his is the most inspiring anti-creed yet offered to a post-religious culture."[55] What could be more "modern" in spirit than this evocation of a crisis of belief? What could be closer to the problematic of crisis that we find in Nietzsche, Heidegger, and Foucault, among many others? Like so many writers, Rieff accepts unquestioningly the notion of a contemporary crisis of thought and commitment.

And yet, Rieff's position is very different from the postmodernism of the thinkers whom we have been considering in this study, for unlike them he responds in a dualistic manner to the presumed crisis. In short, he is not simply "modern" (that is, committed to crisis) but "modernist"—and thus not "postmodern." In Rieff's perspective, antinomian implications (i.e., crisis) are rigorously countered (i.e., the anironic moment) but not denied, so that we are left with the anxiety of analysis—a controlled anxiety, one that enables us to go on living a life that would otherwise be unbearable. Note, in *Freud: The Mind of the Moralist*, Rieff's account of the "mixture of detachment and forbearance" that he sees in Freud: "To detach the individual from the most powerful lures in life, while teaching him how to pursue others less powerful and less damaging to the pursuer—these aims appear high enough in an age rightly suspicious of salvations. Freud had the tired wisdom of a universal healer for whom no disease can be wholly cured."[56] Note how Rieff sees the successful patient as having "learned to withdraw from the painful tension of assent and dissent in his relation to society by relating himself more affirmatively to his depths."[57] Note how Rieff describes the meeting between patient and analyst as "an oasis in the desert of reticence in which the patient lives."[58]

In *The Triumph of the Therapeutic*, the dualisms become utterly pervasive. Note the obsessive recurrence in the later book of the opposition between demand and remission, between the interdictory and the counter-interdictory, between control and release.[59] And note Rieff's assertion that "the Freudian doctrine was never to be put in systemic service to either interdiction or release, under pain of ceasing to be analytic."[60] The position that Rieff articulates here is identical in structure to the literary modernism of such figures as Eliot, Pound, and Yeats. If I may describe his position in the language proposed by Wilde, Rieff maintains that the analytic attitude—equivalent, as we can see, to Wilde's "absolute" irony—looks down upon both fragmentation and order, identifying itself with neither. Thus, Freud, the therapist and disabused moralist, proposes a detached and self-protective strategy of existence that he sees as peculiarly appropriate to the potentially overwhelming uncertainties of "modern" life.

Freud and interpretation

But to postmodernists such an ideal is anathema. One thinks of Nietzsche's attack on the "last man" in *Zarathustra* and of Heidegger's dismissal of "calculative thinking" in *Discourse on Thinking*. One thinks, too, of the whole animus of postmodern art against the notion of depth in any guise—its replacement of modernism's "characteristically vertical orderings of disconnection" with an ambiguous and disconcerting horizontality, an eerie flatness.[61] It is in consequence not surprising that the modernist Freud has increasingly been countered by the postmodernist Freud. Postmodern intellectuals have turned to the Freudian text, seeking and to a large extent finding traces of a postmodern view. The postmodern interpretation of Freud eliminates the anironic moment, any hint of Freudianism as providing a strategy of life (to be sure, a strategy of life may be implicit in postmodernism, but it is part of postmodernism's style that this strategy can never be articulated). The postmodernist Freud propounds no doctrine, conveys no message. He is not a moralist in any sense but is rather (like Nietzsche) an antimoralist. He teaches us not how to live but how to read. In short, the postmodern Freud is Freud the interpreter—not the interpreter of dreams, or of the psyche, or of culture, but the interpreter *tout court*.

This is the Freud pointed out by the translator of *Of Grammatology*, Gayatri Spivak, when she asserts that for Derrida, psychoanalysis is "not a science that necessarily provides a correct picture of the psychic norm and prescribes cures for the abnormal, but rather teaches, through its own use thereof, a certain method of deciphering any text" (*GRAM*, pp.—/xxxvii).

In the eyes of his postmodern interpreters, Freud's most significant work is *The Interpretation of Dreams,* which they value not for the theoretical advances that it is alleged to have made but rather for the wealth and copiousness of its interpretive flights. Admittedly, modernist interpreters, too, have noted Freud's skill at interpretation: thus, Rieff points out that for Freud "nothing falls outside the range of the 'meaningful and interpretable'.... Freud's interpretive method ... reaches out to embrace all subjects."[62] But the interpretation that Rieff here envisages is interpretation in the first of Derrida's two senses, that is, "rabbinical" interpretation, whereas postmodern interpreters find in Freud a model for interpretation in the second of Derrida's two senses, interpretation not as an attempt to decipher a truth but as self-justifying play. Alternatively, we might characterize Rieff's Freud as an epistemologist and the postmodern Freud as an exponent of hermeneutics, in Rorty's senses of those terms.

It is perfectly clear that neither Freud himself, nor any of those who have interpreted and extended Freudian doctrine, could possibly accept the postmodern revision of psychoanalysis. Freud always saw himself as concerned with "reality"—more especially, with "psychical reality."[63] Though he acknowledged that this reality was difficult of access, he nonetheless saw it as unambiguously present—not a cave behind a cave behind a cave, but something solid and unequivocal, an *interpretandum* and not a mere *interpretans.* This is true even of Lacan, whatever his structuralist penchant for defining psychical reality as language. Freud would never have subscribed to the Derridean view that "there is nothing outside of the text." Nor, despite his frequent use of the metaphor of writing (pointed out by Derrida in "Freud and the Scene of Writing"), would he have conceded that his practice of interpretation was "textual" in the poststructuralist and postmodernist sense. Freud was fundamentally a "realist." This is evident not only in the fact that he saw his scientific lifework as a search for "reality," but also in his persistent rejection of the idealisms both of nostalgia and imagination.[64]

The point that Freud was a realist is clearly enough made by Derrida himself at the beginning of "The Purveyor of Truth." Here he discusses Freud's account in *The Interpretation of Dreams* of the "secondary revision of the material" in Sophocles' *Oedipus Rex.* Freud holds that the "key" to *Oedipus Rex* lies in the son's love for his mother and hatred for his father. All the other elements in the tragedy are mere disguises intended to hide its sexual core.[65] As Derrida puts it, accurately summarizing Freud's argument, "whenever critics have considered *Oedipus Rex* to be a tragedy of fate, a conflict between men and gods, a theological drama, etc., what they have considered to be the essential element of the play was actually an afterthought, a garment, a disguise, a fabric added to the *Stoff* itself in order to mask its nakedness " (*CARTE*, pp. 442–443/33). What, then, is the aim of interpretation in the Freudian scheme of things? Its aim is to expose the "secondary revisions" that have distorted the dream, the play, the legend, the myth, thus allowing us to get down to the psychic material out of which these were originally created. Derrida's formulation is again worth quoting: "The baring of this *Stoff,* the discovery of the semantic material: such would be the terminus of the analyst's deciphering. Baring the meaning behind these formal disguises, undoing the work, this deciphering exhibits the primary contents under the secondary revisions" (*CARTE*, pp. 443/33).

And yet, the "realist" character of psychoanalysis in general and of Freud's text in particular is not nearly so unequivocal as it might seem at first glance. As Derrida observes, one can find in Freud a "blurring of the boundary lines between 'imagination' and 'reality,' between the 'symbol' and the 'thing it symbolizes'" (*DISS*, pp. 249/220). Firstly, the "reality" with which Freud is concerned turns out to be highly elusive. In dream interpretation, for example, Freud of necessity analyzes not the dream itself but only an imperfect recollection of the dream. Similarly, in the psychoanalytic treatment of patients, he usually knows nothing about the events of the patient's early life other than what the patient tells him. To be sure, Freud persists in speaking as if he has grasped these realities. But as Rieff puts it, in a passage that helps us to see how well Freud lends himself to the postmodern view, when Freud "presumes that he has disinterred the determinant thoughts of the past, actually his method fundamentally alters the sense of the past and its reality. When he speaks of the dream, he admittedly does not mean the dream as such, as it 'really' happened, but only the dream as constructed afterward with the aid of the interpreter."[66]

Freud defends this procedure with the argument that the determinism operating in psychic life guarantees that every distortion of reality is a telling distortion. Consequently, the fact that we do not know the dream *wie es eigentlich gewesen ist* is of no account. The same holds true for the patient's early life: it is not what actually happened to him in childhood that is important, but his fantasies about what happened. Thus, it does not matter whether the patient was actually seduced by her father; it is sufficient that she imagines having been seduced. As Rieff says, discussing the "Dora" analysis, "Freud ... does not listen to what the brute symptoms might be trying to say. Because he saw *all* behavior as symptomatic, he could concentrate entirely on Dora's statement. To track down a dream, or any actual event, was inessential."[67] In short, psychic determinism justifies the practice of entering into an understanding of the psyche at points far along the interpretive chain. Freud worked, here, by analogy with the eminently respectable field of physics in its mid-nineteenth-century form, where a simple, mechanical determinism reigned supreme.[68] But given the obviously *a priori* nature of his particular deterministic assumptions, the effect of this procedure in Freud's work is anything but scientific. Far from being highlighted, the "really real," the "thing itself," tends to disappear.

Secondly, along with this subtle effacement or reconstruction of "reality" goes a tremendous interpretive exuberance. What most impresses the postmodern (and indeed the post-postmodern) reader of Freud is not his alleged discoveries. At an earlier stage in the reception of Freud's work, these "discoveries" were exciting, and in a certain sense liberating. But now, whether or not we are convinced by Freud's rhetoric, they are common coin. Rather, we find ourselves attracted by the breathtaking scope and freedom of his interpretive practice. In the matter of dreams, for example, Freud could have contented himself with merely collecting and cataloguing. But he was not one to play it safe in this way. On the contrary, he had the courage and imagination to build, on a foundation terrifying in its exiguousness, an immense interpretive edifice. It is this that makes *The Interpretation of Dreams* so patently a work of genius, and it would remain a work of genius even if every statement in it were proved wrong. It is this, moreover, that connects Freud with the postmodern thrust in contemporary thought, making him of such immense interest to recent critics.[69]

Freud's official biographer, Ernest Jones, rightly observes that "daring and unrestrained imagination always stirred Freud." But characteristically (for Jones's Freud is preeminently Freud the scientist), he goes on to say that Freud "rarely gave full rein" to this part of his nature, since it had been tamed "by a skeptical vein."[70] One screams with laughter at this point, for—Jones to the contrary—Freud's interpretive practice is anything but skeptical. He gives the game away in *The Interpretation of Dreams* when he tells us that "in analyzing a dream, I insist that the whole scale of estimates of certainty shall be abandoned and the faintest possibility that something of this or that sort may have occurred in the dream shall be treated as complete certainty."[71] This sentence gives the model of his whole interpretive practice. Note, for example, the brilliant charlatanry of the "Dora" analysis, with its fantastic play of implausible interpretations, its confident conclusions based on no evidence whatsoever. At one point in "Dora," he insists that he is not a "man of letters engaged upon the creation of a mental state ... for a short story" but rather "a medical man engaged upon its dissection."[72] But in abandoning the scales of certainty and in depriving us of the means to know what could possibly serve as counter-evidence to his conclusions, he surely destroys his claim to be the scientific analyst of modern man. In revenge, however, he opens himself up to a rhetorical energy and verve, to a brilliance of performance that well accords with the whole postmodern valuation of interpretation for interpretation's sake.

Freud, Derrida

It is easy to see, then, why Derrida should find Freud's enterprise fascinating. To be sure, on an explicit level Freud stands in opposition to the whole "grammatological" project. The other side of Freud's attachment to science is his hostility to art, a hostility that marks him off from aestheticist thinkers.[73] But at the same time, it is not hard to find, in his enthusiastic pursuit of interpretation, much more than a hint of a postmodern perspective. As Rieff observes, Freud plunges us into an "incredible world: fantastic realities beneath reasonable appearances; worlds composed of absurd conjunctions—events that never happened and yet control those that do; cure coming through a stranger who aims to know another more intimately than his intimates have ever known him; thoughts that wander in an over-determined way. Consider alone the absurdity, and yet the demonstrated inevitability of that faith the patient develops in his analyst—there you have a hint of the profound and true absurdity of psychoanalysis."[74]

For Rieff, this absurdity is purely honorific in character. It is not something that he wishes to examine. And we can easily see why he holds himself back—for a real confrontation with the absurdity of psychoanalysis would utterly destroy it as an object of modernist veneration. Derrida's great merit here is that he undermines the modernist use of Freud. At the beginning of "Freud and the Scene of Writing," he informs us that "our aim is limited: to locate in Freud's text several points of reference, and to isolate, on the threshold of a systematic investigation, those elements of psychoanalysis which can only uneasily be contained within logocentric closure" (*E&D*, pp. 296/198). In carrying out this "limited" aim, Derrida is attacking an intellectual position that continues to carry immense prestige.

Note the following passage, also from "Freud and the Scene of Writing": "The conscious text is ... not a transcription, because there is no text *present elsewhere* as an unconscious one to be transposed or transported. . . . The text is not conceivable in an originary or modified form of presence. The unconscious text is already a weave of pure traces, differences in which meaning and force are united—a text nowhere present, consisting of archives which are *always already* transcriptions. . . . Everything begins with reproduction" (*E&D*, pp. 313–314/211). Whatever the difficulties of this passage (and it is less difficult than most in Derrida), its point is clear, and in large measure correct. Derrida calls attention to Freud's tendency to assimilate *interpretans* and *interpretandum*. He thus makes clear how hard it is to find, in Freud's various analytic endeavors, a reality prior to its own interpretation. The effect of this is to cast into doubt all attempts to "use" Freud, to take him as conveying, however tentatively or indirectly, a truth to live by. "The Purveyor of Truth," for example, is a devastating attack on Lacan, and by implication on all those interpreters who insist on taking Freud's "discoveries" seriously, on finding in his writings a "lesson" or "message" or "truth" that must be protected from misinterpretation (see, e.g., *CARTE*, pp. 454–455, 464, 478, 483–484, 495–498/46–47, 57, 72–73, 78–79, 88–90).

One can read "Fors" as an opposition piece to "The Purveyor of Truth." Whereas "The Purveyor of Truth" mounts an attack on the scientism of Lacan (actually, an unintentional parody of scientism), "Fors" is cast as an appreciation of the psychoanalytic work of Nicolas Abraham, whose inclination was to stress, as Derrida does, the fictive aspect of psychoanalysis. Derrida notes that Abraham and Torok's analysis of "The Wolf-Man" reads like "a novel, a poem, a myth, a drama," and the two authors themselves acknowledge their analysis to be a fiction.[75] Abraham and Torok's "poetic" interpretation of Freud is the contrary of Lacan's "rabbinical" interpretation; here *pietas* before the Holy Text gives way to interpretive play.

This same playfulness prevails in the Freudian dream-work itself: abolishing the difference between text and interpretation, postmodernism opens itself up to precisely those interpretive modes that Freud finds at work in the unconscious mind. It is thus illuminating to reflect on the affinities between the dream-work as depicted by Freud and the texts of Derrida. (If my intentions were more exclusively literary, I might want to delve deeply into the interpretive affinities between a characteristic text of Derrida's—say, *Glas*—and *Finnegans Wake*, but in the present context this is perhaps not necessary: for remember, *Finnegans Wake* is a book about a dream.)

Consider, firstly, how the movement of a text by Derrida is directed less by the logic of an argument than by word play, free association, and an almost obsessive recurrence of a limited number of motifs. To take an example that lies close at hand, in "Freud and the Scene of Writing" Derrida uses the motifs of "trace" and "writing" to tie together, in a patently forced and illogical way, three widely separate Freudian texts: *Project for a Scientific Psychology* (1895), *The Interpretation of Dreams* (1899), and "Note on the Mystic Writing-Pad" (1925).

Glas is a better example, with its play on the verbal similarity between *Hegel* and *aigle*, with its pursuit of the association *glas, sa, savoir absolu, signifiant* (abbreviated as "sa"), and *id* (rendered in French as *ça*), with its recurrent motif of flowers, and with countless other apparently accidental linkages of this sort. These associations are oddly powerful; it is difficult to convey *Glas*'s rich hilarity, its serenely joyful joking quality. And the hilarity is apt to be best appreciated if one keeps in mind the dream analogy. *Glas* is an intellectual fantasy, constructed from the detritus of 2,500 years of Western culture in rather the same way that a dreamwork is constructed from the detritus of our personal lives. In many other of Derrida's writings, both before and after *Glas*, there is a greater pretense of logical argument and rational connectedness. In *Glas*, pretense is seen as pretense. As Freud points out, in the dream "we find associations based on homonyms and verbal similarities treated as equal in value to the rest"—treated, that is, as equal in value to the logic of rational connection to which we adhere in waking life.[76] So also in *Glas*.

Or recall the beginning of *The Psychopathology of Everyday Life* (1901), where Freud attempts to explain why on a certain occasion he forgot the name of the artist (Signorelli) who painted the frescoes of the "Four Last Things" in the Cathedral of Orvieto. Freud's explanation, with its very complicated and farfetched association of names (Signor, Herzegovina, Herr; Botticelli, Bosnia; Boltraffio, Trafoi), reads exactly like a page from one of Derrida's more exuberant works.[77] If nothing else, Derrida makes us wonder why for such a long time we took Freud so seriously—indeed, why we took Freud seriously at all.

Consider, too, the all-important questions of meaning and intention. Freud tells us in *The Interpretation of Dreams* that "the productions of the dream-work... *are not made with the intention of being understood*."[78] More than this, the purpose of the dream is actively to obscure truth, so that if dreams are "not made with the intention of being understood," they are also, in a more forceful rendering of these words, made with the intention of *not* being understood.

Freud does hold that (within limits) the meaning of dreams *can* be understood; this, after all, is the point that he wants to establish in *The*

Interpretation of Dreams. Yet, he also concedes that powerful forces are at work seeking to render illegible the original ideas, preoccupations, and wishes underlying the dream. Insofar as these forces are successful in their task, the dream resembles the sustained attempt at the erasure of meaning that one finds in Derrida: an erasure that nonetheless leaves traces of what has been erased. When Derrida says in *Positions* that "in the literal sense writing does not wish to say/mean anything," we could easily substitute *dream* for *writing*: the dream, too, does not wish to say anything.

As we have amply seen, Derrida contends that the desire to convey a message, or the related desire to "read" a message into a text already written, is inextricably tied up with the logocentrism of the whole Western tradition. All messages are by definition metaphysical. Derrida's aim, it appears, is a systematic dismantling of message-sending structures, a task that he tends to disguise as merely the dismantling of a canon. This dismantling—a dismantling, ultimately, of "destination"—is closely tied up with his dismantling of the *Geschick* of Western history, which I considered in Chapter 7.

Deconstructing Kant

Freud observes in the "Dora" analysis that neurotics "are dominated by the opposition between reality and fantasy"; yet, "if what they long for most intensely in their fantasies is presented them in reality, they none the less flee from it."[79] But Freud, too, is dominated by this opposition: what is wrong with neurotics is not that they adhere to the opposition but rather that they make the wrong choice between the two sides. This helps us to see a further point about Freud: that if he is a realist in Berki's sense, he is realistic in an incomplete way. For he conceives of the real in the guise of the *necessary,* viewing reality as "the realm of unchangeable, inevitable and in the last resort inexorable occurrences, a world of eternity, objectivity, gravity, substantiality and positive resistance to human purposes."[80] Why does Freud conceive of reality in this way? He does so partly because he establishes, at least on an explicit level, a sharp opposition between dream and reality—and similarly between art and reality, between "poetry" and "truth." Dreams and fantasies, of course, play an important role in the Romantic scheme of things. It is not surprising, when one considers their connections to Romanticism, that the early Nietzsche lays great stress on the dreamlike character of the Apollonian and that the early Foucault stresses the affinity between dreams and madness. Freud moves in the other direction. By postulating a rigid opposition between dream and reality and by opting unequivocally for the latter, he hopes to protect himself from the accusation of harboring illicit, unscientific, Romantic tendencies.

Nietzsche, Heidegger, Foucault, and Derrida all call this opposition into question, though they do so in different ways. Nietzsche, Heidegger, and Foucault challenge the opposition by attempting to raise "art" to the level of "reality." Recall Nietzsche's characterization of "the world" as a "work of art" and his insistence that language and interpretation can themselves bring about a transformation of reality. Recall Heidegger's insistence that the work of art opens up a world and keeps it in force. Recall Foucault's insistence that art and discourse perform a critical function, compelling the world to "a task of recognition, of reparation." All these assertions come out of the post-Kantian, post-Schillerian, Romantic valuation of art—an historical connection that is perhaps most clearly displayed not in these writers but in the more pedestrian work of Hans-Georg Gadamer.

In thus raising art to the status of reality, Nietzsche, Heidegger, and Foucault engage in a mythmaking enterprise—taking *myth*, here, to mean a justificatory art, an art that seeks to establish and support a form of life. The mythic moment is especially strong in Nietzsche and Foucault, for both thinkers demand, in a very obvious way, a radical change in the extant order (though, for reasons that are now clear to us, they are entirely incapable of describing the new, transfigured order that they wish to see come into being). They view their own writings as attempts to construct a myth that will justify the new order, or at least the effort to construct that order. Heidegger is perhaps a more difficult case, for it could be argued that he wants no change in society whatsoever, and hence has no need for a myth designed to effect such a change. But if Heidegger does not want to change *society*, he clearly does want to change our *way of thinking,* and his writings are an art whose intention is to justify such a transformation.

In Derrida, however, I see nothing of this mythic moment. If Nietzsche is an ironic mythmaker, Derrida seems only ironic: the radicality of his irony undermines any pretension to myth. Thus, instead of articulating a justificatory art, he chooses to question the myth of art itself. He most frequently characterizes his enterprise as an attack on the whole Western tradition of logocentric, phonocentric thought. But I am inclined to see in this characterization a residue of the same enhancement of origins that we found in Heidegger. It is more illuminating, I think, to see Derrida as attacking post-Romantic thought. One object of this attack is Hegel (or

"Hegel"), whose conception of History he deconstructs. Its second object is Kant (or "Kant"), whose view of Art he deconstructs. Nietzsche, Heidegger, and Foucault are unwitting Hegelians, as Derrida shows. But they are also unwitting Kantians, for their notion of the creative power of art depends on the initial Kantian distinction between art and not-art.

It is in *Truth in Painting* that Derrida most directly addresses the philosophy of art. The occasion for this reflection is provided by Cézanne's avowal: "I owe you truth in painting, and I will tell it to you" (*VenP*, p. 6). Derrida explores the relation between this promise and the notion of the truth of art as it is found in Hegel and in Heidegger. As he points out, the philosophy of art presupposes the existence of works of art. Thus, in his *Lectures on Aesthetics,* Hegel assumes implicitly that there *are* works of art, and he evinces no difficulty in deciding which objects, among the many in the world, these are. But as Derrida indicates, this is already to assume that art, as a word, a concept, and a thing, has "a unity and . . . an originary meaning, an *etymon,* a *single* and *naked* truth that it would be sufficient to unveil *over the course of* history" (*VenP*, pp. 24–25). There is a double assumption here, for Hegel is attributing a unity not only to art but also to history itself (cf. Chapter 7). In other words, we see a philosophy of identity at work, which Derrida undermines in its aesthetic and historicist guises. The assumption of the unity of art over time in turn supports the notion that art has a meaning—that underneath the multifarious forms of *technē* displayed in art there exists a single, simple kernel of truth. Thus, we have the "ontological" view of art, of which Hegel is the progenitor and Heidegger the most prominent twentieth-century exponent.

Derrida is especially illuminating on the extent to which the ontological view of art subordinates art to the form of *saying,* even when it is a matter of works of art (plastic or musical) in which the form is not at all that of saying. Of course, it is notorious that this is what Hegel does. Hegel sees the true meaning of the work of art as something that can be translated into discourse; not surprisingly, he places the discursive arts above the nondiscursive. But it is also true of Heidegger, for as Derrida points out, Heidegger subordinates all art "to speech and, if not to poetry, at least to the poem, to the said, to language, to the word, to nomination (*Sagen, Dichtung, Sprache, Nennen*)" (*VenP*, pp. 26–28). To be sure, Heidegger claims to go back before the classic philosophical oppositions that have dominated the philosophy of art: meaning/form, interior/exterior, content/container, signified/signifier, represented/representer, and so on (*VenP*, p. 26). But Derrida argues that Heidegger, too, is caught within the phonic, antigrammatological perspective that dominates the history of the West. (I have noted, following George Steiner, how it seems surprising that Heidegger does not appeal to music in the course of his consideration of art—for the peculiar self-containedness of music seems especially appropriate to Heidegger's preoccupation with the "world" of the work of art. Derrida's exposure of the logocentric, discursive bias of Heidegger's view of art helps to explain this omission.) In short, there is not really much difference between Hegel and Heidegger in matters of art—hardly surprising, in light of the fact that Heidegger himself acknowledges the importance that Hegel's *Aesthetics* had for his own work. "Truth in painting": a phrase that can be understood, Derrida says at one point, in four different senses (*VenP*, p. 9). But in the "classic" philosophy of art, all these senses are subjected to "the discursive arts, to voice and to the *logos*" (*VenP*, p. 27).

Though a seeming liberation, then, art is as much under the sway of the Greek logos as philosophy is. But beyond these "ontological" reflections on art there are the "aesthetic" reflections of the *Critique of Judgment*. Heidegger sees Hegel's *Aesthetics* as the most comprehensive reflection on art that we possess. But as Derrida points out, the place that Heidegger thus accords to Hegel's *Aesthetics* "can only be established within an historical topography laid out by the *Critique of Judgment*, Kant's third critique, in which he sought to find a middle term capable of overcoming the abyss between nature and spirit" (*VenP*, p. 42). Kant suggests in the *Critique of Judgment* that there is an aesthetic domain distinct from all other domains—a domain that is the special territory of the aesthetic judgment. Thus, in judging the beauty of a palace (to take one of his examples), one excludes from consideration all nonaesthetic criteria—for example, criteria of empirical psychology, of economic production, of political structure, of technology, and so on. In short, one presupposes a sphere within which "disinterested pleasure" can take place (*VenP*, p. 53). It is Derrida's merit to point out how questionable this assumption is. He is not the first to attack Kant—far from it. Nietzsche, for example, engages in a polemic against the whole Kantian notion of disinterestedness in art; Heidegger argues that pleasure as a criterion in art is either superfluous or insufficient (*VenP*, p. 54). But Derrida is the first to carry this attack to the point of undermining the aestheticist view itself.

Crucial here is the idea of the *cadre*, or frame. The first of the four essays making up *Truth in Painting* deals not with the work of art as such but with the "parergon"—that is, with what is "around" or "by" the work. Neither inside nor outside the work, neither above nor below it, the parergon upsets the classical oppositions of the philosophy of art. The frame, part of this parergon, turns out to be crucial to the being of the work of art, for it is the frame that separates art from what is not art. The frame is "the decisive structure of the risk, invisible at its limit to . . . the interiority of meaning (screened by the whole hermeneutizing, semiotizing, phenomenologizing, formalizing tradition) *and* . . . to all the empiricisms of what is extrinsic, which, knowing neither how to see nor to read, miss the question" (*VenP,* p. 71). Derrida's reflection on the frame is exuberant in its development. For example, he brings into consideration a number of artworks—such as Fantuzzi's "Ornamental Panel with Empty Oval" (1542–43)—in which the frame itself is the work of art. Derrida's use of examples must surely be irritating to anyone reading him for his arguments alone—anyone reading him as one "normally" reads a philosophical text. But his point is precisely that one cannot rigorously distinguish between a philosophical text and a work of art: hence, he can characterize his own work as a "theoretical fiction" (*VenP,* p. 93). Derrida argues that the "formalism" of Kant's aesthetics is connected to "the possibility of a system of framing that is at the same time imposed and effaced" (*VenP,* p. 79). That is, if one is to adhere to a Kantian or post-Kantian position, one needs to keep hidden the fact that an arbitrary division has been made between art and not-art. Exposing this division— casting a spotlight on the frame or parergon—undermines the philosophy of art as it has been developed not only by Kant but also (ontologically) by Hegel and Heidegger. And it also undermines aestheticism—for aestheticism, too, depends on this Kantian division.

Such is one way, at any rate, of reading Derrida. Derrida warns against the "impatience of the bad reader" (*CARTE,* p. 8/ —). Whether this reading of his corpus is *too* impatient remains to be seen. But whatever the fate of this reading (which I concede to be only one possible interpretation among others), one thing seems undeniable: namely, that central to Derrida's project is an importing into the realm of ideas of what was already present in practice in the realm of art. His attack on the frame is anticipated in Duchamp, in all those forms of modern sculpture that take ordinary objects as their material, in the mixture of novel and *reportage* in, for example, Mailer, in the street theater of the 1960s and early '70s, in video art. Derrida's particular genius is his ability to see connections and implications that others have missed. In so doing, he treads an uneasy ground between "philosophy" (crossed out) and "art" (also crossed out).

Most of the stratagems that Derrida employs come quite specifically out of the realm of postmodern art. In many ways, Derrida, too, seems to fall under the postmodernist rubric (however shifting and uncertain the rubric may be). Like postmodernists, he deconstructs the frame—the division between "art" and "reality." Like postmodernists, he substitutes for the modernist faith in depth and penetration an adherence to surfaces (a substitution most clearly displayed in the allegorical feminism of *Spurs*). Yet, I do not believe that Derrida can finally be seen as a postmodernist. Firstly, his attack on crisis theory undermines the rationale for postmodernism, as it does the rationale for modernism. And secondly, postmodernism still retains a residual attachment to the "Kantian" division between the theoretical, the practical, and the aesthetic realms, for in its peculiar sort of playfulness and laughter it treats art in isolation from ethical considerations. It practices a demoralized, derealized, dehistorical art.

This is not, I think, the end toward which Derrida's work points. If Derrida champions a postmodernist, "poetic" interpretation, he also champions, as Reb Derrida, the "rabbinical" interpretation that still seeks a truth in things. Thus, though there could have been no Derrida without Nietzsche, he is not a Nietzschean—as Heidegger and (even more) Foucault still are. On the contrary, Derrida deconstructs not only "Hegelianism," but also that Nietzscheanism and post-Nietzscheanism that took Hegel as its primary target. One therefore has, in Derrida, the sense of an ending—an ending not only of Hegelianism and Kantianism but also of the Nietzscheanism that followed these. But one also has— having worked through the Derridean critique—what is perhaps the possibility of a beginning: one that would liberate us from the historicism and aestheticism that, in one way or another, have dominated Western thought since the beginning of the nineteenth century.

Conclusion

It is my contention that Nietzsche, Heidegger, Foucault, and Derrida mark out an epoch in modern Western intellectual history. The present work has, I hope, demonstrated why I hold this to be so. Nietzsche, Heidegger, and Foucault are crucially important visionaries, and Derrida the antivisionary who follows in their wake. We find in their writings a utopian response to certain well-known features of "the modern age"; we also find a deconstruction of that response. Looking at our two earlier writers, I do not think that there can be any doubt about their importance for the intellectual history of our century. Nietzschean and Heideggerian assumptions have become deeply rooted in Western intellectual life. Nietzsche and Heidegger articulated in rhetorically compelling form notions that later became common coin; they formulated responses to situations that now seem to face us. It is this anticipation that makes them historically significant thinkers. As for Foucault and Derrida, it is difficult to know what impact they will have on the history of ideas. Obviously, the results are not yet in. But if their historical importance remains in question, their working out of the possibilities and limits of Nietzschean and Heideggerian thought gives them, from the perspective of this study, an undeniable theoretical importance.

According to Hegel, in what remains one of his most celebrated dicta, "the owl of Minerva spreads its wings only with the falling of the dusk."[1] But Minerva's owl—that is, philosophy—has repeatedly, over the last three hundred years, played a morning role, preceding rather than following social and political history. Cartesianism, with its separation of ego from external world and its consequent emphasis on control and manipulation, anticipates the bureaucratic, technological society within which we in the twentieth century so obviously live. The philosophy of the Enlightenment, with its rational humanitarianism, anticipates the French Revolution and the rise to prominence of those political ideologies that find their roots in the Revolution: liberalism, radicalism, and socialism. The thought of Saint-Simon and Marx, however wrong those two thinkers were in matters of detail, interestingly illuminates the economic, social, and political developments of the present century. And the crisis thought that Nietzsche initiated likewise seems to find confirmation in subsequent events.

It is clear, I think, that modern Western intellectual history has up to now been mainly defined by the thought of the Enlightenment. Admittedly, in large degree the successoral movements to the Enlightenment saw themselves as rebellions against it. But this is itself significant, for it means that Enlightenment thought set the terms of subsequent discussion. In any case, these movements often owed more to their Enlightenment predecessors than they were willing to admit. Nineteenth-century Romanticism and historicism were reactions against, but also continuations of, the Enlightenment. In the present century, the whole structure of the social sciences and humanities is based on Enlightenment presuppositions. Of course, there are those who seek in the East a counterbalance to the Enlightenment. But current intellectual debates in, say, India or China often have an eerily nineteenth-century quality to them. Westerners are sometimes taken aback by the extent to which Easterners maintain an implicit and largely unquestioning faith in such Enlightenment and post-Enlightenment values as science and progress.

Yet, for all its importance in defining our problems and in justifying our institutions, my guess is that the primacy of the Enlightenment—its importance in setting the terms of our discourse—will not continue much longer. I concede that I have little that is solid to substantiate this guess. I can appeal only to what seems to me to be the evident decline of the old Kantian, Cartesian, and Hegelian certainties, and to the obvious and continuing malaise in our politics and institutions—politics and institutions that are themselves the products of Enlightenment moral, social, and political theory.

Following Rorty, I have characterized Nietzsche, Heidegger, Foucault, and Derrida as "reactive" thinkers. Clearly, it is against the Enlightenment project, and against the elaboration and modification of that project in Romanticism and historicism, that these thinkers react. Nietzsche could perhaps be regarded as the fourth, deconstructive moment in a sequence that begins with Descartes, Kant, and Hegel. But what is to happen now that Descartes, Kant, and Hegel are so far behind us? Marxism has been the most durable remnant of that earlier dialectic, embodying a Cartesian faith in science, a Kantian faith in human nature, and an Hegelian faith in reason and history. Yet, Marxism, as a doctrine that one can continue to take seriously, is clearly in trouble. The reasons for this trouble go far beyond the oppression, ranging from the petty to the tyrannical, that reigns in the Communist bloc. Rather, the "crisis of Marxism" is connected with a more general "crisis of the Enlightenment." This "crisis" in turn connects with the persistent failure of our institutions to live up to expectation. These considerations lead me to suspect that we are standing on the brink of an important transformation in the history of ideas, for which the thought of the prophets of extremity, and most especially of Nietzsche and Heidegger, is likely to play an important role.

To be sure, there are some who believe it possible to dismiss these thinkers out of hand. The most comprehensive charge that can be leveled against them is that they overlook or totally misconstrue the truly pressing realities of human life. In their idealism, they try to come to grips not with gravity but with "the spirit of gravity." It can be argued that the point about such apparent banalities as "What about the workers?" and "What about the starving millions?" is that they refer to an underlying social reality with problems far weightier than the issues that interest crisis thinkers. Rorty has made a suggestive connection between "nineteenth-century idealism" and "twentieth-century textualism."[2] The story is more complicated than this, of course: it is a long journey from "idealism" to "textualism." But as will be obvious from my own account of the provenance of aestheticism, I agree that the linkage to an earlier idealism is important. Indeed, in reading those who see themselves as belonging to the revolutionary wing of aestheticism, one is often uncannily reminded of Bruno Bauer.

Yet, simply to reject these thinkers is to deprive oneself of what is valuable in their work. Nietzsche, Heidegger, Foucault, and Derrida speak an "edifying" discourse—a discourse designed, as Rorty puts it, to "take us out of our old selves by the power of strangeness, to aid us in becoming new beings."[3] To make the same point in another way, these writers are trying to encourage our capacity for *ekstasis*—that imaginative ability that we possess to transcend our own situations, to get outside ourselves in time and space. This is a highly important project, for it is precisely the capacity for *ekstasis* that enables us to function as moral beings, allowing us to see *ourselves* in the guise of those upon whom we act. Yet, it is a project that for all practical purposes has been excluded from the domain of the social sciences, and has been repressed within the humanities. The thinkers whom we have considered in this book are committed to ending this exclusion or repression. They aim to bring back to thought a concern that in the Enlightenment view finds its place, if it finds any place at all, in art and religion.

There is reason to believe that this attempt to reintegrate what in the Enlightenment view remains divided answers a widely felt need. This is why I think that these thinkers—especially the two founding fathers of this thought, Nietzsche and Heidegger—are likely to be important for the future. Ever since the eighteenth century, those intellectual projects that have been historically significant have all sought to provide better, more detailed, more sophisticated answers to questions first raised by eighteenth-century philosophers. It has been a matter of carrying out projects that these philosophers first conceived, or (a minority position) of trying to show that these projects were unworkable. In short, in one way or another it has been a matter of coming to terms with the Enlightenment. I do not think that this confrontation with the Enlightenment will continue. I suspect, rather, that in the future it will be a matter of developing or criticizing the thought that Nietzsche and Heidegger have given us. Foucault and Derrida are engaged in just such an enterprise. I have argued that Derrida, in particular, undermines certain fundamental assumptions of the prophecy of extremity. I do not think, however, that this is the end of the story. On the contrary, assuming that our culture survives—and this is, admittedly, a risky assumption—I believe that the issues raised by Nietzsche and Heidegger will more and more move into the center of intellectual debate.

What, then, is aestheticism? In broadest terms, it can be viewed as an attempt to bring back into thought and into our lives that form of edification, that reawakening of *ekstasis,* which in the Enlightenment and post-Enlightenment view has been largely confined to the realm of art. More specifically, it can be regarded as a collection of related propositions having their origin in Romantic and post-Romantic aesthetics. To approach aestheticism critically, one must move from the general assertion that aestheticism seeks to edify to these more specific propositions.

Ontologically, the aestheticist development of aesthetics finds its justification in the conviction that "the world" is "a work of art that gives birth to itself"—or, in another formulation, in the conviction that "the world itself is nothing other than art" (Nietzsche, *KGW,* 8. Abt., 1. Bd., p. 119). The notion that the world is a work of art can and does lead in two radically different directions. On the one hand, it leads in the direction of passive contemplation. In this view, since the world is a work of art we ought to relate to it as we do to works of art in the narrow sense. That is, we ought to stand before the world in awed rapture, allowing it to manifest to us its deeply veiled truth. This is the position adopted by the later Heidegger. On the other hand, aestheticist ontology leads in an activist direction. Here it is not contemplation but radical creativity that comes to be stressed. The artist creates out of nothing. Since in aestheticism the aesthetic has centrality, all human activity comes to be interpreted on the model of the creativity attributed to the (Romantic) artist, who himself stands as the successor to the radical creativity of God. The very words of the poet bring into being the world. Discourse creates its own reality. This view is prominent in the Nietzsche of the 1880s, is an important subtheme in the later Heidegger, and came to be espoused, in a de-aestheticized form, by Foucault in the late 1960s.

One would have to be either a madman or a fool to believe literally in these aestheticist theses. I am not accusing Heidegger, or Foucault, or Nietzsche before his breakdown, of being either. For it is clear that the aestheticist statements of Heidegger and Foucault, and before them of Nietzsche, are not to be taken literally. Rather, they are examples of the trope of hyperbole. They are exaggerations put forward with specific rhetorical ends in view. Yet, there is a problem here, for the rhetorical effectiveness of these assertions very much depends on their being taken literally. Here lies the great danger or defect of aestheticism.

In his *Aesthetic Letters,* Schiller observes that aesthetic semblance cannot be prejudicial to truth, for "one is never in danger of substituting it for truth, which is after all the only way in which truth can ever be impaired."[4] But this statement is surely false—as Nietzsche, for example, sensed. Aesthetic semblance, discursive invention, interpretive sally— these do come to be substituted for truth. This substitution occurs so frequently that it is hardly worth commenting on individual instances. It is perhaps most noticeable not in the writings of Nietzsche, Heidegger, Foucault, and Derrida themselves but in those of their followers. In the movement from master to disciple, a certain crudity intervenes. Consider the reception of Foucault's writings. Time and again, these are taken as presenting the literal truth of the past. A statement in *The Order of Things* or *Discipline and Punish* or *Birth of the Clinic* will be accepted uncritically, and a structure of allegedly historical interpretation will be built on top of it. Such a reading of Foucault leaves out of the picture the whole polemical impulse embodied in his project. Granting no status to the tension between Foucault's interpretations and the actual past, it fundamentally alters the character of that project.

Clearly, the question of truth is decisive here. This question arises in its most striking form in the notion of "the truth of the work of art." Moreover, the "truth value" notion acquires added significance by virtue of the fact that it is adhered to well beyond the territory charted out by the four thinkers with whom we have here been concerned. It is a notion widely diffused in modern Western intellectual culture. The appeal is frequently made, for example, to "the testimony of modern art."[5] Our reading of Nietzsche, Heidegger, Foucault, and especially Derrida ought to teach us to be highly suspicious of such appeals. For surely the testimony of art is so Delphic that it really amounts to a reflecting back of the prejudices of the interpreter, protecting them from the critical examination to which they ought to be subjected. The effect of this reflection is clear: it imparts a greater prestige and authority to those prejudices.

George Steiner observes that meaning in art "can be plain and compelling but untranslatable into another code."[6] Steiner speaks here of music, about whose untranslatability, it seems to me, he is entirely right. But this raises a question: what is the status of a "meaning" that is untranslatable? Further, how can we determine that this "meaning" is true? These are difficult questions. Perhaps it is best to avoid them altogether by the simple expedient of ceasing to speak of the "truth value" of art. This is what Foucault seems to suggest to us. "Madness," he says in *History of Madness*, "is no longer the space of indecision through which it was possible to glimpse the original truth of the work, but the decision beyond which this truth ceases irrevocably" (*HF1*, pp. 642/287 [translation altered]; *HF2*, p. 556). Even more does Derrida call into question the notion of art's truth, as we see in his devastating exposure of the ideological tendencies buried in the truth that Heidegger seeks to extract from van Gogh.

If we must look with suspicion on the notion of the truth of the work of art, we must look with equal suspicion on that of the creative lie, which occupies so important a place in the writings of Nietzsche and Foucault. Indeed, this notion is but a variant of the "truth value" position. It is distinguished from Heidegger's version of that position only by a slightly different twist in the definition of truth. Heidegger tends more to think of truth as already *there*, and only waiting to be actualized by the interpreter. Nietzsche, on the other hand, tends to think of truth as something that is unequivocally fabricated. Schiller distinguishes between aesthetic sem-

blance on the one hand and truth on the other. Rejecting Schiller's distinction between art and truth, Nietzsche rejects his notion of "mere semblance" as well. Art—and language, and interpretation—are indeed
semblance, in Nietzsche's view. But the semblance, far from being opposed to truth, is constitutive of it. The difference between Nietzsche and
Heidegger amounts to a difference of emphasis in their definitions of
truth, with Nietzsche focusing mainly on the creation of truth, and
Heidegger mainly on its supposedly continuous presence.

Just as the "truth value" notion risks reflecting and thus confirming the
interpreter's unexamined prejudices, so also does the notion of the creative lie. All too easy is the neglect or even the dismissal of a natural and
historical reality that ought not to be neglected or dismissed. Consider
again Foucault, the most systematic practitioner of the Nietzschean notion of truth. Foucault's insights most decidedly ought to be put to use,
but only with great circumspection. For if one adopts, in a cavalier and
single-minded fashion, the view that everything is discourse or text or
fiction, the *realia* are trivialized. Real people who really died in the gas
chambers at Auschwitz or Treblinka become so much discourse. Again, I
do not accuse Foucault himself of forgetting that discourse and world are
finally different. I am merely pointing out how easy, and how dangerous,
this kind of misreading is.

With this in mind, we ought to read Foucault, and the prophets of extremity in general, not literally but ironically. We ought to take them not as
guides but as opponents. We ought to view their writings, as we view the
work of the artist, as existing in a state of tension with the given. Foucault,
for example, is most clearly the double of conventional historians, who
challenge, and ought to be challenged by, his work. The same applies to
Nietzsche, who stands as a double to the whole range of conventional
scholarship. Derrida's deconstruction—his brilliant self-parody—helps
bring to light the latent absurdity residing on both sides of this opposition, and thus helps us to see the limitations of each.

In short: we ought to approach aestheticism in a spirit of sympathetic
skepticism. If, upon hearing of the manifest truth of the work of art or of
the textual, fictional character of the world, the reader will let a knowing
smile play upon his face where previously he maintained an attitude of
high seriousness, then the aim of this book will have been in part achieved.
Yet, at the same time, we shouldn't forget the therapeutic intent of these
assertions—their intent to help us break out from a deadening routine,
from the petrification of which Weber warned. The prophets of extremity

put up a distorting mirror against our world—but one which, properly attended to, can tell us something about that world, and about the possibilities of changing it, or changing ourselves.

I have argued extensively in this work that aestheticism is dependent on crisis. The crisis view needs to be approached with the same skeptical attitude that we bring to aestheticism itself. Against the crisis notion, I have deployed a logical argument. I have argued that the notion of a crisis in history presupposes what it sets out to destroy—the idea of history as a continuous process, history with a capital H. Crisis theorists attack the historicist notion of directionality in history. But in postulating a crisis or turning in history, they assume just such a directionality. Hence, to the extent that the proponents of the crisis notion are successful in making their point, they undermine the basis of their own view.

One can also deploy against the crisis notion a rhetorical argument. Currently, the notion of "the crisis of our time" is widely diffused and mindlessly repeated. In its original context, it did serve a useful purpose, whatever its logical weaknesses. It constituted a radical attack on historicism, and on the arrogance and self-satisfaction that historicism sustained and justified. Yet, this context is hardly ours. Historicism is no longer a view seriously articulated (though it continues, I think, to play something of a role in the less articulate levels of American political mythology). In present-day discussion, "the crisis of our time" has become a thought-cliché—an idea that serves as a substitute for, rather than as a stimulus to, thought.[7] It has become a stale platitude, obscuring more layers of reality, more aspects of experience, than it reveals. It brings not the shock of unfamiliarity but the comfort of recognition. Nietzsche, Heidegger, Foucault, and company are essentially therapeutic thinkers, as we have seen. This brings with it its own limitation. A therapeutic thinker, by definition, seeks to attack received ideas, to demolish previous platitudes. But what happens when he has succeeded in this task—when the hated platitudes have all been driven out? Where is his new mission to be found? How are we to read these writers then?

Finally, one can deploy against the crisis notion a third, pragmatic argument. Briefly: let's suppose that there *is* a "crisis of our time." And let's suppose, moreover, that this crisis is the same crisis of belief and authority that our prophets speak of. The question that then needs to be posed is: what difference does it make? It is my argument that it makes no difference whatsoever—at least not a helpful difference. Professors are being mugged in Manhattan, reliable household help is hard to find, wars are continually breaking out, and the world generally is in a sorry state. Quite possibly these facts have nothing to do with the death of God, the crisis of values, the eclipse of authority, or the breaking of the tradition. And even if they *are* connected with these supposed events, the question remains what the practical significance of this connection would be.

What are we supposed to do about the death of God, the crisis of values, the eclipse of authority? And how exactly would any action that we might take on these fronts have an effect on the practical difficulties of our political and social life? The problem with the crisis notion, from a pragmatic point of view, is that whether or not these difficulties are related to the crisis, they have causes of a more immediate sort that are in all likelihood far more amenable to improvement than is the supposed crisis of values or belief. The problem with the crisis notion is that it can only speak in vague generalities. It does not properly address concrete cases. In fact, it tends to obscure concrete cases—in the same way that Heidegger allowed his vision of the "National Socialist Movement" to be obscured in 1933.

Concerning crisis, one further point needs to be made. I have attacked the crisis notion in this study. Yet, I am well aware that there is one sense in which crisis is more disturbingly real at this time than at any time in the past. For it is clear that human history could indeed come to an end. It could do so with frightening speed and viciousness. The "end of history" is a practical possibility: the technology that would bring about such an end is already in place. Nietzsche, Heidegger, and Foucault are all believers in the apocalypse. At any rate, they project a reasonable facsimile of such a belief. Unfortunately, such prophecies have a tendency toward self-fulfillment. Heidegger's conviction that only a god can save us is hardly calculated to help us evade the crisis of which he speaks; Foucault's belief in unending protest—his hostility to every order—may only move us closer to disaster.

In short, I see the crisis notion itself as a danger. I have already noted that Nietzsche and Heidegger are better seen as post-Christian than as anti-Christian thinkers, a point that I made in connection with their commitment to the creativity of art. But if the notion of radical creativity is a Christian notion, so also is that of crisis and apocalypse. The crisis of the City of Man—its destruction, making way for the City of God—is an important part of the Christian myth. At some times it has been more emphasized than at others. It has received much emphasis recently among American religious fundamentalists. Some of these fundamentalists give a quite precise political interpretation to the apocalypse that they envisage. The apocalypse means an all-out war between the forces of Good and the forces of Evil. The war is imminent. What's more, it is to be welcomed: for it heralds the Coming. The possibility of nuclear destruction is thus transformed into a herald of salvation. I am not holding Nietzsche or Heidegger or Foucault responsible for the presence of such views. I am merely pointing out that these thinkers are fascinated by crisis. They are fascinated by crisis because they see therein the possibility, or at least the vision, of something better than the degraded present. But for those who do not believe that the present is so utterly degraded, or who lack a faith in the cleansing power of crisis, there ought to be a compulsion to actively oppose the crisis notion.

Yet, this does not mean that we ought to reject the prophets of extremity. For we do live in an age of uncertainty. For many of us, this uncertainty is more appealing than the self-satisfaction of historicism. As historical actors, we barely know the shape of the world in which we act; and while it is an error to glorify this ignorance, it is surely no error to recognize it. Crisis, for all its faults, is perhaps the best metaphor for inculcating a sense of this uncertainty. Moreover, closely connected with the notion of crisis in these thinkers is their attack on the primacy of literal truth. In attacking the primacy of literal truth, they are attacking the notion that there is "One True Way"—a single truth privileged above all other truths. This connects with their role as artist-philosophers, for they follow modern artists in seeking to widen our imaginations, in seeking to open us up to multiple possibilities. Nietzsche and his successors call literality into question, returning us to a situation where there is no longer a single literal truth, a privileged meaning to which all other meanings point.

I find this a supremely important development. It is a development that ties in very closely with what seems to be the most compelling reality in modern history—namely, the existence of weapons of such massive destructive capacity that their use would quite possibly mean the destruction of civilization itself. If we have any commitment to that civilization— and it is hard to know how we cannot be committed to that of which we are the products—then we ought to look with suspicion on the notion of a single, privileged way. For the notion that there is "One True Way" clearly works as an exclusion of those who do not adhere to the way. It tends to reduce them to a position beneath contempt. It leads to a distinction between the Chosen and the Unchosen—or, in Levinas's terminology (taken up by Foucault and Derrida), to a distinction between the Same and the Other. Such a work of exclusion is perhaps bearable when the community that is being excluded does not have the power to destroy the community that is doing the excluding—and vice versa. At least in these cases something will survive. But when each community has the capacity to destroy the other, the situation changes radically. Here total destruction becomes a real possibility.

The thinkers whom we have considered in this book remind us that there are compelling reasons for disbelieving in the One True Way. Note how the historicism against which Nietzsche and his successors reacted was Europocentric and Americanocentric in its bias. Xenophobia and historicism are close companions. The movement of history in a given direction excludes all other movements, making Europe or America or some other chosen entity the culmination of history in general. By implication, this endpoint becomes the model for all social, political, and intellectual orders. The One True History and the One True Way go together. Against such views, Nietzsche and Heidegger—and, in a more engaged and immediate fashion, Foucault and Derrida—must be seen as struggling. As critics of such a way, they are of immense importance. Yet, paradoxically, it is our task as readers to creatively oppose their works, lest they, too, be seen as inculcating a privileged truth.

I end with a reflection on my own stance as a commentator and historian. I find it necessary to do so for reasons that I hope will be obvious to my readers. For the prophets of extremity call radically into question all claims to objectivity, all conventional logic. While they are certainly not irrational thinkers, they are not rational thinkers either. They are perhaps best seen as writing from some sort of "nonrational" stance. This makes trouble for the commentator. Were I dealing with conventionally rational thinkers, I would be able to avoid questioning my own stance, for I would share that stance with the objects of my commentary. There would thus be a continuity of assumptions linking us, and a resulting continuity between exegesis and critique. But as I pointed out at the beginning, such a continuity does not exist here. I have clearly not engaged in the tactic of "immanent critique," practiced by Schleiermacher, Ranke, Dilthey, and their successors, where the critique of an author claims to come out of the author's own assumptions. Nor, for that matter, have I engaged in the other, external type of critique, which appeals not to authors' assumptions but to the presumably universal canons of rationality. Both hermeneutics (in its Romantic, not its Rortyan sense) and the opposing "positivistic" approach seem inadequate for coming to grips with Nietzsche, Heidegger, Foucault, and Derrida. They seem inadequate because they avoid confronting the main question at issue—namely, the status of conventional rationality. It is my argument that Nietzsche, Heidegger,

Foucault, and Derrida, as therapeutic thinkers, need to be read in tension with the conventional rationality that they attack. Unfortunately, the latter-day Diltheyan adopts for his own the aestheticism of these writers, while the "positivist" critic comes armed with the buckler of "normal" logic. On the one hand, the prophets of extremity are seen as speaking an uncompromised truth, while on the other they are seen as spreading lies. In both instances, the whole point of the polemic (of which the prophets of extremity are one pole) is lost.

Perhaps the reader will better understand what I am getting at if I note the difficulties that I had in approaching Derrida. To be sure, I had difficulties of an almost identical sort with Nietzsche, Heidegger, and Foucault. I do not want to single out Derrida as greatly different from the other three. Nonetheless, the difficulties are more obvious with Derrida than with the others. For it is possible to find ways of evading the aestheticism of Nietzsche, Heidegger, and Foucault. It is possible to view Nietzsche as a protoexistentialist, Heidegger as a phenomenologist, and Foucault as a peculiar sort of neopositivist. Elements of these positions are present in these writers, and can easily be emphasized at the expense of their aestheticism. But it is difficult to treat Derrida in this way. He seems *sui generis,* unconnected with any such tradition as existentialism or phenomenology or neopositivism. Moreover, whereas the other three thinkers display a logic of sorts—admittedly, a kind of nonlogical logic— in working out their positions, Derrida seems to tear logic to pieces. In consequence, I could not evade the extremity of Derrida's thought, whereas I might have been able to evade the extremity of the other three.

In my early attempts to write on Derrida, I mentally classified the trouble that I was having in dealing with him under the heading of the "inside/ outside" problem. On the one hand, I seemed to have the choice of writing about him from "inside" his own perspective—or at least from a point *claiming* to be inside his perspective. In writing such a commentary, I would employ Derrida's language and categories. On disputed points, I would appeal to Derrida's authority. My definitions would come from Derrida, and I would allow him to decide which issues were important and which not. But such a style of commentary would have raised serious problems. In the first place, a commentary written in that style would have been all but incomprehensible to anyone outside the band of Derrida's disciples. To repeat Derrida is obviously not to explain him. Secondly, there would have been no clear sense of the purpose of such a commentary. Surely, if a commentary merely repeats Derrida, the reader interested in Derrida would be better off reading Derrida himself. And finally, despite appearances, such a commentary would not be "faithful" to Derrida. Taking up a stance close to that of classical hermeneutics—a stance that Derrida, obviously, rejects—it would completely miss that element of playful infidelity that is so important an aspect of his enterprise.

On the other hand, I seemed to have the choice of writing about Derrida from "outside" his perspective. Not many people have attempted this, for if one is "outside" the Derridean perspective, one is unlikely to find enough merit in his writings to make them seem worthy of commentary. Still, such an approach to Derrida is at least a possibility. Yet, this approach, too, simply does not work. Adopting a "normal" perspective on Derrida, one inevitably misrepresents what he is doing, for one attempts to make his categories conform to the categories of "normal" thought. Moreover, one begs the question again, for it is precisely the categories of "normal" thought that Derrida is concerned to attack. And the same problem arises, though in a somewhat less obvious way, when it is a matter of dealing with Nietzsche, Heidegger, and Foucault. I seemed constitutionally incapable of becoming a disciple, yet on the other hand I could not operate out of the confident standards of rationality (essentially: Enlightenment standards) that I found so many deploying against these thinkers.

Rejecting both discipleship and outright opposition, I found myself weaving a line between the two. This was a strategy adopted *faute de mieux,* not one whose rationale I was able to think out in advance. And yet, I did eventually discover a rationale for it. It is a rationale that arises out of the rhetorical situation that these writers willy-nilly have brought into being. Perhaps it is simplest to speak of Nietzsche in this regard, but what I say of Nietzsche also applies to the other three. Nietzsche privileges himself as an artist-philosopher: this is the persona that, for better or for worse, he creates for himself. Nietzsche's experience is the "extraordinary" experience of Zarathustra on his mountaintop; it is the experience of the artist liberated from all mundane constraints. Yet, in adopting the persona of the artist-philosopher, Nietzsche *demands* an audience. This audience is necessarily made up of us folks here—living in the "ordinary" world, earning money, raising families, catching buses, experiencing pleasure/leisure of various sorts, and undergoing the vagaries of nature. And what do we do when Nietzsche confronts us? Do we wander off in search of mountaintops for ourselves? Or, before thinking of doing this, do we not try to understand what Nietzsche is saying? I believe that we try—or at least that we ought to try—to understand what he is saying. And this is exactly what I have sought to do. My discussion of Nietzsche and his successors is based on the premise that the stance that these writers have adopted requires such an effort of understanding.

My leaps from exegesis to criticism are dictated by their own insistence that *we* be their audience. Note the peculiar position that these writers occupy. There is a radical dissonance in what they do. They are playful (and sometimes somber) ironists, making a dance out of the problems that we confront in the "ordinary" world, transforming these problems into the material of art. The adherents of science and method—those who follow in the tradition of the Enlightenment—cultivate a distance between their allegedly objective scientific stance and the passions motivating the world. Despite their opposition to science and method, the prophets of extremity do the same thing, for only out of *aesthetic* distance does their art become possible. When they ravel and unravel the myriad ironies of discourse, they are as distant from morality and suffering as the supreme rationalist. Zarathustra's withdrawal to the mountaintop is paradigmatic of the prophecy of extremity in general. The "authority" of Heidegger and Foucault is of a similar kind to Nietzsche's. In short, as a kind of compounded irony, the prophets of extremity fall victim to the same distancing that they criticize (above all, in the guise of the subject/ object division) in "normal" science. The task of the commentator becomes that of trying to span this distance—for, after all, the prophets of extremity do demand that it be spanned. Yet, the distance is so great that I cannot hope to act as a transparent translator, conveying unchanged what Nietzsche and his successors said and meant. Any such translation would be just as mystifying as the original it seeks to translate. I have tried, rather, to nimbly negotiate their project, exploring its nooks and crannies and getting at its general shape—knowing all the while that I cannot any more convey their project than I can hope to move a mountain from one place to another.

The present work is in the first instance a work of history, not a work of criticism—though I hold it as axiomatic that the two cannot be separated. I have sought to display both aestheticism and the crisis notion that makes aestheticism possible. I have done so in the hope of encouraging intelligent discussion of a highly significant perspective. I have advanced certain critical views of my own, but I have seen this as subordinate to the task of unveiling the perspective itself. For this I see as the historian's task: to bring important but obscure happenings to the eyes of the public.

Notes

Introduction

1. Alasdair MacIntyre, *After Virtue: A Study in Moral Theory* (Notre Dame, Ind.: Notre Dame University Press, 1981), especially pp. 49–75. For an earlier attempt to deal with this theme, see Judith N. Shklar, *After Utopia: The Decline of Political Faith* (Princeton: Princeton University Press, 1957), pp. 3–25.

2. Stanley Rosen, *Nihilism: A Philosophical Essay* (New Haven: Yale University Press, 1969), pp. xvii, 39, 67, 74, 81, 104, 106–107, and 126–127.

3. Ibid., p. 81.

4. The best-known exponent of this view is Arthur O. Lovejoy, "On the Discrimination of Romanticisms," in his *Essays in the History of Ideas* (Baltimore: Johns Hopkins University Press, 1948), pp. 228–253.

5. Leonard Krieger, *Kings and Philosophers, 1689–1789* (New York: Norton, 1970), pp. 208–228.

6. Erich Auerbach, *Introduction to Romance Languages and Literature: Latin, French, Spanish, Provençal, Italian,* trans. Guy Daniels (New York: Capricorn Books, 1961), p. 237.

7. Georg Lukács, *The Destruction of Reason,* trans. Peter Palmer (Atlantic Highlands, N.J.: Humanities Press, 1981), pp. 95–305. See especially pp. 151–155.

8. Ernst Behler, "Nietzsche und die Frühromantische Schule," *Nietzsche-Studien,* 7 (1978), 59–96. See especially pp. 60–64 and 72–87.

9. Behler discusses Nietzsche's "image of Romanticism," in ibid., pp. 64–70.

10. Benjamin Bennett, "Nietzsche's Idea of Myth: The Birth of Tragedy out of the Spirit of Eighteenth-Century Aesthetics," *PMLA,* 94 (1979), 427.

11. Wilhelm Windelband, *A History of Philosophy,* trans. James H. Tufts (New York: Macmillan, 1901), p. 530.

12. John T. Wilcox, *Truth and Value in Nietzsche: A Study of His Metaethics and Epistemology* (Ann Arbor: University of Michigan Press, 1974), pp. 98–126.

13. William Wordsworth, *The Prelude, or Growth of a Poet's Mind,* ed. Ernest de Selincourt, 2nd edition, revised by Helen Darbishire (Oxford: Clarendon Press, 1959), Book XI, p. 419, lines 301, 305.

14. Immanuel Kant, *Critique of Judgment,* trans. J. H. Bernard (New York: Hafner, 1972), Introduction, sect. II, p. 12.

15. Ibid., §57, p. 185.

16. Ibid., §59, pp. 198–199.

17. Ibid., §49, p. 157; §57 Remark I, p. 187.

18. Richard Kroner, *Von Kant bis Hegel,* 2nd edition (2 vols. in 1; Tübingen: J. C. B. Mohr [Paul Siebeck], 1961), Vol. II, p. 46.

19. Friedrich Schiller, *On the Aesthetic Education of Man in a Series of Letters*, ed. and trans. Elizabeth Wilkinson and L. A. Willoughby (Oxford: Clarendon Press, 1967), letter 6, §§2–6, pp. 31–35.

20. Ibid., letters 12 and 13, pp. 79–93.

21. Ibid., letter 15, §1, p. 101.

22. Ibid., letter 10, §4, p. 65.

23. Ibid., letter 26, §5, p. 193.

24. Ibid., letter 26, §9, p. 197.

25. Ibid., letter 26, §10, p. 197.

26. See Hölderlin's letter to Schiller of September 4, 1795: "I seek to develop the idea of an unending progress of philosophy, I seek to show that the insistent demand that must be made of every system, namely, that it should unite subject and object in an absolute—Ego, or whatever one wants to call it—is indeed possible aesthetically, through intellectual intuition, but theoretically it is possible only through an endless approximation" (Friedrich Hölderlin, *Sämtliche Werke*, 7 vols. [Stuttgart: Cotta, 1943–77], Vol. VI, pp. 196–197).

27. On the much-debated question of authorship, see especially Otto Pöggeler, "Hegel, Der Verfasser des Ältesten Systemsprogramms des deutschen Idealismus," *Hegel-Studien*, Beiheft 4 ("Urbino Hegel-Tage 1965: Vorträge," ed. Hans-Georg Gadamer), (Bonn: Bouvier, 1969), pp. 17–32; and H. S. Harris, *Hegel's Development Toward the Sunlight, 1770–1801* (Oxford: Clarendon Press, 1972), pp. 249–257.

28. The German original of the "Earliest Systematic Program" is conveniently available in Georg Wilhelm Friedrich Hegel, *Werke*, 20 vols., ed. Eva Moldenhauer and Karl Markus Michel (Frankfurt am Main: Suhrkamp, 1970–71), Vol. I, pp. 234–236. I quote from Harris's translation of this document, in *Toward the Sunlight*, pp. 510–512.

29. Friedrich Wilhelm Joseph von Schelling, *System des transzendentalen Idealismus*, in *Werke*, 6 vols., ed. Manfred Schröter (Munich: Beck, 1956–60), Vol. II, p. 349.

30. Ibid., p. 370.

31. Ibid., p. 617.

32. Ibid., p. 625.

33. Ibid., pp. 627–628.

34. Ibid., p. 629.

35. Friedrich Schlegel, *"Dialogue on Poetry" and "Literary Aphorisms,"* ed. and trans. Ernst Behler and Roman Struc (University Park: Pennsylvania State University Press, 1968), §§116, 125, pp. 140–141.

36. J. P. Stern, *Nietzsche* (London: Fontana, 1978), pp. 144–146.

37. See, on this point, Ricarda Huch, *Die Blüthezeit der Romantik* (Leipzig: Haessel, 1899), pp. 83–118.

38. M. H. Abrams, *Natural Supernaturalism: Tradition and Revolution in Romantic Literature* (New York: Norton, 1971), p. 413.

39. Ibid., p. 139.

40. Ibid., especially pp. 91–92, 125, 150–154, 179, and 190–195.

41. J. Hillis Miller, "Tradition and Difference" (review of M. H. Abrams, *Natural Supernaturalism*), *Diacritics*, 2 (Winter 1972), 11.

42. Abrams, *Natural Supernaturalism*, pp. 316–318.

43. As Philippe Lacoue-Labarthe comes close to doing in his *Sujet de la philosophie (Typographies 1)* (Paris: Aubier-Flammarion, 1979), pp. 93–99.

44. Hans-Georg Gadamer, *Truth and Method* (New York: Continuum, 1975), p. xvii.

45. Ibid., p. 263.

46. The classic work on this Romantic theme is Jean Starobinski, *Jean-Jacques Rousseau: la transparence et l'obstacle* (Paris: Plon, 1957).

47. Gadamer, *Truth and Method*, p. xix. See also p. 263.

48. For Kant's discussion of genius, see *Critique of Judgment*, §§46–50, pp. 150–164.

49. Gadamer, *Truth and Method*, p. 38.

50. Ibid., p. 362.

51. Hans-Georg Gadamer, "Aesthetics and Hermeneutics" (1964), in his *Philosophical Hermeneutics*, ed. and trans. David E. Linge (Berkeley and Los Angeles: University of California Press, 1976), pp. 95–96.

Chapter 1

1. Walter Kaufmann, *Nietzsche: Philosopher, Psychologist, Antichrist,* 4th edition (Princeton: Princeton University Press, 1974). I write the present essay in the margins of Kaufmann's Nietzsche interpretation. Because Kaufmann lends himself so well to my polemical purposes and tactical needs, I am entirely explicit about this in the body of the essay. I write also in the margins of Paul de Man's very different Nietzsche interpretation. Alas, I have found it impossible to unravel de Man's writings on Nietzsche without tangling my readers in de Man's skein. Since I aim to write on Nietzsche, not on de Man, I have had to let the reference to de Man remain largely implicit. In a sense, de Man elides the movement from Nietzsche to Derrida that I am concerned in this book to elucidate. This limits his value for my purposes. But interested readers may consult Paul de Man, *Allegories of Reading: Figural Language in Rousseau, Nietzsche, Rilke, and Proust* (New Haven: Yale University Press, 1979), especially pp. 79–131. For a similarly derrideanized reading of Nietzsche, see Rudolf E. Kuenzli, "Nietzsche's Zerography: *Thus Spoke Zarathustra,*" *Boundary 2,* 9:3 and 10:1 (Spring/Fall 1981), 99–117.

2. For an exploration of this and other striking affinities between Nietzsche and earlier, Romantic writers, see (briefly) my Introduction and (at greater length) Ernst Behler's "Nietzsche und die Frühromantische Schule," *Nietzsche-Studien,* 7 (1978), 59–96. I am not here concerned with *Quellenkritik,* and I cannot pursue the Romantic connection in detail. But whatever the precise lines of influence, it is clear that many of Nietzsche's ideas concerning art and myth bear a close resemblance to things that were being said, circa 1795–1800, by the Schlegels, Schelling, Novalis, and other early German Romantic writers—and there are more general, family resemblances with Romanticism considered in a broader sense. My argument, nonetheless, is that there is a break between Nietzsche and the Romantics. His thought finally escapes a Romantic framework because, unlike the Romantics, he is committed to the notion of a radical cultural crisis or (what is the same) to the notion of the absolutely derelict character of the present.

3. Nietzsche, *Ecce Homo,* Preface, §4: "Among my writings my *Zarathustra* stands to my mind by itself. With that I have given mankind the greatest present that has ever been made to it so far. This book, with a voice bridging centuries, is not only the highest book there is, the book that is truly characterized by the air of the heights—the whole of man lies *beneath* it at a tremendous distance—it is also the *deepest,* born out of the innermost wealth of truth." See also, on Zarathustra as poet, *Thus Spoke Zarathustra,* Part I, "Of Poets," p. 149.

4. Maurice Blanchot, "Nietzsche et l'écriture fragmentaire," in his *Entretien infini* (Paris: Gallimard, 1969), p. 244.

5. On Nietzsche's "extensive" use of the concept of art, see Arthur C. Danto, *Nietzsche as Philosopher* (New York: Macmillan, 1967), pp. 44–45; on his general penchant for using words simultaneously in both a narrow and a wide context, see ibid., pp. 11–12. While, as Kaufmann has pointed out (*Nietzsche,* p. 359n), Danto's book is flawed by some elementary linguistic and philological deficiencies, and while he also wrongly imagines that the Nietzschean corpus is a collection of discrete fragments that "may be read in pretty much any order, without this greatly impeding the comprehension of his ideas" (Danto, *Nietzsche as Philosopher,* p. 19), on some important points of interpretation, such as here, on art and on language, Danto hits the mark.

6. On Blanchot and Heidegger, see Geoffrey H. Hartman, "Maurice Blanchot: Philosopher-Novelist," in his *Beyond Formalism: Literary Essays, 1958–1970* (New Haven: Yale University Press, 1970), pp. 97–103.

7. Cf. the preface (written in the spring of 1886) to Part I of *Human, All-Too-Human,* where Nietzsche tells us that "life . . . *demands* illusion, it lives by illusion" (*Human, All-Too-Human,* Part I, §1, p. 3).

8. I depend, for the contrast between an early, modernist Nietzsche and the later postmodernist, on Frank Lentricchia's suggestive comments in his *After the New Criticism* (Chicago: University of Chicago Press, 1979), pp. 42, 55, 58–59. I discuss modernism and postmodernism more extensively in the later parts of this book.

9. As Kaufmann has shown, the apparent reference to the Apollonian in *The Gay Science*, §370, is an illicit insertion by Nietzsche's editors. See Kaufmann, *Nietzsche*, p. 375*n;* and Nietzsche, *The Gay Science*, p. 330*n.*

10. I base this conclusion on *Twilight of the Idols,* "Expeditions of an Untimely Man," §§8–10, pp. 71–73, where "intoxication" (*Rausch*) is seen as the psychological precondition for art, with the Apollonian and Dionysian being reduced to two types of intoxication; and on the fragment "Zur Physiologie der Kunst," in *Gesammelte Werke, Musarionausgabe,* Vol. XVII, p. 355. These references date from 1888. For a number of other late references to the Apollonian, see *The Will to Power,* §798 (March–June 1888), §1049 (1885–86), and §1050 (March–June 1888) (*Werke: Kritische Gesamtausgabe,* 8. Abt., 3. Bd., pp. 27–28, 16–17). In the last of these references, the Apollonian/Dionysian distinction does seem to take on something approaching its former scope, but I do not think that this fragment can legitimately be said to outweigh the all but total disappearance of the Apollonian from Nietzsche's later writings. For more on this point, see the following note.

11. A simple quantitative confirmation. Oehler's index to the chronologically ordered *Musarionausgabe* gives ninety-six references to the Apollonian in the first nine volumes (incorporating Nietzsche's writings up to 1879), and only nine references to the Apollonian thereafter. Many of the former references are to multiple pages; all of the latter to one page only. In contrast, there are still fifty-two references to the Dionysian after Volume IX, compared to seventy-six up to Volume IX.

12. Kaufmann, *Nietzsche*, p. 129. For the conflict between Dionysus and "the Crucified," see *Ecce Homo,* "Why I am a Destiny," §9, in *Basic Writings,* p. 791; and *The Will to Power,* §1052 (*Werke: Kritische Gesamtausgabe,* 8. Abt., 3. Bd., pp. 57–59).

13. As is pointed out by, among others, Tracy B. Strong, *Friedrich Nietzsche and the Politics of Transfiguration* (Berkeley and Los Angeles: University of California Press, 1975), p. 315, note 62; and Werner J. Dannhauser, *Nietzsche's View of Socrates* (Ithaca: Cornell University Press, 1974), pp. 39–40.

14. Maurice Mandelbaum, *History, Man, and Reason: A Study in Nineteenth-Century Thought* (Baltimore: Johns Hopkins University Press, 1971), p. 349.

15. Ibid., p. 350. Mandelbaum's concern is with epistemology. For a discussion of literary (and ontological) aspects of this theme, see Geoffrey H. Hartman, *The Unmediated Vision: An Interpretation of Wordsworth, Rilke, and Valéry* (New Haven: Yale University Press, 1954), especially pp. 127–173.

16. He refers to it by title in the preface that he added to Part II of *Human, All-Too-Human* in 1886, citing it as evidence that already in that period he believed "in nothing at all any more." See *Human, All-Too-Human,* Part II, Preface, §1, p. 2.

17. The translation of this work included in the Levy edition is inadequate, and I have had repeatedly to make alterations in quoting from it. For a better translation (though I still prefer my corrected rendering of the Levy text), see Friedrich Nietzsche, *Philosophy and Truth: Selections from Nietzsche's Notebooks of the Early 1870's,* ed. and trans. Daniel Breazeale (Atlantic Highlands, N.J.: Humanities Press, 1979), pp. 77–79. Breazeale also includes translations of Nietzsche's notes for a projected continuation of "On Truth and Lie." For the German original, see *Werke: Kritische Gesamtausgabe,* 2. Abt., 2. Bd., pp. 367–391.

18. Friedrich Nietzsche, "On the Uses and Disadvantages of History for Life," chap. 1, in his *Untimely Meditations,* trans. R. J. Hollingdale, with an introduction by J. P. Stern (Cambridge: Cambridge University Press, 1983), pp. 60–61.

19. To casual readers of Nietzsche, this commitment to immediacy will be most evident in his account of morality. Take, for example, that striking passage in *The Genealogy of Morals,* First Essay, §11, where he speaks of those free, uncomplicated nobles who, in dealing with those outside their community, "go *back* to the innocent conscience of the beast of prey, as triumphant monsters who perhaps emerge from a disgusting procession of murder, arson, rape, and torture, exhilarated and undisturbed of soul, as if it were no more than a students' prank" (Nietzsche, *Basic Writings,* p. 476). What Nietzsche finds good about this behavior is precisely that it is immediate, that it involves no structure of justification but is simply a question of spontaneous and presumably authentic action. See also, in the Second Essay, §11 (*Basic Writings,* p. 511), the important distinction between the "active" and the

"reactive," and the declaration, in *The Will to Power,* §430, that "as the soldier exercises, so should man learn to act. In fact, this unconsciousness belongs to any kind of perfection" (*Werke: Kritische Gesamtausgabe,* 8. Abt., 3. Bd., p. 80).

20. See, for example, Georg Wilhelm Friedrich Hegel, *Phenomenology of Spirit,* trans. A. V. Miller, with an analysis and foreword by J. N. Findlay (Oxford: Clarendon Press, 1977), Preface, §§7, 10, pp. 4–5, 6.

21. And *Zarathustra* can be viewed as a counter to Hegel's *Phenomenology*—as is pointed out by Strong, *Friedrich Nietzsche and the Politics of Transfiguration,* p. 332, note 25.

22. Strong, *Friedrich Nietzsche and the Politics of Transfiguration,* p. 262.

23. Harold Alderman, *Nietzsche's Gift* (Athens: Ohio University Press, 1977), pp. 14, 18. Alderman's book, incidentally, is the only commentary of which I am aware that faces up to the absolute centrality of *Zarathustra* for the whole Nietzschean enterprise. Though Alderman declares that his book is "only a recommendation . . . to read Nietzsche in a certain way" (p. 13), it seems to me that it is more than this—that it is in some important respects *correct* in its reading of Nietzsche. Not the least of its merits is that it emphasizes, contra Heidegger himself, "the important *formal* identity" between Heidegger's and Nietzsche's work (p. 171; more generally, pp. 164–173). In this, it manages to give a genuinely Heideggerian interpretation of Nietzsche, which Heidegger does not. My only objection to the book (albeit a major one) is that it is insufficiently critical regarding its own Nietzschean and Heideggerian presuppositions.

24. Hence, the importance of "initiation" for Nietzsche's enterprise—as also for the enterprises of Heidegger and Foucault. As Alderman puts it, "the teaching of eternal recurrence is the culminating movement of Nietzsche's philosophy. It is only by making the affirmation demanded by this teaching that we become fully initiated into Nietzsche's perspective. Only with this initiation can we come to understand the epiphanous roles of laughter, dance, and song" (*Nietzsche's Gift,* p. 17). But one question is left unanswered: why accept the initiation in the first place?

25. Danto, *Nietzsche as Philosopher,* pp. 231–232.

Chapter 2

1. On the art-myth connection in the early Nietzsche, see Benjamin Bennett, "Nietzsche's Idea of Myth: The Birth of Tragedy out of the Spirit of Eighteenth-Century Aesthetics," *PMLA,* 94 (1979), 420–433. Bennett is right, it seems to me, in seeing that Nietzsche's idea of myth belongs to "the history of aesthetics, as a direct development of eighteenth-century thinking on the phenomenon of artistic illusion" (p. 420).

2. I return to Nietzsche's critique of vision in my discussion of structuralism-as-metaphysics in the Foucault essay, below. For another, somewhat elusive pursuit of this theme, see Richard Rorty, *Philosophy and the Mirror of Nature* (Princeton: Princeton University Press, 1979), pp. 11, 13, 38–39, 371, and passim.

3. Friedrich Nietzsche, *Daybreak: Thoughts on the Prejudices of Morality,* trans. R. J. Hollingdale, with an introduction by Michael Tanner (Cambridge: Cambridge University Press, 1982), §448.

4. A contrast emphasized by Tracy B. Strong, *Friedrich Nietzsche and the Politics of Transfiguration* (Berkeley and Los Angeles: University of California Press, 1975), p. 181.

5. See, most importantly, "David Strauss, The Confessor and the Writer" (1873), chap. 2, the first of his *Untimely Meditations,* trans. R. J. Hollingdale, with an introduction by J. P. Stern (Cambridge: Cambridge University Press, 1983), p. 10, where Nietzsche refers to "the brew of fantastic and language-twisting philosophies and tendentious historiographies, a carnival of all the gods and myths, which the Romantics had mixed together." Ernst Behler's discussion of how we ought to take such statements is indispensable. See again his "Nietzsche und die frühromantische Schule," *Nietzsche-Studien,* 7 (1978), 64–70.

6. Nietzsche, "On the Uses and Disadvantages of History for Life," chap. 7, in his *Untimely Meditations,* p. 96.

7. Walter Kaufmann, *Nietzsche: Philosopher, Psychologist, Antichrist,* 4th edition (Princeton: Princeton University Press, 1974), p. 27.

8. Ibid., pp. 140–141.

9. Friedrich Wilhelm Joseph von Schelling, *The Ages of the World,* ed. and trans. Frederick de Wolfe Bolman, Jr. (New York: Columbia University Press, 1942, pp. 84, 91. On the parallel between Schelling's project and Nietzsche's, see Philippe Lacoue-Labarthe, *Sujet de la philosophie (Typographies 1)* (Paris: Aubier-Flammarion, 1979), pp. 93–99. Here Nietzsche's Romantic connection—and Heidegger's strange refusal to acknowledge those connections—are importantly, if elliptically, canvassed.

10. Paul de Man, "Genesis and Genealogy," in his *Allegories of Reading: Figural Language in Rousseau, Nietzsche, Rilke, and Proust* (New Haven: Yale University Press, 1979), especially pp. 93–101.

11. Nietzsche, "On the Uses and Disadvantages of History for Life," chap. 10, in *Untimely Meditations,* p. 116.

12. Friedrich Nietzsche, "Richard Wagner in Bayreuth," chap. 8, in *Untimely Meditations,* p. 230.

13. Ibid., chap. 9, pp. 236–237.

14. Ibid., chap. 4, p. 209.

15. Nietzsche, "Entwürfe und Gedanken zu den unausgeführten Theilen des Zarathustra," in *Werke,* Vol. XII, p. 400.

16. Nietzsche uses the terms "return" (*Wiederkehr*) and "recurrence" (*Wiederkunft*) "more or less interchangeably," as Joan Stambaugh points out in *Nietzsche's Thought of Eternal Return* (Baltimore: Johns Hopkins University Press, 1972), p. 29.

17. See Allan Megill, "Martin Heidegger and the Metapolitics of Crisis," in John S. Nelson, ed., *What Should Political Theory Be Now?* (Albany: State University of New York Press, 1983), especially pp. 303–304.

18. A number of the *Nachlass* fragments do, however, deal with it; see especially *The Will to Power,* §§1053–1067, pp. 544–550.

19. Kaufmann, *Nietzsche,* p. 323.

20. Michel Foucault, "Nietzsche, Marx, Freud," in Colloque de Royaumont, *Cahiers, philosophie* no. 6, *Nietzsche* (Paris: Minuit, 1966), pp. 183–200. I discuss this essay in the section of Chapter 6 entitled "Depth and interpretation."

21. On the relationship between "rationalism" and "cognitivism," see John T. Wilcox, *Truth and Value in Nietzsche: A Study of His Metaethics and Epistemology* (Ann Arbor: University of Michigan Press, 1974), pp. 11–13. I note here that Wilcox's book is concerned with the nature of Nietzsche's metaethics and not with his view of interpretation *per se.* Nonetheless, the two problems are closely related.

22. Ibid., p. 98.

23. Ibid., pp. 6–7.

24. Ibid., p. 201.

25. Ibid., p. 124.

26. Ibid., pp. 224, 226.

27. See, for example, Nietzsche, *The Anti-Christ,* §52, in *"Twilight of the Idols" and "The Anti-Christ,"* p. 69: "Another mark of the theologian is his *incapacity for philology.* Philology is to be understood here in a very wide sense as the art of reading well—of being able to read off a fact *without* falsifying it by interpretation [*Interpretation*]...." Cf. *The Will to Power,* §479: "to be able to read off a text as a text without interposing an interpretation [*Interpretation*] is the last-developed form of 'inner experience'—perhaps one that is hardly possible——" (*Werke: Kritische Gesamtausgabe,* 8. Abt., 3. Bd., p. 254). It is undoubtedly significant that the particular "thing" that is here being interpreted is a "text"—that is, an object produced by human will, and presumably also accessible to it.

28. See also *Beyond Good and Evil,* §4, where utility and truth are likewise distinguished: "the falseness of a judgment is for us not necessarily an objection to a judgment.... The question is to what extent it is life-promoting, life-preserving, species-preserving, perhaps even species-cultivating." For other passages of similar bearing, see Kaufmann, *Nietzsche,* p. 356. See also Maurice Mandelbaum, *History, Man, and Reason: A Study in Nineteenth-Century Thought* (Baltimore: Johns Hopkins University Press, 1971), pp. 340–341, which deals clearly and succinctly with this point.

29. Nietzsche, *Daybreak,* §119, p. 120.

30. Nietzsche, *The Gay Science,* "Joke, Cunning, and Revenge," §44: "Ein Forscher Ich? O spart dies Wort!—/Ich bin nur schwer—so manche Pfund!/Ich falle, falle immerfort/ Und endlich auf den Grund!"

31. To be sure, in "On Truth and Lie" and also in *The Birth of Tragedy,* Nietzsche does not yet acknowledge, or acknowledges only imperfectly, the radically "creationist" tendency of his own position. See again, for example, the passage quoted from "On Truth and Lie" above, where Nietzsche seems quite clearly to want to say that there *are* "trees, colours, snow, and flowers" independent of our perception of them, and where he treats object and subject as "absolutely distinct spheres" rather than the former as a "modus" of the latter. As Wilcox points out (*Truth and Value in Nietzsche,* p. 114), Nietzsche tends to move from "the Kantian position that there is a thing-in-itself, through a period of doubt about whether there is any thing-in-itself, toward the conclusion that the very concept of the thing-in-itself is contradictory or fundamentally confused." And even in the early Nietzsche, the notion of the "thing-in-itself" is undercut by, for example, his assertion in *The Birth of Tragedy,* chap. 18, that the tragic view of life that he is advocating is illusory rather than veridical (*Truth and Value in Nietzsche,* p. 109; Nietzsche, *Basic Writings,* pp. 109–110). Of course, to reemphasize my difference with Wilcox, it is my view that Nietzsche is *not* talking simply about the Kantian thing-in-itself, but more generally about "things themselves." Hence, he is questioning not only "*transcendent* knowledge, in Kant's sense," but also the very possibility of knowledge in general.

32. Some of this is well brought out in Bennett's article, "Nietzsche's Idea of Myth."

33. Arthur C. Danto, *Nietzsche as Philosopher* (New York: Macmillan, 1967), p. 97.

34. See Danko Grlic, "L'Anti-esthéticisme de Nietzsche," Colloque de Royaumont, *Cahiers,* philosophie no. 6, *Nietzsche* (Paris: Minuit, 1966), pp. 177–182.

35. Bennett, "Nietzsche's Idea of Myth," pp. 422, 425.

36. Ibid., p. 422.

37. On the opposed idealisms of nostalgia and imagination, see R. N. Berki, *On Political Realism* (London: Dent, 1981), pp. 192–263.

Chapter 3

1. Heidegger, "The Word of Nietzsche: 'God is Dead'" (based on Heidegger's Nietzsche courses of 1936–40; "major portions were delivered repeatedly in 1943 for small groups"; first published in 1950), in *The Question Concerning Technology and Other Essays,* trans. and with an introduction by William Lovitt (New York: Harper & Row, 1977), pp. 54–55.

2. This comes out very clearly in Harold Alderman, *Nietzsche's Gift* (Athens: Ohio University Press, 1977), pp. 164–173.

3. I do not deny that *Being and Time* is susceptible to such analyses. For one example, see Richard Schmitt, *Martin Heidegger on Being Human: An Introduction to Sein und Zeit* (New York: Random House, 1969).

4. John Stuart Mill, *Collected Works,* Vol. XVI, ed. Francis E. Mineka and Dwight N. Lindley (Toronto: University of Toronto Press, 1972), Letter of November 4, 1867, p. 1323.

5. Carnap's discussion of Heidegger is available in Michael Murray, ed., *Heidegger and Modern Philosophy: Critical Essays* (New Haven: Yale University Press, 1978), pp. 23–24.

6. A. J. Ayer, "Reflections on Existentialism," in his *Metaphysics and Common Sense* (London: Macmillan, 1969), especially pp. 206–208 and 212–214; W. V. O. Quine, *Word and Object* (Cambridge, Mass.: MIT Press, 1969), p. 133.

7. Thomas S. Kuhn, *The Structure of Scientific Revolutions,* 2nd edition, enlarged (Chicago: University of Chicago Press, 1970), p. 111.

8. Paul Feyerabend, *Against Method: Outline of an Anarchistic Theory of Knowledge* (London: NLB, 1975), p. 295.

9. Hannah Arendt, "Martin Heidegger at Eighty," in Murray, ed., *Heidegger and Mod-*

ern Philosophy, p. 297. See also, on the same point, Otto Pöggeler, *Der Denkweg Martin Heideggers* (Pfullingen: Neske, 1963), pp. 8–9.

10. Karl Löwith, *Heidegger: Denker in dürftiger Zeit,* 3rd edition, revised (Göttingen: Vandenhoeck & Ruprecht, 1965), p. 110.

11. Robert Musil, *The Man Without Qualities,* 3 vols., trans. Eithne Wilkins and Ernst Kaiser (London: Secker & Warburg, 1953–60), Vol. I, p. 59.

12. Alan Wilde, *Horizons of Assent: Modernism, Postmodernism, and the Ironic Imagination* (Baltimore: Johns Hopkins University Press, 1981), especially pp. 19–49.

13. Roy Pascal provides a general discussion of this transition in *From Naturalism to Expressionism: German Literature and Society, 1880–1918* (New York: Basic Books, 1973). On apocalypse as an expressionist theme, see Frederick S. Levine, *The Apocalyptic Vision: The Art of Franz Marc as German Expressionism* (New York: Harper & Row, 1979), especially pp. 3, 6–7, 100–103.

14. Cf. Heidegger's evocation of the "crises" in mathematics, physics, and biology in the Introduction to *Being and Time,* pp. 9–10.

15. For Simmel's reflections on this theme, see *Georg Simmel: Sociologist and European,* ed. Peter Lawrence (New York: Barnes & Noble, 1976), p. 251 and passim.

16. See Georg G. Iggers's excellent study, *The German Conception of History: The National Tradition of Historical Thought from Herder to the Present* (Middletown, Conn.: Wesleyan University Press, 1968), especially pp. 124–195.

17. Ezra Pound, "Hugh Selwyn Mauberley" (1920), in *Selected Poems* (New York: J. Laughlin, 1957), p. 64; Paul Valéry, "La Crise de l'esprit" (1919), in *Oeuvres,* 2 vols., ed. Jean Hytier (Paris: Gallimard, 1957), Vol. I, pp. 988–1000; Oswald Spengler, *The Decline of the West,* 2 vols., trans. Charles Francis Atkins (New York: Knopf, 1926–28).

18. See, on this theme, Robert Wohl, *The Generation of 1914* (Cambridge, Mass.: Harvard University Press, 1979), pp. 42–84 and passim.

19. See R. N. Berki, *On Political Realism* (London: Dent, 1981), pp. 192–263.

20. These two opposing sides, it should be observed, stand closer to each other than we might think. In practice, each tends to turn into the other. As Berki puts it, "the idealism of nostalgia, if pushed far enough, . . . turns, not so miraculously, into the idealism of *imagination,* for that is where the very remote past belongs" (Berki, *On Political Realism,* p. 222). And vice versa, I might add.

21. One striking indication of the importance of this sensibility is to be found in the similarities between Heidegger's discussions of *"das Man"* (the anonymous "they"), and of technology and the account of capitalism that Georg Lukács gives in his *History and Class Consciousness* (1923). See Lukács, "Reification and the Consciousness of the Proletariat," in *History and Class Consciousness: Studies in Marxist Dialectics,* trans. Rodney Livingstone (Cambridge, Mass.: MIT Press, 1971), especially pp. 83–110. I attribute this similarity not to Heidegger's having read *History and Class Consciousness* during the writing of *Being and Time* (there is no evidence that he did) but rather to certain fundamental similarities in the intellectual formation of the two writers. See Lucien Goldmann, *Lukács and Heidegger: Towards a New Philosophy,* trans. William Q. Boelhower (London: Routledge and Kegan Paul, 1977); also Rainer Rochlitz, "Lukács et Heidegger (suites d'un débat)," *L'Homme et la société,* 33–34 (1977), 87–94. The fact that Lukács turned one way and Heidegger the other is no denial of these similarities.

22. For a recent example, see Mark Blitz, *Heidegger's Being and Time and the Possibility of Political Philosophy* (Ithaca: Cornell University Press, 1981), especially p. 20.

23. Heidegger, "My Way to Phenomenology" (first published in 1963), in *On Time and Being,* pp. 74–82; "A Recollection" (1957), in Thomas Sheehan, ed., *Heidegger: The Man and the Thinker* (Chicago: Precedent, 1981), pp. 21–22; "A Dialogue on Language," in *On the Way to Language,* p. 7. All these are late texts, and I suspect that at least to some extent Heidegger is reading back into the earliest period of his intellectual development concerns that only became important for him later on. One notes, for example, that most of the volumes of Dilthey's *Gesammelte Schriften* appeared well after 1914. Nonetheless, his dependence on the notions of cultural crisis and alienation that were being put forward before, during, and after World War I is clear.

24. Arendt, "Martin Heidegger at Eighty," p. 293; Pöggeler, *Der Denkweg Martin*

Heideggers, p. 27. Heidegger did lecture at Freiburg in the winter semester of 1915–16, the summer semester of 1916, and the winter semester of 1916–17, but was then drafted for auxiliary war service and returned to teaching in the summer semester of 1919.

25. See Michael E. Zimmerman, *Eclipse of the Self: The Development of Heidegger's Concept of Authenticity* (Athens: Ohio University Press, 1981), for a lucid account of Heidegger's notion of authenticity.

26. Following what has become established practice, I shall leave this Heideggerian *terminus technicus* untranslated. Literally, it can be rendered as "there-being"; more loosely, as "human existence."

27. One notable exception is T. W. Adorno, who shrewdly points out the existence, in *Being and Time*, of "the mental posture of a permanent 'back to' " (Theodor W. Adorno, *Negative Dialectics*, trans. E. B. Ashton [New York: Seabury Press, 1973], p. 62).

28. A translation of the Introduction to *Being and Time* by Joan Stambaugh in collaboration with J. Glenn Gray and David Farrell Krell, rather more fluent than Macquarrie's and Robinson's, is available in Heidegger, *Basic Writings*. For the most part, I shall follow this version.

29. Heidegger's notion of Dasein as coming back to itself futurally, and his assertion that the call of conscience calls us back in calling us forth, well illustrate something that I have already noted—namely, the close proximity of the nostalgic and the imaginative orientations. Similarly, Foucault speaks of a "wholly new form of thought"—a "future thought" that is somehow tied up with a "return" of "language" (*Les Mots et les choses*, pp. 314–318, 396–398; *The Order of Things*, pp. 303–307, 384–386). I note, further, that neither Heidegger nor Foucault should be seen as seeking to move to a literal past or future. In the passages in question here, for example, Heidegger seems quite clearly to want to call us back to *ourselves*.

30. The key passage in *Being and Time* is on p. 25; for a representative statement from the later Heidegger, see his letter of April 1962 to William J. Richardson, *Heidegger: Through Phenomenology to Thought* (The Hague: Nijhoff, 1963), pp. xii, xiii.

31. See Søren Kierkegaard, *Two Ages: The Age of Revolution and the Present Age, a Literary Review*, ed. and trans. Howard V. Hong and Edna H. Hong (Princeton: Princeton University Press, 1978), especially pp. 90–95.

32. As Fredric Jameson puts it, *Fables of Aggression: Wyndham Lewis, The Modernist as Fascist* (Berkeley and Los Angeles: University of California Press, 1979), p. 128. The *locus classicus* of this interpretation of *Being and Time* is Lukács, *The Destruction of Reason*, trans. Peter Palmer (Atlantic Highlands, N.J.: Humanities Press, 1981), pp. 489–522.

33. Otto Pöggeler, *Philosophie und Politik bei Heidegger*, 2nd edition, with a new afterword (Freiburg: Karl Alber, 1974), p. 25.

34. Heidegger, "Plato's Doctrine of Truth," trans. John Barlow, in *Philosophy in the Twentieth Century: An Anthology*, 3 vols., ed. William Barrett and Henry D. Aiken (New York: Random House, 1962), Vol. III, p. 267 (translation altered).

35. Heidegger, *Die Selbstbehauptung der deutschen Universität* (Breslau: Korn, 1934). For a more accessible edition, see Heidegger, *Die Selbstbehauptung der deutschen Universität/Das Rektorat 1933/34: Tatsachen und Gedanken* (Frankfurt am Main: Klostermann, 1983), pp. 9–19.

36. Ibid., p. 13. On Heidegger's forbidding of the "Jewish placard," see "Das Rektorat," p. 31.

37. Heidegger, "Der Ruf zum Arbeitsdienst," January 23, 1934, in Guido Schneeberger, ed., *Nachlese zu Heidegger* (Bern, 1962 [privately published]), p. 181.

38. Karl Jaspers, *Philosophische Autobiographie*, new, enlarged edition (Munich: Piper, 1977), p. 101. See also Karl Jaspers, *Notizen zu Heidegger*, ed. Hans Saner (Munich: Piper, 1978), which exhaustively documents Jaspers's pained reaction to Heidegger's course from 1933 onward.

39. "Only a God Can Save Us: *Der Spiegel*'s Interview with Martin Heidegger," trans. Maria P. Alter and John D. Caputo, *Philosophy Today*, 20 (1976), 267–284. The interview is also available, in a translation by William J. Richardson, in Sheehan, ed., *Heidegger: The Man and the Thinker*, pp. 45–67.

40. For those who wish to pursue the matter, George Steiner manages to convey in brief

compass something of its complexities in his *Heidegger* (London: Fontana, 1978), pp. 111–121. On pp. 156–157, Steiner lists some of the more interesting literature on Heidegger's involvement with the Nazis. For another listing, see Winfried Franzen, *Martin Heidegger* (Stuttgart: Metzler, 1976), pp. 78–85. So far as I know, the most detailed factual survey of Heidegger's involvement with the Nazis is contained in an unpublished doctoral dissertation (available from University Microfilms): Karl A. Moehling, "Martin Heidegger and the Nazi Party: An Examination" (Northern Illinois University, 1972). Moehling includes transcriptions of several documents that do not seem to be available elsewhere. Unfortunately, he is deaf to the moral equivocacy of many of Heidegger's pronouncements of 1933–34, but this does not invalidate his assemblage of facts. Moehling summarizes his findings in "Heidegger and the Nazis," in Sheehan, ed., *Heidegger: The Man and The Thinker*, pp. 31–43. The articles and interviews by Maurice de Gandillac, Alfred de Towarnicki, Karl Löwith, Alphonse de Waehlens, and Eric Weil which appeared in *Les Temps modernes* in 1946 and 1947 represent the first outbreak of the controversy over the depth of Heidegger's implication in the Nazi debacle. They are still worth reading. So, too, are such more recent contributions as Stanley Rosen, *Nihilism: A Philosophical Essay* (New Haven: Yale University Press, 1969), pp. 119–124; Henry Pachter, "Heidegger and Hitler: The Incompatibility of *Geist* and Politics," *Boston University Journal*, 24 (1976), 47–55 (reprinted in his *Weimar Etudes* [New York: Columbia University Press, 1982], pp. 208–224), and Karsten Harries, "Heidegger as a Political Thinker," in *Heidegger and Modern Philosophy*, pp. 304–328. Blitz's account of the Nazi episode in *Heidegger's Being and Time and the Possibility of Political Philosophy*, pp. 210–222, is disappointing.

4 1. Karl Löwith, "Les Implications politiques de la philosophie de l'existence chez Martin Heidegger," trans. Joseph Rovan, *Les Temps modernes*, 14 (November 1946), 351.

4 2. Ibid., pp. 358–359. See also Pachter, "Heidegger and Hitler," pp. 51, 55; and Steiner, *Heidegger*, p. 117. In my view, however, these writers underestimate the extent to which Heidegger's preoccupation with the notion of a nihilistic crisis postdated 1927, and hence overestimate the continuity between *Being and Time* and Heidegger's words and actions in 1933.

4 3. Heidegger, "Deutsche Studenten," in Schneeberger, ed., *Nachlese zu Heidegger*, pp. 135–136.

4 4. Heidegger [Bekenntnis zu Adolf Hitler und dem Nationalsozialistischen Staat] in Schneeberger, ed., *Nachlese zu Heidegger*, p. 148.

4 5. Heidegger, "Nationalsozialistische Wissensschulung," in Schneeberger, ed., *Nachlese zu Heidegger*, p. 200.

4 6. Heidegger, "What is Metaphysics?" in Walter Kaufmann, ed., *Existentialism from Dostoevsky to Sartre*, revised and expanded edition (New York: New American Library, 1975), p. 242.

4 7. Heidegger, *Selbstbehauptung*, pp. 7–8.

4 8. Ibid., pp. 10–11.

4 9. Ibid., p. 12.

5 0. Ibid., p. 11.

5 1. Ibid., p. 14: "Die deutsche Studentenschaft ist auf dem Marsch." Note also the words on a poster to be seen at bookburnings in 1933: "Deutsche Studenten marschieren wider den undeutschen Geist" (photograph, *Der Spiegel*, May 31, 1976, p. 196).

5 2. Heidegger, *Selbstbehauptung*, p. 22.

5 3. Plato, *The Republic*, trans. H. D. P. Lee (Harmondsworth, Middlesex: Penguin Books, 1955), p. 294.

5 4. Heidegger's letter is given in full in Moehling, "Martin Heidegger and the Nazi Party," pp. 263–268. The passage quoted is on p. 263 (my translation).

5 5. Schneeberger, ed., *Nachlese zu Heidegger*, plate following p. 192.

5 6. Heidegger, *Selbstbehauptung*, p. 13.

5 7. Zimmerman's comments on this point in his *Eclipse of the Self*, p. xxv, seem to me to be apt. As Zimmerman observes, Heidegger sought to demythologize the Christian notion of redemption through divine intervention, but "in his talk of how Being 'conceals itself' and thereby governs human history, [he] seems to have developed a mythology of his own."

5 8. Ibid., pp. 216–218. I have for the most part followed the translation of this address by Thomas Sheehan in Sheehan, ed., *Heidegger: The Man and the Thinker*, pp. 27–30.

59. Spengler, *Decline of the West*, Vol. II, especially pp. 89, 96, 435. With its contrast between country and city, soul and intellect, Spengler's chapter "The Soul of the City," pp. 85–110, is particularly "Heideggerian" in its resonances.

60. David Schoenbaum, *Hitler's Social Revolution: Class and Status in Nazi Germany* (Garden City, N.Y.: Doubleday Anchor, 1966), p. 3.

61. See George L. Mosse, *The Crisis of German Ideology: Intellectual Origins of the Third Reich* (New York: Grosset & Dunlap, 1964), especially pp. 1–87, for an illuminating account of *völkisch* notions.

62. On neo-conservatism, see Klemens von Klemperer, *Germany's New Conservatism: Its History and Dilemma in the Twentieth Century* (Princeton: Princeton University Press, 1957), especially pp. 117–188; see also Moehling, "Martin Heidegger and the Nazi Party," pp. 135–136.

63. "Only a God Can Save Us," p. 273.

64. Heidegger, *Selbstbehauptung*, p. 22.

65. "Only a God Can Save Us," p. 277 (translation altered).

66. See especially Hannah Arendt, *The Life of the Mind*, 2 vols. (New York: Harcourt Brace Jovanovich, 1978), Vol. II (*Willing*), p. 173. See also Arendt, "Martin Heidegger at Eighty," pp. 302–303.

67. "Schlageterfeier der Freiburger Universität," in Schneeberger, ed., *Nachlese zu Heidegger*, pp. 47–49.

68. Steiner, *Heidegger*, p. 126; see also pp. 18 and 46–47.

69. "Only a God Can Save Us," p. 277.

70. Hannah Arendt, *Eichmann in Jerusalem: A Report on the Banality of Evil*, revised and enlarged edition (New York: Viking Press, 1963). See also Arendt's *The Human Condition* (Chicago: University of Chicago Press, 1958), which is likewise profoundly Heideggerian in its bearing, though Arendt never mentions Heidegger's name.

71. Herbert Marcuse, *One-Dimensional Man: Studies in the Ideology of Advanced Industrial Society* (Boston: Beacon Press, 1964), especially chap. 6, "From Negative to Positive Thinking: Technological Rationality and the Logic of Domination," pp. 142–169. For discussions of Marcuse's connection with Heidegger, see Martin Jay, "Metapolitics of Utopianism," *Dissent*, 17 (1970), 342–350; and Michael E. Zimmerman, "Heidegger and Marcuse: Technology as Ideology," in *Research in Philosophy and Technology*, vol. 2, ed. Paul T. Durbin and Carl Mitcham (Greenwich, Conn.: Jai Press, 1979), pp. 245–261.

72. See, for example, Dolores LaChapelle's remarkable book *Earth Wisdom* (Los Angeles: The Guild of Tutors Press, 1978).

Chapter 4

1. See also Nietzsche, *Twilight of the Idols*, §§ 8, 9, and 24, pp. 71–72, 81–82. Note again Nietzsche's plan for a physiology of art in *Gesammelte Werke, Musarionausgabe*, Vol. XVIII, p. 355.

2. "Only a God Can Save Us: *Der Spiegel*'s Interview with Martin Heidegger," trans. Maria P. Alter and John D. Caputo, *Philosophy Today*, 20 (1976), 280.

3. Ibid.

4. As William Barrett reports, "Heidegger and Modern Existentialism: Dialogue with William Barrett," in Bryan Magee, ed., *Men of Ideas* (New York: Viking Press, 1979), p. 94.

5. As Stanley Rosen aptly puts it, "beneath the Nietzschean surfaces of Heidegger's thought, we may detect a continuing Hegelian resonance" (*Nihilism: A Philosophical Essay* [New Haven: Yale University Press, 1969], pp. 127–128). See also Hans-Georg Gadamer, "Heidegger and the Language of Metaphysics" (1969), in his *Philosophical Hermeneutics*, ed. and trans. David E. Linge (Berkeley and Los Angeles: University of California Press, 1976), pp. 230–231: "Heidegger's thought has revolved around Hegel until the present day in ever new attempts at delineation."

6. See R. N. Berki, *On Political Realism* (London: Dent, 1981), pp. 67–69, 72, 77–80, 197, and passim. As Berki indicates, the post-Hegelian tradition of "German idealism," with its split between "Left" and "Right" Hegelians, can be seen as a departure from Hegel's realism (p. 197).

7. John G. Gunnell, *Political Theory: Tradition and Interpretation* (Cambridge, Mass.: Winthrop, 1979), especially pp. 65–93. Specifically on Heidegger, see also Richard Rorty, "Overcoming the Tradition: Heidegger and Dewey," in Michael Murray, ed., *Heidegger and Modern Philosophy: Critical Essays* (New Haven: Yale University Press, 1978), pp. 250–252, 256–258 (reprinted in Richard Rorty, *Consequences of Pragmatism* [Essays: 1972–1980] [Minneapolis: University of Minnesota Press, 1982]; see pp. 46–48, 52–54).

8. Georg Wilhelm Friedrich Hegel, *Lectures on the History of Philosophy*, 3 vols., trans. E. S. Haldane and Frances Simson (London: Routledge and Kegan Paul, 1955), Vol. III, pp. 551–552.

9. Karl Löwith, "The Historical Background of European Nihilism," in his *Nature, History, and Existentialism, and Other Essays in the Philosophy of History*, ed. Arnold Levison (Evanston: Northwestern University Press, 1966), pp. 10–13.

10. Heidegger, "Hegel und die Griechen," in *Wegmarken*, ed. Friedrich-Wilhelm von Herrmann (Frankfurt am Main: Klostermann, 1976), p. 427.

11. Hegel, *Lectures on the History of Philosophy*, Vol. III, p. 551.

12. Ibid., Vol. I, p. 40.

13. On this Hellenophilia, see the useful study by Jacques Taminiaux, *La Nostalgie de la Grèce à l'aube de l'idéalisme allemand: Kant et les Grecs dans l'itinéraire de Schiller, de Hölderlin et de Hegel* (The Hague: Nijhoff, 1967).

14. Georg Wilhelm Friedrich Hegel, *Aesthetics: Lectures on Fine Art*, 2 vols., trans. T. M. Knox (Oxford: Clarendon Press, 1975), Vol. I, p. 11.

15. On Sartre's misinterpretation of Heidegger, see Dominick LaCapra, *A Preface to Sartre* (Ithaca: Cornell University Press, 1978), pp. 29, 52–53, and 129–130.

16. On Heidegger's conception of truth, see especially *Being and Time*, §44, pp. 213–226.

17. Georg Lukács, "Die Subjekt-Objekt-Beziehung in der Aesthetik," in his *Heidelberger Aesthetik (1916–1918)*, ed. György Márkus and Frank Benseler (*Werke*, vol. 17) (Neuwied am Rhein: Luchterhand, 1974), especially pp. 91–102.

18. Georg Lukács, *Soul and Form*, trans. Anna Bostock (Cambridge, Mass.: MIT Press, 1974), especially the essay "The Metaphysics of Tragedy," pp. 152–174.

19. Georg Lukács, *History and Class Consciousness: Studies in Marxist Dialectics*, trans. Rodney Livingstone (Cambridge, Mass.: MIT Press, 1971), pp. 139–140.

20. For an illuminating account of this distinction and the context of its emergence, see Karsten Harries, "Hegel on the Future of Art," *Review of Metaphysics*, 27 (1973–74), 677–696.

21. Immanuel Kant, *Critique of Judgment*, trans. J. H. Bernard (New York: Hafner, 1972), §49, p. 157; §57 Remark I, p. 187; §59, pp. 198–199.

22. Hegel, *Aesthetics*, Vol. I, pp. 7–10, 55.

23. Maurice Blanchot, "Nietzsche et l'écriture fragmentaire," in his *L'Entretien infini* (Paris: Gallimard, 1969), pp. 227–255.

24. On this point, see especially Hans-Georg Gadamer's afterword to the Reclam edition of "On the Origin of the Work of Art," available in English as "Heidegger's Later Philosophy," in his *Philosophical Hermeneutics*, pp. 219–224. Gadamer, too, attacks what he sees as the illegitimate subjectivization of art, as we have seen.

25. Maurice Blanchot, *L'Espace littéraire* (Paris: Gallimard, 1955), pp. 230–231.

26. Ibid., pp. 242, 249, 252.

27. On Heidegger's view of language in the *Habilitationsschrift*, see Richard Schmitt, *Martin Heidegger on Being Human: An Introduction to Sein und Zeit* (New York: Random House, 1969), pp. 55–73. The text of the *Habilitationsschrift* is available in Heidegger, *Frühe Schriften*, ed. Friedrich-Wilhelm von Herrmann (Frankfurt am Main: Klostermann, 1978), pp. 189–411.

28. Heidegger, *Sein und Zeit*, ed. Friedrich-Wilhelm von Herrmann (Frankfurt am Main: Klostermann, 1977), p. 117, note c.

29. Ludwig Wittgenstein, *Tractatus Logico-Philosophicus,* trans. D. F. Pears and B. F. McGuinness (London: Routledge and Kegan Paul, 1974), §6.4 to end. See also Wittgenstein, "On Heidegger on Being and Dread," in Murray, ed., *Heidegger and Modern Philosophy,* pp. 80–83.

30. Rorty, "Overcoming the Tradition," p. 257 (*Consequences of Pragmatism,* p. 52).

31. David A. White, *Heidegger and the Language of Poetry* (Lincoln: University of Nebraska Press, 1978), p. 13.

32. See Hans-Joachim Schrimpf, "Hölderlin, Heidegger und die Literaturwissenschaft," *Euphorion,* 51 (1957), especially pp. 308–311.

33. Stefan George, "Hölderlin," in *Werke,* 2nd edition, 2 vols. (Munich: Küpper, 1958), Vol. I, pp. 518–521.

34. Friedrich Hölderlin, "Bread and Wine," in *Poems and Fragments,* enlarged edition, ed. and trans. Michael Hamburger (Cambridge: Cambridge University Press, 1980), pp. 244–247.

35. Georg Wilhelm Friedrich Hegel, *Phenomenology of Spirit,* trans. A. V. Miller, with an analysis and foreword by J. N. Findlay (Oxford: Clarendon Press, 1977), §741, p. 449.

36. Hölderlin, *Poems and Fragments,* pp. 248–249.

37. See "Only a God Can Save Us," p. 281.

38. Heidegger, *Erläuterungen zu Hölderlins Dichtung,* 4th edition, enlarged (Frankfurt am Main: Klostermann, 1971), p. 7.

39. Robert Minder, "Heidegger und Hebel oder die Sprache von Messkirch," in his *Dichter in der Gesellschaft: Erfahrungen mit deutscher und französischer Literatur* (Frankfurt am Main: Insel, 1966), pp. 210–264.

40. Meyer Schapiro, "The Still Life as a Personal Object—A Note on Heidegger and van Gogh," in Marianne L. Simmel, ed., *The Reach of Mind: Essays in Memory of Kurt Goldstein* (New York: Springer, 1968), pp. 203–209.

41. George Steiner, *Heidegger* (London: Fontana, 1978), p. 137.

42. Rosen, *Nihilism,* pp. 41–42.

Chapter 5

1. Martin Puder, "Der böse Blick des Michel Foucault," *Neue Rundschau,* 82 (1972), 315–324. In the present essay, I am mainly concerned with Foucault's work up to the years 1975–76. The last major works to which I have access are *Discipline and Punish* and *The Will to Knowledge,* the first volume of his projected six-volume *History of Sexuality.* As I write this, the second and following volumes of the *History of Sexuality* have not yet appeared. Foucault is not averse to shifting his positions, and what he will do in these and subsequent books remains to be seen. The uncertainty is especially acute because his writings of the 1970s seem to point in at least two possible future directions, one of which would certainly take him beyond the aestheticist and discursive focus emphasized in this essay.

2. Michael S. Roth, "Foucault's 'History of the Present,'" *History and Theory,* 20 (1981), 43.

3. Jean-Louis Ézine, "[Entretien avec] Michel Foucault," *Nouvelles littéraires,* 2477 (March 17–23, 1975), 3.

4. The silence was broken by Hubert L. Dreyfus and Paul Rabinow, *Michel Foucault: Beyond Structuralism and Hermeneutics,* with an afterword by Michel Foucault (Chicago: University of Chicago Press, 1982). See especially pp. 11, 38–39, 42–43, and 57. A major difference between their focus and mine, however, is that whereas they emphasize the affinities between Foucault and the early Heidegger, I am more interested in Foucault's affinities with the crisis thought of the later Heidegger.

5. Michel Foucault, "Hommage à Jean Hyppolite," *Revue de métaphysique et de morale,* 74 (1969), 136.

6. As Vincent Descombes points out in his useful introduction to contemporary French philosophy, *Modern French Philosophy,* trans. L. Scott-Fox and J. M. Harding (Cambridge: Cambridge University Press, 1979), p. 4.

7. Fons Elders, interview with Michel Foucault and Noam Chomsky, in *Reflexive Water: The Basic Concerns of Mankind,* ed. Fons Elders (London: Souvenir Press, 1974), p. 167. But see Foucault's somewhat more accurate statement in the interview "Questions on Geography," in *Power/Knowledge,* p. 66: "And for all that I may like to say that I am not a philosopher, nonetheless if my concern is with truth I am still a philosopher."

8. Alan Sheridan, *Foucault: The Will to Truth* (London: Tavistock, 1980), p. 5. For Foucault's own comments on his relations with musicians, see Paolo Caruso, "Conversazione con Michel Foucault," in his *Conversazioni con Claude Lévi-Strauss, Michel Foucault, Jacques Lacan* (Milan: Mursia, 1969), p. 117.

9. Georges Bataille, *Oeuvres complètes,* Vol. I: *Premiers écrits, 1922-1940,* présentation de Michel Foucault (Paris: Gallimard, 1970), p. i.

10. Philippe Sollers, "Pourquoi Artaud, Pourquoi Bataille," in Centre Culturel de Cerisy-la-Salle, *Artaud* (Paris: Union générale d'éditions, 1973), p. 10. This volume and its companion, *Bataille* (Paris: Union générale d'éditions, 1973), give a good deal of insight into the preoccupations of some radical French intellectuals in this period.

11. For perhaps the most compact indication of Foucault's indebtedness to Bataille, see Foucault's "A Preface to Transgression," in *Language, Counter-Memory, Practice,* pp. 29–52. Robert Sasso provides an account of Bataille's work in *Georges Bataille: le système du non-savoir, une ontologie du jeu* (Paris: Minuit, 1978).

12. Dreyfus and Rabinow, *Michel Foucault,* pp. viii, 1–103.

13. See, for example, Raymond Bellour, "Deuxième entretien avec Michel Foucault: Sur les façons d'écrire l'histoire," *Les Lettres françaises,* 1187 (June 15–21, 1967), 6 and 9; and "Foucault: Non au sexe roi" (Foucault interviewed by Bernard-Henri Lévy), *Nouvel observateur,* 644 (March 12, 1977), 93 and 113. An English translation of the Lévy interview, by David J. Parent, is available under the title "Power and Sex: An Interview with Michel Foucault," in *Telos,* 32 (Summer 1977), 152–161; see pp. 152–153 and 159.

14. Alexandre Kojève, *Introduction to the Reading of Hegel: Lectures on the Phenomenology of Spirit,* assembled by Raymond Queneau, ed. Allan Bloom, trans. James H. Nichols, Jr. (New York: Basic Books, 1969), pp. 41–63.

15. Friedrich Nietzsche, "On the Uses and Disadvantages of History for Life," chap. 6, in his *Untimely Meditations,* trans. R. J. Hollingdale, with an introduction by J. P. Stern (Cambridge: Cambridge University Press, 1983), p. 93.

16. On this theme, see Richard Rorty, *Philosophy and the Mirror of Nature* (Princeton: Princeton University Press, 1979), pp. 11–13 and passim.

17. R. N. Berki, *On Political Realism* (London: Dent, 1981), p. 195.

18. See Karl Mannheim, *Ideology and Utopia: An Introduction to the Sociology of Knowledge,* trans. Louis Wirth and Edward Shils (New York: Harcourt, Brace, 1936).

19. Berki, *On Political Realism,* p. 221.

20. See, e.g., *Histoire de la folie* (1961 edition), pp. i, v, vi–vii, ix, 31, 34–35, 44, 47, 51, 57, 135, 166, 411, 424–425, 459; *Histoire de la folie* (1972 edition), pp. 36, 39–40, 47, 49, 53, 58, 124, 150, 359–360, 371, 399–400; *Madness and Civilization,* pp. 27, 35.

21. Sheridan, *Foucault,* p. 5. See also Foucault, *Power/Knowledge,* p. 64.

22. Michel Foucault, "La Recherche du psychologue," in *Des Chercheurs français s'interrogent* (Paris: Presses universitaires de France, 1957), especially pp. 173–175, 183, 186–187, 190–193, 197–201.

23. Ludwig Binswanger, *Le Rêve et l'existence,* trans. Jacqueline Verdeaux, with an introduction by Michel Foucault (Paris: Desclée de Brouwer, 1954), pp. 9–10.

24. Ibid., p. 12.

25. Michel Foucault, *Maladie mentale et personnalité* (Paris: Presses universitaires de France, 1954), pp. 53–54. Available in English as *Mental Illness and Psychology,* trans. Alan Sheridan (New York: Harper & Row, 1976), based on the radically revised (and retitled) French edition of 1962. The chapter that I cite here, however, remains unchanged, pp. 44–57.

26. R. D. Laing, *The Divided Self: A Study of Sanity and Madness* (London: Tavistock, 1960).

27. On structuralism and the subject, Descombes, *Modern French Philosophy,* pp. 75–77, is illuminating.

28. In this regard, it is interesting how in his essay "Science and Reflection" (1954) Heidegger already suggests the position that Foucault works out in *History of Madness*. Heidegger declares in this essay that psychiatry represents the life of the human soul "in terms of the objectness of the bodily-psychical-spiritual unity of the whole man. At any given time human existence, which is already presencing, displays itself in the objectness belonging to psychiatry. The openness-for-Being in which man as man ek-sists, remains that which for psychiatry is not to be gotten around" (Heidegger, *The Question Concerning Technology and Other Essays*, trans. and with an introduction by William Lovitt [New York: Harper & Row, 1977], pp. 174–175).

29. Ferdinand de Saussure, *Course in General Linguistics*, ed. Charles Bally and Albert Sechehaye, with the collaboration of Albert Riedlinger, trans. Wade Baskin (New York: Philosophical Library, 1959), Introduction, chap. 3, §3, p. 15.

30. Philip Pettit, *The Concept of Structuralism: A Critical Analysis* (Berkeley and Los Angeles: University of California Press, 1975).

31. Ibid., p. 29.

32. Ibid., pp. 68–69.

33. For the Mallarméan theme in Foucault, see *Les Mots et les choses,* especially pp. 58–59, 95, 316–317, 394; *The Order of Things,* pp. 43–44, 81, 305–306, 382–384. On the importance of Blanchot for Foucault, see Bellour, "Deuxième entretien avec Michel Foucault," in which Foucault tells us that "it is Blanchot who has made possible all discourse on literature." He also informs us in this interview that "I differ from those who are called structuralists in that I am not greatly interested in the formal possibilities presented by a system such as language. Personally, I am haunted rather by the existence of discourses, by the fact that utterances have taken place" (p. 8).

34. Pettit, *The Concept of Structuralism*, p. 33.

35. François Wahl, "La Philosophie entre l'avant et l'après du structuralisme," in Oswald Ducrot et al., *Qu'est-ce que le structuralisme?* (Paris: Seuil, 1968), p. 10.

36. Ibid., pp. 10–11.

37. Ibid., p. 304.

38. For references to discourse, see *Les Mots et les choses,* pp. 95–96, 249, 315, 321–322, 397; *The Order of Things,* pp. 81, 236, 304, 311, 385–386. It should be noted that in *The Archaeology of Knowledge* Foucault uses the word *discourse* much more broadly, to include—so it seems—virtually every systematic use of language. As he himself notes, "instead of gradually reducing the rather fluctuating meaning of the word 'discourse,' I believe that I have added to its meanings: treating it sometimes as the general domain of all statements, sometimes as an individualizable group of statements, and sometimes as a regulated practice that accounts for a certain number of statements; and have I not allowed this same word 'discourse,' which should have served as a boundary around the term 'statement,' to vary as I shifted my analysis or its point of application, as the statement itself faded from view?" (*L'Archéologie du savoir*, p. 106; *The Archaeology of Knowledge*, p. 80; see also pp. 140–141, 153, 220–221 of the former, and pp. 107, 117, 169 of the latter).

39. I borrow the expression "direction of meaning" from Northrop Frye, *Anatomy of Criticism: Four Essays* (Princeton: Princeton University Press, 1957), pp. 73–74.

40. For more on this theme, see Foucault, *Language, Counter-Memory, Practice*, especially the four essays—"A Preface to Transgression," "Language to Infinity," "The Father's 'No,'" and "Fantasia of the Library"—that the editor has classified under the general rubric of "Language and the Birth of 'Literature.'"

41. On representation, signification, and their mutual relations, see *Les Mots et les choses*, especially pp. 77–81, 221–224, 314–315; *The Order of Things,* pp. 63–67, 208–211, 303–304.

42. Saussure, *Course in General Linguistics*, pt. 2, chap. 4, §4: "Dans la langue il n'y a que des différences."

43. Ducrot et al., *Qu'est-ce que le structuralisme?*, pp. 339, 349.

44. Ibid., p. 306.

45. Ibid., p. 307.

46. Ibid., pp. 308–309.

47. Ibid., p. 309.

48. Incidentally, it is highly significant that Foucault, Derrida, and their followers tend to blur the distinction between the "signified" (which constitutes one half of the signified/signifier couple making up the sign) and the "referent" (to which this signifying couple refers). The signified is expanded to cover the territory of the referent; the referent itself mysteriously disappears.

49. Pettit, *The Concept of Structuralism*, p. 33.

50. Ducrot et al., *Qu'est-ce que le structuralisme?*, p. 10.

51. Jean Piaget, *Structuralism*, trans. Chaninah Maschler (New York: Basic Books, 1970).

52. Ibid., p. 5.

53. Ibid., p. 132.

54. Ibid., pp. 132–133.

55. Ibid., pp. 134–135.

56. Ducrot et al., *Qu'est-ce que le structuralisme?*, p. 419.

Chapter 6

1. Foucault, "Nietzsche, Marx, Freud," in Colloque de Royaumont, *Cahiers*, philosophie no. 6, *Nietzsche* (Paris: Minuit, 1966), pp. 183–200. Foucault's use of the term *exteriority* in this context has much to do with his reading of Blanchot. See Raymond Bellour, "Deuxième entretien avec Michel Foucault: Sur les façons d'écrire l'histoire," *Les Lettres françaises*, 1187 (June 15–21, 1967), 7–8; and Foucault, "La Pensée du dehors," *Critique* (Paris), 229 (June 1966), 23–46.

2. Foucault, "Nietzsche, Marx, Freud," p. 189.

3. Ibid., p. 187.

4. See "What is an Author?" in *Language, Counter-Memory, Practice*, pp. 112–138; and *L'Archéologie du savoir*, pp. 31–39, 121–126, 161; *The Archaeology of Knowledge*, pp. 21–27, 92–96, 122.

5. But for a commentator who denies that Foucault should be treated as a methodologist, see Larry Shiner, "Reading Foucault: Anti-Method and the Genealogy of Power-Knowledge," *History and Theory*, 21 (1982), especially 382–383 and 396–397.

6. For a suggestive discussion of Foucault's relation to parody in general, see Margaret A. Rose, *Parody/Metafiction: An Analysis of Parody as a Critical Mirror to the Writing and Reception of Fiction* (London: Croom Helm, 1979), especially pp. 128–157.

7. Bellour, "Deuxième entretien," p. 9.

8. Ibid., p. 7.

9. "Foucault: Non au sexe roi" (Foucault interviewed by Bernard-Henri Lévy), *Nouvel observateur*, 644 (March 12, 1977), 113 (pp. 158–159 in the English translation).

10. Alan Sheridan, *Foucault: The Will to Truth* (London: Tavistock, 1980), p. 113.

11. Hubert L. Dreyfus and Paul Rabinow, *Michel Foucault: Beyond Structuralism and Hermeneutics*, with an afterword by Michel Foucault (Chicago: University of Chicago Press, 1982), pp. 101, viii.

12. As Patricia O'Brien points out in *The Promise of Punishment: Prisons in Nineteenth-Century France* (Princeton: Princeton University Press, 1982), pp. xi–xii, 7–8. See, too, Michelle Perrot, ed., *L'Impossible Prison: Recherches sur le système pénitentiaire au XIXe siècle* (Paris: Seuil, 1980).

13. *Moi, Pierre Rivière, ayant égorgé ma mère, ma soeur et mon frère... Un cas de parricide au XIXe siècle*, ed. Michel Foucault (Paris: Gallimard/Julliard, 1973), p. 12; translated by Frank Jellinek as *I, Pierre Rivière, having slaughtered my mother, my sister and my brother... A Case of Parricide in the 19th Century* (New York: Random House, Pantheon Books, 1975), p. x.

14. Vincent Descombes, *Modern French Philosophy*, trans. L. Scott-Fox and J. M. Harding (Cambridge: Cambridge University Press, 1979), p. 7.

15. Dreyfus and Rabinow, *Michel Foucault*, p. 113.

16. Frank Lentricchia, "Reading Foucault (II)," *Raritan*, 2:4 (Summer 1982), 51.

17. Jacques Léonard, "L'Historien et le philosophe: À propos de *Surveiller et punir: Naissance de la prison*," in Perrot, ed., *L'Impossible Prison*, pp. 14–16.

18. "Foucault: Non au sexe roi," p. 113 (p. 158 in the English translation).

19. See, also, on the "decentering" of structures, *L'Archéologie du savoir*, pp. 22–23; *The Archaeology of Knowledge*, pp. 12–13; and especially the essay "Theatrum Philosophicum" (1970), in *Language, Counter-Memory, Practice*, pp. 165–196.

20. John K. Simon, "A Conversation with Michel Foucault," *Partisan Review*, 38 (1971), 192, 201.

21. Jean-Louis Ézine, "[Entretien avec] Michel Foucault," *Nouvelles littéraires*, 2247 (March 17–23, 1975), 3.

22. Richard Weaver, *The Ethics of Rhetoric* (Chicago: Regnery-Gateway, 1953), pp. 19–20.

23. Ibid., p. 15.

24. Richard Rorty, "Beyond Nietzsche and Marx," *London Review of Books*, February 19–March 4, 1981, p. 5.

25. Michel Foucault, "Pour un morale de l'inconfort" (review of Jean Daniel, *L'Ère des ruptures*), *Nouvel observateur*, 754 (April 23, 1979), 83.

26. Jean-Paul Sartre, "La République du silence," in his *Situations III* (Paris: Gallimard, 1949), p. 13.

27. Otto Friedrich, "France's Philosopher of Power," *Time*, November 16, 1981, p. 148.

28. Michel Foucault, "Is It Useless to Revolt?" *Philosophy and Social Criticism*, 8 (1981), 8 (first published in *Le Monde*, May 11, 1979). Among Foucault's other writings on Iran, see "À quoi rêvent les Iraniens?" *Nouvel observateur*, 726 (October 16, 1978), 48–49; "Lettre ouverte à Mehdi Bazargan, *Nouvel observateur*, 752 (April 14, 1979), 46; and especially "L'Esprit du monde sans esprit," an interview with Claire Brière and Pierre Blanchet appearing in their *Iran: La révolution au nom de Dieu* (Paris: Seuil, 1979), pp. 225–241.

29. Walter Kaufmann, *Nietzsche: Philosopher, Psychologist, Antichrist*, 4th edition (Princeton: Princeton University Press, 1974), p. 203.

30. Ibid., p. 218.

31. Ibid., p. 242.

32. Ibid., pp. 261, 259.

33. Ibid., p. 293.

34. Carlin Romano, "Michel Foucault's New Clothes," *Village Voice*, April 29–May 5, 1981, p. 40.

35. Foucault depends here on Blanchot's interpretation of Sade: see Maurice Blanchot, "Sade," in his *Lautréamont et Sade* (Paris: Minuit, 1949), pp. 215–265.

36. "Foucault: Non au sexe roi," p. 113 (p. 158 in the English translation). Foucault discusses Marcuse in the interview "Body/Power" (1975), in *Power/Knowledge*, p. 59.

37. On philosophy as therapeutic, see Richard Rorty, *Philosophy and the Mirror of Nature* (Princeton: Princeton University Press, 1979), pp. 5–6.

38. Hayden White, *Metahistory: The Historical Imagination in Nineteenth-Century Europe* (Baltimore: Johns Hopkins University Press, 1973), pp. 22–23n.

Chapter 7

1. Søren Kierkegaard, *The Concept of Irony with Constant Reference to Socrates*, trans. Lee M. Capel (New York: Harper & Row, 1965), p. 85. Let me note that in the present essay I am concerned with Derrida's work up to 1980. The last substantial work to which I have had full access is *Postcard*. Only at a very late stage in my writing did I see his essay "D'un ton apocalyptique adopté naguère en philosophie," in Colloque de Cerisy, 23 juillet–2 août 1980, *Les Fins de l'homme: à partir du travail de Jacques Derrida* (Paris: Galilée, 1981), pp. 445–479 (now published in slightly revised form as a short book, Galilée, 1983). Derrida's essay touches interestingly on my account of him in this and the following chapter. I have chosen, however, not to deal with it here, lest my task become unending.

2. Kierkegaard, *The Concept of Irony*, p. 85.

3. Geoffrey H. Hartman, *Saving the Text: Literature/Derrida/Philosophy* (Baltimore: Johns Hopkins University Press, 1981), p. 24.

4. Kierkegaard, *The Concept of Irony*, p. 85.

5. As the philosopher Robert Cumming points out: "Not too long ago one coped with 'The Availability of Wittgenstein.' Little did we anticipate how soon we would have to cope with another elusive invader from the Continent. Insofar as Jacques Derrida has become available, it has been mainly through widespread literary imitation of his philosophical procedure of 'deconstruction'" (Robert Denoon Cumming, "The Odd Couple: Heidegger and Derrida," *Review of Metaphysics*, 34 [1980–81], 487).

6. The literature is already large. Much of it is in the form of articles appearing in such journals as *The American Scholar, Boundary 2, Critical Inquiry, Diacritics, The Georgia Review, Glyph, MLN, New Literary History, The New York Review of Books*, and *Salmagundi*. I shall not give an individual listing here. Among books explicating or exemplifying the controversy, see, for example, Harold Bloom et al., *Deconstruction and Criticism* (New York: Continuum, 1979); Gerald Graff, *Literature Against Itself: Literary Ideas in Modern Society* (Chicago: University of Chicago Press, 1979); Frank Lentricchia, *After the New Criticism* (Chicago: University of Chicago Press, 1979); Geoffrey H. Hartman, *Criticism in the Wilderness: The Study of Literature Today* (New Haven: Yale University Press, 1980); and Jonathan Culler, *On Deconstruction: Theory and Criticism after Structuralism* (Ithaca: Cornell University Press, 1982).

7. See Paul de Man, "Criticism and Crisis," in his *Blindness and Insight: Essays in the Rhetoric of Contemporary Criticism* (New York: Oxford University Press, 1971), pp. 3–19.

8. "Anironic" is Alan Wilde's term: *Horizons of Assent: Modernism, Postmodernism, and the Ironic Imagination* (Baltimore: Johns Hopkins University Press, 1981), pp. 10n, 30–34. Also illuminating on the modernist preoccupation with countering a hostile reality is Lentricchia, *After the New Criticism*, pp. 53–60.

9. See Karsten Harries, "Hegel on the Future of Art," *Review of Metaphysics*, 27 (1973–74), 677–696.

10. A prime example of this is Northrop Frye. See Lentricchia's analysis of Frye's criticism, in *After the New Criticism*, pp. 18–26. Heidegger, too, though less obviously than Frye, depends on Kantian assumptions in his pursuit of the "truth value" of art.

11. Maurice Mandelbaum, *History, Man, and Reason: A Study in Nineteenth-Century Thought* (Baltimore: Johns Hopkins University Press, 1971), p. 42.

12. Northrop Frye, *Anatomy of Criticism: Four Essays* (Princeton: Princeton University Press, 1957), p. 43.

13. George Steiner, *The Death of Tragedy* (New York: Knopf, 1961).

14. Hartman, *Saving the Text*, p. 24.

15. Cf. Mikhail Bakhtin, *Rabelais and His World*, trans. Helene Iswolsky (Cambridge, Mass.: MIT Press, 1968), pp. 119–122.

16. See Rudolf E. Kuenzli, "Derridada," *L'Esprit créateur*, 20 (1980), 12.

17. "Entre crochets: Entretien avec Jacques Derrida, première partie," *Digraphe*, 8 (April 1976), 112.

18. Ludwig Wittgenstein, *Philosophical Investigations: The English Text of the Third Edition*, trans. G. E. M. Anscombe (New York: Macmillan, 1973), pp. v, 49, 144.

19. Georg Wilhelm Friedrich Hegel, *Phenomenology of Spirit*, trans. A. V. Miller, with an analysis and foreword by J. N. Findlay (Oxford: Clarendon Press, 1977), Preface, §1, p. 1.

20. "Entre crochets," p. 100.

21. I borrow the notion of four-thinking from John S. Nelson, "Political Theory as Political Rhetoric: A Sophistic Correction of Current Political Theory," in Nelson, ed., *What Should Political Theory Be Now?* (Albany: State University of New York Press, 1983), pp. 184–185.

22. Herbert Spiegelberg, *The Phenomenological Movement: An Historical Introduction*, 2nd edition, 2 vols. (The Hague: Nijhoff, 1965), Vol. II, pp. 396–397.

23. Vincent Descombes, *Modern French Philosophy*, trans. L. Scott-Fox and J. M. Harding (Cambridge: Cambridge University Press, 1979), p. 3.

24. Note, too, that many of those American literary critics who turned to Derrida (and Foucault) in the 1970s were "fascinated in the 1960s by strains of phenomenology"—as Lentricchia points out in *After the New Criticism*, p. 159. See also the illuminating chapter "Versions of Phenomenology," in which Lentricchia explores the affinities between phenomenology and post-Kantian notions of aesthetic experience.

25. Alexandre Kojève, *Introduction to the Reading of Hegel: Lectures on the Phenomenology of Spirit*, assembled by Raymond Queneau, ed. Allan Bloom, trans. James H. Nichols, Jr. (New York: Basic Books, 1969), especially pp. 43, 47, 148, and 162–163. Though published only in 1947, Kojève's book was a transcription of lectures that he delivered at the *École des Hautes Études* from 1933 to 1939. Many prominent intellectuals attended.

26. Descombes, *Modern French Philosophy*, p. 136.

27. Jean Wahl, *Vers la fin de l'ontologie: Étude sur l'Introduction dans la Métaphysique par Heidegger* (Paris: Société d'édition d'enseignement supérieur, 1956).

28. Maurice Merleau-Ponty, *The Visible and the Invisible, followed by Working Notes*, ed. Claude Lefort, trans. Alphonso Lingis (Evanston: Northwestern University Press, 1968), p. 165. It is tempting to speculate what direction Merleau-Ponty might have taken had he not died in 1961. His faith in the primacy of perception coupled with his conviction of its precariousness, his attunement to the "silences" amid the "prose of the world," his notion of synthesis as incomplete, and his sense of the "burden of consciousness" bring him to the verge of postmodernism—as Wilde points out in *Horizons of Assent*, pp. 14–16.

29. Maurice Blanchot, *L'Espace littéraire* (Paris: Gallimard, 1955), pp. 252, 255, 260.

30. Ibid., pp. 31–35.

31. Wilde, *Horizons of Assent*, especially pp. 43–45.

32. Derrida's references to Blanchot's critical writings are few. But see *L'Écriture et la différence*, pp. 150–151, 253–258; *Writing and Difference*, pp. 102–103, 169–173. More telling as an indicator of Derrida's relation to Blanchot is his taking up of themes that Blanchot previously suggested—e.g., the attack on the preeminence of oral over written discourse (I note the relevant texts below). In his more recent work, Derrida has turned to a consideration of Blanchot's fictional writings. See Jacques Derrida, "Living On," trans. James Hulbert, in Bloom et al., *Deconstruction and Criticism*, pp. 75–176; and "The Law of Genre," trans. Avital Ronell, *Critical Inquiry*, 7 (1980–81), 55–81.

33. See Margaret A. Rose's suggestive comments on Magritte's use of parody in her *Parody/Metafiction: An Analysis of Parody as a Critical Mirror to the Writing and Reception of Fiction* (London: Croom Helm, 1979), pp. 140–144.

34. Ibid., p. 131.

35. Robert Minder, "Heidegger und Hebel oder die Sprache von Messkirch," in his *Dichter in der Gesellschaft: Erfahrungen mit deutscher und französischer Literatur* (Frankfurt am Main: Insel, 1966), especially pp. 211–213, 224–227. On the notion of unwitting parody, see Hans Kuhn, "Was parodiert die Parodie?" *Neue Rundschau*, 85(1974), 604–605.

36. See Richard Poirier, "The Politics of Self-Parody," in his *The Performing Self: Compositions and Decompositions in the Languages of Contemporary Life* (New York: Oxford University Press, 1971), especially pp. 27–28.

37. Jacques Derrida, "Mallarmé," in *Tableau de la littérature française de Madame de Staël à Rimbaud* (Paris: Gallimard, 1974), p. 370.

38. See, for example, *Zen and the Art of Motorcycle Maintenance* (New York: Bantam, 1975), Robert M. Pirsig's telling meditation on the *Phaedrus*.

39. Maurice Blanchot, "The Beast of Lascaux," trans. David Paul, in *René Char's Poetry: Studies by Maurice Blanchot, Gabriel Bounoure, Albert Camus, Georges Mounin, Gaëtan Picon, René Ménard, James Wright* (Rome: de Luca, 1956), pp. 30–31.

40. Ibid., p. 31.

41. Ibid., p. 32.

42. S. L. Goldberg, *The Classical Temper* (New York: Barnes & Noble, 1961), pp. 66–99.

43. Ibid., pp. 23–24. Significantly, *Finnegans Wake* was deeply influenced by Joyce's reading of Mallarmé, as David Hayman argues (too single-mindedly, but nonetheless with an essential accuracy) in *Joyce et Mallarmé*, 2 vols. (Paris: Lettres modernes, 1956). Indeed,

Hayman sees *Finnegans Wake* as a "crystallization" of "'*l'oeuvre pure*' mallarméenne" (p. 69). See also Goldberg, *The Classical Temper*, p. 16.

44. Richard Rorty, *Philosophy and the Mirror of Nature* (Princeton: Princeton University Press, 1979), p. 321.

45. The "Book," for Derrida, is a figure of Hegelianism. See *L'Écriture et la différence*, p. 393; *Writing and Difference*, p. 267; and Kojève, *Introduction to the Reading of Hegel*, p. 148.

46. See Mandelbaum, *History, Man, and Reason*, pp. 41–138.

47. Ibid., pp. 369–370.

48. See ibid., pp. 59–60.

49. Gilles Deleuze, *Nietzsche and Philosophy*, trans. Hugh Tomlinson (London: Athlone Press, 1983), p. 195.

50. On the "reactive" character of edifying, hermeneutical thought in general, see Rorty, *Philosophy and the Mirror of Nature*, pp. 365–366.

Chapter 8

1. See Martin Heidegger, *Erläuterungen zu Hölderlins Dichtung*, 4th edition, enlarged (Frankfurt am Main: Klostermann, 1971), p. 7.

2. Michel Foucault, *Raymond Roussel* (Paris: Gallimard, 1963); Michel Foucault, *This Is Not a Pipe*, with illustrations and letters by René Magritte, trans. James Harkness (Berkeley and Los Angeles: University of California Press, 1983).

3. Jean-Paul Sartre, *Saint Genet: Actor and Martyr*, trans. Bernard Frechtman (New York: Braziller, 1963), pp. 587–588.

4. Georges Bataille, *Literature and Evil*, trans. Alastair Hamilton (London: Calder & Boyars, 1973), pp. 160–161.

5. Harold Rosenberg, *The De-definition of Art* (New York: Horizon Press, 1972).

6. Jacques Derrida, "Où commence et comment finit un corps enseignant?" in Dominique Grisoni, ed., *Politiques de la philosophie: Châtelet, Derrida, Foucault, Lyotard, Serres* (Paris: Grasset, 1976), pp. 55–97; and "L'Âge de Hegel," "La Philosophie et ses classes," and "Réponses à la Nouvelle Critique," in Groupe de Recherches sur l'Enseignement Philosophique, *Qui a peur de la philosophie?* (Paris: Flammarion, 1977), pp. 73–107, 445–450, 451–458.

7. I borrow the distinction between three sorts of Derridean texts from Derrida's interviewer in "Entre crochets: Entretien avec Jacques Derrida, première partie," *Digraphe*, 8 (April 1976), 97.

8. Ibid., pp. 102–107.

9. Geoffrey H. Hartman, "Preface," in Harold Bloom et al., *Deconstruction and Criticism* (New York: Continuum, 1979), p. ix.

10. Northrop Frye, *Anatomy of Criticism: Four Essays* (Princeton: Princeton University Press, 1957), pp. 40–41.

11. And as Levinas acknowledges: see Emmanuel Levinas, "Signature," in his *Difficile liberté: Essais sur le judaïsme contemporain* (Paris: Albin Michel, 1963), p. 323.

12. Ibid., pp. 323–324. See also Levinas's *Totality and Infinity: An Essay on Exteriority*, trans. Alphonso Lingis (Pittsburgh: Duquesne University Press, 1969), p. 29.

13. Emmanuel Levinas, *The Theory of Intuition in Husserl's Phenomenology*, trans. André Orianne (Evanston: Northwestern University Press, 1973), p. xxxiii.

14. Ibid., p. 119.

15. Emmanuel Levinas, *Existence and Existents*, trans. Alphonso Lingis (The Hague: Nijhoff, 1978), p. 19.

16. Levinas, *Totality and Infinity*, pp. 46–47.

17. Ibid., p. 43.

18. Ibid.

19. Ibid., pp. 44–45.

20. Ibid., p. 45.

21. Ibid., pp. 45–46.

22. Levinas, "Judaïsme et temps présent," in *Difficile liberté*, pp. 232–235.

23. Levinas, *Totality and Infinity*, pp. 22–23.

24. For another, more conventional account of the Judaic dimension in Levinas's thought, see Edith Wyschogrod, *Emmanuel Levinas: The Problem of Ethical Metaphysics* (The Hague: Nijhoff, 1974), pp. 159–199.

25. Geoffrey H. Hartman, *Saving the Text: Literature/Derrida/Philosophy* (Baltimore: Johns Hopkins University Press, 1981), p. 17 (also pp. xix–xx, 18–19, 63, 95, 112–113).

26. Harold Bloom, *A Map of Misreading* (New York: Oxford University Press, 1975), pp. 42–43.

27. G. Douglas Atkins, "Dehellenizing Literary Criticism," *College English*, 4 (1980), 773.

28. I depend on Jonathan A. Goldstein, "The Origins of the Doctrine of Creation *Ex Nihilo*," *Journal of Jewish Studies*, 35 (1984) pp. 127–135.

29. Georg Wilhelm Friedrich Hegel, "The Spirit of Christianity and Its Fate," in his *Early Theological Writings*, trans. T. M. Knox, with an introduction by T. M. Knox and fragments translated by Richard Kroner (Chicago: University of Chicago Press, 1948), pp. 182–301.

30. Karl Löwith, "Les Implications politiques de la philosophie de l'existence chez Martin Heidegger," trans. Joseph Rovan, *Les Temps modernes*, 14 (November 1946), 347.

31. Ibid., p. 348. Thomas Sheehan documents the impact on Heidegger of his reading of St. Paul, in "Heidegger's 'Introduction to the Phenomenology of Religion,' 1920–21," *The Personalist*, 60 (1979), 312–324; see especially pp. 315 and 321–322. Also see Thomas Sheehan, "Heidegger's Early Years: Fragments for a Philosophical Biography," in Sheehan, ed., *Heidegger: The Man and the Thinker* (Chicago: Precedent, 1981), pp. 10–11; and Husserl's letter of March 5, 1919 to Rudolf Otto, in Sheehan, ed., *Heidegger: The Man and the Thinker*, pp. 24–25. As Hans-Georg Gadamer has recently observed, "now that we know more about Heidegger's first philosophical ventures and lectures in the early 1920's," we can see that his question was: "how can one successfully resist the alien influence of Greek philosophy upon the Christian message?" ("Heidegger and the History of Philosophy," trans. Karen Campbell, *The Monist*, 64 [1981], 435).

32. Note also the affinities between Heidegger's later thought and the prophetic writings of the Old Testament, discussed by Michael E. Zimmerman, *Eclipse of the Self: The Development of Heidegger's Concept of Authenticity* (Athens: Ohio University Press, 1981), pp. 227–228.

33. Stanley Rosen hits the nail on the head when he observes that for Heidegger "the function of foundational, recollective, or 'poetic' thinking is to return man to the origin, in a way sufficiently reminiscent of both pagan and Hebrew thought as to lead to the greatest confusion" (Rosen, *Nihilism: A Philosophical Essay* [New Haven: Yale University Press, 1969], p. 130).

34. See Paul de Man, *Blindness and Insight: Essays in the Rhetoric of Contemporary Criticism* (New York: Oxford University Press, 1971), especially pp. 16–19, 105–111, 140–141, 184–186.

35. On *gematria*, see Gershom Scholem, *Kabbalah* (New York: Quadrangle, 1974), pp. 337–342.

36. Harold Bloom, *Kabbalah and Criticism* (New York: Continuum, 1975), pp. 51–92.

37. Thomas Pynchon, *Gravity's Rainbow* (New York: Viking Press, 1973), p. 520.

38. For Pynchon's relation to these thinkers, see Thomas S. Smith, "Performing in the Zone: The Presentation of Historical Crisis in *Gravity's Rainbow*," *Clio*, 12 (1982–83), 245–260.

39. See especially George Steiner, *Language and Silence* (New York: Atheneum, 1967), pp. 46–54 and passim.

40. Edmond Jabès, *Le livre des questions*, Vol. III: *Le Retour au livre* (Paris: Gallimard, 1965), p. 88.

41. Edmond Jabès, *Le Livre des questions* (Paris: Gallimard, 1963), pp. 9, 17–18, 108–109, 132; translated by Rosemarie Waldrop as *The Book of Questions* (Middletown, Conn.: Wesleyan University Press, 1976), pp. 11, 19, 100–101, 122.

42. Derrida's translator omits the reference to Nazism at this point.

43. Jacques Derrida, "Fors: Les mots anglés de Nicolas Abraham et Maria Torok," in Nicolas Abraham and Maria Torok, *Cryptonymie: Le verbier de l'homme aux loups* (Paris: Aubier-Flammarion, 1976), pp. 7–82. This is translated by Barbara Johnson as "Fors: The Anglish Words of Nicolas Abraham and Maria Torok," *Georgia Review,* 31 (1977), 64–116.

44. Lorin Anderson, "Freud, Nietzsche," *Salmagundi,* 47–48 (Winter–Spring 1980), 3–29.

45. On the displacing of the axis of social theory toward subjectivity in this period, see the useful synoptic work by H. Stuart Hughes, *Consciousness and Society: The Reorientation of European Social Thought, 1890–1930* (New York: Random House, 1961).

46. Seymour Fisher and Roger P. Greenberg, *The Scientific Credibility of Freud's Theories and Therapy* (New York: Basic Books, 1977), p. 5.

47. Sigmund Freud, *Civilization and Its Discontents,* Chap. VIII, in *The Standard Edition of the Complete Psychological Works of Sigmund Freud,* 24 vols., translated from the German under the editorship of James Strachey, in collaboration with Anna Freud, assisted by Alix Strachey and Alan Tyson (London: Hogarth Press, 1953–74), Vol. XXI, p. 451.

48. See Roland Barthes, *The Pleasure of the Text,* trans. Richard Miller, with a note on the text by Richard Howard (New York: Hill and Wang, 1975).

49. Richard Wollheim, *Freud* (London: Fontana, 1971), p. 17.

50. Alan Wilde, *Horizons of Assent: Modernism, Postmodernism, and the Ironic Imagination* (Baltimore: Johns Hopkins University Press, 1981), pp. 19–49, especially pp. 24–27, 29–34, and 43–45.

51. Philip Rieff, *Freud: The Mind of the Moralist* (Garden City, N.Y.: Doubleday Anchor, 1961). Other noteworthy modernist interpreters of Freud include Lionel Trilling and Peter Gay. See Trilling, *Freud and the Crisis of Our Culture* (Boston: Beacon Press, 1955); and Gay, "Sigmund Freud: A German and His Discontents," in his *Freud, Jews, and Other Germans: Masters and Victims in Modernist Culture* (New York: Oxford University Press, 1978), pp. 29–92. But Rieff is more useful for our purposes, since in his writings Freud's modernism is rigorously explored, whereas in Trilling and Gay it tends simply to be assumed.

52. Rieff, *Freud: The Mind of the Moralist,* pp. 391–392.

53. Ibid., p. 361.

54. Philip Rieff, *The Triumph of the Therapeutic: Uses of Faith After Freud* (New York: Harper & Row, 1966), p. 261.

55. Ibid., p. 40.

56. Rieff, *Freud: The Mind of the Moralist,* p. 359.

57. Ibid., p. 362.

58. Ibid., p. 364. See also, on Freud's dualistic tendencies in general, pp. 377–378.

59. Rieff, *The Triumph of the Therapeutic,* especially chaps. 2 and 8, pp. 48–65 and pp. 232–261.

60. Ibid., p. 238.

61. See Wilde, *Horizons of Assent,* p. 3 and passim.

62. Rieff, *Freud: The Mind of the Moralist,* p. 116.

63. See, for example, Sigmund Freud, *The Interpretation of Dreams,* Chap. VII (F), in *Standard Edition,* Vol. V, pp. 613, 620.

64. As Rieff puts it: "Freud was not hopeful; nor was he nostalgic. Retrospectively, he treasured no pagan or primitive past. He looked forward to no radically different future. . . . Freud's own attitude toward a variety of historical dualisms, including Christianity, was always respectful, for he considered that they were but versions of a more fundamental dualism in the nature of man and in the cosmos. For this reason he never seriously entertained any utopian aspiration" (*Freud: The Mind of the Moralist,* pp. 377–378).

65. Sigmund Freud, *The Interpretation of Dreams,* Chap. V (D), in *Standard Edition,* Vol. IV, pp. 260–264.

66. Rieff, *Freud: The Mind of the Moralist,* p. 126.

67. Ibid., pp. 81–82.

68. On Freud's debt to physics, see Frank J. Sulloway, *Freud, Biologist of the Mind: Beyond the Psychoanalytic Legend* (New York: Basic Books, 1979), especially pp. 9–131.

69. See, for example, Edward W. Said, *Beginnings: Intention and Method* (New York:

Basic Books, 1975), p. 161: "The *Interpretation* deals as much with the nature of psychological reality as with the meaning of dreams, but the book's fascination lies in the fact that Freud does not choose between illusion and reality until the very end." This statement, by a literary critic much influenced by Foucault and other recent French figures, seems to me exactly right. But note that Freud *does* choose—or at any rate claims to.

70. Ernest Jones, *The Life and Work of Sigmund Freud,* ed. and abridged by Lionel Trilling and Steven Marcus (Harmondsworth, England: Penguin Books, 1964), p. 418.

71. Sigmund Freud, *The Interpretation of Dreams,* Chap. VII (A), in *Standard Edition,* Vol. V, p. 516.

72. Sigmund Freud, *Fragment of an Analysis of a Case of Hysteria ("Dora"),* Chap. I, in *Standard Edition,* Vol. VII, p. 59.

73. See Rieff's perceptive comments: "[Freud] inherited a good deal of that hostility to art which has accompanied the scientific attitude so long as it has been empirical in pretension and practical in orientation.... Art ... is seen as a distortion of reality, a dangerous incitement against reason.... Freud implied that science, to the degree to which it is successful, renders art that much less necessary. The great rationalist slogan of psychoanalysis—*Where id was, there shall ego be*—implicitly offers science as the successor not only to religion but to its original handmaiden, art" (*Freud: The Mind of the Moralist,* pp. 133–135). Compare this with Hegel—or with the Nietzsche of 1879.

74. Ibid., p. xxii.

75. Derrida, "Fors," in Abraham and Torok, *Cryptonymie,* p. 31; see also pp. 32–35. In the English translation (see note 43, above), p. 82, also pp. 84–86. Abraham and Torok acknowledge the fictional character of their analysis in *Cryptonymie,* p. 131.

76. Freud, *The Interpretation of Dreams,* Chap. VII (E), in *Standard Edition,* Vol. V, p. 596.

77. Sigmund Freud, *The Psychopathology of Everyday Life,* Chap. I, in *Standard Edition,* Vol. VI, pp. 2–5.

78. Freud, *The Interpretation of Dreams,* Chap. VI (D), in *Standard Edition,* Vol. V, p. 341 (Freud's emphasis).

79. Freud, *Fragment of an Analysis of a Case of Hysteria,* in *Standard Edition,* Vol. VII, p. 110.

80. R. N. Berki, *On Political Realism* (London: Dent, 1981), p. 8.

Conclusion

1. Georg Wilhelm Friedrich Hegel, *Philosophy of Right,* trans. T. M. Knox (Oxford: Clarendon Press, 1952), p. 13.

2. Richard Rorty, "Nineteenth-Century Idealism and Twentieth-Century Textualism," *The Monist,* 64 (1981), 155–174; reprinted in Rorty, *Consequences of Pragmatism (Essays: 1972–1980)* (Minneapolis: University of Minnesota Press, 1982), pp. 139–159.

3. Richard Rorty, *Philosophy and the Mirror of Nature* (Princeton: Princeton University Press, 1979), p. 360.

4. Friedrich Schiller, *On the Aesthetic Education of Man in a Series of Letters,* ed. and trans. Elizabeth Wilkinson and L. A. Willoughby (Oxford: Clarendon Press, 1967), letter 26, §5, p. 193.

5. William Barrett, *Irrational Man* (Garden City, N.Y.: Doubleday Anchor, 1962), pp. 42–65.

6. George Steiner, *Heidegger* (London: Fontana, 1978), p. 126.

7. See, on the "thought-cliché," Jacques Barzun, *The House of Intellect* (New York: Harper & Brothers, 1959), pp. 51–59.

A Note on Texts

In quoting Nietzsche, I have used the English translations indicated in the Key to Abbreviations, appearing after the Preface. Wherever I depart from these translations I note this, except where the changes are conventional rather than substantive in character (e.g., "Apollonian" for "Apollinian"). These departures have been infrequent for the translations by Kaufmann and by Hollingdale, and more frequent elsewhere. Because most of Nietzsche's published writings are divided into short, almost aphoristic sections a page or less in length, page references have not usually been necessary. As a general rule, only where the section or chapter in question is two or more pages long do I give a page number. The section numbers will usually enable the reader to find his way easily to Nietzsche's text no matter what edition he chooses to consult and in no matter which language.

As for those texts not available in English translation, or where there are compelling scholarly reasons for going back to the German original, I have cited three different editions of Nietzsche's writings. These are the second edition of the so-called *Grossoktavausgabe,* entitled simply *Werke* and published in Leipzig in nineteen volumes from 1901 to 1913; the *Musarionausgabe,* entitled *Gesammelte Werke* and published in Munich in twenty-three volumes from 1920 to 1929; and the most recent edition, entitled *Werke: Kritische Gesamtausgabe,* edited by Giorgio Colli and Mazzino Montinari and published in Berlin by de Gruyter beginning in 1967. The last of these is the most reliable, but so far, at least, it lacks an index or even a general table of contents and is thus inconvenient for some purposes.

Nietzsche's *Nachlass* presents special problems. The "book" that his original editors published under the title *The Will to Power* was no such thing, but only a collection of fragments from his notebooks. It therefore has to be used cautiously. Still, the editors' falsification was largely confined to their presenting as a finished work something that they themselves had cobbled together. Consequently, unlike some commentators, I do not deny to this collection all evidential value. Nor, for that matter, do I deny evidential value to those of Nietzsche's fragments that were not included in *The Will to Power*. On the contrary, I regard the *Nachlass* as an extremely useful supplement to the interpretation of Nietzsche's thought. Especially when one can find similar passages in works that Nietzsche actually did publish, the *Nachlass* fragments do cast additional light on his thinking. I have checked the passages that I cite from *The Will to Power* against the Colli-Montinari edition. In most cases, I was able to find the fragments in question. The Colli-Montinari renderings rarely varied, and then only in minor detail, from the renderings in *The Will to Power*. I have retained my references to that collection because it is readily available and easy to use, and because it does have the advantage of topically organizing an otherwise disorderly body of writing.

Heidegger, too, presents textual problems. Firstly, there is the question of dating. The writings whose publication Heidegger himself oversaw are usually accompanied by some indication of the times of first composition and revision, but this does not tell us what, exactly, was revised when. Since those writings were often written to be delivered as lectures, they presumably had to be revised for publication, and we cannot always be certain when these revisions were carried out and how extensive they were. Works printed very soon after their initial composition do provide a valuable check. But these are frequently very sparse, since for one reason or another Heidegger tended to hold onto his manuscripts for years before publishing them. I am well convinced that when Heidegger says that a given piece was first composed in a certain year, the gist of it was indeed composed at about that time. Nonetheless, the skeptical historian remains the skeptical historian, and we must consider datings to be somewhat tentative.

Secondly, there is no standard, critical edition of Heidegger's writings. The first volume of the monumental Heidegger *Gesamtausgabe*, being published in Frankfurt by Klostermann, appeared in 1976, but will not be completed for many years. Besides, the *Gesamtausgabe* does not constitute a critical edition in the accepted sense of the term, but is claimed rather to be an edition "of the last hand." But *whose* hand? In many instances, the final hand at work would seem almost necessarily to be that of an editor. Heidegger's manuscripts, heavy with emendations, frequently admit of alternate readings. Some indication of the difficulties can be gleaned from David Farrell Krell's "textual appendix" on pp. 223–229 in the first volume of his translation of Heidegger's *Nietzsche*. Krell includes on pp. 224–225 a facsimile of what one gathers to be a typically messy manuscript page.

In the face of these difficulties, one is tempted to wait another hundred years, by which time a truly critical edition might be available. Unfortunately, most of us will be dead by then, and Heidegger's thought is a matter of current importance. Moreover, while we shall undoubtedly be able to learn a good deal more about the details of Heidegger's intellectual odyssey, I do not think that the textual and editorial difficulties prevent us from discerning its general outlines now.

Wherever they are available, I cite English translations of Heidegger's writings and not the original German. The only exception to this rule is *Being and Time*, where the English translation includes in its margins the pagination of the later German editions of the work. Since I have used these page numbers in my citations, the reader will be easily able to locate the cited passages in most of the available German editions. I do not otherwise give page references to the original German texts, because the question arises which editions to cite, and because I believe that most of my readers will find such citations a distraction rather than a help. In any case, the English translations are readily available—usually more readily available than any single German edition of the works concerned—and the reader is perfectly free to find his way back from these translations to whichever German original he chooses.

A word is in order concerning the quality of the translations, some of which have been severely criticized in certain quarters. This is true, for example, of the Macquarrie and Robinson translation of *Being and Time* (see John Wild, "An English Version of Martin Heidegger's *Being and Time*," *Review of Metaphysics,* 16 [1962–63], 296–315), and a new English rendering of that work is in preparation. But in all fairness it ought to be said that no translation can be entirely satisfactory, and that even with the best of all possible translations one would still want the original German at hand in doing any serious work on Heidegger. The Macquarrie and Robinson translation may not be the best possible, but it is in many ways very serviceable; its indices, for example, are of considerable use. And the other English translations are also in some ways very convenient: many of them, for example, are available in inexpensive paperback editions. On occasion I have departed from these translations, usually for reasons of consistency or emphasis. Once again, I indicate where I have made alterations except where these are merely conventional in character. Hence, I have not hesitated to substitute, without notice, "tradition" for "Tradition," "Being" for "being," "beings" for "essents," "destruction" for "de-struction," and so on.

Foucault and Derrida present fewer bibliographical problems than do their German predecessors. Usually there is only one French edition to cite. I have also cited the English translations of their books, with the exception of one translation which seems to me to be irredeemably bad. Naturally, I have sometimes departed from these translations also, and make note of every departure that is significant. Many of Foucault's essays and interviews are conveniently available in two English-language collections. I do not cite the original French versions of these, which appear in widely scattered and not always easily available periodicals.

Index